THE SEYMOUR FAMILY

QUEEN JANE SEYMOUR.
From an engraving in the British Museum after a portrait by Holbein.

THE
EYMOUR FAMILY

BY

A. AUDREY LOCKE

ILLUSTRATED

BOSTON AND NEW YORK

HOUGHTON MIFFLIN COMPANY

1914

Seb

CONTENTS

LIST OF ILLUSTRATIONS

THE SEYMOUR FAMILY

INTRODUCTORY

In the early history of the Seymour or St. Maur family so much is vague, that although it is possible to carry back their presumptive pedigree to pre-Conquest times such a task seems useless in the lack of genuine evidence. Tradition has it that a family of St. Maur lived in the eighth century in a little village of Touraine, St. Maur-sur-Loire, which took its name from a certain black hermit called St. Maur or Mauras.[1]

That such a family existed is probable,[2] but that it directly represented the family, which was to come into predominance in Tudor times, is nowhere proved. Indeed the most important link in the facts which are supposed to connect the two families is based on pure hypothesis. Even the best authorities[3] can only assign a possible

[1] This Maur is said to have lived in the village in the seventh century and to have claimed, like other Abyssinian princes, an informal descent from Solomon and the Queen of Sheba. He is probably a myth; at any rate the village certainly took its name from the St. Maur (an Italian monk sent from Nursie to France at the request of the Bishop of Mans), who founded a monastery, the oratory of which still exists, in the little village then called Glenfeuil and later St. Maur-sur-Loire. See *Vita S. Mauri*, p. 274, etc.

[2] See pedigree of family as given by La Chenaye des Bois [1873], xviii, 183.

[3] H. St. Maur, *Annals of the Seymour Family*, p. 4. After quoting the pedigree from La Chenaye des Bois the author goes on to state that the William son of Goscelin (who according to La Chenaye des Bois died without issue), 'seems to have had a son Wido.'

A

father to the Guy de St. Maur who, according to the most unreliable evidence of the Battle Abbey Roll, is said to have followed the Conqueror to England. And since it is from this Guy that all the branches of the family are supposed to descend, it is clear that the position is weak and untenable.

Who then, we may ask, were the ancestors of Queen Jane Seymour ? In the lack of certainty we must pass aside the crowd of those bearing her name, who in the twelfth and thirteenth centuries figure in the early assize rolls and other ordinary documents, in all parts of England. When we have done this we can centre our attention on one William St. Maur, who in the first half of the thirteenth century was holding lands in Monmouthshire, and bore as his coat-of-arms the pair of wings which still form part of the arms of the Seymours or St. Maurs, Dukes of Somerset.

The first that is heard of this William is that in 1235 he entered into a questionable agreement with Gilbert Marshall, fourth Earl of Pembroke (of the second creation), to wrest the manor of Undy from a Welshman, Morgan ap Howell, Lord of Caerleon. This they proposed to do *according to English law*, and agreed that when they had acquired the manor they should divide it equally between them, and Gilbert, Earl of Pembroke, should pay William St. Maur £10 of the whole manorial rent of £20, and, whatever circumstances might arise, William should remain in possession. Further intent on improving his possessions and estates, William enlarged the castle at Penhow, which belonged to him, built a church at Penhow which he dedi-cated in honour of the Abbot St. Maur (now changed to St. John the Baptist). He had already assured his position in the country by marrying the third daughter of William Marshall, first Earl of Pembroke (of the second creation).

Penhow Castle, though so small in extent that it has been described simply as an early manorial residence, with no

outworks, no drawbridge, gate-house or portcullis, and no
embattled towers, is nevertheless of great interest as one
of the earliest known homes of the St. Maurs. It stands
on a high headland, overlooking the country, and is
approached by a road winding up the steep hill on the
western side. From the road can be seen the modern dwell-
ing-house, built some two centuries ago, in front of the
original buildings. The earliest work in the castle, namely,
the tower, usually miscalled 'the old Norman Tower,' is
thirteenth century,[1] and stands, with some alterations, as
it was first built by William de St. Maur. At a somewhat
later period, possibly by William himself, the castle was
evidently, from internal evidence, enlarged and completed,
being enclosed by walls of great thickness. Until the
fifteenth century the castle presumably remained un-
altered, but long before that time Penhow had passed from
the direct line of the St. Maurs, who were to become Dukes
of Somerset.

William St. Maur, the builder of Penhow, had two sons,
William and Roger. William, the elder, living in 1270, became known as of Penhow; Roger, the younger, as of Undy.
Of these two sons William presumably died without children,
since Roger, son of Roger his younger brother, from whom
the Dukes of Somerset descended, was holding both
Penhow and Undy in 1314. This Roger married Joan,
the daughter of one of the Damarels of Devon, and left
two sons, John and Roger. John, the elder son, held
Penhow, and died in 1385, leaving a son Roger, aged eighteen.
Roger left an only daughter and heir, Isabel, who married
(c. 1382) John Bowler or Bowlay of Penhow, and carried
Penhow Castle into the Bowlay family.

---

[1] It is thus, with the exception of the great Norman keep at
Chepstow Castle, one of the earliest domestic buildings in this part
of the country. (See C. O. S. Morgan, *Notes on Penhow Castle*
[Caerleon Antiq. Ass.], 1867.)

Meanwhile Roger, the younger son of John Seymour, lord of Undy manor, had left Wales, and chosen instead to live at Even Swindon (in Wiltshire). His marriage to Cecily, daughter of John de Beauchamp, third Lord Beauchamp of Hache in Somerset, had brought him into union with one of the most noble and wealthy families in the kingdom, and in 1868, on the death of her brother John without heirs, Cecily became co-heir with her sister, to all the Beauchamp estates.[1] Roger and Cecily had five children, of whom William, the elder, married Margaret, daughter of Simon de Brockbarn, and resided for the most part of his life at Undy. He died before his mother in 1390, seised of the manors of Hatch Beauchamp (in Somerset) and Brockbury Erdesleye and Undy (in Hereford and the Marches of Wales). His son and heir, Roger, succeeded not only to the paternal estates, but also to the wealth and property of his grandmother, Cecily, on her death in 1398.

This Roger (1366-1420) possessed the family capacity for making a fortunate marriage. He married Maud, one of the daughters and co-heirs of William Esturmy,[2] knight, Lord of Wolf Hall (co. Wilts), the bold and fearless Speaker of the House of Commons, best remembered as the leader of the Layman's Parliament of 1405, which proposed the application of the revenues of the Church to State pur-

---

[1] Her share comprised the manors of Hatch Beauchamp, Shepton Beauchamp, Murifield, and a third of Shepton Malet (co. Somerset); certain lands in Sturminster Marshall (co. Dorset); the manors of Bolbury and Harberton (co. Devon); the manor of Dorton (co. Bucks); Little Hawes (co. Suffolk), and two-thirds of Snelling (co. Kent).

It was in memory of this ancestress that Henry VIII. created Edward Seymour (brother of his Queen Jane), Viscount Beauchamp.

[2] The Esturmys had been bailiffs and guardians of the forest of Savernake from the time of Henry III., and their hunter's horn of huge size, tipped and mounted with silver, was in the possession of the Seymour family for many generations (Camden).

poses. John, son of Roger and Maud, became Sheriff of Southampton, and held many important offices in Wiltshire. In 1424 he married Isabel, daughter of Mark Williams of Bristol, who, after her husband's death in 1464, took vows of chastity and became a nun at Westbury. Their son John was married to Elizabeth, daughter of Robert Coker of Lydiard St. Lawrence (in Somerset), and died in 1468, predeceasing his father. Their son John, known as John Seymour of Wolf Hall (1450-1491), married as his first wife Elizabeth, daughter of Sir George Darrell of Littlecote (in Wiltshire), by whom he had several children, the eldest of whom was another John. By his second wife, a daughter of Robert Hardon, he had a son, Roger, and four daughters.

John, the son and heir (1474-1536), who in 1491 became Lord of Wolf Hall, alone interests us here. Of Wolf Hall, his favourite residence, we know from a survey of Edward VI.'s reign that the whole manor contained approximately 1270 acres, including 'Suddene Park,' 'Horse Park,' and 'Red Deer Park.' Of this extent, two and a half acres were garden and orchard, of which 'half an acre lyeth in a gardyne within the walls and half a yard lyeth in the gardyne next the said gardyne.' There was an orchard called Cole-house orchard, a garden called 'the Great Paled Garden,' another called 'My Young Lady's Garden,' and another called 'My Old Lady's Garden.' Of the house itself we know little, and at the present day nothing of it survives except the fine old wooden and thatched barn in which it is said high wedding festivities took place on the occasion of Jane Seymour's marriage with Henry VIII.[1] There was certainly a chapel in the house, for in one of the Household Books of the Manor which Canon Jackson brought to light, there is an account of 17d. paid for a 'pastall '[2]

---

[1] See below, p. 15.

[2] A large wax candle used at Easter. See *Wilts Arch. Mag.* xv. 140 *et seq.*

for the chapel of 1lb weight ; 6d. for two tapers for the chapel, and £2 a year salary for the priest of the chapel. There was also a kennel of hounds attached to the manor ; while the household establishment consisted of forty-four men and seven women. The highest salary, £8 10s. a year, was paid to the steward, the lowest, 13s. 4d., to the two turnspits.

Such in its main outlines was the household of John Seymour of Wolf Hall in the early sixteenth century. He himself was in great favour both with Henry vii. and Henry viii. He fought for the king in 1497 against the Cornish rebels under the command of Lord Audley, and Henry vii., seeing his military genius, knighted him for his services. Being engaged in the campaigns in France and Flanders during the early years of the reign of Henry viii., he was present at Terouenne and Tournay and at the Battle of the Spurs. Later, he was made Sheriff of Dorset, Somerset, and Wiltshire, and one of the knights of the body to the king. In 1517 he and his son Edward held the office of Constable of Bristol Castle ; in 1520 he attended at Guisnes and Ardres at the meetings between Henry and Francis i. of France, and in 1582 accompanied the king to Boulogne as Groom of the Bedchamber on the occasion of the second interview between Henry and Francis. He had married Margery. daughter of Sir Henry Wentworth of Nettlestead in Suffolk, who was descended from John of Gaunt. Hence royal blood was brought into the family as if in preparation for the honours that were to come to the children of John and Margery.

CHAPTER I

'JANE THE QUENE'

'Whenas King Henry ruled this land
He had a queen, I understand,
Lord Seymour's daughter, fair and bright.'—*Ballad.*

'Comme le phénix elle meurt en donnant la vie à un autre phénix.
—Callier, *Reines d'Angleterre.*

IN the timber-framed house of the manor of Wolf Hall in
the 'Great Paled Garden,' or in 'My Young Lady's
Garden,' or in the 'orchard called Cole-house orchard,'
lived and played the eight children of Sir John Seymour.
Three of these were to play a chief part in the drama of the
history of their day. One was to become third queen of
Henry VIII., and mother of the boy in whose reign reform
was to sweep forward to the utmost limits, to the inevitable
rebound. Of the two others, one, by force of personal
magnetism and fortunate or unfortunate circumstance,
was to determine the course of the early events of that
reign; the other with as great, if not greater personality,
and certainly with as much strength of character, was to
give colour to events in another and not less vital way.

It is not difficult to conjure up some picture of the early
life of Jane Seymour. Born about 1509, the eldest daughter
of the family of eight, she probably lived the quiet and
somewhat humdrum life of fifteenth-century girlhood, working at her books little and at her tapestry much. Some
of the needlework that she did when a girl at Wolf Hall was
in existence as late at least as 1652. 'Five Pieces of

chequered hangings of a coarse making having the Duke of Somersett's Arms in them. . . . One furniture of a Bed of Needlework with a chaise [chair] and cushions suitable thereunto . . . said to be wrought by the Queene the Lady Jane Seymour ' were in that year compounded for with Parliament by William, Marquis of Hertford, by payment of £60. The work had come into the possession of the Crown, probably on the marriage of Jane with Henry VIII., and had remained as Crown property until given to the Marquis of Hertford in 1647 by Charles I.

Outside the quietness of the country home there had been wars and rumours of wars in the early years of Jane's life. Her father had served at Terouenne and Tournay, and had won the honour of Knight Banneret by his bravery. Less than ten years later there was a fashion of jousts and tournaments and Cloth of Gold displays at court, and in these her father and her elder brothers joined. Soon for Jane herself some taste of court life came, as, like Anne Boleyn, she seems to have been early trained in the accustomed etiquette and intrigue in the French court as maid-of-honour to Marie, Queen of Louis XII. This fact, however, rests on the somewhat insecure evidence of a picture in the Louvre of one of the French Queen's maids, identified, but with no certainty, as Jane Seymour. Anyhow there is no doubt that already, before Katherine of Arragon was discarded, Jane Seymour was attached to her household as lady-in-waiting. When Anne Boleyn became Queen in 1533, Jane Seymour's services were transferred to the new queen. Of their relation with one another nothing is known or hinted until the beginning of the course of incidents which was to change the whole course of their two lives, and to bring one to the scaffold, the other to the throne.

Already, before Henry's infatuation for Jane Seymour had begun, Anne Boleyn had had good reason to suspect his fickleness. Within eighteen months after their marriage he was, according to Chapuys the Imperial ambassador, paying marked attention to a young and handsome lady of the Court.[1] 'The credit and pride of the concubine (Anne Boleyn) are decreasing,' he wrote in October 1584, 'and there is good hope that if the said *amour* continues, the affairs of the queen and the princess, to whom the lady is very much attached, will go well.' The Boleyn faction resorted to diplomacy, the imperialist favourite was defeated in the king's affection by Anne's own cousin, Margaret Shelton, a friendly rival. Chapuys wrote to the emperor, Charles v., in February 1585. 'The lady who formerly enjoyed the favour of this king does so no longer; she has been succeeded in her office by a first cousin of the concubine, daughter of the new governess of the Princess.'[2] But the king's fancies changed quickly. In the following September, when going on progress through the south-western counties, he visited Wolf Hall, and there, in her father's house, probably began to notice Mistress Jane Seymour, whom he knew to be a lady-in-waiting to Anne. Here was a new opportunity for the imperialist party. They watched the king carefully, they watched the new lady carefully. They found her wise and tactful in her demure gentleness, and reckoned that here was one whom they could use as a catspaw, whose beauty was less, but whose influence might be greater than that of the favourite on whom they had relied less than two years before. Within a few weeks after the royal visit to Wolf Hall the French ambassador reported that the king

---

[1] *Cal. S. P. Engl. and Spain*, v. pt. i. 264. The index to this Calendar identifies this lady with Jane Seymour, upon no evidence whatever. Friedmann (*Anne Boleyn*, ii. 35) definitely states that she was not Jane Seymour.

[2] This and the preceding letter are quoted by Friedmann from the Vienna archives.

had a new love, and Count Ferdinand de Cifuentes wrote the same news to the emperor. As yet, however, matters could go no further. As long as Katherine of Arragon lived, Henry, if he discarded Anne, must take back Katherine. By fair means or foul—the possibility is foul —a solution of that difficulty came in the January of the next year. Katherine died on the seventh day of that month, as a result, as Doctor de Lasco suspected, of 'some slow and cleverly composed drug,' without the symptoms of ordinary poisoning.

Anne Boleyn, in spite of her first transport of joy, soon saw what this meant. On the very day of the interment of Katherine ' the Concubine had an abortion which seemed to be a male child.' 'It was ascribed,' wrote Chapuys, 'to a fear that the king would treat her like the late queen, especially considering the treatment shown to a lady of the court named Mistress Semel (Seymour), to whom, as many say, he has lately made great presents.' [1]

According to Wyat the miscarriage was the result of a shock that Anne Boleyn received on one day surprising the king alone with Jane Seymour, who was calmly receiving his caresses. However that may be, when the king, receiving the news of the abortion as an insult to himself, upbraided Anne with the loss of his boy, ' some words were heard breake out of the inward feeling of her hart's dolours,' [2] and she retorted that he had no one to blame but himself since the misfortune had been caused by her distress of mind ' about that wench Jane Seymour.'

Later, in the March of the same year, Chapuys reported to the Spanish court that the new amours of the king with the young lady of whom he had before spoken, still

---

[1] This and the succeeding letters in this chapter, except where otherwise referenced, are quoted from the *Calendar of Letters and Papers, Henry VIII., sub annis.*

[2] George Wyat, *Life of Queen Anne Boleigne* (1817), 19-20. See Miss Strickland, *Lives of the Queens of England*, ii. 663.

went on 'to the intense rage of the concubine,' and that, fifteen days before, the king had 'put the young lady's brother [Sir Edward Seymour] in his chamber.' It was at this time doubtless that Anne, noticing a jewel which Jane Seymour wore round her neck, asked to look at it. Jane drew back, and the queen, noting her confusion, snatched it violently from her, and found that it contained a portrait of the king. Jane Seymour was no brainless beauty to be drawn into a rash flirtation with the king and be cast aside after the idle moment was over. She was flying at higher game, and there was the imperialist party behind her ready to back her up with insidious advice. She herself and her personal ambition counted for nothing to them, wider issues of politics and religion were bound up in their enmity for Anne and the Boleyn faction, and Jane was a convenient and reliable catspaw. Thus, in April 1586, Chapuys wrote to Charles v. reporting on the progress of matters. The king having been lately in London, and 'the young lady Mrs. Semel whom he serves,' at Greenwich, he had sent her a purse of sovereigns and a letter. The young lady, well versed in her lines, after kissing the letter returned it unopened to the messenger, and throwing herself on her knees, begged him to pray the king on her part to consider that she was 'a gentlewoman of good and honourable parents without reproach, and that she had no greater riches in the world than her honour, which she would not injure for a hundred deaths, and that if he wished to make her some present in money she begged it might be when God enabled her to make some honourable match.

The effect on Henry can be imagined. The man in him was piqued, the king surprised. His love and desire towards the said lady were wonderfully increased by this, Chapuys reported. Moreover, the king declared she had behaved most virtuously, and to show her he only loved her honourably he did not intend henceforth to speak with her except in the presence of some of her kin. This was an easy compromise. Within a few days Thomas Cromwell was ordered to remove from a chamber to which the king had access by a secret gallery, and Jane Seymour's brother Edward and his wife were lodged there instead. Nothing could have been better devised. The king could see Jane whenever he wanted, and she had been well drilled by the enemies of Anne Boleyn 'by no means to comply with the king's wishes except by way of marriage, in which,' as Chapuys wrote, 'she is quite firm.' Moreover, she was advised to tell the king boldly how his marriage was detested by the people and how none considered it lawful. She was also to choose her opportunity when none were present but titled persons who would say the same on their oath, if the king put the question to them. 'Certainly it appears to me,' Chapuys informed Charles v., 'that if this matter succeed it will be a great thing both for the security of the Princess (Mary) and to remedy the heresies here of which the Concubine is the cause and principal nurse, and also to pluck the king from such an abominable, and more than incestuous marriage.' The ambassador himself soon took a definite step in favour of Jane's cause. He refused to dine with Anne and the king, and saying it was not without good reason, waited instead in the hall until the royal party had dined. Afterwards, while watching Cromwell and Henry discussing the possibility of alliance with Spain, he 'conversed and made some acquaintance with the brother of the young lady to whom the king is now attached.'

Before the end of April the ambassador reported to Charles v. that 'the conspiracy against the concubine was in full swing. . . . The grand ecuyer, Mr. Caro (Sir Nicholas Carew), continually counselled Mrs. Semel and other conspirators, "pour luy faire une venne."' In the next month he wrote to Antoine Perrenot, the Emperor's Secretary of

State, telling him, 'something of the quality of the king's new lady.' She was of 'middle stature and no great beauty, so fair that one would call her rather pale than otherwise.' As for her age the ambassador reported her over twenty-five, and added, 'I leave you to judge whether, being English and having long frequented the court, "si elle ne tiendroit pas a conscience de navoir pourveu et prevenu de savoir que cest de faire nopces." ' She was not, Chapuys judged, a woman of great wit but she might have good understanding. She was said to be proud and haughty, but to bear great reverence to the Princess (Mary). Honours might make her change, but that as yet no one could tell.

Already, before Anne Boleyn's arrest on the second day of May, the king and Mistress Seymour had planned out their future marriage, and evidently part of the plan was that after the death of Anne the king should wait until he was requested by Parliament to marry. Thus, to cover his affection for Jane, she was lodged seven miles away, in the house of the master of the horse (Sir Nicholas Carew), and the king announced publicly that he had no desire in the world to marry again unless he should be constrained by his subjects to do so.

Meanwhile Jane still played her part well and, to the ambassador's satisfaction, used all means in her power to persuade the king to replace the Princess Mary in her former position. The king only called her a fool, and told her she ought rather to solicit the advancement of the children they would have between them and not any others. She had thereupon replied that in asking for the restoration of the Princess she conceived she was seeking the rest and tranquillity of the king, herself, her future children and the whole realm. 'I will endeavour by all means to make her continue in this vein,' Chapuys wrote to the emperor.

In the meantime, while Anne was awaiting her con-

demnation in the Tower, the king was 'going about
banqueting with ladies, sometimes remaining after midnight and returning by the river.'   For the most part of
the time he was accompanied 'by various musical instruments' and by the singers of his chamber. On May the
15th, Anne Boleyn was condemned to death for treason.
The day before her condemnation the king sent for 'Mrs.
Semel' by the grand esquire and some others, and made
her come within a mile of his lodging where, most richly
dressed, she was splendidly served by the king's cook
and other officers. On the morning of the condemnation
the king sent to tell her that he would send her news of
the condemnation by three o'clock, and did so by M. Briant
(possibly Sir Francis Brian), 'whom he sent in all haste.'
'To judge by appearances,' wrote Chapuys, 'there is no
doubt that he will take the said Semel to wife, and some
think the agreements and promises are already made.'

Four days afterwards, the execution which the king
was awaiting with all impatience, took place, and though
there were general rejoicings at Anne's death some mur-
mured at the mode of procedure against her, and some
'spoke variously of the king.' And there was little likelihood of 'pacifying the world' when it was known what
had passed and was passing between the king and Jane
Seymour. On the very day of the execution Cranmer
issued a very unnecessary dispensation to Henry and Jane
Seymour to marry without publication of banns, although
in the third and third degree of affinity (tertio et tertio
affinitatis gradibus), and on that same day the king,
immediately on receiving the news that the deed was
done, entered his barge and went to visit 'Mistress Semel.'

All difficulties seemed now cleared away from Jane's
path to the throne. An obsequious Parliament had
evidently petitioned the king to marry again before Anne
Boleyn was dead, and, condescending to consent, the king

met his future bride the morning after the execution, and at nine o'clock in the morning the betrothal ceremony was completed. 'Mrs. Semel came secretly by river this morning to the king's lodging,' wrote Chapuys to his master, 'and the promise and betrothal were made. . . . The king meant it to be kept secret until Whitsuntide, but everybody already began to murmur by suspicion.' Ten days later the wedding celebration took place, not at Wolf Hall, as is popularly supposed, though the ten days between the betrothal and the wedding may have been spent there, but in the queen's closet at York Place or manor, as John Husee[1] wrote to Lord Lisle on the same day. The bride was gorgeously apparelled, for according to Lord Herbert,[2] 'the richer she was in cloaths the fairer she appeared; whereas the richer the former queen was apparelled the worse she looked.' It was not, however, until Whitsunday (the 4th of June 1586) that Jane was 'openly showed as queen,' and even then the coronation was to be postponed until Michaelmas. Yet already congratulations and complimentary flattery poured in upon the king and his new queen. The Princess Mary, into whose favour Jane had already ingratiated herself, wrote her congratulations to her father on the first day of June, and begged that she might wait on the queen and do her service. Chapuys reported that both the king and queen were wonderfully pleased with the wise and prudent letters the Princess Mary had written. Eight days later, the Princess wrote hoping God would preserve the king and queen and send them a prince. Again in the next month she wrote praying that God might preserve His Grace and her 'very natural mother, the queen,' and bring them issue.

By her gentleness and demureness, and an air of silent submissiveness, Jane Seymour gained popularity with

---

[1] See p. 18 *n*.   [2] *Life of Henry VIII.*, 387.

courtiers and people. Sir John Russell wrote early in
June to Lord Lisle, 'she is as gentle a lady as ever I
knew, and as fair a queen as any in Christendom, the king
has come out of hell into heaven for the gentleness in this
and the cursedness and the unhappiness in the other.' A
few days later Cardinal Pole wrote to Cardinal Cartarini that
'some good things were said about the new bride.' Thomas
Cromwell wrote to Stephen Gardiner, Bishop of Winchester,
then ambassador in France, that the king had chosen 'as
all his nobles and council upon their knees moved him to
do, the most virtuous and veriest gentlewoman that liveth.'
Chapuys wrote to Charles v. that he had kissed and congratulated the queen for the king's satisfaction, and had
told her that whereas her predecessor had borne the device
'La plus heureuse' she herself would bear the reality.
Chapuys, of course, looked on her success as a means to
an end. Hence even in his complimentary address he
informed the queen that it was 'not her least happiness
that, without having had the labour of giving birth to her
she had such a daughter as the princess (Mary), of whom
she would receive more joy and consolation than of all
those she could have herself.' He begged her further to
favour the interests of the princess, and to win for herself
the name 'pacific.' The king, in the flush of his new
happiness, seems to have answered for his bride, telling
the ambassador that he quite believed the queen desired
the name of 'pacific,' for 'besides that her nature was gentle
and inclined to peace she would not for the world that he
was engaged in war, that she might not be separated from
him.' The crowds that had watched the triumph of Anne
Boleyn now gathered to watch the new queen whenever
she and the king went in procession through the city, being
anxious to see her, since she was counted 'a very amiable
lady of whom all had great hope.'

Jane Seymour's unclouded triumph was to be of short

duration. The first sign of this was her delayed coronation. As early as the beginning of July 1586, Chapuys had written to Charles v. that the coronation was to be delayed unt᾿¹ after Michaelmas, and suspicious rumours were on fo that this was to see if the queen should be with child. I. she were found to be barren, then 'occasion might be r ade to take another.' Already rumour had it, the ᵏ ng would not have the 'prize of those who do not repent in marriage,' for within eight days after the publication of his marriage with Jane Seymour, having twice met two beautiful young ladies, he 'said and showed himself some- what sorry that he had not seen them before he was married.'

At any rate, whatever truth there was in this, Jane Seymour had learnt once and for all that the only effec- tive way to preserve both her dignity and her head was to follow out the letter, if not the spirit of her own motto, 'Bound to obey and serve.' On the one occasion that she tried to assert her opinion in the interests of the papal and imperialist party, against the king's, she was igno- miniously snubbed. The pendulum of the king's mind, as concerned religious matters, was swinging towards the reforming party now that the dissolution of the monasteries was offering such a tempting booty. Hence, when during the Yorkshire rebellion of 1586, Jane, looking upon it as a punishment of God, fell on her knees and begged the king to restore the abbeys, he roughly bade her get up and 'attend to other things,' reminding her that 'the last queen died in consequence of meddling too much with state affairs,' which was 'enough to frighten a woman who is not very secure.' Yet the queen's sympathies were well known. Luther wrote to Nicholas Hausmann that she was 'an enemy of the gospel,' and in the October of 1586 the Prioress of Clementsthorpe in Yorkshire did her best to move the queen to do what she could in the interests of the nunnery. Sir Robert Constable, a prisoner after

B

the Yorkshire Rebellion, wrote to his nephew, Sir Marmaduke Constable, 'to entreat my lord of Rutland to get the queen to sue to the king for my life.'

The news that the queen was with child, bruited as early as October 1536, when the Vicomte de Dieppe reported it to John Hutton, but not confirmed until the spring of the next year, gave her a new standing both with king and people. The Duke of Norfolk wrote to the king in March 1537, thanking him for the good news of the likelihood of the queen being with child, and telling him how five or six days before the rumour had been received with ' as much joy as anything he ever saw.' Letters of instruction were also given to the Pursuivant of Berwick to deliver the news to the Regents of Scotland, and to say how every man was ' rejoicing and thinking to have his part therein.' In April John Husee [1] wrote to Lady Lisle, 'It is said the queen is with child. Jesu send her a prince,' and again in May, ' It is said the queen is with child twenty weeks gone. God send her a prince.' On the first day of June Sir William Sandys wrote from Guisnes to Lord Lisle at Calais that Queen Jane was with child: 'I have this afternoon received from you the most joyful news ever sent me. No greater comfort ever came to my knowledge next to the prosperous estate of our sovereign lord. You inform me that fires are to be made, and the Te Deum sung and guns shot off at Calais at four o'clock. Too much honour cannot be done to the occasion, and I will do the same here, but

---

[1] John Husee was servant of the Lord and Lady Lisle, who were stationed at Calais, where Lord Lisle was Lord Deputy. Among the Lisle papers there is an amusing and interesting correspondence between John Husee, who remained in London, and Lady Lisle, informing her ladyship of all the changes in fashion, advising her as to the cut and make of her new gowns, and those of her daughters, and suggesting whose favour should be curried at court, and to whom gifts should be made.

the day is too far spent to do it publicly, and I have warned
the curates of this country to meet at the parish church
to-morrow morning and have a solemn mass and Te Deum
after it.' A fire was also to be made in the market-place
of Guisnes and guns shot so that the news might be made
known to all neighbours round; the signals might even
be heard at Calais, Sir William thought, if the wind were
favourable.

The news flew over England; bonfires and Te Deums
and festivities abounded everywhere. Thus from York the
Duke of Norfolk reported to Cromwell how the Te Deum
was to be sung at night and bonfires lighted throughout
the city. Four hogsheads of wine were also to be laid
abroad at night to be drunk in divers places freely. And
the king was happy 'He is in good health and disposition,'
wrote Cromwell to Sir Thomas Wyatt, 'the more because
the queen is quick with child. God send her good
deliverance of a prince.' He himself wrote to the Duke
of Norfolk postponing his journey to the North 'because
the queen . . . might be in danger from rumours blown
abroad in our absence, and it is thought we should go no
further than sixty miles from her.' The real fear which
haunted the queen was of the sickness that was scourg-
ing the country in the summer of 1537. John Husee
wrote to Lady Lisle, 'Your Ladyship would not believe how
much the queen is afraid of the sickness.' However, she
escaped the infection, and on the sixth day of October the
news came that 'the queen had taken her chamber' (at
Hampton Court). Six days later, on Friday, the 12th of
October, the queen herself wrote to Cromwell informing
him of the birth of her son, 'conceived in lawful matrimony.'
The same day Cromwell wrote to Sir Thomas Wyatt,
ambassador to Charles v., bidding him tell the emperor the
news. The king himself, he thought, would write of it to
all the princes. 'Incontinent after the birth Te Deum

was sung in Paul's and other churches of the city, and great fires [were made] in every street, and goodly banqueting and triumphing cheer with shooting of guns all day and night, and messengers were sent to all the estates and cities of the realm to whom were given great gifts.'   As Latimer wrote to Cromwell, there was 'no less rejoicing at the birth of our prince whom we hungered for so long, than there was at the birth of John the Baptist . . . God . . . has overcome all our illness with his exceeding goodness . . . we have now the stop of vain trusts and the stay of vain expectations.' The following Monday the christening took place, precautions having been taken that none should come to the court on the christening day without special letters from the king or some of his council, on account of the plague, which was still raging.   No duke was to bring more than six persons in his company, no marquis more than five, no earl above four, no baron above three, no knight or squire above two, no bishop or abbot above four, and none of the king's or queen's chaplains above two.

There is extant [1] a full account of the whole ceremony of the christening by torchlight in the chapel of Hampton Court; of the course of the procession; of the decorations of the chapel; of 'the crysome richly garnished borne by the lady Elizabeth . . . the same lady for her tender age in her turn borne by the Viscount Beauchamp [2] with the assistance of the lord (Morley)'; of the three days' old prince, borne under a canopy by the lady Marquis of Exeter; and of the lady Mary, the lady godmother, following after the canopy.   When the ceremony was ended the prince was brought to receive the blessing of the king and queen.   The latter, according to the rules of state ceremonial,

---

[1] *L. and P. Hen. VIII.*, xii. (ii), 1060.

[2] Sir Edward Seymour had been created Viscount Beauchamp on the day of Prince Edward's birth.

had been removed from her bed to a state pallet where she waited, Henry sitting by her side, through the two long hours of the ceremony, until the flare of trumpets at her chamber door announced the return of the procession, and she was called upon to rouse herself and give the maternal benediction. It was not wonderful that the exertion and excitement proved too much. Within a week her life was despaired of. On the morning of the 24th of October the Earl of Rutland and others who were attendant on the sick-chamber wrote to Cromwell that although the queen had had ' an naturall laxe ' on the afternoon of the day before, by reason of which she seemed to amend, yet towards night a relapse had come, and all night she had been very ill, and now they feared ' appares ' rather than amends. That morning her confessor had been with her, and was then preparing to administer the sacrament of unction. At eight o'clock that same night the Duke of Norfolk wrote to Cromwell, praying him to be at Hampton Court early the next morning ' to comfort our good master, for as for our mistress there is no likelihood of her life, the more pity, and I fear she shall not be on live at the time ye shall read this.'

About midnight Jane Seymour died. The king ordering the Duke of Norfolk, the Earl Marshal, and Sir William Paulet, the Treasurer of the Household, to see to her burial, himself ' retired to a solitary place to pass his sorrows.' The heavy tidings passed in a few days over the country, and ' never was lady so much plained with every man, rich and poor.' At the end of the month Cromwell wrote to Lord William Howard and Stephen Gardiner, Bishop of Winchester, ambassadors in France, bidding them inform Francis that though the prince was well and ' sucketh like a child of his puissance,' the queen, ' by the neglect of those about her, who suffered her to take cold and eat such things as her fantasy in sickness called for,' was dead.

The ambassadors were to add that the king, though he ' took
the chance reasonably ' was ' little disposed to marry
again.' But both Cromwell and the council knew the
king, and thought it ' meet to urge him to it,' for the sake
of his realm. Henry assumed an attitude of indifference
' both to the thing and to the election of any person
from any part that with deliberation should be thought
meet.'

Queen Jane was not yet buried, but by the beginning
of the next month Windsor was decided upon as her last
resting-place. The body had been embalmed, and had
lain in state in the chamber of presence with twenty-four
tapers about the hearse. And the ladies and gentlemen
had ' put off their rich apparel, doing on their mourning
habit, and white kerchers hanging over their heads and
shoulders,' and there knelt about the hearse during mass
afore noon and Dirige after. A watch was kept at night
until the last day of the month. On the first Wednesday
in November the great chamber and the galleries leading
to the chapel, and the chapel itself were hung with black
cloth and garnished with rich images. A hearse ' garnished
with eight banner-rolls of descents ' was prepared in the
chapel, and the body was that afternoon carried there,
the king's officers and servants standing in double rank
from the chamber to the chapel with torches not lighted,
whilst the Bishop of Carlisle, her almoner, assisted by
the Bishop of Chichester and others, ' did the ceremonies,
as censing with holy water and De Profundis.' The
Lancaster Herald then said with a loud voice ' Of your
charity pray for the soul, etc.'—Then Dirige was sung,
and all departed to the queen's chamber. Watch was
kept every night in the chapel by priests, gentlemen ushers
and officers of arms, who in the morning early were relieved
by ladies, and went to ' breakfast, which was provided as
two chines of beef, with bread, ale and wine thereunto

sufficient.' On Monday, the twelfth day of November, the body was removed to a chair drawn by six chariot horses. Two attendants with black staves headed the procession, followed by two hundred poor men, wearing the queen's badges, who at Colbrooke, Eton and Windsor lined the streets. Then came minstrels with trumpets, and the lady Mary chief mourner, her horse trapped in black velvet, followed by an endless cortège, among which were two almoners distributing alms along the way. The Dean of Windsor and all the college met the body at the outer gate, and accompanied it to the chapel, where a solemn watch-night was held. After the services of the next day, and the offering of seven palls, the mourners went to the castle, 'where they were sumptuously provided for' and the body was solemnly buried 'in presence of many pensive hearts.'

Two almost contemporary ballads exist, showing the general opinion throughout the country that the queen had died as the result of a Cæsarian operation, and this story was afterwards repeated by the Jesuit Nicholas Sanders in his history of the times of Henry VIII. The facts above presented show that this was obviously not the case.[1] Yet the ballads are interesting as embodying the popular belief of the following years. One ballad compares the loss of the queen with that of the royal warship, the *Mary Rose*, which foundered off Spithead in 1540, and tells how, after the queen had passed thirty 'woful hours and more' in pain, one of her ladies repaired to the king

'And said : "O king, show us thy will
The queen's sweet life to save or spill."

---

[1] Edward VI. in his journal writes thus of his own birth :—' The year of our Lord 1537 a prince was born to King Henry VIII. by Jane Seymour then queen, who, *within a few days* of the birth of her son died, and was buried at Windsor' (*Lit. Rem. of Edw. VI.*).

"Then as she cannot saved be,
Oh, save the flower though not the tree."
O mourn, mourn, mourn, fair ladies,
Your queen, the flower of England's dead!'

The other ballad, fragmentary only, was taken down in
the early nineteenth century from the singing of a gipsy
girl, to whom it had been handed down orally. It runs
thus :—

'Queen Jane was in travail
For six weeks or more,
Till the women grew tired
And fain would give o'er.
"O women, O women!
Good wives if ye be,
Go, send for King Henrie
And bring him to me."

King Henrie was sent for,
He came with all speed,
In a gownd of green velvet
From heel to the head.
"King Henrie, King Henrie!
If kind Henrie ye be,
Send for a surgeon,
And bring him to me."

The surgeon was sent for
And came with all speed,
In a gownd of black velvet
From heel to the head;
He gave her rich caudle,
But the death sleep slept she.
Then her right side was opened
And the babe was set free.

The babe it was christened
And put out and nursed,
While the royal Queen Jane
She lay cold in the dust.

.   .   .   .

So black was the mourning
And white were the wands,
Yellow, yellow the torches
They bore in their hands.
The bells they were muffled
And mournful did play,
While the royal Queen Jane
She lay cold in the clay.

Six knights and six lords
Bore her corpse through the grounds,
Six dukes followed after
In black mourning gownds.
The flower of old England
Was laid in cold clay,
While the royal King Henrie
Came weeping away.'

With the exception of Katherine Parr, who survived the king, Jane Seymour, though never crowned, was the first and only wife of Henry VIII. to be undisputed queen. It was this fact, as well as her status as mother of his heir, that caused the king to command the body of his 'loving queen Jane' to be laid in his own tomb. Moreover, he directed that a tomb should be raised to their mutual memory in Windsor Chapel. Statues of Jane and himself were to be placed on the tomb, that of Jane reclining 'not as in death but as one sweetly sleeping'; children with baskets of red roses made of precious stones, jasper, cornelian and agate, were to sit at the corners of the tomb, 'showing' to take the roses in their hands and 'cast them down on and over the tomb and down on the pavement.' And the roses they cast over the tomb were to be enamelled and gilt, and the roses they cast on the steps of the said precious stones, and some were to be inlaid on 'the pavement.' This scheme, though it reached a further stage than many other of the schemes of Henry VIII., and was actually begun, was never accomplished. However, Henry was laid by the side of Jane in the vaults of St. George's Chapel, and in the nineteenth century George IV., when searching for the headless body of Charles I., found that the Round-heads had placed it close by the tomb of Henry and his queen.[1] The skeleton of King Henry was accidentally un-earthed, but the coffin of Queen Jane was intact and the vault was finally walled up.

It is not, however, at Windsor that Queen Jane's ghost is said to walk, but at Hampton Court, where, in spite of all structural alterations, ever as the anniversary of Edward the Sixth's birth-night returns, the spectre of Jane Seymour, ' clad in flowing white garments with a lighted lamp in her hand,' is said to ascend the great staircase.

Jane Seymour was fortunate in her death, gaining by it an added glory, since it took place not only before her royal husband had tired of her, but at the very moment when he was in the fulness of his joy at the birth of his heir. That memory of her remained both to people and king, that and the memory of her gentleness, which, looked at from afar, became a dearer if a negative virtue. It was the good she seemed to be that was remembered, the rest was buried in her grave and forgotten, and she was and has been acclaimed the fairest, discreetest, and the most meritorious of all Henry VIII.'s wives. As her fairness was paleness, so her discretion was near to hypocrisy, and her merit to un-scrupulous attainment of her own ends. Granted that her position was difficult, she was not the only ' gentlewoman of honour ' to whom Henry made advances, and to whom the same difficulties were presented. Granted that her religious tendencies biassed her against the Boleyn faction, and Anne as its head, Katherine of Arragon was still alive while Jane's intrigues with the king were at their height, and Katherine of Arragon was the true representative of

[1] Byron's ' too *farouche* ' satire on this event is well known. See *Works* (ed. 1904), vii. 35-36.

the Roman faction. Granted that she was swept along by a force greater than herself, that her head was turned by flattery or even by the persuasions of her family; the night of the condemnation of her rival was hardly the time to receive and make merry with her royal lover, and the day of the execution was hardly the time to sit attired in rich raiment, and eat of the sumptuous delicacies prepared by the royal cook. Granted even that she loved the king, the 'discreet conduct' which Chapuys so much praised was hardly compatible with the heart of a woman who loved. Jane Seymour's character and conduct cannot be justified unless unscrupulous personal ambition can be looked upon as a justification of any action. Under the semblance of gentleness and tenderness and modesty, the keynote of Jane Seymour's life was inordinate ambition. It was by this ambition, and by this only, that she tuned her every action, and became queen of England, and the mother of an heir to the English throne.

CHAPTER II

THE BROTHERS OF A QUEEN

'Affection shall lead me to court, but I'll take care that interest keeps me there.'—' *Maxims of the Seymours,*' *Sloane MSS.*, 1523.

IT has been the pleasure of historians to contrast rather than compare the character of the two brothers of Jane Seymour, who, as uncles of Edward VI., came into power and predominance in the early years of his reign.   One historian will create a hero in the person of the elder of the two brothers, Edward the Protector, and to make the dramatic situation complete, further create a villain in the person of the younger brother Thomas, the Lord Admiral.   Another will see in the Protector a Cæsar Borgia, and yet another will see in the Lord Admiral one of his victims.   Those who have not found themselves called upon to draw so violent a contrast have granted ambition to both, but have looked on that of the Lord Admiral as a purely personal ambition, animated only by mean and selfish motives, on that of the Protector as impersonal and animated by broad and un-selfish motives.   It is not difficult to see how this concep-tion appears to be proved by facts if both are judged by their actions alone.   But a man must be judged by more than his actions, and in attempting to compare the two men not only their actions but their circumstances must be taken into account.   For it is always an easy thing for the man in possession to assume a lofty and dignified attitude, and seem not to care for the thing he has ; the ambition that was once personal is easily translated into an ambition that has all the attributes of greatness. For the rival who desires but does not attain, the attitude is not so dignified nor the translation so easy. The Protector was the man in possession, the Lord Admiral was the rival.

It is not a simple task to crowd into a few pages the varied incident and vivid romance of the lives of these two men. Though they themselves were unscrupulous enough, and of strong enough personality to have in any case left their mark in history, it was the ambition of their sister and her royal marriage that lifted them to the high course along which each travelled his own way to ruin. Of the other sons of Sir John Seymour, John, the eldest of the family, had died unmarried in 1520, while Henry, the third son, of a different mettle from the two others, lived the life of a country gentleman, appearing seldom if ever at court, and seeking no honours or preferments. For him his sister's marriage brought only the solid, and, to him, satisfactory benefit of an estate carved out of the See of Winchester.

Edward, the second and eldest surviving son, seems to have been born about 1500, and to have been educated both at Oxford and Cambridge. As early as 1515, as ' le fils de messe (*sic*) Seymour,' he was ' enfant d'honneur ' to Mary Tudor on her marriage to Louis xii. of France, and two years later he and his father were granted the constableship of Bristol castle. Chapuys notices him as having been in the service of Charles v., probably in 1522, and in the next year he accompanied the Duke of Suffolk's expedition to France, where, on account of his prowess, he was knighted by the duke. In the following year he was taking part as one of the Challengers in a grand feat of arms, was, with his father, one of those chosen to take part in Wolsey's embassy to France in 1527, and was in the royal train at the meeting of the Field of the Cloth of Gold in 1582. (See the picture at Hampton Court,

in which he and his father undoubtedly figure.)   During
the year 1534, as numberless letters among the state papers
of Henry VIII. show, he was involved in a dispute with
Lord Lisle, afterwards Governor of Calais, concerning some
lands in Somerset.   The next year, 1535, was momentous
for the Seymour family, and Sir Edward, being brought
into the king's favour, not only received a grant of lands
in Hampshire, but also a visit from the king at his manor
of Elvetham in that county.

In the meantime his younger brother Thomas, born about
1508, had not come so much into public notice.   The first
mention of him is in 1530, when he was employed on
frequent embassies by Sir Francis Brian, into whose service
he had entered.   From 1536, the year of the royal marriage,
both brothers started on a further course of preferments.
The elder brother was immediately (5th June 1536) created
Viscount Beauchamp with a pension of twenty marks a year.
The next day the King granted him manors and lands in Wiltshire, the manors of Broad Town, Sherston and Amesbury,
Winterbourne and Alleworthbury ; the site of the late priory
of Holy Trinity, Easton, the manors of Easton, Froxfield,
Grafton, Corsley, Monkton, Tidworth, Barwick Basset,
Richardston, Langden, Midghall, Stodley and 'Costowe';
the site of the late priory of Farley, and the manors of
Farley, Chippenham, Thornhill, Broome, Urchfount and
All Cannings, with remainder in tail male to the issue of his
wife Anne (Stanhope), or in default of such to the issue of
any future wife.   In the following month he was given the
office of keeper, governor and captain of the Island of Jersey,
and the castle of Gorey, *alias* Montorguill (Mont Orgueil)
with fees as enjoyed by the late governors.   In August he
was made Chancellor and Chamberlain of North Wales, and
was one of the seventeen peers summoned to the council at
Westminster that year.   Further, in the August of 1537,
came a grant of the Wiltshire manors of Slaughtenford,

Allington, Maiden Bradley, Yarnfield, and Kingston Deverell. Although not keeping pace in honours with his brother, Thomas Seymour was one of the Gentlemen of the Privy Chamber in 1537, and was that year granted for life, in conjunction with one George Cotton, the offices of Chief Master and Constable of the Castles of Lyons, alias Holte, Bromfield, Yale and Chirk, and also Constable and receiver of the manors of Lyons, Bromfield, Yale, Chirk, Chirkland, Kenloth and Owen in the marches of Wales.

The birth of Edward VI. brought new honours to both. Thomas Seymour was knighted and Viscount Beauchamp was created Earl of Hertford. Some reaction necessarily came with the death of Queen Jane, and, in the following years, the Earl of Hertford was described as ' young and wise,' but ' of small power.' It seemed, indeed, at that time that fortune, that is to say the king, was favouring the younger brother.[1] In March 1588, he was granted the site of the monastery of Coggeshall, together with various manors and lands in Suffolk. There was also some talk of his marriage with Mary, Duchess of Richmond, the only daughter of Thomas Howard, third Duke of Norfolk. Indeed, the Duke of Norfolk told the king that ' he could well find in his herte and wold be glad standing so with the kinges pleasure to bestowe his doughter on Sir Thomas Seymour, as well for that he is so honestly advaunced by the Kinges Maiestie as also for his towardness and other his comendable merytes.' The marriage never took place because, it seems, the lady's ' fantezey would not serve to marry with him.'

Breaking for a moment into the course of events it seems well here to consider some of the moot questions that have arisen concerning the marriages of the Earl of Hertford. By his first wife, Katherine, daughter of Sir William Filliol

[1] For a detailed account of his life, see Sir John Maclean's *Life of Sir Thomas Seymour of Sudeley.*

of Woodlands in Horton, Dorset, to whom he was married
before 1519, he had two sons, John and Edward. The
supposed repudiation of Katherine, and the later entail which
settled his estates and titles on the issue of his second wife,
Anne, have been explained in various ways. One story given
by Peter Heylyn states that when the Earl, then Sir Edward
Seymour, was in France, he ' did there acquaint himself
with a learned man, supposed to have great skill in magick ;
of whom he obtained by grat rewards and importunities,
to let him see, by the help of some magical perspective, in
what estate all his relations stood at home. In which im-
pertinant curiosity he was so far satisfied as to behold a
gentleman of his acquaintance in a more familiar posture
with his wife than was agreeable to the honour of either
party. To which diabolical illusion, he is said to have given
so much credit that he did not only estrange himself from
her society at his coming home, but furnished his next
wife with an excellent opportunity for pressing him to the
disinheriting of his former children.' Another bit of evidence,
which Horace Walpole quoted with great gusto, is found in
Vincent's *Baronage* in the College of Arms. There a note is
added to the statement that Katherine Filliol was Sir Edward
Seymour's first wife, to this effect,—' *repudiata quia pater ejus
post nuptias, eam cognovit.*' A later point of view has been
to reject all this evidence as false, to suppose that Katherine
was dead before the second marriage, and that the entail
was due to the influence of the second wife, ' a lady of a
high mind and haughty undaunted spirit,' or, as Baker's
Chronicle puts it more forcibly, ' a woman of haughty
stomach.' One piece of evidence that has not yet been
used throws more light on the subject than any as yet
brought under consideration. The inquisition post mortem
taken on the death of Sir William Filliol in 1528 shows
three things. In the first place, that his relations with his
daughter and her husband were entirely changed between

EDWARD SEYMOUR, DUKE OF SOMERSET AND LORD PROTECTOR.
From an engraving in the British Museum.

1519 and 1528 ; in the second, that his daughter had already been repudiated by her husband and was henceforward to live in a nunnery; and, in the third, that his attitude towards her husband was even less friendly than it was towards her. In a previous indenture, made in 1519, Katherine, his daughter, wife of Sir Edward Seymour, was named one of his executors, and, in her default, her son John should take her place. In 1528 he declared his will and intent ' for many dyverse causes and considerations ' to be that neither his ' doughter Katherine nor hir heires of hir boody ne Sir Edward Seymour hir husbonde in any wyse have any part or parcell ' of his manors or estates, except certain lands of his inheritance lying within the county of Sussex. Instead, his executors were to take the yearly revenues, etc., for the performance of his will and ' duryng the lyff of . . . Dame Katherine Seymour,' were to pay her £40 a year from the profits ' for hir necessarie lyvyng . . . as longe as shee shall lyve vertuously and abide in some house of relegion of wymen.' ' Yf,' the will continues, ' my seid doughter do not lyve vertuously and abide in some honest house of relegion of wymen to the pleasing of God, then I will that my said doughter have no parcell of the said £40, but the said executors do dispose thereof towards the performance of my testament and last will and other good deeds of charitie.' Moreover, Sir Edward Seymour was to have no part in the said £40, but it should be delivered into the hands of the daughter. And ' if her husbond will not suffer hir to dispose it att hir pleasure for hir honest and necessarie lyving,' then the executors should deliver no part of the £40 to her, but of the same should ' paye for hir apparell and all hir other necessarie thinges as long as she shall order hir self.' If her husband would not suffer them to do this, then the money should be applied to the performance of the will. Less than eight years later, in April 1536, Sir Edward Seymour and his second wife, Anne

c

Stanhope, were lodged in the royal palace at Greenwich. Anne Stanhope had been associated with his sister Jane in the service of Anne Boleyn, and with her high lineage, her friendship with Jane and her position at court, she was a far more suitable wife for the aspiring young courtier than Katherine Filliol, whatever the faults of the latter may or may not have been. As for the fate of Katherine, considering the strained relations that existed in 1528 and the conditions of her father's will, it is probable that if she were not dead by this time she was still living in 'some honest house of relegion of wymen.'

Sir Thomas in the meantime remained unmarried, but for the next two years was employed as bearer of despatches in the various embassies connected with the matrimonial speculations of the king. The culmination of these in the marriage with Anne of Cleves in December 1539 is well known. Both the brothers were among the English nobles who met the new bride at Calais and supped with her there. Hertford wrote to Cromwell that nothing since the birth of Edward VI. had pleased him so much as this marriage. He also, like his brother, had been employed abroad during the past year, having been sent in March 1538-9 to provide for the defence of Calais and Guisnes. On his return Chester Place, without Temple Bar, was granted him as his reward. He had, moreover, entertained the king at Wolf Hall in the autumn of that year, and as further reward had received a grant of the Charterhouse at Sheen. One of the steward's account books of Edward Seymour, Earl of Hertford, preserved at Longleat, shows how on ' Setterday the ix[th] Daye of Auguste the King's Majesty with his nobility and hole Household,' and 'my Lord and my Lady with thare Hole Household ' were entertained at Wolf Hall. The king and his nobility appear to have supped apart from the earl and his family, as there is a separate account of the two suppers, and of the diet for the Sunday, Monday and

Tuesday while the royal party remained. The expenses
for the whole week, including the king's visit, amounted to
£288, 19s. 10d. (representing about twenty times as much
as the same amount at the present day), but the whole
expense does not seem to have fallen on the earl, the
king's officers paying the greater amount. They also seem
to have paid the earl for the ' hides, fells and tallow of
the beifes and muttones expended whiles the king was at
Wolf Hall.'

During the next few years, the eight years before
Henry VIII. died, while Hertford was winning his brilliant
victories in Scotland and France, his brother was not only
employed as ambassador to Hungary and the Netherlands,
but was employed also in a new sphere of duty, being created
admiral in October 1544.

Let us turn first to the events of those years as connected
with the Earl of Hertford. Already, from the fall of Cromwell in 1540, as a result of the pitiful failure of Anne of
Cleves to please the king, Hertford began to have some
taste of the power that was to be his when Henry was dead.
During the king's progress through the north of England in
the autumn of 1541, Hertford, Cranmer and Audley had the
complete management of state affairs in London. In 1542 the
earl was appointed Warden of the Scotch marches, but failed
to serve there for more than a few weeks since ' the country
knew him not nor he them.' However, on the 5th of March
1543-4, on account of the new alliance between France and
Scotland, he was appointed lieutenant-general of the North,
and in the following May, having been unable to compel the
unconditional surrender of Edinburgh, he allowed the Canon-
gate to be blown in and the city pillaged for two days. A
month later he returned to England and was appointed lieutenant of the kingdom under the Queen Regent during the
king's absence in France. But his services were needed
abroad. In August he reached Boulogne, and was present at

the surrender of the town—the following January he took
command at Boulogne, and when surrounded there by a large
besieging army sallied out with only about 4000 foot and
700 horse, took the French by surprise, and completely routed
them. Boulogne was then safe, and Hertford was needed
in Scotland, where the king's forces had suffered defeat at
Ancrum Muir. Hence he was recalled and once more made
lieutenant-general of the North. In the autumn of 1545 he
entered Scotland and, meeting with no opposition, sacked
and burnt monastery and castle, as they came in his way, on
a march of about twenty days. In October he was recalled
to London, and was in attendance at the Council until the
following March, when he was once again appointed lieutenant-general of Boulogne, replacing the Earl of Surrey,
whose miserable military blunders he had to remedy. Peace
followed in the summer of that year, and for the next
few months Hertford remained constantly at court and in
attendance on the Council.

Indeed, unless the Imperialist party were to triumph, it
was necessary that Hertford should be at hand. The king's
days were numbered, and a child of nine would be king.
The question was who should be king over the king. The
influence of Hertford was strong and was growing in
strength. Van der Delft, the Spanish ambassador, wrote,
in September 1546, to the Queen Dowager of Spain and
the emperor concerning the changed attitude of the king
towards the emperor, and how certain persons (the Earl
of Hertford and the then Lord Admiral, John Dudley)
had come into great favour with the king, ' so that he [the
ambassador] wished they were as far away as they were
last year.' The fall of the Howards, the Duke of Norfolk
and the Earl of Surrey, the only important rivals of Hertford,
in December 1546, practically ended the party struggle.
The reforming party, with Hertford at its head, was left
triumphant. 'Affairs here change almost daily,' Van der

Delft wrote to the emperor, '. . . the councillors are now of a different aspect, and much inclined to please and entertain the earl and the admiral [Dudley], neither of whom have ever been very favourably disposed towards your Majesty's subjects. This being the case . . . these two have entirely obtained the favour and authority of the king, . . . nothing is done at court without their intervention, and the meetings of the Council are mostly held in the Earl of Hertford's house. It is even asserted that the custody of the prince and the government of the realm will be entrusted to them, and the misfortunes that have befallen the house of Norfolk may well be said to have come from the same quarter. As regards the diversity of religion, the people at large are to a great extent on their (Seymour and Dudley's) side, the majority being of these perverse sects and in favour of getting rid of the bishops.' The ambassador continues later, ' I have always found the king, personally, strongly in favour of preserving the friendship with your Majesty, and I understand he will never change in this respect: but it is to be feared, if God take him, which I trust will not be the case for many years, the change will cause trouble and plunge everything here into confusion.'

A few days later Chapuys, the other Imperial ambassador, wrote to the queen dowager of his fears that, in the coming parliament, the bishops would be divested of their property and authority, and receive nothing but certain pensions from the king's coffers. This plan he thought the Earl of Hertford had first conceived through the teaching of Cromwell, who, ' as soon as he doubted his ability to reconcile the emperor with the king, adopted the expedient of entering into this heresy, and so to place the whole of the realm at issue with his Imperial Majesty.' ' If,' he adds, ' (which God forbid) the king should die, which would be more inopportune for us than it would have been twenty years ago, it is probable that these two men (Seymour and Dudley) will have the management of affairs, because, apart from the king's affection for them and other reasons, there are no other nobles of a fit age and ability for the task.' The king's death came sooner than either Chapuys or Van der Delft expected. On the night of Thursday, the 27th of January 1547, while the Duke of Norfolk lay in the Tower, a condemned prisoner awaiting execution, Henry lay in his palace at Westminster, the victim whom Death had chosen in the other's stead. As, overcome by weakness, the king slept a little through the night, outside in the gallery there paced the Earl of Hertford and his ally Sir William Paget, the king's chief secretary, watching each moment for the momentous change to come. At two o'clock in the morning Henry passed away, and, as the reins of authority fell from his hand, Hertford and Paget concerted together outside in the gallery to secure the handling of those reins for themselves. Handing over the king's will to Paget, Hertford himself set off to secure the person of Edward vi., then at Hertford, deciding meanwhile to keep secret the news of the king's death. On Monday he was returning to London with the young prince, and on that day Henry's death was announced in parliament by the Chancellor, while Paget read aloud the greater part of the king's will. At three o'clock in the afternoon ' the kinges maiestie . . . rode in at Algate and so along the wall by the Crossed Friars to the Towre Hill and entred at the Redd Bulwarke where Sir John Gaze, Constable of the Toure, and the Lieutenant receaved his maiestie on horsebacke, the Erle of Hertforde ryding before the king and Sir Anthonie Broun riding after the kinge.' ' Le Roi est mort, vive le Roi ! '

Turning back to consider what those last years of the reign of Henry vIII. had meant in the life of Sir Thomas Seymour, one gains some idea of the capacities and character of the man who was to be so deadly a rival to

the kingly pretensions of his brother. He had, as we have
seen before, been frequently employed on embassies,[1] and
thus, in the spring of 1542, he was despatched on a mission
to Ferdinand, King of Hungary, to ascertain the state of
that country and its possible attitude to England in the
event of a war between England and France. He seems
to have been well received in Vienna, where he found
Ferdinand engaged in preparations for an attack on Buda
and Pesth. Writing from the thick of the preparations
early in July, Sir Thomas gave an account of the forces of
the King of Hungary, and also mentioned the delivery
of Henry's missive concerning the engagement of troops
to Baron Heydyke, a pensioner upon England, ' who,' he
states, ' friendly doth offer us all the pleasure that in hym
ys.' ' It may plesse Your Heynes,' he continues, ' to hold
me exkewsed with this elle hand and grosse indytyng of
this letter, for this tyme and I trost shortly, for lake of a
better to trobell Your Heynes with the lieke thereof.' Six
days later he wrote the king a full account of the strength
of weapons and men of the King of Hungary and his chances
in the coming expedition against Buda. Of the attitude
of the country to the French he writes, ' Here hath ben a
proclamation made that all Frenche men do forth with
avoyde the camp, and that if any be founde within the
presynk of the same that he shall losse hys hede. I assure
Your Heynes, as ferre as I can perseve, that never nashon
was worse beloved in a camp than they be here.' Early
the next month he reported to Henry that the news concerning the approaching attack on Buda was ' so unserten '
that he was ' in fere to wreyght them ' to the king lest
what he should ' wreyght shuld prove contrarey.' In
effect the preparations of Ferdinand were fruitless, as the
attack on Buda and on Pesth failed utterly, and the Turks

[1] See *Cal. S. P. Dom.*, vols. xvii.-xx., for letters written by Sir
Thomas Seymour.

were left in possession. Sir Thomas, who had gone with
the army to Pesth, was recalled by Henry in the following
autumn, being finally commissioned to ascertain what
force of mercenaries could be put at the disposal of
England. Further, the king bade him ' to conduct and
hier there for Us at such wages as you shall think mete,
ten taborynes on horsbak after the Hungaryons facion ;
and if it be possible, whatsoever we pay for them, to get
oon or two of that sorte that can both skilfully make the
sayd taborynes and use them : and likewise we wolde you
shuld provyde us of ten good dromes and as many fifes.'
Seymour wrote back to England that he would do his best
to arrange for the hire of mercenaries, and had already sent
a man with ' all delegence to the campe to provyde the
dromes and fyffes.' As for the drums and fifes he wrote,
' as I passe throw the contre I shall inquyre for the ketell
dromes that you wolde have provyded, for in the camp
thar warre but 2, the on was with the Hongeryns and the
other with the Generall.'

   In the following December Seymour was despatched
to Nuremberg to treat for the hire of mercenaries, but
the negotiations fell through, and he was recalled in
January 1542-3. In the following May, as a result of
his treaty with the emperor, Henry decided to send
ambassadors to reside with the Queen Regent of Flanders,
and chose Sir Thomas Seymour and Dr. Nicholas Wotten
for ' the express purpose of communicating to her matters
and things respecting the said closer friendship and
alliance.' Chapuys himself wrote to the Queen Regent
in favour and commendation of ' Mons. de Semel,' as he
styled Sir Thomas, ' both out of respect for the king, who
sends him to reside at your majesty's court as on account
of that gentleman's qualifications and honourable parts,
for this king's satisfaction, and the many obligations under
which I stand towards him and his brother, the Earl of

Hertford, lord high chamberlain of the king.' In June the queen wrote to Chapuys telling him how the English ambassadors, by that time resident at her court, had earnestly requested her to exempt the English merchants from the duty of 1 per cent., saying they had a mandate to that effect from the king their master. Though unwilling to sustain the loss such an exemption would bring, the queen, by their persuasion and 'considering the present state of affairs and fearing that if we went on refusing the application they (the English) might delay the settlement of matters of greater importance' decided to postpone the collection of the duty from English merchants until some further agreement should be made with the king.

Early in the next month, before the matter was settled, Sir Thomas Seymour was recalled. War had been declared against France by the King of England, and Sir Thomas Seymour was appointed marshal of the army sent to Calais under Sir Thomas Cheyne. Dr. Nicholas Wotten, who was now left alone to represent England at the Queen Regent's court, wrote to Henry 'His (Sir Thomas Seymour's) departure hence must nedis be most discomfortable to me, for that burden of the whiche hitherto I have supporttide the lesse parte, now by his departure restithe holelye yn my necke, the whiche to sustayne I knowe and knowledge my self moste insufficient.' Meanwhile the command of the army in France had been transferred from Sir Thomas Cheyne to Sir John Wallop, and Sir Thomas Seymour was made second in command. On the 24th of July, Seymour was sent in command of a strong force against the Castle of Rinxent in the Boulonnais. The siege was successful and the castle was destroyed. Next, he attacked another castle called ' Arbrittayne,' ' one of the strongest piles within Bullonoiz,' with the same success. Thence he marched towards Ligne, and Wallop reported that 'The fyers that was made . . . merching towardes Leskes (Ligne) left feawe villages unburned in all that countrey.' At Ligne Seymour forced the Abbey, a strong castle, to surrender, and found it was garrisoned only by eighteen men and boys. After a council of war in August the army, reinforced by imperial allies, was for a time quartered at Font de l'Angle, awaiting the King of England's orders. While there, Sir John Wallop fell sick of the ague and was removed to Valenciennes, Sir Thomas Seymour taking command during his absence. In October the emperor wrote to Chapuys that Master Wallop fulfilled his duties admirably, but 'as to the marshal, he has shown himself colder and more difficult to meet than we should have wished ; but this,' he adds, 'is merely intended for your particular ear.' [1] Early in the next month the English army took leave of the emperor and retired into winter quarters in Calais.

During the next year Henry rewarded Sir Thomas Seymour for his services in this campaign of 1543, granting him a licence for the exportation of wood and oats in the January of 1543-4, and another for the exportation of beer. In March, 'for his good, true and faithful services already given and to be given in future,' he was granted the office of keeper of the King's Park of Farleigh Hungerford, and in April he was appointed Master of the Ordnance for life.

In the campaign of 1544, Seymour was present during the unsuccessful siege of Montreuil, and at the close of the campaign in the autumn of that year returned to England. The news that a French fleet had put to sea, in the autumn of 1544, in order to cut off communication between

---

[1] It is well to note that in the Public Record Office *Calendar of State Papers, England and Spain*, vol. vi., from which most of this information is taken, the references to Sir Thomas Seymour are wrongly ascribed to the Earl of Hertford in the index.

Boulogne and England, brought a new honour for Sir Thomas Seymour. He was appointed Admiral of the King's Navy with instructions to convey a great quantity of provisions to Boulogne. This accomplished, he was ordered to station the warships in mid-channel, and at the same time, if possible, to ' appoint a convenient numbre of the small shallopps and other small vessels to passe in the River Estaples, and there burne and bring away suche vessells of thenmies as may be there found, or do such other annoyaunce to thenmies as the tyme will serve.' On the 6th of November Seymour wrote to the Council advising that he should attack the coasts of Brittany, ' yf it shall plesse you to sende the shepes that kepe the narow sees to meett me at the Wyghte ande geve us leve to go into Brettayne I am in beleffe to sarve the Kynges Majeste well.' The king consented, but Seymour's designs were met with failure. A violent storm spoilt an intended attack on some of the enemy's ships which were lying at Dieppe and in the Seine, and, being obliged to take recourse to the open sea, his ships were so battered that the next day he reached the Isle of Wight with only part of the fleet, all the boats having been lost during the night.

The king, being quick to anger, evidently conveyed his dissatisfaction at the failure of the enterprise to the admiral through the Privy Council. Thus, on the 18th of November, Seymour wrote to the Council that he had received their letters and ' perseve be the same that I am thowght neclegent in the accomplechement of the Kynges Heynes plesur. Yf it can be so provede, I am both worthey of ponychement and blame ; and havyng don the best that in me was, I am to be exkewsed.' He then proceeds to give some account of the night at sea, and to show how impossible it had been to combat the elements. ' Wharfor,' he continues, ' I deseyer your Lordshepes to cawlle all the captaynes ande masteres that ware in this jorne and yf any of them be abell to say that we myght lay lenger in Dover Road, the Downes or Bollen Rode, as the wynde dede change without pottynge ourselves ande the Kynges shepes in gretter danger, then let me barre the blame ; and yf we have don but as the wether wolde serve I shuld desyer your Lordeshepes to blame the wether ande lett me, with the rest in my company be exkewsede, to incorage us to serve on the see a nother tyme, rather then to blame us with out deserttes.' This manly letter and appeal to his commonsense won the king's forgiveness, for, in the following January, 1544-5, he granted Sir Thomas Seymour the manor of Water Eton in the county of Berks. The following July Sir Thomas was stationed at Dover, but by September he had joined the fleet at Portsmouth, and, on the 11th of that month, wrote to the king concerning the plague that was raging among the ships. ' Dyvers of the shippes whiche Your Majestie appointed to kepe the seas with me, Sir Thomas Seymour, are infected as it may appere by the margyne of a boke of the said shippes names being noted with a pricke against every of the said shippes.' In the following November Henry granted the admiral a house called Hampton Place, in the parish of St. Clements, without Temple Bar. During the next year he was appointed English commissioner ' to settle the delimitation of the territories in the Boulognais and the questions about the fortifications. Paulin, the General of the Galleys of France, was the French commissioner. Van der Delft wrote to the emperor, in December 1546, that the two commissioners had been unable to agree on the spot, and had therefore both come to England to settle about it. However, the Imperial ambassador believed rather that Paulin had arranged the coming to England ' more for the purpose of promoting the intrigue,' of which he (Van der Delft) had given information to the King of England, ' who was very glad to know of it.'

There were only a few more weeks for Henry to live, and, strangely enough, there seems to be no indication of Sir Thomas Seymour's doings during those weeks in which his brother was becoming the most powerful noble in the kingdom, and was preparing to become ruler over the king to be.

CHAPTER III

THE UNCLES OF A KING

'Debellare pares !—occumbere pares !
—Ex quo discordia fratres
Perducit miseros.'

'DELIBERATE maturelye in all things. Execute quyckelye the Determynations. Do justice without respecte. Make assured and stayed wyse men mynisters under you—Maynetayne the Mynisters in their offices. Punnyshe the disobedient according to their deserts. In the King's causes give comyssion in the King's name. Rewarde the King's worthye servants liberallye and quicklye. Give your owne to your owne and the King's to the King's frankelye. Dispatche suyters shortlye. Be affable to the good and sterne to the evill. Follow advise in Counsaill. Take Fee or Rewarde of the King's onlye. Keep your Mynisters about you uncorrupte. Thus God will prosper youe. The King favour youe and all men love youe.'

Such was the advice that Sir William Paget sent to his friend, the Earl of Hertford, as a New Year's gift, in one of the late years of Henry VIII.'s reign. Already, as we have seen, it was a foregone conclusion that Hertford would need this advice when Henry VIII. should die, for it was he who would inevitably be chosen Protector. And the inevitable came. The prophetic dread of Chapuys was fulfilled. The will of Henry VIII., whether genuine or not, was potent in effect, and its sixteen executors were unquestionably accepted as governors of the young king not by their right as Privy Councillors, but in their capacity as executors of the will. Fifth only in the list came the Earl of Hertford, but this placing had no meaning. On the 31st of January the councillors met in the Tower and almost unanimously nominated Hertford as Protector. Wriothesley alone raised objection, but deferred his will to that of the majority, and announced the nomination to the king. The minutes of the proceeding ran thus :—' We . . . by oone hole assent, concorde and agrement, uppon mature consideration of the tendrenes and proximitie of bludde between our Soveraigne Lorde that now is and the Erle of Hertforde, being his uncle, and of the grete experience which he hath in all affayres of this realme and all other the Kinges Maiesties realms, dominions and cuntreys have . . . gevin unto him the furste and chief place amonges us, and also the name and the title of the Protectour of all the realmes and dominions of the Kinges Majestie that nowe is and of the Governour of his most royal persone : with this special and expresse condicion that he shall not do any Acte but with thadvise and consent of the reste of the coexecutors in such maner, ordre and fourme as in the said wille of our said late Souveraigne Lorde and moste Gracious Maister is apoynted and prescribed.' On Sunday, the 6th of February, Paget announced the honours that were to be conferred on the executors, and among them Hertford himself was made Duke of Somerset, and was given the barony of Seymour of Hache, and the Duke of Norfolk's offices of Lord High Treasurer and Earl Marshal. His brother, Sir Thomas, who was one of those appointed to assist the executors, was created Lord High Admiral and Baron Seymour of Sudeley.

The preliminaries over and his position so far assured, Somerset, within a fortnight of his promotion, turned to clear away from his path the only rival he, for the moment, feared. Wriothesley, as Lord Chancellor and as a convinced Romanist, would inevitably oppose every attempted reform, both social and religious, and would endanger all Somerset's

ambitious schemes.   He well knew of Wriothesley what Sir
Richard Morison wrote of him at a later date, that he was
' an earnest follower of whatsoever he took in hand, and did
very seldom miss where either wit or travail were able to
bring his purpose to pass.'   Hence Somerset was ready to
seize the first opportunity of attack on so dangerous a foe.
The opportunity came quickly.   Before the end of February
Wriothesley, as Lord Chancellor, had empowered four
civilians to hear cases in Chancery in his absence.   Complaints were immediately made to the Council by ' divers
students of the Common Lawes,' the question was referred
to the judges, and Wriothesley was sentenced to lose his
office and incur such penalty and fine as the king should be
pleased to inflict, and imprisonment at the king's will.   His
offence, as stated by the Protector, was not only that he had
' menassed divers of the said lerned men and others for their
service to the King's Majesty in this behalfe but also used
unfitting wourdes to me, the said Protectour, to the prejudice of the Kinges estate and thindrance of His Majesties
affayres.'   When Wriothesley's power was thus crippled
Somerset was content.   His foot had been on his rival's
throat ; he did not wish to kill.   Wriothesley was paid the
legacy left him by Henry VIII., and soon afterwards was
admitted to the new Privy Council, and Somerset was
commended by the world for ' gentleness.' [1]

Wriothesley's fall accomplished, Somerset was able to
influence the Council to change the status both of his powers
and of their own.   The young king was persuaded to ' moste
graciously condescend and graunte ' a commission stating
the powers of the Protector to execute ' all and every other
thing ' which should belong to the office of a ' Governour

---

[1] See Gardiner's letter to Somerset (Foxe, vol. vi.) : ' Your grace
showed so much favour to him (Wriothesley) that all the world
commended your gentleness.'

of a king,' and to ' procure and execute all and every other
thing and thinges, acte and actes of what qualitie or effecte
soever they be or shalbe concerning our affayres . . . both
private and public . . . in such like maner and fourme as
shalbe thought by his wisedome and discrecion to be for
the honour, suretie, prosperitie, good order, wealth and
comodite of us.'   Moreover, the king nominated twenty-six
councillors, breaking up the appointment by Henry VIII.'s
will, and gave the Protector full power to summon ' suche
and so many as he from tyme to tyme to thyncke convenient,' or to add new members at his will.

Somerset was now at the height of his power. The difficulty of the task before him cannot be overestimated. The
results of the social and religious changes of the reign of
Henry VIII. were now ripening in full force, and were involving England in a dangerous policy abroad, and in an
economic and religious dislocation at home. It is not necessary or in place to enter into any actual account of Somerset's
methods of government. That has been done often enough
elsewhere. It is enough here to make some attempt to
summarise the character of the man himself as shown by
his work during his brief authority, and to suggest how the
policy which he inaugurated might have made the reign of
Mary an impossibility if it had been less rashly hurried
forward and less hurriedly brought to a close on personal
motives.

It is not easy to gather any clear idea of the growth of
Somerset's religious views, or to come to any conclusion as
to the part they played in his life apart from their political
and financial meaning. However, by the end of the last
reign he had been looked upon as an ardent Reformer, and
the leader of those who were in favour of ' getting rid of
the bishops.' Certainly the early events of the Protectorate bore out this assertion. Cranmer, with Somerset's
support, embarked on a rapid succession of sweeping

D

reforms, culminating in the Communion service in the English tongue and the first Book of Common Prayer. Added to this doctrinal change came the confiscation of the chantries and the tearing down of images. Pamphlets expressing the views of the extremists flooded the country while the Romanist point of view was everywhere suppressed.

The effect on the country population, still buried deep in the old religion, can be imagined. The agrarian discontent already stirred up in the last reign by the policy of enclosures and by the dissolution of the monasteries was aggravated by the confiscation of chantry lands, and by the excessive greed and aggrandisement of the already rich. Somerset himself, one of the most rapacious of a generation of property thieves, among other things seized on a vast amount of ecclesiastical property, and pulled down a parish church to build his palace, the original Somerset House, where the modern building now stands. The gap between rich and poor was being steadily widened, and at this moment Somerset chose to substitute for the accustomed time-honoured service what to the unlearned seemed ' a Christmas game.' He, doubtless, saw the mummery of the old Latin service, and, seeing that the future would bring the ordinary man to the reformers' standpoint, seems to have little expected the opposition of the western counties. But here, as always, he showed his unwisdom in acting according to his own impulse, without keeping his finger on the pulse of the nation, as the Tudor genius for government might have taught him to do. The unwisdom of forcing extreme and unwelcome reform at the moment when social discontent was brewing everywhere was to preclude even his most biassed admirers from counting Somerset a statesman. Yet he has been praised for placing a stone in the temple raised in the honour of Liberty because of his attempted social and economic reforms, and his opposition to enclosures, and because of his repeal of the statute giving proclamations the force of law, and of the new felonies and treasons acts.   In the abstract his ideal may have been liberty, but in the practical the liberty he allowed was the liberty he enforced, that is to say, liberty, granted obedience to him.   This, at any rate, was presumably, without the justification of being a religious fanatic, the result of his extremist reform policy.

His foreign policy as the issue of his religion was of necessity opposition to Spain; and his rash, impatient warfare in Scotland ruined every possibility of a union between England and Scotland, and instead drove Scotland once more into the arms of France, already England's enemy on account of the constant bickerings about the fortifications of Boulogne.

Yet it was not his policy, religious, economic, or foreign, that brought Somerset to the scaffold.   It was rather the ambition and greed for power that made it impossible for him to share his authority with any other, and the arrogant impatience with which he thrust a policy which he knew to be ultimately acceptable on a nation whose instinct is to receive reform only if it comes imperceptibly and, as it were, by accident.   There was yet another element in his character, a contrast to all the rest, but as sure a factor in his fall; a limitation and yet a strength in so far that, although failure is written across his life, it has won and still wins him a certain popularity.   It was a peculiar sensitiveness that kept him, with but one exception, from the unscrupulousness of a Napoleon, and won him the title of ' verie gentle and pitifull.'

It was a strange mixture, this arrogant monarchic instinct which made the man the enemy of his equals, and of none more than his own brother; this sensitiveness which made him the friend of the people, ' the poore commynaltie of Englande' and a seeker after popular support.   Had he had less ambition, and had he been less blind in the impatient pursuit of his own will and less jealous of power, the sensitive gentleness of his character would have stood him in good stead. As it was, the two elements blended in such a ratio could not act together in one man for any good end. At the one moment when most of all his ' gentleness ' should have outcried his ambition, it failed lamentably. He allowed his brother to be sacrificed not on high state motives, not as dangerous to the king or nation, but on purely personal motives, as dangerous to himself and his own monarchic power.

While Somerset had been acquiring kingly power his brother Thomas, the Lord Admiral, Lord Seymour of Sudeley, had been grasping at authority in another way. Henry viii. died in January 1546-7. In February the Lord Admiral wrote to the Princess Elizabeth ' the most eloquent letter in the world ' asking her hand in marriage.[1] She wrote ' contenting herself with unfolding to him in a few words her real sentiments.' The letter, she confesses, has surprised her, for she writes, ' besides neither that my age nor my inclination allows me to think of marriage, I never could have believed that any one would have spoken to me of nuptials at a time when I ought to think of nothing but sorrow for the death of my father.' She must, at least, have two years to mourn for her father's loss, ' and how,' she adds, with a characteristic touch, ' can I make up my mind to become a wife before I shall have enjoyed for some years my virgin state, and arrived at years of discretion ? ' Finally she winds up by dwelling on his virtues and merits and her esteem of them, begging that she may preserve for herself the privileges of recognising him as ' *a disinterested person* ' without entering into that strict bond of matrimony which often ' causes one to forget the possession of true merit.'[2] Rebuffed   by   Elizabeth's   worldly   wisdom,   the   Lord

[1] Gregorio Leti, *Elisabetta* (1693), Pt. i. Bk. i., 173-5.   [2] *Ibid.*, 176-7.

Admiral turned his advances in another direction and, by the following May, he was writing to the Queen Katherine Parr as her favoured suitor. ' I shall ombeley desyr your highness to geve me one of your small pictures, yf ye hav any left, who with his silence shall geve me occahson to thynk on the frendly chere that I shall reseve when my sawght (suit) shalbe at a nend.' His next letter was signed ' from hym that ys your loving and ffaithful hosbande dewyrng hys lyffe.' A letter from Katherine Parr at about the same date suggests something of romance in their courtship in spite of the previous proposal to Elizabeth, and indicates that Seymour had been an old time lover. ' I wold not have yow to thynke,' she writes, simply and candidly, ' that thys myne onest good wyll towarde yow to proceed from any sudden motion or passion ; for as truely as God ys God my mynde was fully bent the other tyme I was at lybertye, to marye yow before any man I knowe howbeyt, God withstode my wyll thereyn moost vehemently for atyme, and throwgh hys grace and goodnes made that possible wyche simeth to me most impossible ; that was, made me to renownce utterly myne one wyll and to folowe hys wyll most wyllingly It wor to long to wryte all the processe of thys matter, yf I live, I shall declare it to yow myself.' [1]

Kathcrine, it seems, like Elizabeth, had asked for two ycars' respite, but Seymour was doing his best to persuade her to change the two years into two months. She wrote to him coyly and teasingly, ' My Lord where as ye charge me with a promys wryttin with myne oune hand to chaunge the two yeres into two monethes, I thynke ye have no such playne sentence wrytten with my hand ; I know not wether ye be a paraphryser or not, yf ye be lerned in that syence yt is possyble ye may of one worde make a hole sentence, and yett nott at all tymes alter the true meanyng of the wryter,

---

[1] Letter in Sudeley Castle collection given in facsimile by Mrs. Dent, *Annals of Winchcombe and Sudeley*, to face p. 163.

as it aperyth by thys exposycyon upon my wrytting.'
The letter continues in another vein, ' When yt shalbe your
pleasur to repayre hether ye must take sum payne to come
without suspect. I pray yow lett me have knowledge (o)ver
nyght at what hower ye wyll come, thet your porteresse
may wayte at the gate to the feldes for you.' This letter
is signed ' By her that ys and schalbe your humble true and
lovyng wyff during her lyff, Kateryn the Quene K. P.'

The lovers knew the opposition they would encounter,
more especially from the Duke and Duchess of Somerset.
Katherine had already hinted to Seymour that coldness and
opposition might well be expected from his brother. ' I
gether,' she wrote to Seymour, ' ye are in sum fere how to
frame my lord your brother to speke in your favour ; the
denyall of your request schall make hys foly more manyfest
to the world.' She advises him not to put his suit to his
brother more than once, but rather to win the goodwill of
the king and the council ' wyche thynge obtained schalbe no
small schame to your brother and lovynge syster in case they
do not the lyke.' In spite of all foreseen difficulties Seymour and the queen were married either in the May or
June of that year, but the fact was kept secret. The young
king, whose affection for Seymour was far stronger than that
for the Lord Protector, was importuned to give his consent
to the marriage, and the Lady Mary was written to for the
same purpose, as though the event were unsettled. The
king seems to have been easily won over, but the Lady
Mary wrote declining to be ' a medler in thys matter con-
sydering whose wyef her grace was of late.' King Edward
made a note of the marriage in his Journal, adding the sig-
nificant comment, ' with this marriage the Lord Protector
was much offended.'

At length, when the marriage was a recognised fact, the
jealousy and mistrust between the two brothers, each bent
on a similar end—his own personal aggrandisement—took

a more decided aspect, and was further nurtured by the position and jealousy of the two wives. Katherine Parr, as Queen Dowager of England, necessarily took precedence of the Duchess of Somerset; but Katherine Parr, as wife of the Lord Admiral, was bound to give way to the pretensions of the wife of the Lord Protector. Already, before the marriage, the two women had been enemies. There is the sarcastic reference, before quoted, to Seymour's 'loving sister.' Then in another letter complaining that Somerset had not kept his promise to come and see her, Katherine adds, 'I thynke my Lady hath tawght hym that lesson; for yt ys her coustome to promys many comynges to her frendes and to performme none. I trust in greatter matters she is more cyrcumspect.'[1] Early in the next year she wrote to her husband informing him that 'my Lord your Brother hathe thys afternone a lytell made me warme—yt was fortunate we was so muche dystant for I suppose els I schulde have bytten him. *What cause have they to fear having such a wyff. Yt ys requysyte for them contynually to pray for a schorte dyspatche of that Hell.*'[2] Another of the queen's letters shows more clearly than anything else the attitude which the Protector maintained against his brother. 'I perceyve ye have had no little trobell and busyness with your mater,'[3] she writes to her husband, 'I supposed my Lorde Protector would have used no delay with his Friend and naturell Brother in a mater wyche ys upryght and just as I take yt. What wyll he do to other that be indyfferent to hym I judge not very well.' After uttering her own 'coler' she bids her husband not to unquiet himself 'with any of his [the Protector's] unfriendly parts, but bere with them for the tyme.' Her letter

[1] Letter at Sudeley Castle, quoted above.
[2] Haynes, *Burghley Papers*, i. 61.
[3] The special matter here referred to seems to have been a dispute that had arisen between the Protector and his brother concerning some jewels that had belonged to Katherine as queen, but had been seized by the Protector, who refused to relinquish them.

ends with a womanly touch contrasting with the rest, 'I gave your lytell knave your Blessing who lyke an onest man styred apase after and before.[1]

In spite of the jealous opposition of the Protector and his wife the romance of the marriage of the Lord Admiral had so far gone well. On the part of the queen at least, as her letters clearly show, the marriage was based on strong personal feeling and attachment to the Lord Admiral. It is a more difficult thing to read the riddle of his feelings, and to judge how much of his attachment to the queen was based on personal affection, how much on his insatiate ambition.

The tragedy of the story was soon to begin. After the death of Henry VIII. the Princess Elizabeth, who firmly guarded the secret of the proposal of the Lord Admiral, had been given into the care of Katherine Parr, with whom she lived at Chelsea while the marriage negotiations were in progress. On the news of the marriage of Katherine, the Princess Mary had in vain tried to bring about the withdrawal of her sister from Katherine's household. It would have been a happier day for Katherine if this had happened. As it was the Lord Admiral was thrown into close contact with this young girl to whom he had lately proposed marriage. Her force and boldness of character appealed to a man of his temperament, while her rank as the sister of the king and possible heir to the throne appealed to his ambition. Evidence was given at a later date as to the familiarity with which he treated the young princess, familiarity in which Katherine seems at first to have laughingly joined, until she realised something of the seriousness of the situation. 'The Admiral loved her [Elizabeth] but too well,' was the witness of Mrs. Ashley, Elizabeth's governess, ' and hadde done so a good while, and the Quene was jelowse on hir and him in so much that one tyme the Quene, suspecting the often accesse of the Admirall to the Lady

[1] Haynes, *Burghley Papers*, i. 62. Katherine was expecting a child.

Elizabeth's Grace, cam sodenly upon them wher they
were all alone (he having her in his armes) wherefore
the Quene fell out both with the Lord Admiral and
hir Grace also.' It seems to have been after this incident
that, early in 1548, Elizabeth was removed from Sudeley
Castle into other custody. Thence she wrote to the queen
thanking her for her many kindnesses, but expressing also
some uneasiness lest she should have forfeited the queen's
good opinion. 'Truly,' she writes, 'I was replete with
sorowe to departe from your highnes especially leving you
undoubtful of helthe and albeit I answered litel I wayed
more dipper whan you sayd you wolde warne me of all
evelles that you shuld hire of me.' Evidently it seems
Katherine remained a friend to her young step-daughter in
spite of her own jealousy. This may have been because many
of the scandals concerning Elizabeth had come about through
the insinuations of the Duchess of Somerset, the queen's
rival, who seems to have reported that Katherine was no
fit guardian for the young princess, since she allowed her,
among other things, to stay out late at night on the river
Thames.

In the autumn of 1548, the queen gave birth not to a 'lytell
knave,' but to a daughter. The Admiral in his joy wrote the
news to his brother, the Protector, who answered congratulating him that the queen, escaping all danger, had made him
the father of 'so pretie a daughter. And altho,' he continues,
'it would have been both to us, and as we suppose to yow, a
more joye and comforte if it had bene this the furst a sonne,
yet thescape of the daunger and the Prophecie and Good
hansell of this to a great sort of happie sons, the which, as
you write, we trust no les than to be trew is no small joye
and comforte to us.' This letter and the good comrade-
ship evinced by the Protector is not easy to interpret
rightly. It is generally taken to imply that the Protector
had no desire to maintain the strained relations between

his brother and himself, and wished to show that he no longer regarded his marriage with disfavour. On the other hand, it may be that the Protector, in view of the greater danger which had since presented itself, the danger of the Lord Admiral's possible aspiration to the hand of Elizabeth, was wise enough to see the value of this new link binding him to the queen.

However that may be, the hope of such was soon shattered. On Wednesday, the 5th of September, 'between 2 or 3 of the clocke in the morninge,' the queen died and was buried, being 'cearid and chestid in lead,' in the chapel of Sudeley Castle.[1] 'Two days afor the deth of the Queen,' as Elizabeth Tyrwhyt, one of her attendants, afterwards gave witnes, 'at my comyng to her in the mornyng she askyd me wher I had been so long, and sayd unto me she dyd fere such Thinges in harself that she was suer she cold not lyve. Whereunto I answaryd as I thowght that I sawe na lyklyhod of Deth in har. She then haveyng my Lord Admirall by the hand and dyvers others standyng by, spake thes wardys, partly as I tooke byt idylly, "My Lady Tyrwhyt I am not wel handelyd, for thos that be about me caryth not for me, but standyth lawghing at my gref, and the moor good I wyl to them, the less good they wyl to me." Whereunto my Lord Admirall answered, "Why, sweet harte, I wolde you no hurt." And she said to hym agayn alowd, "No, my Lord, I thinke so," and immediately she sayed to hyme in hys eare, "but, my Lord, you have geven me many shrowed tauntes."' Perhaps the queen herself suspected or had realised that treachery had accomplished her death, or it may have been that this inquietude was the result of the distorted imagination of a dying woman. In Wriothesley's Chronicle the death of the queen is noticed with no suspicion of the story of poisoning which the Admiral's enemies were only too eager to seize upon as likely

---

[1] The little daughter lived only a few days after the mother.

or true. As a matter of fact the suspicion is unfounded, except for this story of the restlessness of the queen, and the fact that her death seemed to come at an opportune moment in the progress of the Admiral's schemes. Anyhow, he was now free to make open suit to Elizabeth, as open, that is, as he dared in the face of the inevitable opposition of his brother.

Already he had spared no efforts to undermine the authority of the Protector, and win the young king and the Council, if possible, to his side. He clearly saw that the way to gain the support of the young king was, on the one hand, to be always ready to give him pocket money, and, on the other, to be frequently persuading him of the unfairness of keeping him so long in ward. With an impetuosity characteristic of the man's temperament, he seems to have spread his ideas concerning the Protectorate wherever he went, and his confidence, easily won, was easily betrayed when the hour of his misfortunes came. It is certain that he took a busy part in the alteration of the Protectorate patent in the October of 1547, since the idea was to make the Protector's tenure of office depend, not on the duration of the king's minority, but on the king's pleasure. On the basis of precedent he declared he would ' never consent or agree that the king should be left as warde till he come to the yeres of eighteen whereby he misliked my Lord Grace's [first] patent.' Obviously he had yet his trump card to play if he could cheat his brother and marry Elizabeth. The Protector's fate would be sealed, and where he stood, or even higher still, perhaps, the Admiral himself would stand ; the position would be reversed.

His actual course of procedure during those four last months of the year 1548 is not easy to follow, but it is clear that rumours of his attachment to Elizabeth were rife everywhere. Wrightman, one of his servants, later confessed a conversation he had had at Sudeley with Nicholas

Throckmorton, concerning his master, soon after the queen's death. They had both thought, so he declared, that the death of the queen should make the Admiral have 'the lesse mynde to the keaping together of worldelye goodes, and also learne him to stande in the more fear and awe of God, who coulde, by the same meane, withdrawe him from the worlde that he had taken so notable a wief from his use.' Moreover, they trusted, 'it wooll make him a good wayter at the courte and . . . more humble in harte and stomache towards my Lord Protectour's grace.' They hoped further that ' he wooll become a newe maner of man bothe in harte and service, for he must remember that if ever anye grudge weare borne towardes him by my Lady of Somerset, it was as most men gesse for the Queen's cause who now, being taken awaye by Death, it wooll undouttedlye followe (oonelesse the fault lie in himself) that she wooll beare him a good Harte as ever she did in her lief.' Throckmorton warned Wrightman that the Admiral was thought to be ' a very ambitious man of Honour,' and it was feared that now ' the Queen was gone ' he would be desirous for his advancement to match with one of the king's sisters. Wrightman promised to do all he could ' to breake the Dance.' The Lord Admiral himself told the Marquis of Northampton that he ' had herde of a wonderfull Thyng, saying he was credibly informed that my Lord Protector had sayd he wolde clappe him in the Tower if he went to my Lady Elizabeth.' The marquis had answered he thought it but ' somme vayne Bruite ' but advised the Lord Admiral to put any suspicion touching the Lady Elizabeth and himself out of the Protector's head. The Lord Admiral declared ' ther was no woman lyving that he went about to marye.'[1]

However, by January 1548-9, the danger had become too serious for the Protector to remain inactive, and he determined to put a decisive end to his brother's career. On

[1] Haynes, *Burghley Papers.*

the 17th of January, the Lord Admiral was committed to
the Tower by the Protector and eighteen of the councillors.
Inquiries were made right and left to gather in every
possible evidence concerning the admiral's relations with
Elizabeth. She herself wrote to the Protector in answer
to his letter asking her to declare what she knew in the
matter. She told how, ' after the Queen was departed,' she
had asked Mrs. Ashley, her governess, ' what newes she
hadde from London,' and she had answered merrily, ' They
say ther that your grace shal have my Lord Admiral ànd
that he will come shortlye to woue you.' The Princess
advised him not to come to see her at Hatfield House, but
she avoids saying whether her advice was followed or not.
The probability is, therefore, that it was not. At the end of
her letter Elizabeth states the actual form which rumours
were then taking concerning herself and the Admiral.
' Master Tirwit and others have told me that ther goeth
rumers abroad wiche be greatly bothe agenste my Honer
and Honestie (wich above al other thinks I estime) wiche be
these ; that I am in the Toure, and with child by my Lord
Admiral.' ' My Lord,' she continues, ' these are shameful
schlanders for the wiche, besides the great desire I have
to see the King's Maiestie, I shall most hasteley desire
your Lordship that I may come to the Court . . . that I
may shewe myselfe there as I am.'

There is an atmosphere of vivid romance hanging over
these years of Elizabeth's life. This letter, and the
clever way in which she avoids committing herself by
any definite statement, although seemingly denying all
charges by designating them shameful slanders, shows
something of the way she was already training for her
evasive policy of later years. It suggests more. It
suggests that Elizabeth had something very real to hide,
and that that ' something ' was her affection for the Lord
Admiral. It is not unlikely that he also had been prompted

by more than his ambition in his suit to her, and that the
relations between them had been the outcome of real personal feeling.   However that may be, it was not easy to
discover the truth where such a skilled actress as Elizabeth
was concerned, and it is still less easy at this date.
Yet a theory is quick to present itself as a working
hypothesis. Is it not possible, one asks, that there was
some ground for the rumours which Elizabeth could not,
or at least did not definitely deny, and is it not possible also
that this explains much of her conduct when queen, and
answers the well-worn question why she did not marry ?
Moreover, her after policy of encouraging the piratical raids
of John Hastings and Francis Drake had perhaps in it a
memory of the good lover of her youth, the pirate Lord
Admiral.[1] Whether this is only idle conjecture or has in
it some elements of truth, it is certain that Elizabeth
maintained a sincere affection for the Admiral, and, at a
later date, received and accepted a poem written by
Nicholas Throckmorton in his praise—

> 'He was hardy, wise, and liberal,
>   His climbing high, disdained by his peers,
>   Was thought the cause he lived not out his years.'

In the meantime, while evidence of all kind was being
collected and concocted against him, the Lord Admiral
remained in the Tower throughout the months of January
and February 1548-9.   On the 28rd of February the
whole Council, except Somerest, Cranmer and Baker, went
to the Tower to examine him on thirty-three articles in
which the charges against him were supposed to be summed
up.   He refused to reply unless confronted by his accusers
in open trial. To avoid this the personal authority of the
king was necessary. Hence the next day the Lord
Chancellor waited on the king after he had dined, and
reported to him the 'heynous and trayterous attempts

[1] See the articles of his trial quoted later.

THOMAS SEYMOUR, LORD SEYMOUR OF SUDELEY.
From an engraving in the British Museum.

and doeings' of the Lord Admiral, and how he had made
'obstinate refusall to answer to the same or to excuse himself if peradventure there might be any hope for him.'
The other members of the Council in turn brought their
persuasions to bear on the young king, and lastly, the
Protector himself declared how sorrowful a case this was
for him, and yet that he would rather regard 'his bownden
dutie to the king's majestie and the crown of England than
his own son or brother, and did wey more his allegiance than
his blood.'   The king, not daring to protest, 'perceyved'
that they 'requyred but justice to be done,' and permitted
them to proceed according to their request.   Once again
the Lord Chancellor and other representatives of the
Council went to the Tower, and declared their commission
to the Lord Admiral, and, 'uppon his stif standyng and
refusall to answer, used as many persuasions and mocions
unto him as thei coulde.'   At last they persuaded him to
answer to the articles which were there read to him in
order.   Whereupon, scorning to consider the others, he
answered the three first articles.

To the first, which charged him with going about to 'undo
the order,' and get into his own hands the government of the
king, he answered that he had said to a certain Mr. Fowler,
a gentleman of the Privy Chamber, 'if he might have the king
in his custodie as Mr. Pag[et] had he wolde be glad, and that
he thought a man might bring him through the galery to his
chamber, and so to his howse,' but this he had spoken 'meaning no hurte.'   To the second article, charging him with going
about to allure His Highness to condescend and agree to
the same 'by corrupting with gifts and fair promises divers
of the Privy Chamber,' he answered that he had given
money to two or three of those who were about the king, and
to Mr. Fowler of the Privy Chamber he had given money
for the king many times, and 'what time Mr. Latymer
preached afore the king' he sent £40 by Mr. Fowler, £20

as a 'good rewarde for Mr. Latymer,' and the other for
the king to bestow among his servants. The third charge
was that he had written a letter for the king (evidently
suggesting that he should be his governor), which the king
was to write to Parliament to be delivered in Parliament
by the Lord Admiral, who would make there a 'broile or
tumult and uprore to the great daungier of the Kinge's
Majesties persone and subversion of the state.' To this
the Lord Admiral answered he had drawn 'suche a Bill
in dede himself and profferid yt to the king or els to Mr.
Cheke,' and before this he had caused the king to be
sounded by Mr. Fowler whether he could be 'contented
that he shulde have the governaunce of him but he knew
not what answer he had.' The ten following articles
practically repeated the same charges in different words,
and as the Lord Admiral saw, therefore needed no further
answer. The fifteenth, sixteenth, seventeenth and
eighteenth articles dealt with the excessive number of
retainers he had gathered round him to the 'great perill
of the state of the realme.' The nineteenth, twentieth and
twenty-first dealt with his marriage with Katherine Parr,
and aspirations to the hand of Elizabeth, accusing him of
marrying the late queen so soon after the king's death,
that 'if she had conceived straight after it shulde have
bene a great doubt whether the childe borne shuld have
been accompted the late king's or his.' The next five
articles accuse him of obtaining the control of the mint at
Bristol from Sir William Sharington, whom he seems to
have protected from a charge of felony. The most interesting articles follow. They charge the Lord Admiral
with encouraging pirates, of having stolen goods in his
hands and distributing them among his servants, of casting
the 'takers of pirates' into prison 'to the discouraging of
suche as truly shulde serve the Kings Majesty,' and of
letting the 'hed pirates' go free, as though he were

authorised to be the chief pirate and to have all advantage thei could bring.' The thirty-third and last article charges him with storing provisions at Holt Castle, placing the country thereby 'in a great mase, dowte and expectacion, loking for some broile, and wolde have been more if by your apprehension it had not bene staied.' [1]

Alarmist lies played the most important part in compassing the death of the Lord Admiral. Whatever may have been his ambition and unscrupulous greed for power, there is no proof that his designs endangered the state or the personal safety of the king. His one object was to wrest from his brother the power which he had usurped, and to gain a greater share in the government which that brother had monopolised. However, the Bill of Attainder against him was passed, the judges in the House of Peers, and all the Council convicted him of treason, and he was sentenced to be executed on Tower Hill. Great stress is laid on the absence of Somerset from this meeting of the Council for, 'from natural pities sake, he desired license to be absent,' but it is obvious that Somerset saw how to play his part and that this was in his part. He had been present at all the previous Council meetings, had attended the House of Lords while the Bill of Attainder was pending, and had lent his own voice to debar the Lord Admiral from fair and open trial. Now there was no need for his presence, the result, he knew, was a foregone conclusion. Moreover, his name headed the list of those who signed the death warrant.

On the 20th day of March, 1548-9, the Lord Admiral was executed. Two days later Latimer, who had often profited by the Lord Admiral's generosity during his lifetime, preached before the king defaming the dead man's character. 'He died very dangerously, irksomely, horribly . . . being in the Tower he wrote certain

[1] See the *Acts of the Privy Council, sub anno*.

E

papers . . . one to my Lady Mary's Grace, and another to my Lady Elizabeth's Grace, tending to this end that they should conspire against the Lord Protector's Grace.' Further, Latimer announced that when he was on the scaffold, and about to lay his head on the block, he had desired his servant should be bidden to ' speed the thing that he wots of.' This, according to Latimer, referred to the two papers which the servant confessed had been found ' sewed within the soles of a velvet shoe.' To make the story more plausible Latimer continued—' He made his ink so craftily and with such workmanship as the like hath not been seen. . . . He made his pen of the aglet of a point he plucked from his hose and thus wrote those letters so seditiously. . . . God had left him to himself, he had clean forsaken him . . . surely he was a wicked man : the realm is well rid of him.' In the following month Latimer was still preaching against the memory of the Lord Admiral, noting how, when ' the good queen that is gone had ordeyned in her house dayley prayer,' he had hidden himself ' lyke a moule diggyng in the earth.' Warming up in his hatred, Latimer then declared, ' He shalbe Lottes wife to me as long as I lyve. He was, I heard say, a covetous man, a covetous man indeede. I would there was no moe in England. He was, I heard say, an ambitious man. I would there were no moe in England. He was, I heard say, a seditious man, a contemner of common prayer : I would there were no moe in England. Well, he is gone, I would he had left none behinde him.' [1]

The death of the Lord Admiral was received with horror. ' Many a noble,' says Hayward, ' cried out upon the Protector, calling him a blood-sucker, a murderer, a parricide and a villain, declaring that it was not fit the

[1] *Latimer's Sermons* (Parker Soc.), i. 161, 228.

king should be under the protection of such a ravenous
wolf.'

As a matter of fact, the death of his brother was a fatal
blow to the Protector's power.   It lost him much of the
popularity among the people he had striven so hard to gain,
and did more than anything else to render him an easy
victim to the cooler and more artful politicians who were
preparing all their forces to bring about his ruin.   They
had not long to wait for their opportunity.   Troubles, as
the result of his general policy, began to fall thick and fast
around him, culminating in Ket's Rebellion in Norfolk.
Warwick's success in crushing the most serious of the various
rebellions, contrasting as it did with Somerset's failures at
home and abroad, encouraged him in his intrigues against
the Protector.   Meetings of disaffected nobles, headed by
Warwick, were constantly held in the autumn of 1549.
Somerset, in order to prepare a counterblow, attempted to
arouse the commonalty on his side, urging them to rise in
his defence.   Ten thousand men are said to have answered
his summons, but Warwick and his adherents won the
support of the city of London, secured the Tower and the
services of fifteen thousand men to defend their cause.
Edward VI. in his journal gave an account of this time :—
' Then begane the Protector to treate by letters sending
Sir Philip Hobby . . . to see to his family, who brought
in returne a letter to the Protector very gentle wich he
delivered to him, another to me, another to my house to
declare his fautes, ambicion, vain glorie entring into rashe
warres in mine youth, negligent looking on Newhaven,
enriching of himself of my treasures folowing his own
opinion and doing al by his owne authorite, etc.' [1]

---

[1] This part of the journal contrasts strangely with the formal
letters written by the young king to his uncle when the latter was in
the height of his power.   In these letters he always acknowledged
most gratefully, so it seemed, the care which the Protector was taking

The Protector, seeing that all hope was lost, promised to submit, and on the 14th of October he was sent to the Tower. Early in January the charges against him, summed up in twenty-nine articles, were placed before Parliament. Somerset confessed everything, and threw himself on the mercy of the Council. He was deprived of his Protectorate by Act of Parliament, deprived of all offices and of land to the value of £2000. Early in February, he was freed from the Tower, and in the next month was again admitted to the Privy Council, and to precedence of all the other members.

However, signs were not wanting of covert enmity towards him in the Council. As early as the next October a slight was put on him by the refusal of the Council to go into mourning for his mother, although she was grandmother to the king. The excuse is admirably stated in the Acts of the Privy Council. The duke is said to have required the opinion of the Council ' what were meetist for him to use concerninge wearinge of doole.' They, thereupon, ' wayed with themselfes that the wearinge of doole not only did not profit the dead but rather used to enduce the living to have a diffidence of the better lief, and did more cause and semple of coldness in faith unto the weak, besides that many of the wiser sort waeing the impertinent chardges bestowed upon black clothe and other instruments of those funerall pompes might worthelie finde fault with the expences thereapon bestowed.' Hence the Council decided that ' doole should not be worn, since in a king's presence, being the herte and lief of his common-

in the promotion of the peace and religion of the kingdom, and thanked him for undertaking the business of the royal office during his own boyhood. With the failure of Somerset's schemes all gratitude, real or formal, disappeared. In all probability some of the young king's covert animosity towards his uncle had been first excited by his other uncle, the Lord Admiral, during the life of the latter, and had been still further increased by the circumstances of the latter's death.

weale, privat men shulde reserve their privat sorowes to their owne howses and not dymme the gladsome presence of their Prince with such doolefull tokens.' In spite of this slight, Somerset's position in the Council improved during the next few months, and, had it not been for the dissolution of Parliament in the February of 1550-1, he might have again resumed the office of Protector; popular opinion had veered round strongly in his favour, and he had the unfailing support of Paget and Arundel in the Council.

The result of this improved position was that he plotted to destroy his great rival Warwick. Such, at any rate, whether true or false, was the news revealed to the king and Council by Sir Thomas Palmer, who stated that he himself with Somerset, Paget, and Arundel, had determined to raise the country and murder Warwick. However, Fate was against Somerset. Whether his plans against Warwick had gone so far or not, his rival was certainly sparing no pains to bring about his ruin, and Somerset's forced absence from the Council meetings in the September of 1551 gave Warwick the opportunity he needed to mature his designs. Early in October Warwick was made Duke of Northumberland, and his adherents were likewise promoted. A few days later Somerset was summoned to answer to the Council concerning his debts to the king. He attended as usual on the 16th of October, was arrested, and sent to the Tower. The *Diary* of Henry Machyn, citizen of London, states that, on the 15th day of October 'was lead to the Toure the Duke of Somerset and the Lord Grey, on the 16th' (the 18th in Wriothesley's *Chronicle*) 'the Duchess of Somerset, Sir Ralfe Vane and Sir John Thyn, as also Sir Thomas Holcroft, Sir Michael Stanhope, Mr. Hammond, Mr. John Seimour, etc.' 'On the 21st was carried to the Toure my lord Pagett by the guard.' On the next day 'was alle the

craftes [of London] commandyd to go to ther halles and
ther yt was [shewed] them that the Duke of Somersett
wold [to] have taken the Towre and to have [destroyed]
the cete and then to go to the ylle of Whytte and so every
craft to ward at evere gatt in London and to have a rydyng
wache through the cete.' Wriothesley's *Chronicle* notes
how the Council, on the 19th of October, declared the mis-
demeanours of the duke to the Commons, and ordered that
' everie cittizen in his owne house shoulde looke to his
familie, and to see that vagabondes and idle persons might
be avoyded out of the cittie.'

'On the xxx day of November,' says Machyn, ' ther
was a grett skaffold mad in Westmynster halle agaynst
the next day, that was the ffurst daye of December, for
the Duke of Somersett, the which was raynyd of treson
and qwytt of ytt and cast of fe[lony] and ther was such
a shutt of men and women for they thought that he had
byne qwytt.' And Wriothesley noted in his *Chronicle*,
' There was such a shoyke and castinge up of caps that
it was heard into the Long Acre, beyonde Charinge
Cross, and also made the lords astonyed, and word [was]
likewise sent to London which the people rejoysed at,
and about v of the clocke at night the duke landed at
the Crane in the Vintre, and so [was] had thorough Can[dle]
Wyke Street to the Toure, the people crying, God save him "
all the way he went.' One party, says Holinshed, cried
with joy that he was acquitted and the other cried out that
he was condemned. The second party was right ; the earl
had been condemned for felony, for having designed to kill
the Duke of Northumberland and others, and, according to
the journal of Edward vi., he had ' seemed to confess he
went about their death.' At last Northumberland's day
had come. Somerset was beheaded on Tower Hill ' afore
ix of the clocke in the forenoon, which took his death very
patiently, but there was such a feare and disturbance amonge

the people sodainely before he suffered that some tumbled downe the ditch and some ranne toward the houses thereby and fell, that it was marveile to see and hear, but howe the cawse was, God knowith.' Such was Wriothesley's testimony. A cry of pardon had been raised but Somerset was not deceived. Protesting his loyalty to the king his nephew, he died; and, more than seven weeks after the trial, the young king made a note in his diary, ' the Duke of Somerset had his head cut off upon Tower Hill on the 22nd January 1551-2, between 8 and 9 o'clock in the morning.'

Peter Heylyn, in his *History of the Reformation*, gives a forcible, if only half true, picture of the two brothers :—
' The admiral was fierce in courage, courtly in fashion, in personage stately, in voice magnificent : the duke was mild, affable, free and open, more easy to be wrought on but no way malicious, and honoured by the common people as the Admiral was more generally esteemed among nobles. The Protector was more to be desired as a friend, the other more to be feared as an enemy. The defects of each being taken away, their virtues would have made one excellent man.'

One last word must be spoken concerning the literary ability of the two brothers. In keeping with their characters, it was the Protector alone who possessed some literary gifts and tastes and knowledge. A doggerel poem, supposed to have been written a few days before his death, is alone ascribed to the Lord Admiral. It deserves quotation because of the sentiments expressed—

> ' Forgetting God
> To love a kynge
> Hath been my rod
> Or else no thynge
> In this frail lyfe
> Being a blast

Of care and stryfe
Till yt be paste
Yet God did call
Me, in my pryde
Leste I shulde fall
And from him slyde
For whom he loves, he
Must correcte,
That they may be
Of hys electe,
Then, death, haste thee,
Thou shalt me gaine
Immortallie
With God to raigne,
Lorde ! sende the kyng
Like years as Noye (Noah)
In governinge
Thys realme in joye,
And, after thys
Frayl lyfe such grace
That in thy blisse
He maie find place.'

There is something very characteristic of human nature suddenly brought face to face with death in these quaint lines, yet although this, together with the contrast they present to the Lord Admiral's everyday character, might suggest in the paradox of things, that they are genuine, the use of the term 'hys electe,' belonging as it does to a later doctrinal period, relegates them rather to the seventeenth than the sixteenth century.

The Lord Protector having read, during his first imprisonment, a translation in manuscript from the German entitled *A most spirituall and most precious Pearl, teaching all men to love and embrace the Cross as a most sweet and necessary thing*, proceeded, on his release, to get the manuscript printed, and himself wrote a characteristic preface. In this book he says is put forth 'a real medycyne for an unquiet mind,' for it is well known that ' whosoever foloweth but worldlye and mans reason to teache comforte to the troubled mynde can geve but a counterfeit medycyne.' ' In our greate trouble,' he continues, ' whyche of late dyd happen unto us (as all the worlde doth know) when it please God for a tyme to attempte us wyth hys scourge, and to prove yf we loved hym : in reading thys book we dyd fynd greate comforte and an inward and godlye workynge power much relevyng to the gryefe of oure mynde.' Hence it seemed to him to be his duty to put this book before all men, as the duty of a Christian ' to be ready to helpe all men by all wayes possible.'   There is in Tottel's *Miscellany*,[1] a poem entitled ' The pore estate to be holden for best,' the first letters of the lines of which (with the last of the last) make the acrostic ' Edwarde Somerset.' It is written in two rhyme royal stanzas of Alexandrines in the style of Wyatt and Surrey, and may have been written by the Lord Protector during one or other of his imprisonments.   His other work of note was the translation of Calvin's *Epistle of Godly Consolation* from French to English.   Religion, whether it had meant little or nothing to him, except from a political standpoint, during the ambitious years of his life—and this, it seems, must remain an unanswered question—certainly brought him, in his last years, the consolation that he expressed in his Preface to *A Spiritual Pearl*, apart from any question of images and shrines and spoliation of church property.

[1] *Songes and Sonettes* (Tottel's *Miscellany*), 1557, ed. Arber, p. 164.

CHAPTER IV

VICTIMS OF ELIZABETH

'Our life is turned
Out of her course wherever man is made
An offering or a sacrifice.'—Wordsworth.

The romantic marriages of the Seymour family were not to end with the death of the Lord Admiral.

The Duke of Somerset, by his first wife Katherine Filliol, had two sons; John, who was sent to the Tower with his father in October 1551, and, dying there in December 1552, was buried in Savoy Hospital, and Edward, who was knighted at the Battle of Pinkie in 1547, and was restored to blood by Act of Parliament in 1553. He settled at Berry Pomeroy, in Devonshire, and was the ancestor of the Seymours of Berry Pomeroy, the present Dukes of Somerset.

For the moment, however, we will concern ourselves with the children of the second marriage of the Protector. These were four sons and six daughters. Two of the sons died young, the others were Edward, Earl of Hertford, whose life is the most interesting, and Henry, the admiral, whose greatest fame is that he was concerned in the fight against the Spanish Armada. Of the six daughters, Anne, the eldest, married firstly, John Dudley, son of the Earl of Northumberland, and, secondly, Sir Edward Unton;[1] Margaret, Jane, and Katherine all died unmarried, the last being maid-of-honour to Queen Eliza-

---

[1] She died in February 1587-8, and there is extant ' A sermon preached at Farington (Faringdon) in Barkeshire the seventeene Daye of Februarie 1587, at the buriall of Anne, Countess of Warwicke, widow of Sir Edward Umpton,' by B. Chamberlaine, London, 1591, 8vo.

beth ; Mary married, firstly, Andrew Rogers of Bryanstone, Dorset, and, secondly, Sir Henry Peyton ; Elizabeth, the youngest, married Sir Richard Knightly of Fawsley, Northamptonshire. The three eldest daughters, Anne, Margaret, and Jane, composed some verses in 1550, on the death of Margaret of Valois, ' Annæ, Margaritæ, Janæ, Sororum Virginum, heroidum Anglarum in mortem Margaritæ Valesiæ Navarrorum Reginæ Hecadistichon.' [1] (Paris, 1550, 8vo.) Jane, as maid-of-honour to Elizabeth, became the bosom friend of Katherine Grey, also maid-of-honour, and encouraged the fatal marriage between Katherine and her brother, Edward, Earl of Hertford. She died at the court on the 20th of March 1560-1, and was buried at Westminster six days later. Henry Machyn describes the funeral in his diary :—' xxvi day of Marche at after-none at westmynster [was brought] from the quen['s] armere (almonry) my ladye Jane Semer, with [all the quire] of the Abbey with iiC of [the] quen's cowrt the wyche she was [one] of the quen['s] mayd[s] and in grett favor, and a iiij[xx] morners of [men and] women, of lordes and lades, and gentylmen and gentyllwomen all in blake, besyd odur of the quen's preve chambur and she [had] a grett baner of armes borne and master Charenshux was the harold and master Skameler, the new byshope of Peterborow, dyd pryche. [She was] bered in the sam chapell whar my ladye of Suffolke was.' She is supposed to have been

---

[1] Ronsard pays tribute to these ' trois belles chanteresses,' in the third ode of his Fifth Book.

> ' Mais si ce harpeur fameux (Orphée)
> Oyoit le chant des Serenes
> Qui sonne aux bords escumeux
> Des Albionnes arenes
> Son luth payen il fendroit
> Et disciple se rendroit
> Dessous leur chanson Chrestienne
> Dont la voix passe la sienne.'

the daughter destined by her father to be wife of Edward vi., and to have taken an active interest in the Reformation, writing a Latin letter, under the direction of her tutor, to the Reformers, Bucer and Fagius, in 1549.[1]

Edward, Earl of Hertford, the eldest surviving son of the Protector, was probably born in 1539, was educated with Prince Edward, and was knighted at his coronation. Between 1547 and 1552 he was styled the Earl of Hertford, and since the attainder of the Protector left his son's titles and estates unaffected, he became *de jure* Duke of Somerset. However, three months later, his father's enemies procured an Act of Parliament limiting the late Duke of Somerset's lands, and declaring forfeit all the lands, estates, dignities and titles of the late duke and his heirs by his second wife.

Queen Mary restored Edward Seymour in blood, and is said to have desired to make him Earl of Hertford, but was dissuaded by her ministers. Elizabeth was inclined to look favourably on the nephew of the Lord Admiral, and, on her accession to the throne, created him Baron Beauchamp and Earl of Hertford in January 1558-9. His popularity with the queen was, however, but short-lived. In less than a year, in December 1560, by the connivance of his sister Jane, he had succeeded in secretly marrying Lady Katherine Grey, one of her companion maids-of-honour to the queen. When the queen had gone one morning to hunt, the Lady Jane and the Lady Katherine, leaving the palace at Westminster by the stairs at the orchard, made their way by the sands to the earl's house in Chanon Row.[3] Lady Jane is supposed to

[1] The letter is published in the third series of Zurich letters (Parker Society), i. 2.

Her monumental tablet in Westminster, with inscription erected by ' her deare brother,' the Earl of Hertford, is shown in an engraving in Dart's *Westminster Abbey*.

[3] Now Cannon Row, between Westminster Bridge Road and New Scotland Yard.

have secured a priest, and the two were married. Then the Earl, accompanying them to the waterstairs of his house, put them into a boat, and they arrived at Westminster before the queen was back from hunting. This was undoubted treason, for Lady Katherine was of blood royal and, by the Act of 1536, it had been made treason for one of blood royal to marry without the consent of the sovereign. In this case the offence was aggravated. Katherine, as great-granddaughter of Henry VII., now that her sister, Lady Jane Grey, was dead, stood next to the throne, barring the Scottish line, after Elizabeth.[1] Already, in 1560, a scheme had been afoot to marry her to Philip of Spain, who should assert her claim to the throne against Elizabeth on the ground that the latter was illegitimate. Now this dangerous rival was secretly married to one who was himself near to blood royal as cousin of the late king. For a few months the marriage was successfully kept

---

[1] Henry VIII. by will postponed the elder line of Scotland in favour of the descendants of his second sister, Mary, whose elder daughter, Frances, married Grey, Marquis of Dorset and Duke of Suffolk, and was the mother of Jane and Katherine. Katherine when only a child had been married, in 1553, to Henry Hubert, afterwards second Earl of Pembroke. There seems to be no evidence that the marriage was ever consummated, and, after the execution of Lady Jane Grey and her father, the Earl found it convenient to break the alliance and Katherine was divorced. Camden says that when she was divorced she was ' so far gone with child as to be very near her time,' and insinuates that the divorce was illegal—but the story looks like one of Camden's own making, or it would surely have been used as evidence against the Earl and Lady Katherine in 1561. If it were not for the youth of Katherine at the time (she could only have been about fifteen) one might perhaps suggest that the infant child referred to by Camden was the Katherine who is said to have been a child of Lady Katherine, and to have died when an infant (*See Dict. Nat. Biog., sub.* Edward Seymour, Earl of Hertford). The infant Katherine could not certainly have been the child of Katherine and Hertford, since they were allowed no communication after the birth of their second son, Thomas, in the Tower, and there had presumably been no attachment between them until after the date of the divorce.

secret. In March 1560-1, Lady Jane Seymour, the one friend in whom Katherine had been able to confide, died of consumption. In the following June, probably to avoid suspicion, the Earl of Hertford went to Paris with Thomas Cecil (afterwards Marquis of Exeter), in whose excesses he possibly joined either willingly or unwillingly, leaving his young wife alone with her deadly secret to face court gossip and court slander.

By the end of the summer she could keep her secret no longer. She first confessed it privately to Mrs. Sentlowe (afterwards Lady Shrewsbury), and then sought a private interview with Lord Robert Dudley, begging him to break her news to the queen, so that he might soften the queen's anger towards her. All to no avail. She was committed to the Tower in August, and there questioned on the subject. She refused to make any statements, but the father of her child was known. Hertford was summoned to England, and was sent to the Tower after his young wife. On the 24th of September [1] she gave birth in the Tower to her elder son, Edward, Lord Beauchamp.

The news roused Elizabeth's bitter anger, and from that moment she spared no pains to make Katherine's life unbearable. Her commission, 'under the broade seale,' was issued to divers commissioners, 'reciting that by public fame it came to her hearinge that the said Ladie had a childe wch was begotten by the saide Earle, wch manie thought to have been begotten by their unlawfull accompanyng together, and yett that the said Earle and Ladie affirmed that the same was begotten in lawfull marriage.' The commissioners were bidden to enquire 'as well of the crime as of the solemnization thereof.' The commission proceeded to examine 'the saide Earle and Ladie severally upon divers articles whereof they both confessed.' On the

---

[1] The exact date of his birth is given in the Bible that Hertford used in the Tower. It is now at Longleat.

12th of May 1562, the commission declared there had been no marriage, and that the child was illegitimate. They were both kept in the Tower with strict orders that they should not see one another. However, the earl, 'having by corruption of the kepers had secrett accesse by night to the Ladye Katherine,' another child, Thomas, was born to them in the Tower in February 1562-3. The earl was called before the Council and the Star Chamber and was fined at £15,000,[1] 'for the payment whereof,' wrote Sir John Mason to Sir Thomas Chaloner, 'an extent is gon uppon his landes: his bodye to remayne in prisone during the queen's pleasure.' Sir John further reported that Sir Edward Warner, the Lord Lieutenant of the Tower, was imprisoned 'uppon suspicion that he was not ignorant of the matter, but the matter falling out otherwise his deliverye is loked for daylie.'

The cause of the young couple was popular. Sir John Mason wrote to Cecil ' There be abrode both in the cite and in sondry other places of the realme very brode speaches of the case of the erle of Hertford summe following theyre lewde affections, and summe others of ignorance make such talles thereof as lyketh them, not lettyng to say they be man and wief, and whye sholde man and wief be lett from comyng together. Theise speaches and others, as I am informed, be very common.' In March 1563 Lord John Grey of Pyrgo (Essex) wrote to Cecil on behalf of his niece, Lady Katherine, ' I cannot but recommende her woefull liffe unto you. In faithe, I wolde I were the Quenes Confessor this Lent that I might join her in penaunce to forgeve and forget : or otherwise able to steppe into the pulpett to tell her Highnes that God will not forgeve her unleast she frelye forgeve all the worlde.' In August 1563, Cecil wrote to Sir Thomas Smith that ' my

[1] Of this Elizabeth remitted £10,000, demanding that £1000 should be paid immediately. Finally, the earl paid £1187.

Lord Hertford and my Lady Katherine because of the plague are thus delyvered ; he with his mother as prisoner, she with her uncle my Lord John Grey.' He adds, ' They die in London above a thousand in the week,' such were the ravages of the plague of this year. From Pyrgo, Lord John Grey wrote to Cecil thanking him for the delivery of his niece to his custody, and assuring him, ' She is a penitent and a soroful woman for the Quene's displeass' and most humblye and heartelye desires you to fynishe that your friendshipp begonne, for the obteyninge of the Quene's favor in the full remission of her faulte.' Lady Katherine herself wrote to her ' Good cosyne Cecill,' thanking him and her ' good cosyne ' his wife, for delivering her to her uncle, and adding that he need not doubt her ' owne deare Lords good wyll for the requitall thereof to the uttermost of hys power.' She ends her letter ' restyng in prayer for the Queen's Majesties long raigne over us, the forgeveness of myne offence, the short enjoying of my owne deare Lord and husband, wyth assured hope, through God's grace and your goode helpe and my Lord Robert for the enjoying of the Queen's Hyghnes favor in that behalfe.' It is clear, not only from this mention of Lord Robert (Dudley), but also from a mention of a letter written by him to Lord John Grey, that he had been moved by the petition of the young mother at an earlier date, and though not able to move his royal mistress, had done all in his power to help to put the unfortunate Katherine into the sympathetic custody of her uncle.

The next month after Lady Katherine left the Tower, the Lord Lieutenant, Sir Edward Warner, sent a description of the furniture of her rooms in the Tower to Cecil, ' it was delyvred by the Quene's commandment, and she hath worn it now two yere's ful, most of it so torn and tattyred with her monkies and dogs as wyl serve to smal purpose.' The inventory of the stuffs, delivered in the August of

1561, when Katherine was sent to the Tower, from the wardrobe of the Tower, follows, with remarks by the Lord Lieutenant. Since the list suggests an interesting picture of the rooms of the young wife, and of the dilapidated state of everything when she left, it is well to give it in full. It runs thus :—' Furst, vi peces of hangings of tapestry to hang her chamber [These be of dyvers sorts and very owld and corse]. Item, iii wyndowe peces of lyke stuffe. Item, a sparver for a bed of changeable sylke damaske [All to broken, not worth x^d]. Item, one silke quylte of red striped with gold [stark naught]. Item, one bed, a bolster of downe with ii pillowes of downe. Item, one whyte linning quylt stuffed with woll. Item, ii payr of fustians thone of vi bredthes, thother of fyve. Item, ii carpets of turkey makyng [The woll is all worne away]. Item, ii small wyndowe carpet. Item, one chayer of clothe of golde, cased with crymson velvet with ii pomels of copper and gylt and the Quene's armes in the backe [nothing worthe]. Item, one cushion of purpell velvet [An owld cast thyng]. Item, ii foote stooles covered with grene velvet, [Old stolys for King Henry's feet]. Item, one cubbard joyned. Item, one bed, one bolster, and a counterpoynt [1] for hyre women [a meane bed].'

In all probability, when once released from the Tower, Katherine and her husband might have remained in comparative peace and seclusion if they had been content to be separated from one another. But Katherine was pining away at Pyrgo, as Lord John Grey wrote to Cecil,[2] hoping to win the Queen's forgiveness through him. 'I assure you cowsigne Cecil (as I have written unto my lorde Robert) the thought and care she takethe for the wante of her Highenes favour, pines her awaye : before God I speake it if it come not the soner, she will not longe live thus, she

---

[1] Counterpoynt=counterpane; deriv. M. Fr. coutrepoincter.
[2] For this and following letters see Lansd. MSS. (Brit. Mus.) 6.8.9.102.

F

eateth not above six morselles in the meale. If I saie unto
her "Good Madam, eate sumewhat to comfort yourselfe,"
she faules a wepinge and goethe upp to her chamber; if I
aske her what the cause is she usethe her self in that sorte,
she aunswers, me, "Alas, Unckell, what a liffe is this to
me, thus to live in the Queene's displeasure; but for my
lorde and my childerne I wolde to God I were buried." '
In November 1568, Lord John Grey wrote again, enclosing a letter from his niece to the queen, and asking Cecil,
if he thought ' onni thyng ' ought to be amended in it,
to send it back before delivering to Lord Robert Dudley for
presentation to the queen. The enclosed petition from
the Lady Katherine craved pardon for the ' disobedient
and rasche matchinge of my selfe withowt your Highenes
consent.' She goes on to acknowledge herself a ' most
unworthye creature to feale so muche of your gracious favor
as I have don,' and declares that her ' great tormente of
minde ' is that she has so forgotten her ' dewtie ' towards the
queen. In spite of this cringing letter the queen would
not be moved. In the following month Lord John wrote
again to Cecil, telling of the ' augmentinge of my Neeces
greiff in the wante of the Quene's Majestie's favour.' She
was now confined to her chamber, and ' she never went to
bed all this time of her sicknes, but they that watched with
her muche dowted howe to fynde her in the morninge, for
she is so fraughted with fleame by reason of thought, wepinge
and settinge still, that many times she is like to be overcume
therewith. In the same month [1] Lady Katherine herself
wrote another pathetic appeal to Cecil, but all to no avail.

---

[1] It was at this time, probably the December of 1563, that false
reports went abroad as to the large sums expended by the Lord John
on his prisoner. Thus he wrote in the following January to Cecil
complaining of the untruth of these reports, and showing that Lady
Katherine was maintained by her husband even when she was a
prisoner at Pyrgo. He then gives a detailed account of ' my Lady of
Hartfords wekelye Rate for her lorde, her childe and her folks here :—

Whether these appeals would ever have accomplished their purpose or not it is impossible to say, but any possibility of such was frustrated by the unfortunate revival of the discussion of Katherine's claim to the succession. John Hales, clerk of the Hanaper, wrote a book called *A Declaration of the Succession of the Crowne Imperiall of England*, throwing aside the Scottish line and supporting the legality of the marriage of Lady Katherine, whose son, in that case, would be next heir to the crown. This settlement was very generally popular in the country, as Elizabeth well knew, but, in her own jealous hatred and half fear of Katherine, she was determined to end the possibility of such. Cecil wrote to Sir Thomas Smith in April 1564—' Here is fallen out a troublesome fond matter. John Hales had secretly made a book in the tyme of the last Parliament wherein he hath taken uppon hym to discuss no small matters, namely the title to this crowne after the Quene's Majesty, having confuted and rejected the lyne of the Scottish Quene and made the lyne of the Lady Frauncesce, mother to the Lady Katherine, only next and lawfull.' Hales was committed to the Fleet ' for this boldness,' especially because he had ' committed it to sundry persons.' ' My Lord John Grey is also in trouble for it,' wrote Cecil, ' and besides this John Hales hath procured sentences and counsells of lawyers from beyond seas to be wrytten in mayntenance of the Erle of Hertfordes marriadg. This dealyng of his offendeth the Quene's Majesty very much. God give her Majesty by this chance a disposition to consider hereof that either by her marriadg or by some common

For my Ladye her selfe lxvi^s viii^d ; For her childe xiii^s iiii^d ; For her childe's nurce vi^s viii^d ; for Mrs. Isham vi^s viii^d ; for Mrs Woodforde vi^s viii^d ; For Mrs. Page vi^s viii^d ; For Nowell v^s ; For Robert v^s ; For W^m. Hampton vi^s ; For a lackye v^s ; For her launder v^s ; For the widow that washethe the childe's clothes v^s ; Total vii^{ll} xvii^s viii^d.' It is evident that Lady Katherine only had one child, her youngest, Thomas, with her.

order we poore subjects maye knowe where to lean and
aventure our lives with contentation of our consciences.'

In May 1564, Cecil wrote further to Sir Thomas Smith,
' The Earl of Hertford is with Mr. Mason [Sir John Mason],
the Lord John [Grey] is here in custody.'   The Lady
Katherine was committed to the care of Mr. Petre (Sir
William Petre) probably at Ingatestone near Pyrgo, where
she remained until May 1566.[1] Cecil himself seems to
have come under suspicion of upholding Lady Katherine's
cause because of the suits which had been directed to
him. 'In this matter,' he wrote, ' I am by commandment
occupied, whereof I could be content to be delivered ;
but I will go upright, neither *ad dextram* nor *ad sinis-
tram*.' In November, he wrote with characteristic discretion, ' I have been also noted a favorer of my Lady
Katherine's title but my truthe therein is tryed, and so I
rest quiet, for surely I am and allways have bene circum-
spect to do nothyng to make offence. The Erle remayneth
with Mr. Mason and my Lady Katherine with Mr. Petre.'
In the following month he wrote again that the queen's displeasure continued towards my Lord Hertford and the Lady
Katherine and my Lord Keeper (Lord John Grey) and that
John Hales was still in prison.

For the next three years the Earl and his wife remained
in custody. In vain Anne, Duchess of Somerset, petitioned
for the release of her son, and in vain Katherine made
constant and pathetic appeals to be allowed to join her
husband. The Duchess of Somerset wrote to Cecil in
January 1565, ' Good Master Secretary, after thys long
sylens and for that as yet myne olde occasyon lettes
myne attendans, I have presumed by leter to renewe my
sute for my sonne to the Quenes Majesty, and have lyke-

---

[1] See *Engl. Hist. Rev.* xiii. 302-7.   The facts above quoted prove,
however, that the writer is in error in stating that Katherine's trans-
ference was due to the death of her uncle in November 1564.

wyse wrytten to my lord of Leycester prayng you to sette
in your helpyng hand to ende thys tedyous sute.' Without setting forth reasons ' how moch her Hyghnes desplesure
ys to long lastyng, or how unmeate yt ys thys yowng
couple should thus waxe olde in pryson, or how farre
beter yt were for them to be abrode and lerne to serve '
she sought that Cecil for 'the beter descharge' of his 'call-
ynges and credyte' should procure that 'thys yowng
couple may fele some lyke of her Majestie's plentyfull
mercy.' A year later the Duchess again wrote to Cecil,
after having kept silent so long, in the hope of the Earl of
Leicester's (Lord Robert Dudley) assistance.   She now
wrote in Holy Week, 'a charytable tyme of forgevenes,'
hoping that Leicester and Cecil between them might
prevail on the queen 'not styll to suffre this cawse
alone to rest withowt all favor and forgevenes.' The
queen was immovable.   In October 1567 the death of
Sir John Wentworth, in whose house, Gosfield Hall,
Katherine had remained since May 1566, brought about
her removal to Cockfield Hall, the country house of Sir
Owen Hopton.   There, in cruel loneliness, she lived the
last days of her life, made bitter by the absence of her
husband, then confined at Althorp under the custody of
Sir John Spencer.

It was not long before Death came as the only merciful
deliverer.   The ' manner of her Departing ' is recorded in
full. All the night of the 26th of January 1567-8, she
continued in prayer, and five or six times in the night
she said the prayers appointed to be said at the hours
of death.   Her ladies tried to rouse her—' Madam be of
good comfort, with God's help you shall live and do
well many years.'   But she would answer, ' No, No, no
life in this worlde but in the world to come I hope to
live ever ; for here is nothing but care and misery, and
there is life everlasting.'   Realising death was at hand,

she looked on those about her and said, 'As I am, so shall
you be,. behold the picture of yourselves.'   About six or
seven in the morning she desired that Sir Owen Hopton
should visit her, and, on his asking ' Good Madam, how
do you ? ' she said, ' Even now going to God, Sir Owen,
even as fast as I can.'   Further, she besought him with
his own mouth to make a request to the queen, ' which
shall be the last suit and request that ever I shall make
unto her Highness, even from the mouth of a dead woman ;
that she would forgive her displeasure towards me as my
hope is she hath done . . . and that she would be good
unto my children and not impute my fault unto them, whom
I give wholly unto Her Majesty ; for in my life they have
had few friends and fewer shall they have when I am dead,
except Her Majesty be gracious unto them : and I desire
her Highness to be good unto my Lord, for I know this, my
death will be heavy news unto him, that her Grace will be
so good as to send liberty to glad his sorrowful heart withall.'

Finally, she desired Sir Owen to deliver certain tokens to
her lord, among them a ring with a pointed diamond in it,
which was the ring she had received of him, she said, ' when
I gave myself unto him and gave him my faith.'   ' What
say you, Madam,' said Sir Owen, ' was this your wedding
ring ? '   ' No, Sir Owen,' she answered, ' this was the ring
of my assurance unto my Lord, and there is my Wedding
Ring.'   Then she took another all of gold, of five links, the
four inner ones containing a ' poesie ' of the earl's making :—

   ' As circles five by art compact shew but one Ring in sight,
     So trust united faithfull mindes with knott of secret might,
     Whose force to breake but greedie Death noe wight possesseth
       power,
     As time and sequels well shall prove. My Ringe can saye no
       more.'

' Deliver this also to my Lord,' she said, ' and pray him
even as I have been to him, as I take God to witness I have

been, a true and a faithful wife, that he would be a loving and a natural Father unto my children, unto whom I give the same blessing that God gave unto Abraham, Isaac and Jacob.' Taking out yet another ring, she bade this also to be delivered to her lord as the picture of herself, for on it was a Death's head, and round the head an inscription 'While I lyve yours.' As death now came quickly towards her she commended her spirit to God, and, 'putting down her eyes with her own hands, she yielded unto God her meek spirit at nine of the clock in the morning, the 27th of January 1567-8.' She was buried in Yoxford Church,[1] but was later removed to Salisbury Cathedral, where there is an inscription to her memory.

The dying woman's petition to the queen for her husband's release had no immediate effect. He had long ago petitioned the Council for 'sum lyberte of walk to Releve myself and contynewe my helthe, sum Repayre of sum of my poore frinds to give me advyse howe furder to humbyll my self with contynewall humbyll suts to hyre hyghnes,' but how far such liberty had been given him is not clear. Until the end of February 1569, he remained at Althorp, but at the end of that year he was at his home, Wolf Hall, and was building a new house a mile distant. The incidents of his life and the years of imprisonment had taught him one lesson, to keep as far as possible from court circles and court intrigues. After his release, he took his M.A. degree at Cambridge, and became a member of Gray's Inn in February 1571-2. But he still harboured a natural desire to have the legitimacy of his children certified. The queen, enraged at his petition on this behalf, with a mean and senseless anger once more committed him to the Tower in November 1595. While his children were declared illegitimate they could have no pretensions to the succession,

---

[1] For an account of her funeral, see S. P. Dom. Eliz. xlvi. 48, 49.

and Elizabeth preferred to have as few possible successors as she could. It would have saved her many struggles with her Parliament if the succession had been settled on this English line.   Perhaps, however, she feared that Hertford or his children might follow in the Protector's footsteps, and might try to be king over the queen ; perhaps, also, she preferred to keep an unpopular rival as her possible successor in order to emphasise the loyalty of her people to herself. Hertford was only kept in the Tower for about two months, being released in the following January.

Meanwhile the queen had written to his second wife, of whom she altogether approved, Frances,[1] daughter of Lord Howard of Effingham, the High Admiral, her 'good Francke,' consoling her for her lord's misfortunes. 'It is not convenient to acquaint you with all the particular circumstances of his offence, neither would it avail you who have been ignorant of all the causes, but (to prevent any misapprehension that this crime is in its nature more pernicious and malicious than an act of lewd and proud contempt against our own direct prohibition) we have vouchsafed to cause a ticket to be shown you by the bearer which may resolve you from further doubting what it is not, and satisfy your mind for caring for that which care now remedies not, being a matter both proved by record and confessed with repentance. It is far from our desire to pick out faults in such as he, being slow to rigour towards the meanest, we will use no more severity than is requisite for other's caution in like cases, and than shall stand with honor and necessity. Your Ladyship will quickly judge when you understand it that his offence can have no color of imputation on you, and you will not therefore be one jot the less esteemed for any faults of his.' On 14th May 1598, the 'good Francke' died without issue and was

---

[1] He had married her before 1582 (Wilts Arch. Mag., xv.).

buried in Westminster Abbey, where there is a monument erected to her memory by her husband.[1]

The earl lived to marry yet again, another clandestine marriage, for performing which the officiating priest was suspended for three years by Archbishop Whitgift. This was in the year 1600, while Elizabeth was yet alive, and the lady was Frances, daughter of Thomas, Viscount Howard of Bindon, widow of Henry Pranell. This lady had been left a young and rich widow by Henry Pranell, and had had many suitors, among whom the most favoured was Sir George Rodney, a gentleman of the west country. 'He,' says a contemporary, Arthur Wilson, 'was suitable to her for person and fortune, but Edward, Earl of Hertford, being entangled with her fair eyes, and she, having a tang of her grandfather's ambition, left Rodney and married the earl.' Thereupon Rodney, 'having drunk in too much affection, and not being able with his reason to digest it, summoned up his sickened spirits to a most desperate attempt; and, coming to Amesbury in Wiltshire, where the earl and his lady were then resident, to act it, he retired to an inn in a town, shut himself up in a chamber, and wrote a large paper of well-composed verses to the countess in his own blood.' These he sent to her and then ran himself upon his sword, 'and so ended that life which he thought death to enjoy.' The lady treated the matter with indifference, but her grateful husband settled £5000 a year on her for life.

It was not until Elizabeth was dead that the earl dared once again to make his old appeal for the legitimation of his children by his first wife. So long as James the First's right to the throne was only one of parliamentary title, the Earl of Hertford's son, Edward, Lord Beauchamp, if he were legitimate, had, as we have seen, as good, if not a more lawful right than James. But it

[1] There is a drawing of the monument with the inscription preserved in Harl. MS. 4199, fol. 51.

was the first measure of a subservient Parliament to set aside the will of Henry VIII. and declare James 'lineally, justly and lawfully next, and sole heir of the blood royal of this realm.' All ambitious schemes, if he had had any such for his son, were now over for Hertford. Elizabeth on her death-bed had declared, 'I will have no rogue's son in my seat, but one worthy to be a king,'[1] when Beauchamp's name was mentioned to her, maintaining her old enmity to the end. James I. was undoubted king. All Hertford could now desire was to clear his first wife's name and legitimise her children. In February 1604 on account of a final petition made by the earl, a commission of inquiry was held. It seems probable, from a story related by Dugdale, that the priest who had solemnised the early marriage, and who could not be found in 1561, when the Earl and Lady Katherine were examined, had now come forward. The validity of this marriage, declares Dugdale, was brought to a trial at common law, 'when the minister who married them being present, and other circumstances agreeing, the jury ... found it a good marriage.' A fragmentary account of the proceedings of the commission seems to suggest that such an ending might have been possible, but fails to give any determination on the subject.[2] The matter was certainly not settled by 1606, when there was a suit between the Earl of Hertford and Lord Monteagle, the main point of which was to prove the lawfulness of the Earl's marriage. The court sat until five o'clock in the afternoon, and the jury had a week's respite to consider their verdict. When it was about to be given, 'Mr. Attorney interposed for the king, and said that the land they both strove for was the king's, and, until his title was decided, the jury ought not

---

[1] Ellis (*Original Letters*, Series ii. vol. iii. p. 194) gives this quotation as ' No base person but a king,' and in a footnote states quite erroneously that the allusion, ' base person,' is to Arabella Stuart. See *Cornhill Mag.*, March 1897, p. 302.

[2] Cotton MS., Vitalis C. xvi., ff. 241, 419.

to proceed, not doubting but the king will be gracious to both lords. But thereby both land and legitimation remain undecided.'

In 1608 Edward, eldest son of the earl, who, under the circumstances, had been styled Lord Beauchamp by courtesy only, took a grant of the barony of Beauchamp, and another of the earldom of Hertford, to take effect on the death of the earl, who was not termed his father in the patent. Beauchamp, however, died before his father, in 1612.[1] James, like Elizabeth, had a peculiar dread of the idea of legitimising Katherine's children. In 1610 that dread was emphasised by the fact that, in the early part of the year, William, grandson of the Earl of Hertford, plighted his troth with the ill-fated Lady Arabella Stuart who, by her high birth, was destined to be the unwilling victim of ambitious designs on the part of the Romanists to place her on the throne. The story of their unhappy love must come later. Suffice it now to say that James, with despicable cowardice, used every effort to prevent the establishment of a legitimacy which had only the remotest degree of danger to himself and his throne. Even as late as 1621, according to the contemporary letters of a certain Joseph Mede, he had some thoughts of openly declaring in Parliament the illegitimacy of Hertford's children. It was even said, ' as a secret,' that Lord Southampton, who, together with Lord Oxford and several commoners, was imprisoned after the dissolution of that same Parliament, owed his commitment to an attempt to collect proofs in defence of the validity of the marriage. William Seymour, then Marquis of Hertford, afterwards second Duke of Somerset, grandson of Katherine, wrote to Buckingham, on the accession of Charles I. in 1625, intreating his favour and help with the king concerning his legitimacy,

---

[1] He was buried first at Wick and then removed to Salisbury Cathedral.

praying that with his majesty's liking he might plead his own right or, by his special favour, be preserved from a troublesome suit, 'when all honest hearts have such a cause for rejoicing I alone am forced to hide myself.' Charles evidently was disinclined to grant any such favour, and it was not until the Civil War and the Commonwealth were over, and Charles II. was king, that Hertford was made Duke of Somerset, and his legitimacy established by recital in the Act for his creation.[1]

Of the two sons of the Earl of Hertford, who both predeceased him, little of interest is known. Edward, Lord Beauchamp, the elder, made an early marriage in 1582, without his father's consent, to Honora, daughter of Sir Richard Rogers of Bryanston, Dorset.[2] He was for this cause visited by Elizabeth's displeasure, though it is difficult to see why, since she denied his legitimacy and hence his blood royal, she should have taken it upon herself to interfere with his marriage. However, upon this offence alone, he was, by her orders, confined in his father's house, whence he frequently petitioned Walsingham to be released. He seems to have been a man of little character, and probably would have made no mark in history, even if he had not been kept under the bann of illegitimacy by the caprices of Elizabeth.

Thomas, the second son, lived only until the year 1600. He managed, however, to be implicated in some treasonable proceedings in Essex, in the year 1596. An abortive plot for stirring up the militia seems to have been brewing, and into this Thomas Seymour was drawn, doubtless because of his name and family. A certain Sir John Smythe rode

[1] Act of Parl., 13 Sept. 1660, confirmed by Act of 20 Dec. 1661.
[2] He had three sons by this marriage, Edward, who married Anne, daughter of the Earl of Dorset, and died in 1618; William, who in 1660 became second Duke of Somerset, and died a few months later; Francis, who in 1640 became first Baron Seymour of Trowbridge, and died in 1664.

with him to the musters at Colchester, and tried to win them to oppose 'the daily consumption of the nation and country in foreign wars,' advising them that there was a press out for 1000 men, but ' those who followed him should go no further than he went,' that there were traitors about the court who had ' confined 9000 men foolishly to weaken the land,' that the common people had been a long time oppressed, and that they should have redress if they should come with him. This companion of his, a nobleman belonging to the blood royal of Lord Beauchamp's house, should be their captain, and he himself would be under him. Thomas Seymour underwent a stern examination on the subject, and declared he had gone over to Sir John Smythe's house on invitation, to make merry, and had had no idea that Sir John would have dealt thus with him, to bring his name in question and thereby undo him. He seems to have escaped after this examination, but lived only a few years, dying in August 1600, leaving a widow, who survived him until 1619, but no children. He has been sometimes mistakenly identified with the Seymour who attracted Arabella Stuart's favour in 1608. The date of his death makes this assumption impossible.

One leaves the story of these lives with a haunting sense of the injustice of fate, and of the cruel interference with the liberty of the subject which was nurtured by the despotism of the Tudors and Stuarts. The death of Lady Katherine Grey lies most surely at Elizabeth's door, and one cannot pass over the events of her life and death without a very definite opinion as to the conduct of Elizabeth. Her action cannot, in this case at least, be explained by any pretence of justifiable timidity. At the bar of posterity she must stand convicted of a cruel panic.

CHAPTER V

THE DIVINE RIGHT OF KINGS

'Nor will that day dawn at a human nod
  When, bursting through the network superposed
  By selfish occupation—plot and plan,
  Lust, avarice, envy—liberated man,
  All difference with his fellow mortal closed,
  Shall be left standing face to face with God.'

MATTHEW ARNOLD.

ROMANCE follows romance, circumstance repeats circumstance, as we turn to the life of the best-known grandchild of the Earl of Hertford, William, the second son of Lord Beauchamp. Destiny had brought his grandfather to unhappy fame; destiny was early to bring to him the same fate. In each case destiny took the shape of a woman who paid the price with her life. Arabella Stuart was now to suffer as Katherine Grey had suffered.

As early as 1602-3, rumour, the foster-mother of royal displeasure, had linked the name of Arabella Stuart with that of Edward, the elder brother of William Seymour. A later tale, connecting this early rumour with the later fact, declared that even then, though William Seymour was only a boy of fourteen, and Arabella a woman of twenty-seven, there had been an attachment between them. A mystery must always, it seems, hang over the story of that year as connected with Arabella's life, since the statements upon which most of the agitation was based were figments of Arabella's brain. However, from what facts there are, the following story is evolved.

Born in 1575, child of the hasty marriage between

Charles Stuart and Elizabeth Cavendish, which roused Queen Elizabeth's accustomed wrath and sent Margaret Countess of Lennox, the mother of Charles, to the Tower, Arabella Stuart shared with James of Scotland the hereditary right of the Scottish line to the throne of England. Her paternal grandmother, the Countess of Lennox, was the daughter of Margaret of England, elder sister of Henry VIII., by her second husband, Douglas, Earl of Angus. James of Scotland was the son of Henry, Lord Darnley, elder son of the Countess of Lennox, and Mary Queen of Scots, herself the grandchild of Margaret of England by her first husband, James IV. of Scotland. Hence James and Arabella were first cousins. By the year 1587 Elizabeth was, in her characteristic way, playing off one possible heir against the other. Treating Arabella in those days as her heiress,[1] she made much of her at court, and showed her one day to the wife of the French ambassador, saying, ' Look at her well ; she will be one day even as I am (toute faite comme moi) and will be a ruling lady (une maîtresse dame).' Gradually, however, the queen's favours cooled, and Arabella was relegated to the stern care of her maternal grandmother, Bess of Hardwick, Countess of Shrewsbury. Embittered by the conduct of his shrewish wife, the old Earl of Shrewsbury died in 1590, foretelling that Arabella would bring trouble on his house by his wife's and daughter's devices. While in favour at court, Arabella had had the upper hand of his wife, but now it was otherwise, since the queen did not wish her to be treated as ' a person of consideration.' For the next twelve years Arabella had to bear the despotic rule of her old grandmother. Plot after plot was wound round her by the Romanists, suitor after

---

[1] Arabella was left an orphan in 1581, her father having died in 1576, a year after her birth, and her mother in 1581. The latter confided her orphan child to the queen's care. See Mrs. Murray Smith, *Arabella Stuart*, for full details of Arabella's life.

suitor was suggested—with all this Arabella had little or nothing to do, she was simply the puppet with which the play was to be acted when the right time came. Elizabeth, however, began to see in her a personal enemy, and the old countess was bidden to keep her as a state prisoner at Chatsworth.

Writhing under the yoke, Arabella brought all her wit to devise some plan of escape. Some marriage, arranged unknown to her grandmother, some marriage to a commoner which could not involve her in the Romanist plots, this seemed the only solution, and it was this she determined to accomplish. Some rumour had reached her, perhaps through her two friendly uncles, Henry and William Cavendish, that the Earl of Hertford had commissioned his lawyer, Kyston, to ' speak to a Mr. Owen Tydder (Tudor) in Wales, an old servant of Lady Shrewsbury's to move my Lady of Shrewsbury about the marriage betwixt his lordship's grandchild, the Lord Beauchamp's elder son, and the Lady Arabella.' Here was an opportunity of thwarting her grandmother. The old countess had refused to listen to the suggestion. Arabella herself would take advantage of the idea, and herself approach Hertford on the subject. John Dodderidge, one of her servants, was commissioned, about three weeks before Christmas 1602, to go to Amesbury and interview Kyston, the Earl of Hertford's lawyer, and to tell him ' that if his master were desirous of the same still, he must take some other course.' Dodderidge half feared to deliver the message, but Arabella finally persuaded him, yet before he left changed his mission to one to the earl himself in London. He was bidden to remind the earl of his promise, to tell him that the matter had been thoroughly considered by some of Arabella's friends who did not think his lordship had taken an ordinary course in his proceedings, but that it would have been fitter that the lady herself ' should have been first moved

in the matter, and that the parties might have had sight
the one of the other to see how they would like each other.'
This very sensible suggestion Arabella then proceeded to
make possible by telling her man to advise the earl ' to send
his grandchild, guarded with whom he thought fit, and he
could come and go easily at his own pleasure either to
tarry or depart.' In her own hand she wrote a note of
instructions, suggesting that the ostensible purpose of the
visit might be to sell land or borrow money, adding that if
they came they must bring some token with them to show
who they were, which proves that she certainly did not know
the boy even by sight.   The best way, she thought, was that
he should come disguised as the son or nephew of one of
his attendants, ' an auncient man,' and bring as proofs of
his identity ' some picture or handwriting of the Lady Jane
Grey, whose hand I know, and who sent her sister [grand-
mother of the boy] a book at her death, which were the
best they could bring, or of the Lady Catherine or Queen
Jane Seymour or any of that family which I know they,
and none but they, have.' [1]

Dodderidge made his way to London and gained admittance to the Earl of Hertford, whom he asked to see alone.
He was pouring out his tale before the earl when a servant
entered the room, and saw Hertford looking ' very much
moved and disturbed.'   Before the tale was finished the
earl stopped Dodderidge, and declaring the marriage was
contrary to his wishes, though he did not deny that he
had sent into Wales 'to deal with one Owen Tydder,' scolded
the unfortunate messenger and ordered him to be shut up
in a private room till he could conveniently send him to
the Privy Council.   About nine o'clock the same evening
the earl examined him again and kept him prisoner.   The
poor wretch wrote from his captivity to Arabella, begging

---

[1] Cecil Papers (Hatfield House), cxxxv. fol. 79.   Most of the facts in
this chapter are contained in this volume of the Cecil Papers.

her to speak for him and tell of her knowledge of his mission; the earl would not believe but that he was concerned in some plot, and that she was in danger.

Whether this letter ever reached Arabella or not is uncertain, but Hertford carried Dodderidge off to Cecil, and from his statements they both came to realise, probably most conclusively from the note of instructions in her handwriting, that Arabella was indeed party to the mission. On the 1st day of January 1602-3 the news came to the queen's ears. Sir Henry Brounker was at once sent to Hardwick Hall to interview both Arabella and the countess. The old countess was filled with rage by the deception practised by her granddaughter; Arabella was equally angry, almost frenzied with repressed indignation and irritation that her plot had failed, and that the harsh severity of the past months was to be repeated. However, her devices were not at an end. She still saw a way to mystify the queen's commissioner, and thwart her grandmother. At once she determined to reveal nothing of the real state of affairs to Sir Henry Brounker. She refused to give any definite statements as to the message to the earl, saying that the suggestion had been merely a blind. Two written statements were forced from her, the second little less indefinite and mysterious than the first, but with these Sir Henry had for the time to be contented. The other side of her policy was calculated to make herself an impossible inmate for her grandmother's house. At last she could have her revenge.

Towards the end of January the countess wrote to the queen in a great state of perplexity since her grandchild kept her in a constant agitation by mysterious speeches and hints that she could be taken out of her hands if she wished, by which Bess of Hardwick suspected that 'another match was in working.' She would not now care how meanly Arabella should be bestowed so that it were not offensive to Her

Highness. The queen's answer came through Cecil and Stanhope, who acted for her throughout. The queen would not relieve the countess of her charge, but the countess must see that the ' young woman ' avoided ' idle talks and rumours,' since the queen was certain that some base companion having taken advantage of Arabella's youth and sex had deceived her into believing that Hertford wished her to marry one of his grandsons, ' which from incongruity of ages on the face of it is untrue.' The queen would forgive Arabella if she would take this mishap as a warning. This letter the old countess evidently showed to Arabella, who was not slow to seize such an opportunity of addressing the queen. In an undated letter, evidently written immediately, she thanks the queen in elaborate language for her clemency, and adds a complaint of her old grandmother without whose knowledge she confessed she had done many things, but in every case things which, if it had not been for the tight hand with which the countess had kept her, ' she should have had more reason to wink at than punish so severely as she hath done.'

Early in February the countess sent a letter which she herself had received from Arabella to the queen, a long discourse full of mysterious hints and allusions to a secret lover. Even Bess of Hardwick was baffled. The unnamed lover was one, Arabella declared, whose name ' so far exceedeth all the examples of her Highnesses best favoured [courtiers] that he dare not see nor by stealth send to her he loves as well as ever they did any. . . . And if it pleases Her Majesty to accept of him I shall think myself most happy if Her Majesty will grace him with her favour, and win his heart from me, if that be possible.' This mysterious lover was an excellent stalking horse. The queen and the Council were completely duped. Towards the end of February the old countess wrote in despair to the queen concerning a fresh move in the game that Arabella was playing—

the game with one end, escape from the countess. ' Arbell,' she writes, ' is so wilfully bent that she hath made a vow not to eat or drink in this house at Hardwick or where I am till she may hear from Her Majesty, so that for preservation of her life I am enforced to suffer her to go to a house of mine called Oldcotes, two miles from here. I am wearied of my life, and therefore humbly beseech her Majesty to have compassion on me.' Sir Henry Brounker was once more dismissed to Hardwick Hall on his ungrateful mission. Arabella, being summoned back thither to meet him, was examined on the statements made in her letter to the countess referred to above. To every question about her mysterious lover she answered it was the King of Scots, the one person in the realm about whom no conjecture as to intrigue with his cousin was possible. Many of her statements she had to confess had been mere conceits, and it was evident that her references to the King of Scots were nothing more. Sir Henry had to depart having accomplished nothing by his errand.

No sooner was he gone, however, than Arabella wrote after him that she would not swear her mysterious friend was the King of Scots. Indeed she was beginning to attempt to show her hand to Sir Henry Brounker. ' Experience,' she writes, ' had taught me there was no other way to draw down a messenger of such worth from her Majesty, but by incurring some suspicion, and having no ground whereon to work but this and this being love.' Almost daily letters followed to Sir Henry each one as mysterious and delusive as the other. About the 9th of March she wrote him the longest, and in this started on a new tack, half hinting and inferring that the Earl of Essex had been her lover. ' They are dead whom I loved,' she complains theatrically, ' they have forsaken me in whom I trusted, I am dangerous to my guiltless friends.' She twitted Stanhope and Cecil with favouring their own kindred against her Majesty's—'Doth Her Majesty favour the Lady Katherine's husband more than the Earl of Essex's friend ? . . . Hath my Lord of Hertford regarded her Majesty's express commandment and threatened and felt indignation so much ? ' Fortunate for her that the failing queen was not able to read this letter, and vent her wrath upon her, for in a kind of mad frenzy, she enlarged upon the harshness of the queen and the attachment of the earl. 'How dare others visit me in my distress when the Earl of Essex, then in highest favour, durst scarcely steal a salutation in the Privy chamber . . . were I not unthankfully forgetful if I should not remember my noble friend who graced me in his greatest fortunes to the adventure of eclipsing part of Her Majesty's favour from him.' In another context she speaks of the King of Scots ' unprincely and unchristian giving ear to the slanderous and unlikely surmises of the Earl of Essex and me '; surmises of her own making. In yet another context in the same letter she writes, ' Admit I had been in love and would have declared his name, I assure you on my faith I would have delivered it you in writing,' yet a few lines later she affirms, ' I have conquered my affection ; I have cast away my hopes.' She presents a strange psychological study ; with a facile wit and a broad imagination, she had, with a definite end in view, wound round herself a halo of romantic fancy, and becoming enamoured of her own fancy, finished by scarce knowing where truth ended and fancy began.

In the meantime, while Arabella was weaving her tales, and her uncle Henry Cavendish was attempting to rescue her from the espionage of her grandmother, Elizabeth was tossing on her deathbed, ' raving of Tyrone and Arabella '; Tyrone representing Ireland and its discontent ; Arabella representing the question of succession, and this self-made mystery surrounding her. On the 19th of March 1603 the queen died, and on the 28th James was quietly accepted, and duly proclaimed king without a voice being raised against him.

In a way she had little expected Arabella's deliverance had come. James was king, her own right had been passed by unnoticed, and she was no longer a suspected rival. The progress of the queen consort, Anne of Denmark, and her children into England, was accompanied with all possible splendour, and although, to Bess of Hardwick's disappointment, Anne refused to lodge at Chatsworth, where Mary Queen of Scots was reported to have been so ill-treated, she stayed at a house near by, and is said to have ' spent the greater part of her time and conversation in the society of Lady Arabella.' It is certain Arabella was not slow to give a vivid account of the severity of her grandmother, how she, a woman of twenty-seven, was treated like an irresponsible child, and hardly allowed the privacy of her own chamber. Her designs succeeded well. Anne on her arrival in London appointed her to a place of honour about her own person, and she was once more installed at court. For the next six years she played a brilliant part, joining in court functions, and in elaborate masque and pageant. Yet sometimes protesting against the demoralised and flighty manners of the day, she would retire to the society of her books, her ' dead counsellors.'

In December 1609 there is a note of the beginning of the tragedy which was hanging over Arabella. Chamberlayne writes in that month, ' I can learn no more of the Lady Arabella but that she is committed to the Lord Knyvet and was yesterday before the Lords. Her gentleman usher and waiting women are close prisoners.' Within a few days she was restored to her former estate at court, and the probability is this arrest referred to her money matters, since she seems to have been normally in a state of debt. However, as though she had some ulterior motive, she obtained leave from the king early in 1610 to marry whom she pleased,

provided the suitor was a subject within the kingdom. The
motive was soon apparent. Beaulieu writing to the British
resident at Brussels, early in February 1610, reports that
' the Lady Arabella who (as you know) was not long ago
censured for having without the king's privity entertained
a motion of marriage [1] was again within these few days
apprehended in the like treaty with my Lord Beauchamp's
second son, and both were called and examined yesterday at
the court about it. What the matter will prove I know not,
but these affectations of marriage in her do give some advantage to the world of impairing the reputation of her constant
and virtuous disposition.'

This time the report was true. On the 2nd of February
1610, Arabella had been betrothed to William Seymour,
in spite of their disparity of age, and had been summoned
with him before the king as soon as the news was
known. William Seymour was only twenty-three years
old, Arabella thirty-five. He had left Magdalen College,
Oxford, in 1607, and had probably gone the next year
to court, where he had met and become friends with
Arabella. She must have remembered the old mystery of
1608, winding itself round the sons of the Earl of Beauchamp, and must have remembered also the old Earl of
Hertford's conduct at that date, and his statement that he
did not wish this marriage for any of his grandchildren. It
may even be that at first she set herself to win the love of
the young Seymour to spite the old earl, but it is certain
that she soon came to love him herself with the whole force
of her being. As for him, he was probably flattered by her
love, and, as he said in his confession, being a younger
brother and sensible of his own good, unknown to the world
and of mean estate, not born to challenge anything by his
birthright, and therefore constrained to advance his fortunes
by his own endeavours, he plainly and honestly endeavoured

[1] This may refer to the arrest mentioned above.

to gain her in lawful marriage, since she was a lady of great
honour and virtue, and as he thought of great means, believing that he could effect the same with His Majesty's most
gracious favour and liking.   'Thence,' he states naïvely,
'grew the first beginning of all my happiness, and therefore
I boldly intruded myself into her Ladyship's chamber in the
Court on Candlemas day last (February 2, 1610) at what
time I imparted my desire unto her which was entertained
but with this caution on either part that both of us resolved
not to proceed to any final conclusion without His Majesty's
most gracious favour and liking, and this was our first meeting.'   Their second meeting was 'at Mr. Baggs his house in
Fleet Street,' and a third 'at Mr. Baynton's.'   Two days later
Seymour was brought before the Privy Council, and, on the
20th of February, made this written statement affirming that
there was '*neither promise of marriage, contract, or any other
engagement whatsoever between her Ladyship and myself, nor
ever was any marriage* [1] by me or her intended' unless the
king's consent were first gained.

   Evidently now that there was a likelihood of royal displeasure Seymour realised that it was safer for his own fortune
and happiness to withdraw.   He wrote instructions for one of
his servants to take a message to Arabella to that effect, and
having seriously considered the proceedings between her
ladyship and himself he well perceived that if he should go
on therein it would prove not only 'exceeding prejudicall' to
her contentment but 'extreame dangerous to hym.'   First,
the messenger was to speak 'in regard of the inequality of
degree between your La: and hym, next, the King's Maties
pleasure and comandment to the contrary wch neyther yor
La: or hymselfe did ever intend to neglect.'   He was then to
tell the lady that Seymour desired to be free.   'Since the
proceeding that is past doth not tye him nor yor La: to any
necessytie but that you may freely commit each other to your

---

[1] These words are underlined in the original.—Harl. MS. 7003, fol. 59.

best fortunes, that you w^d be pleased to desist from your
intended resolution concerning hym, who lykewyse resolveth
not to trouble you any more in this kind, not doubting but
yor Ladyship may have one more fitter for your degree (he
having alredy presumed too hygh) and hymselfe a meaner
match with more securyty.'   Whether this letter of instructions was written before the examination of Seymour and
Arabella in February 1610 is not certain, as it is undated.
Anyhow Arabella evidently followed Seymour's lead, given
in the written statement to the Lords, disclaiming contract
of marriage without the royal consent, and as a result both
were discharged with a reprimand, and Arabella received
in her old position at court.

But Arabella could not let him go.   He was a man after
her own heart, 'grave and serious . . . loving his book
above all other exercises . . . and of studious habits,' finding
greatest wisdom among his 'dead counsellors.'   Probably
she made advances to him on the old terms, when the king
was quieted, and probably it was then that he sent the above-
quoted message by his servant.   It was very natural that
Seymour should fear the consequences.   He had the example
of his grandfather before him, and moreover, feared to dis-
obey that grandfather who, taught by the experience of his
own early folly, was sternly opposed to such a match.   But
his conscience bound him to his promise to the Lady Arabella
since she was unwilling to break the contract they had
made.   Maybe it was his conscience only, maybe it was
both his conscience and his love.   Arabella believed it was
the latter, and defended him 'at a later date, when he was
censured before her for his public revocation of their betrothal,
saying, 'He did no more in this case than Abraham and
Isaac had done who disclaimed their wives for a time.'

However, for three months Arabella remained in favour at
court, while she was secretly plotting for the consummation
of her marriage with Seymour.   About Whitsuntide 1610,

meeting a friend, Edward Rodney, at Lambeth, Seymour
took him into his secret confidence, and told him he found
himself bound in conscience by reason of a former pledging
of his faith to the Lady Arabella and that he had therefore
resolved to marry her, fearing ' no other let nor obstacle
than his grandfather.' It was not until the middle of
June that the marriage arrangements were ready.   On
the 21st day of that month Seymour fetched his friend
Rodney as witness to the marriage, and Rodney agreed to
go, ' nothing doubting of the king's consent.' The two went
by boat to Greenwich at midnight, and sat in the Lady
Arabella's chamber until between three and four in the
morning, when the marriage was solemnised. Four of
Arabella's servants were present as witnesses, Mr. Biron
and Mrs. Bradshaw, Edward Kirton and Edward Reeves,
besides her gentleman usher and her faithful steward, Hugh
Crompton. ' One Blagew, sonne to the Deane of Rochester,'
was the minister who married them.   Such is the account
given both by William Seymour in his confession, and by
Hugh Crompton in his account-book for those years, found
by Canon Jackson at Longleat.[1] Crompton finishes his
brief but expressive notes on the event :—

> ' The 8 of July Mr Sey (*sic.*)
> Was comyted to Tower
> The 9 of the same month
> My La. to Sr Thos. Parryes.'

The warrant to Sir Thomas Parry ordered him to restrain
Arabella in close confinement in his house at Lambeth.
The confinement soon became easy by the indulgence of
her gaoler, and, by means of a certain servant called
Smyth, Arabella was able to carry on a secret correspondence with her husband, who on the plea of decaying health
had successfully petitioned the Privy Council to allow him
the liberty of the Tower. Unfortunately only one of these

---

[1] *Wilts Arch. Mag.*, xv. 203.

LADY ARABELLA (STUART) SEYMOUR.
From an engraving in the British Museum. (John Whittakers sculpt.)

letters, one written by Arabella, still exists. If only some of Seymour's letters had also been preserved it might enable posterity to form a truer idea of his attitude towards his royal wife. Arabella's own letter gives a touching picture of her love and unselfish courage. ' I am exceeding sorry to hear you have not binne well,' she begins, '. . . . if it be a cold I will impute it to some sympathy betwixt us, having myself gotten a so swollen cheeke at the same time with a colde.' Nothing terrified her but the fear of her own failing health, and that she might only live to have enjoyed ' so great a blessing,' as himself so little a while. ' No separation,' she writes, 'but that deprives me of the comfort of you, for whearsoever you be in what state soever you are it sufficeth me you are mine.' ' I assure you,' she continues later, ' nothing the State can do with me can trouble me so much as this neues of your being ill doth, and you see when I am troubled I trouble you too with tedious kindnesse, for, so I think you will account so long a letter, yourself not having written to me this good while so much as how you do, but, sweet Sir, I speak this not to trouble you with writing, but when you please.' [1]

Meanwhile, Arabella was addressing petition after petition to the king and queen, begging for her own and her husband's release. She bids James consider that she could have taken no other course, seeing that after the betrothal of February she was ' then the wife of him that now I am,' and that she could ' never have matched with any other man, but to have lived all the days of my life as an harlot.' In every case the petitions seem to have been delivered through the mediumship of the queen, who told Lady Drummond that the only answer his Majesty had given was that Arabella had ' eaten of the forbidden tree.' The queen herself preserved her friendship for Arabella as far as she dared, and sent messages and tokens to her

[1] Harl. MS. 7003, fol. 150.

through Lady Drummond.   Still, Arabella persevered in
her petitions, little realising that she should rather have
been thankful for her present easy confinement in the face
of worse punishment in store.   The king, hearing of the
indulgence of her gaoler, and probably suspecting her communication with Seymour, designed to remove her to the
North of England under stricter guardianship.   For this
purpose he condemned Seymour to double restraint in the
Tower, and wrote to Dr. James, Bishop of Durham, in
March 1610-11, bidding him take Arabella into his care and
custody, and authorising him to carry her down in his
company to any such house as should seem to him best and
most convenient, there to remain so long as it should be
ordered him by the Privy Council.   Four days later, at
eight o'clock in the morning, the Bishop received her into
his care at Lambeth and conveyed her, protesting, to
Highgate.   Thence she declared she could not move.
Tears, entreaties and illness prevailed.   The latter began
to be of a dangerous nature and, though James was loth to
abandon his project of having her conveyed to the North,
he was obliged after her second removal, on March the 21st,[1]
to Barnet, to listen to the verdict of the physicians and
postpone her journey for a month.   She was once more
removed, on the 1st of April, having been transferred to
the care of Sir James Croft in place of the Bishop of
Durham (who thankfully made his way north), from Barnet
to East Barnet, where she was lodged in the house of a certain
Mr. Coniers.   In the middle of April, Sir James Croft wrote
begging for further instructions.   He was under orders to
convey her north as soon as the first month had ended,

---

[1] Concerning this removal the Bishop of Durham wrote to the
Council that on account of Arabella's extreme reluctance to proceed
on her journey he was compelled to use the means ' prescribed, which
were employed with all decency and respect' (S. P. Dom. vol. lxii.
fol. 39, 1).

and as yet she 'had not walked the length of her bed-chamber.' Arabella was using her opportunity. Ill she undoubtedly was, but she had determined to make the most of her illness. Against his own desire, James was forced to allow her a second month's respite from the 11th of May. On this news she wrote promising to undergo the journey at the end of that time, without any resistance or refusal. At the beginning of June she was still at the house of Mr. Coniers at East Barnet, and the doctors were discussing medicines for her recovery.

While they were discussing medicines she and her maid, Anne Bradshaw, with the secret help of Arabella's aunt, Mary Talbot, Countess of Shrewsbury, were discussing ways and means of getting into touch with Seymour and effecting an escape. The second month of respite was to end on the 8th of June. By the 2nd of June all arrange-ments had been made. On that day Edward Rodney, again the friend of the ill-fated couple, went to a house by St. Mary Overy and engaging some rooms, sent goods there the same night, of such weight and evident value that the landlady became suspicious.[1] The next morning came a flaxen-haired gentleman with 'a tall person not richly apparelled and very pale . . . having a wart . . . on her face upon her cheek.' They stayed in the house until two o'clock seeing the goods conveyed to Great Tooley Wharf. The landlady, her suspicions aroused, sent to watch them when they left, and discovered that they went off from Pickle Herring Station. The goods of weight and value were the jewels and luggage of Arabella; the flaxen-haired gentleman was Edward Reeve, one of her old servants, and the tall person with the wart was her maid Anne Bradshaw.

On Monday, the 3rd of June, Arabella walked out of Mr. Coniers' house disguised as a man, accompanied by her servant Markham. She had persuaded her attendant,

[1] Harl. MS. 7003, fol. 126.

Mrs. Adams, 'a minister's wife,' that she wished to see her husband for this last time before going North, and promised to return early next morning. The good woman had believed her, and with her own hands had helped her to put on the French hose, the doublet and peruke, the black coat and hat, the boots with the red tops, and the sword which the faithful steward, Crompton, had provided for his mistress's disguise. After a walk of a mile and a half, Arabella and her companion reached 'a sorry inn' near Barnet where Crompton was waiting with packhorses. The unaccustomed strain of walking told on Arabella, and the ostler remarked, 'The young gentleman looks ill, and will hardly last out to London.' But her pluck carried her through, and riding harder through the day, she and her two companions reached Blackwall about six in the evening.

According to Sir John More's report[1] they then started immediately, but one of the watermen who rowed them stated later that they had tarried at Blackwall tavern for one and a half hours. They were evidently waiting for Seymour, who had not come at the arranged time, and might, Arabella naturally feared, have been prevented escaping from the Tower. Finally they started in two boats, the three men, Markham, Crompton and Reeve in one, Arabella and Anne Bradshaw in the other. Even now, after they had started Arabella ordered that the boats should loiter in case Seymour should appear. Still he did not come, and it was not until early dawn that the two boats arrived at Lee, where they failed to sight the French bark that had been chartered to wait for the fugitives and convey them to Calais. Hailing a brig bound for Berwick, they tried to persuade the captain, John Bright, to alter his course and take them to Calais. He refused, but taking a careful note of the party was able at a later date to give evidence to the Government. 'Being demanded what manner of men the three men were, he

[1] Winwood, iii. 280.

saith the one [Markham] was about forty, with a large flaxen beard . . . the other [Crompton] yonge, with a black beard, who was the man that most desired him to receive and carry them, the last man [Reeve] he observed not.' Further he stated that ' In the other wherie ther was tow women, the one [Anne Bradshaw], bare-faced in blacke ridinge safgard with a blacke hatt havinge nothing on her head but a blacke hatt and her hayr which he tocke by her face to be Moll Cuttpurse,[1] thought so to himsealf that it was she, and that she had maide some fault and so was desirous to escape. The other woman [Arabella] satt verie clooze cooverid with a blacke whod or vaylle over her head and face so that he could not see her, only saw that under her whode she had a whitt atyre, and that puttinge of her glove he observed her to have a marvellous fayre whitt hand.'[2] All Bright had done was to point out to them that the French ship they were looking for was probably the one riding at anchor seven or eight miles beyond Lee. Thither the little party had made, but Arabella, desperate at the non-appearance of her husband, once more delayed until he should come. The delay was fatal. The tide went down, and the ship could not sail for some hours. The time which would have undoubtedly put her out of reach of her pursuers was uselessly wasted. When the vessel was at last ready to sail, Arabella's flight had been discovered, a proclamation was issued, and orders sent out for her pursuit.

Her husband, in the meantime, having tricked his servant with the same promise that Arabella had made to her waiting woman, had managed to escape from the Tower. His barber, Batten, afterwards committed to the Tower for his offence, brought him the disguise of a carter, and in this he escaped by following a waggon and team of horses, which

---

[1] A well-known criminal of the day, whose real name was Mary Frith.
[2] S. P. Dom. Jas. i., lxiv. 3.

had brought materials to the Tower for repairs. His friend Rodney was waiting with a boat and horse at the Tower stairs. Seymour took the boat and rowed to Blackwall, while Rodney rode thither. Arrived there, they found that Arabella and her companion, after having waited at the tavern for an hour after the appointed time, had been forced by the grumbling of the watermen hired to row them to Lee to make their way down the river. Rodney joined Seymour in the boat and they rowed together after Arabella. However, they arrived at Lee too late for the French boat, and after searching some time for it, finally induced a New-castle collier to take them to Calais, for a sum of £40. After much cruising they finally arrived at Ostend about eight o'clock in the morning of the following Friday (7th June), and sent messages along the coasts to ' hearken after the arrival of the Lady Arabella.'

By that time, however, Arabella was a prisoner, and Rod-ney, though he little knew it, had been, through Seymour's delay, one of the means of bringing the story of her flight to the king's ears. Before leaving the house of William Seymour's younger brother Francis, with whom he lodged, Rodney had written to Francis, informing him of the flight, in a letter which was to be delivered on the following (Tuesday) morning at eight o'clock, by which time he calculated that the fugitives would be beyond pursuit. But, as we have seen, William Seymour, either from an indolence of which he has often been accused, or from an inability to leave the Tower sooner, had arrived at the meeting-place an hour late, and Arabella had waited for him and risked her own chances of escape. Hence Francis Seymour had the letter in his possession before the fugitives were safe. The news was too dangerous for him to attempt to keep it concealed, he was piqued that all had been done without his knowledge, whereas he might now be wrongly suspected of complicity. Finally, he probably reckoned with Rodney that the escape was by that time accomplished. Anyhow he went immediately to the Tower, found that his brother was indeed gone, and showed Rodney's letter to the lieutenant of the Tower, Sir William Wood, who made known the escape to the king and Salisbury at Greenwich. Meanwhile Sir William Monson, a retired admiral, had also gathered the same news from gossip of the watermen who had rowed the mysterious passengers of the night before. He had thereupon written to Salisbury, on the morning of June the 5th, that the French bark had set sail about six o'clock in the morning, but that counting on the contrary wind, he was sure they could not reach Calais that night. He had already sent to the narrow seas for a ship to stand over for Calais and had stayed an oyster-boat and put men and shot into her, and was now about to hasten after the fugitive bark.

The king was thrown into a terror and despair quite unwarranted by the cause. The Council obediently followed his lead. Lord Nottingham wrote in a sensible style to Salisbury, that he was sorry for the escape since he knew it would trouble his Majesty, 'else England wyll find no lose by ther absence.' 'I am verely perswaded,' he adds, 'that if they be not relyved from ther frends here they shall find but lyttle relyfe wheresoever they shall be come.' Further his advice is 'that it doe not appeer to the world that ther is here any gret acount moved of them.' He was certain the fugitives could not be 'fare gone' since the wind was contrary and all that was necessary was to send notice with all possible speed 'to the shypes in the Narro Seas.'[1] But the king refused to be comforted until Arabella was safely in the Tower.

In the meantime, Sir William Monson was already in pursuit of the French brig, and had sent orders to a pinnace (*The Adventure*) that lay in the Downs to put to sea, first to Calais Roads, and then to scour up the coast towards

[1] S. P. Dom. Jas. I., lxiv. 4.

Dunkirk. The captain of *The Adventure*, Griffen Crocket, having had orders from Sir William Monson, ' stood off and under the South sandhead and seeing a "smale saill" gave chase. As there was little wind he sent forward the ship's boat with shot, and "half channel over" the boat overtook the sail and "making some shoatt she yielded." ' Thus the captain wrote from the Downs on the afternoon of Wednesday (5th June), his boat having already returned thither from mid-channel with the Lady Arabella. ' Hast, hast, hast, post hast, hast, post hast for your lyffe,' he wrote on the back of his letter. The various postmasters marked the time of delivery at their stations on the letter, showing that it reached Sittingbourne at five o'clock on the morning of the 6th of June, Rochester at six o'clock, and Dartford probably at seven.[1] Hence the Lord Admiral knew of the capture early on the Thursday morning. By the next morning, between seven and eight o'clock, Sir Edward Zouche and Sir William Button came to *The Adventure*, and Sir William Monson wrote to Salisbury that everything should be done according to his directions. ' For the more convenientcy and spead,' Sir William wrote, ' we do imbarke in the french barke wherein they where taken and goeth with her to the North Forland where we shall have choyce of keatches to put my Ladie and her servaunts in . . . and least the wind doe overblowe and hange westerly as yt is licke to doe both. I have wrytten to the officers of the Navye to hasten doune with all spead, the light horsemen to meet us at the east end of the Swale: and so to rowe direcktly up to London : but least your Lordship should not know the meaning of the Swale, yt is the easternmost part of Sheppey whear we shall rowe betwixt the yland and the mayne.' Thus was Arabella Stuart captured and carried off to the Tower, exhausted by the excitement of the past days, and the terrible uncertainty as to her husband's

---

[1] Harl. MS. 7003, fol. 128.

fate, 'yet not so sorry for her own restraint as she should be glad if Mr. Seymour might escape, whose welfare she protesteth to affect more than her own.'

The Seymour family feared lest suspicion should fall on them of abetting the escape. The old Earl of Hertford was furious. The rumour even went abroad that he had died of the shock. Viscount Fenton wrote to Salisbury, bidding him discover whether the rumour was, as he suspected, false, in which case Hertford was to be brought to court to answer for himself. Already Salisbury had received a protesting letter from the old earl from Netley, enclosing the letter which his grandson Francis had sent from his temporary confinement in his own house (Hertford House). Francis Seymour's letter is endorsed in the old earl's handwriting :—'My nephew [1] (*sic*) Francis Seymour his letter (received) at Netley, Wednesday night at eleven of the clocke on night of 5 June 1611.' In his own letter the old man recalls his own early days ; the news of his grandson is, he says, 'no lesse troublesome to me than straung to think I should in these my Last dayes be grandfather of a child that instead of Patience and tareeing the Lordes Leisure (Lessons that I learned and payed for when I was in ysame place whear[fr]om Lewdly he is now escaped) would not tary for ye good houre of favor to come from a gratious and mercifull king as I did and enjoyed in the end (though long first) from a most worthy and noble queene, but hath plounged himself further into His Highnesses just displeasure.' He bids Salisbury signify from him to the king, ' how distastfull this his [William Seymour's] foolish and boyish action,' is unto him and assure his Majesty that even as he had at first misliked ' the unfitnesse and inequality of the match,' so he condemned this last action ' as worst of all in them both.' He winds up his letter

---

[1] This word was in ordinary use as signifying grandchild or nephew coinciding with the use of *nepos* in Latin.

[written at four o'clock in the morning of Thursday the 6th of June] with ' an unquiet mind to thinck (as before) I should be grandfather to any child that hath so much forgotten his dewty as he hath now doon, and having sleape never a winck this night (a bad medycyne for one that is noe fully recovered of a second greav coald I tooke).' One can picture the old man receiving and reading his grandson's letter late at night, holding it, in his agitation, too near the light, and so burning in it the hole which is still to be seen at the bottom of the letter.[1] He apologises to Salisbury for the accident in a postscript to his own letter, filling in the obliterated words. Francis Seymour further wrote to his grandmother from his temporary confinement, that he had ' noe nues to write but that my heart tremble trembles (*sic*) to think on, when I first hard of it I was amazed knowing yit would be their and Her undoing, a gref unto theire frinds and good to none, most hurt unto themselves what is now become of them is yet uncertaine.' As for himself he was ' as cleare of their escape or of any of their practises as is the child that was but yesterday borne.' Indeed it was not by the help of his own family that William Seymour had escaped, and it was not the Seymour family which was to suffer. The friends of Arabella had provided the means, and they and she suffered.

On Saturday (the 8th of June) Mary Talbot, Countess of Shrewsbury, whose schemes for her niece were not only personal but touched wider issues, since she was a Papist and hand in glove with Romanist schemers, followed her niece to the Tower. In her turn she was followed by Sir James Croft ; Dr. Moundford, Arabella's physician ; Mrs. Adams, the minister's wife whom Arabella had duped ; and several servants and friends. The Earl of Shrewsbury was kept a prisoner in his own house, but nothing could be found against him. An examination of the chief prisoners before

---

[1] Harl. MS. 7003, fol. 122.

the Lords of the Privy Council followed. Arabella, relieved now that her husband was safe, answered 'with good judgment and discretion,' but the countess was 'utterly without reason,' crying out that all was 'but tricks and giggs,' and that she would answer nothing in private, but if she had offended the law she would answer it in public. She was said to have amassed 'a great summe of money to some ill use,' £20,000 were known to be hers in cash, while she had made 'provision for more Bills of Exchange to her niece's use than she had knowledge of.' And although the Lady Arabella had not as yet been found inclinable to Popery, yet 'her aunt made account belike that being beyond the seas in the hands of Jesuits and priests either the stroke of their arguments or the Pinch of Poverty' might have forced her to their side.

There was strange diversity of opinion as to the possible danger that might have arisen from Arabella's escape. Some said that 'the Hott alarm taken at the matter' would make the husband and wife more illustrious in the world's eye than . . . (being let alone) they ever would have been. Others compared the case with 'the Powder Treason,' and so filled His Majesty with 'fearfull imaginations' and with him the Prince [Henry]. Indeed the ravings of the Countess of Shrewsbury about mysterious dealings with Romanist powers, were sufficient to make James, clutched by his ever attendant fears, tremble on his throne. Aunt and niece were both sent back to prison, and the countess was sentenced to a second trial because of her 'high and great contempt.' At this Sir Francis Bacon presided, and played the time-serving courtier, pandering to the terror of the king. 'That this flight or escape into foreign parts might have been seed of trouble to this state is a matter whereof the conceit of a vulgar person is not incapable . . . in another sphere [than England] she [Arabella] must have moved in motion of that orb' (not under the guidance, that is, of the most noble and terrified James). As a result of the trial Lady Shrewsbury was fined £20,000 and confined during the king's pleasure. In 1613 she attempted to escape, with the only result that she was more close kept than at any time before, nor was she released until 1616, the year after Arabella's death.

Meanwhile, from June 1611 until death released her, Arabella was a close prisoner. The confinement and loneliness preyed upon her mind, and in 1612 she was said to be 'distracted, which (if it be so) comes well to pass for some Body whom they say she hath nearly touched.' However, a careful study of all the possible evidence shows that her madness was only periodical, and sometimes, as many of her letters show, she was in possession of all her faculties. She directed her own expenditure from the Tower, and by the help of her faithful steward, Crompton, was able to send various sums of money to her exiled husband as Crompton's account-books clearly show. Her faithful, generous love for her young husband never failed [1] even though sometimes she was visited by a natural despair, since he seems never to have risked any attempt to communicate with her. He

---

[1] It is necessary to here confute the utterly unjustifiable accusation of coquetry brought against Arabella by the author of *The Annals of the Seymour Family*, p. 192. She is there accused of having in 1613 been concerned in some love-affair with the Lord Grey, also a prisoner in the Tower. The facts of the incident are these. The Prince Palatinate having come to England in 1613, for his bride, was influenced to petition James to release Lord Grey. James ungraciously refused. In the same year Lord Grey was discovered in conference with one of Arabella's waiting women, who, being strictly examined, was forced to confess 'that it was only a matter of Love and Dalliance.' The king, alarmed lest some plot was brewing, of which the Prince Palatinate had known, caused both Lord Grey and Arabella, 'whose brain still continued crackt,' to be more closely restrained (Winwood, iii. p. 454). The 'love and dalliance,' if it were not, as seems most probable, a blind to cover some plan of escape, obviously did not concern Arabella.

had tarried first in Holland with the Archdukes [1] who had
refused to deliver him up, and constantly tried to persuade
James to pardon ' so small a fault as a clandestine marriage.'
James, however, was obdurate; what they termed a small
fault was to him ' a mountain of iniquity,' and the English
minister at Brussels was ordered ' to carry always a watch-
ful eye to observe what entertainment he [Seymour] doth
find there, how he is respected, to whom he most applies
himself, who especially resort to him, and what course he
purposeth to take either for his stay or remove.'

In September 1611, finding Brussels impossible, Seymour
removed to Paris, where he seems to have fallen among evil
company and to have made many debts. In October 1618
the old Earl wrote to him censuring him for his late
wilful repair to Dunkirk, contrary to the king's orders
and to the instructions sent him from his grandfather
through his tutor Pellinge.[2]   This repair to Dunkirk,
according to a fragment of a burned letter among the
Cottonian Manuscripts, was made in order to escape his
creditors, who had ' putt divers serjeants in waitt for him
and threatened to putt him [in prison].' The letter continues, that ' Mr. Seymour being discontented in his minde,
hath declared unto C.T. that he [will not] have any longer
patience, because that he perceyved that the king had noe
[mind to] bestow any grace upon him, nor to lett him and
his Ladye come together so [that she hath] [be]come distracted of mind, whereby he knew that she could not live
long. And [therefore he] was resolut to take some other
counsel and to shew ere it was long that he was not beaste
nor foole, but that he hath courage enough to anger the

[1] Albert and Isabella were so called, since the title was held in the
latter's right.
[2] The old earl, fearing lest his grandson (who was only twenty-
four years of age) should be corrupted both in morals and religion, sent
Pellinge to him in Paris in November 1611.

best of them, that £400 a yeare[1] shoulde not keepe him, for his grandfather would not [allow him] any more nor pay his debts in France.' He seems to have had a further scheme for remaining with the King of Spain, and taking a pension which would be ' honorabile used.' This, of course, was with the idea of intimidating James. He may even have had some real project of allying with Romanist powers, and attempting an invasion of England. At least he was probably given a vast amount of verbal encouragement. For instance, a certain Captain Dekester called him openly a Prince of England, and declared that Henry VII. went out of Brittany into Wales with 1000 men and that Mr. Seymour might carry himself so that he might have 20,000 men. This braggardy had little practical value, however. Seymour remained in exile, Arabella in prison.

Having in nowise lost her old gift of words, she addressed letter after letter, and verse after verse from her solitude to her adored young husband.

'Thou hast forsaken me. I feel, I know,
There would be rescue if this were not so.
Thou 'rt at the chase, thou 'rt at the festive board,
Thou 'rt where the red wine free and high is poured,
Thou 'rt where the dancers meet—a magic glass
Is set within my soul and proud shapes pass,
Flushing it o'er with pomp from bower to hall.
I see one shadow, stateliest there of all—
THINE! What dost THOU amidst the bright and fair,
Whispering light words and mocking my despair?
It is not well of thee—my love was more
Than fiery song may breathe, deep thought explore,
And there thou smilest while my heart is dying
With all its blighted hopes around it lying,
Ev'n thou, on whom they hung their last green leaf—
Yet smile, smile on ! too bright art thou for grief.'

---

[1] This was the allowance his grandfather made him, and bade him consider sufficient considering the poorness of his own estates, crippled by debt at that time. Later, in 1615, William wrote a complaining letter to his brother Francis, asking the old earl to release him from his debts, and promising in future to cut his coat according to his cloth.

Towards the autumn of 1615, her weakness of body became more intense, and her mind more distracted. On the 25th of September she died, in the Tower, not a raving lunatic, as has been stated, but quietly and peacefully ending a troubled and unsatisfied life, and was secretly buried by night in Westminster Abbey. Even after her death, a concocted story of a pretended child she had borne to William Seymour disturbed her weary shade. In January 1616 the idea was first broached, and James, alarmed in an instant, caused one of her old servants to be examined. The servant denied all possibility of the story, but as late as June 1618 the suggestion still worried the king, and Lady Shrewsbury was summoned before the Star Chamber, for not answering inquiries which had been made to her as to the existence of such a child. She scornfully declared her disbelief in the impossible tale.

William Seymour meanwhile had hastened to take advantage of his wife's death. Only a few months had elapsed when he wrote a humble letter to the king, and in February 1616 he was allowed to return to England. In 1617 he chose his second wife Frances, daughter of the Earl of Essex, and in the next year Fortune favoured his aspirations, since by the death of his elder brother, he became heir apparent of his grandfather, the Earl of Hertford. Hence on the death of the latter in 1621 he received his grandfather's estates and honours by the provision of 1608, though as we have seen before, his legitimacy and royal descent were not acknowledged. For the remaining years of the reign of James I. he lived in comparative retirement in the country, being out of favour at court. Early in the next reign, being naturally on the side of opposition to royal tyranny, he became popular among the country gentlemen of the kingdom, and Charles, who, by the way, had refused to sanction his legitimacy [1] seeing his potential usefulness, brought him into

[1] See above, p. 91.

employment in the years when danger was looming, and in 1640 created him Marquis, with £80 a year out of the customs of the port of London. Charles had reckoned well. Hertford, though a friend of the people, had too much of the blood of kings in his veins to countenance the extravagant claims of Parliament, and he became king's man in heart and goods. In the critical year of 1641, the Earl of Newcastle resigned his post as governor of the young Prince of Wales (Charles II.). The choice of a new governor at this moment was difficult. Newcastle suggested Hertford as popular with the people, and a friend of the king. Charles wisely agreed, and on the 17th of May Hertford was appointed.

Here we must pause a moment to notice an almost incredibly mistaken impression which the character of the Marquis of Hertford has made on the mind of the authoress of a modern book on Catherine of Braganza.[1] Speaking of the moral character of Charles II. she states that many of his evil ways and dissolute tastes owed their colour to the instruction given to him by Lord Hertford. It is hard, she insists, to account for the change of governorship, from the Earl of Newcastle, who was silly but not vicious, to the Marquis of Hertford, who was 'given over to dissipation, without religion or morality,' and ' made it his pleasure to instil knowledge of every kind of evil into the mind of his young pupil.' The change is the more puzzling to her considering ' the attitude of moral rectitude ' held by Charles I. The solution, she decides, must be found in political reasons, or that the life of the Marquis was unknown to the king.

Now all this is quite wrong. One needs only to turn to Clarendon, if one happens to have no previous knowledge of the life and character of Hertford, and ascertain his idea of the man to whom the prince was committed. He was, says Clarendon, 'a man of great honour, interest and estate,

---

[1] Lilias Davidson, *Catherine of Braganza*, p. 21.

and of an universal esteem over the whole kingdom . . . not
to be shaken in his affection for the government of the church,
though not biassed to the person of any churchman.   It is
very true he wanted some of those qualities which might have
been wished to be in a person to be trusted in the education
of a great and hopeful Prince and in the forming of his mind
and manners in so tender an age.[1]   He was not of an age
fit for much activity and fatigue, and loved and was now
wedded so much to his ease that he loved his book above
all exercises . . . and had even contracted such a laziness
of mind that he . . . could never impose on himself the
pain necessary to be undergone in such a perpetual attendance [on the prince] : but then those lesser duties might
be provided for, and he could well support the dignity of a
governor and exact that diligence from others which he
himself could not exercise, *and his honour was so unblemished
that none durst murmur against the designation.'* [2]

If one is not satisfied with this appreciation by Clarendon
there are many points in the life of Hertford that give the lie
to the accusation brought so airily against him.   It was as
a student that he first attracted the love of Arabella Stuart.
If his conduct to her is brought into question, one must at
least remember it is possible that his love for a woman so
many years older than himself may have been short-lived,
if ever existent, and that it was practically impossible for
him to help her in her later years of sorrow and suffering.
The debts he contracted and his supposed youthful folly
in Paris cannot be counted against him in his later years.
If that were so, few could go uncondemned.   The years
of his life in the political world before the Civil War, and
the years of his life, when, in the emergency of need, he
dropped the habit of the student and became the successful general supporting the cause of king and church, as the

[1] And none recognised this better than Hertford himself.
[2] The italics are mine.

embodiment of an abstract moral ideal, speak more for his character and his strong upright spirit than any word-picture of Clarendons.'

Can it possibly be that in this history of Catherine of Braganza he has been confused with an *undated* memory-picture which the authoress holds of his far-off kinsman of the nineteenth century, the third Marquis of Hertford, the 'Lord Steyne' of *Vanity Fair*? Or can it be that he has been confused with the third governor of the prince, that Earl of Berkshire on whom Clarendon poured such scorn as the 'man of any who bore the name of gentleman the most unfit for that province'? Even so the Earl of Berkshire was only a born fool, not a dissolute man, and, as every one knows, it was Mrs. Windham, wife of the Governor of Bridgewater, who had the most demoralising influence upon the young prince.

It belongs to the lover of things military to enter into a detailed account of the brilliant campaigns of the Marquis of Hertford in the west (1642-8); of his gallant defence of Sherbourne; of his capture of Taunton, Bridgewater and Dunster Castle, with Prince Maurice as his second in command; of his march, in conjunction with Hopton, on Bath, the headquarters of Waller, whom he defeated at Lansdown, and of his recall to Oxford on account of the jealous rivalry of Prince Rupert and Prince Maurice at Bristol. The knowledge of his faithful, self-sacrificing service suffices for us, and the memory of his attendance on the king during his confinement. After a brief restriction to his own house at Netley on Southampton Water, subsequent to the king's death, he was allowed to go free, and won the high opinion even of Oliver Cromwell, who, though he could not win him to his cause, desired to keep him for a friend.

Upon the Restoration of Charles II. 'it was considered what should be done for the Marquis of Hertford, whose merit was very great,[1] his advanced age making him decline place—neither did he desire addition to his fortune.' As the most adequate reward it was determined to revoke the attainder of the first Duke of Somerset, thus creating the Marquis second duke. Accordingly a bill to that effect was brought into the House of Commons. Then, to the surprise of all, Henry (Somerset), Lord Herbert, son of the Marquis of Worcester, declared before the king that Charles I. had granted his father a patent to be Duke of Somerset. Secretary Nicholas and ' all that had been old courtiers ' could not find ' any footstep or warrant of anything of that nature.' Meanwhile, Lord Herbert was easily prevailed upon to acquiesce in the creation of Hertford as Duke of Somerset, the king in return promising that he should have a dukedom in time. After the bill was passed it was discovered that the Marquis of Worcester (better known as the Earl of Glamorgan) having by some accident got the Great Seal into his possession and ' being very skilful in mechanics,' actually sealed a commission to himself to make Lords, and accordingly put the seal to several blanks, and a formal patent for himself to be Duke of Somerset. This discovery rather naturally gave great disgust to Charles II. and his old servants, and it was many years before the king would be persuaded to keep his promise to make Lord Herbert a duke[2] (he was created Duke of Beaufort in 1682).

Dugdale in a private letter gives a rather different account of the incident, yet suggests the same facts.[3] The Marquis of Worcester, he says, exhibited a patent under the Great Seal, pretending it to have been granted to him by the late king at Oxford. The patent was suspected of being forged,

---

[1] During the whole of his exile, Hertford had regularly given Charles £5000 a year from his own income.

[2] Lansd. MS. 825, ff. 108, 110.

[3] *Hist. MSS. Com. Rep.* v., App. 178.

since no vestige of it was found at the signet or privy seal, and Lord Hertford was prepared to make such objections ' as might have tended much to the dishonour of my Lord of Worcester.'   Hence the latter ' was pleased to tell the Lords he must confess that there were certain private considerations on which that patent was granted to him by the king which he performing not on his part, he would not insist thereon, but render it to His Majesty to cancel if so he pleased.'   We have already indicated what the ' certain private considerations ' were.

Once more a Seymour had become Duke of Somerset, and William Seymour the ' younger brother' who had been so ' sensible of his own good,' and had early attempted to ' raise his fortunes by his own endeavour,' had succeeded even beyond his own ambitions.   Yet he was only to enjoy his last and well-deserved honour a few weeks.   The patent was granted in September 1660, and on the 26th day of October, Secretary Nicholas wrote to Sir Henry de Vere ' the Duke of Somerset died at Essex House on Monday (24 October) of a general decay of nature.'   Of the four children born to him by his second wife the elder son Henry, Lord Beauchamp, was already dead, being worn out by the hardships he had endured during active service at his father's side throughout the Civil War, followed by a five months' imprisonment in the Tower (from April to September 1651) on a charge of treason.   He had married Mary, daughter of Arthur, Lord Capel of Hadham, and his only son William, who was to succeed his grandfather as third Duke of Somerset, was born in 1651, the year of his father's imprisonment.

The young duke lived only a few years after his grandfather.   On the 16th of December 1671, Henshaw reported to Sir Robert Paston :—' Here died on Wednesday last, at Worster House, the Duke of Somerset, a youth of great beauty and hopes, aged about twenty.   He was lately let go out of his mother's constant care and inspection to come up to court the Countess of Northumberland, who would not be persuaded to marry one five or six years younger than herself. This occasion gave him the acquaintance of the chief young men about the town, and introduced him into the liberties before unknown to him, and some little disorder the Thursday before began such a fermentation in his blood as produced a violent malignant fever, the meazells or smallpox were expected the first three days, but there never appeared any evident signs of either, so that we must now think that if any of that numerous company of doctors that attended had prevailed to have him let blood it had saved his life.' No remark on the suggested remedy is necessary. The death of the young duke was deplorable, continued Henshaw, since it meant that the title and estates went to his uncle John (the old duke's other son), who was ' never like to have children,' and after him the honour would go ' to his uncle Trowbridge's children,' and the land would be divided between the old duke's daughters Frances, Mary and Jane.[1] Deplorable it was in this, that it meant the shattering of the old duke's ideas and plans for his descendants. His son John, the fourth duke, died without issue on the 29th of April 1675,[2] and the dukedom passed to the grandsons of Francis Seymour of Trowbridge, the Francis who had brought the news to the Lieutenant of the Tower when his brother the old duke, then young William Seymour, had escaped in the attempt to join his ill-fated wife Arabella Stuart.

The obvious is not slow in suggesting itself, and here the

[1] *Hist. MSS. Com. Rep.* vi., App. p. 368. Frances married three times, first, Viscount Molyneux, second, Thomas, Earl of Southampton, and third, Lord Darcy ; Mary had married Heneage Finch, second Earl of Winchelsea ; Jane married Charles Boyle, Lord Clifford of Lanesborough.

[2] He had married Sarah, widow of G. Grimston, and daughter of E. Alston.

obvious idea is to hark back to the comparison with which
this lengthy chapter opened, comparison that is, between
the events in the lives of Edward, Earl of Hertford and
his grandson William. Except that one suffered under
the tyranny of Elizabeth, and the other under that of James,
and that the younger man suffered a shorter time, the
comparison between the two men holds good. Each
lived the best years of his life after the unhappy event
that cost the life of a woman. Between the women
the contrast is this, that however Katherine Grey suffered,
she yet had her children and the knowledge of the love
of the husband from whom she was separated. Moreover,
she was allowed to spend the last days of her life in
comparative freedom in the country. Arabella Stuart was
denied all this. She barely saw her husband after their
secret marriage, and she was kept in a constant gnawing
doubt as to whether, in the face of his silence, he remained
faithful to her; and it was this doubt that killed her.
Finally, the last days of her life were spent in close and
merciless confinement in the grim atmosphere of the Tower.

We may perhaps end this story by telling it in the words
of an almost contemporary ballad, entitled '*The True Lovers'
Knot Untied*: Being the right Path whereby to advise
Princely Virgins how to behave themselves by the example
of the Renowned Princess the Lady Arabella and the
2nd son of the Lord Seymer late Earl of Hartfort.'

To the tune of *Frog's Gaillard.*

'As I to Ireland did pass
I saw a ship at anchor lay,
Another ship likewise there was
That from fair England took her way.

The ship that sail'd from fair England
Unknown unto our gracious king,
The Lord Chief Justice did command
That they to London should her bring.

I drew more near and saw more plain
Lady Arabella in distress,
She wrung her hands and wept amain,
Bewailing of her heaviness.

When near fair London Tower she came
Whereas her landing-place should be,
The king and queen with all their train
Did meet this lady gallantly.

" And now, Arabella," said our king,
Unto this lady straight did say,
" Who hath first tyed ye to this thing,
That you from England took your way?"

" None but myself, my gracious Liege,
These ten long years I've been in love
With the Lord Seymor's second son,
The Earl of Hartfort, so we prove

Though he be not the mightiest man
Of goods and livings in the land,
Yet I have lands us to maintain,
So much your Grace doth understand.

My lands and livings are well known
Unto your Books of Majesty
Amounts to twelve score pound a week,
Besides what I do give," quoth she.

" In gallant Darbyshire likewise
I nine score beadsmen maintain there,
With Hats and Gowns and House rent free,
And every man 5 marks a year.

I never raiséd Rent," said she,
Nor yet opprest the Tennant poor ;
I never took no Bribes for fines,
For why, I had enough before.

.   .   .   .   .

I would I had a milkmaid been,
Or born of some more low degree,
Then I might have loved where I like[d],
And no man could have hindred me.

I

Once when I thought to have been Queen,
But yet that still I do deny,
I knew your Grace had right to the Crown
Before Elizabeth did dye.

You of the eldest sister came,
I of the second in degree,
The Earl of Hartfort of the third,
A man of royal blood was he.

Once more to prison must I go,"
Lady Arabella then did say,
"To leave my love breeds all my Woe,
The which will be my Life's decay.

Love is a knot none can unknit,
Fancy a liking of the Heart,
Him whom I love I cannot forget
Though from his presence I must part.

The meanest People enjoy their mates,
But I was born unhappily,
For being crost by cruel Fates
I want both Love and Liberty.

But Death I hope will end the strife.
Farewel, farewel, my Love," quoth she,
"Once I had thought to have been thy wife,
But now am forc'd to part with thee."

At this sad meeting she had cause
In heart and mind to grieve full sore,
After that time Arabella fair
Did never see Lord Seymor more.

CHAPTER VI

THE SEYMOURS OF TROWBRIDGE

'Common souls pay with what they do; nobler souls with that which they are.'

IT is strange that in spite of the many details known of the life of Francis Seymour, first Baron of Trowbridge, he himself should still remain such a faint and indistinct figure. Fuller dubs him 'a wise and religious knight': Clarendon describes him as 'a man of interest and reputation who had always been very popular in the country, where he lived out of the grace of the court, while his parts and judgment were best in those things which concerned good husbandry and the common administration of justice to the people.' His religious views are known, his political career is distinct, yet his personality seems always to elude one's grasp. He is one of those of whom one may know much but whom one may never know.

He was, as we have already indicated, the youngest son of Edward, Lord Beauchamp (1561-1612), and was brought up with his brother William, under the care of his grandfather, Edward, Earl of Hertford. Unlike his brother William, he seems to have been of a quiet and amenable disposition, careful always to do nothing to arouse the displeasure of the old earl. Yet he certainly sympathised with, and was probably kind to his brother and Arabella Stuart while they were in captivity. This is witnessed by letters addressed to him by them both, especially by those of Arabella, who addresses him 'Sweet brother Francis.' On the other hand, fearing for himself, he helped to betray their flight in June 1611, and was profuse in his protestations of innocence as to his knowledge of their escape. In October 1613, James I. knighted him at Royston. In the spring of 1620, he fought a duel in the Low Countries with John Savage of Worcester, and, in the winter of the same year, he began his public life as member of Parliament for Wiltshire. From 1620 to 1626 Sir Francis Seymour was one of the most zealous opponents of Roman Catholicism in Parliament. In May 1621, he made a memorable speech advocating the infliction of heavy penalties on Edward Floyd, whose crime was nominally that he had spoken slighting words concerning the Elector Palatine and his wife, but in reality that he was a Roman Catholic. 'Let him be sentenced,' demanded Seymour, ' to go from Westminster at a cart's tail with his doublet off, to the Tower, the beads about his neck, and to receive as many lashes by the way as he has beads.' The whipping was too much, even for a bigoted Parliament, and it was omitted, though the rest of the sentence was carried out. Three years later Seymour advocated war with Spain, deriding the suggestion of the Spanish match, and suggesting that the promised portion might turn out to be merely a pension even as the jewels might be counterfeit. At the same time, he opposed sending a force to the Palatinate on account of the heaviness of the king's debts.

In June 1625, he moved a request to the king for the proper execution of the laws against the Romanists, and, in the following July, proposed to limit the grant to the crown for that year to one subsidy and one-fifteenth, that is to say, about one-tenth of the amount that Charles needed to fulfil his engagements. It was obvious that Seymour was becoming a powerful leader in the House, and the Duke of Buckingham set himself out to win him over to the king's side by showing himself willing to put aside all engagements with France, and to oppose Romanists in England. Seymour

rejected all his overtures.   Then the duke tried another
scheme.   Knowing Seymour's dislike for the Lord Keeper,
Williams, who was a partisan of both France and
the Romanists, Buckingham determined to remove him
from office, and approached Seymour upon the subject
through a friend.   The idea was that if the Commons should
' set upon ' the Lord Keeper, they should be backed by ' the
greatest men in the kingdom.'   Seymour, realising that the
duke was secretly abetting the plot, would have nothing to
do with it.   Instead, he answered sharply, ' I find nothing
in the Lord Keeper but the malice of those great men.'   The
duke had utterly failed, and the next month Seymour renewed his attacks on the Government for its foreign policy,
for peculation in high places and the sale of court offices.
In this way he attacked the Duke of Buckingham, and,
further, on these grounds, dissuaded the House from granting supplies.   This was more than Charles could endure.
Seymour was re-elected to the new Parliament, summoned
in February 1625-6, but like Coke and Phelps, two others
of his own views and calibre, he was made Sheriff to prevent
his sitting.   As Justice of the Peace he was one of those who
opposed the illegal loan which Charles wished to raise
without Parliament, and hence, in July 1625-6, his name
was struck off the commission of the peace.

However, there were signs that his policy of opposition
was undergoing modification.   Already the popular party
was becoming too fierce and unreasonable for his liking, and
he began to realise that he must throw in his lot rather with
Wentworth's moderating policy than theirs.   His correspondence with Wentworth was frequent, and he joined the latter
in advocating, against Eliot, a joint committee of the two
Houses on the vital question of the Petition of Right in 1629.
Ship-money aroused his wrath once more against the Crown,
and he joined in the refusal to pay.   Further, in the Long
Parliament (to which he was re-elected for Wiltshire, as he

had been to the Short Parliament), he took prominent part in opposing the ecclesiastical grievances. But it is clear that he was gradually turning still further from the popular party, and his revulsion against the death of Lord Strafford (Wentworth) completed the change. Already, on the 19th of February 1640-1, he had been created Baron Seymour of Trowbridge, in Wiltshire, and had insisted in voting in the Lords against Strafford's attainder, although his right was denied by the popular party on the ground that when the charges had been made against Strafford he (Seymour) was not yet a peer. Evidently his change of front was not allowed to go unnoticed by his erstwhile friends. In the journals of the House of Commons there is an interesting note that Mr. Charles Gore was, on 15th February 1641, sent for as a delinquent ' for speaking very scandalous words (not specified) against Sir Francis Seymour as member of the House.' This was ten days before Seymour became Baron Trowbridge, and went to the Lords. Two days after this Gore had to protest his sorrow before the Speaker, and say that he did not remember the words he had spoken, they had evidently ' slipped from him.'

Henceforth, like his brother, the Marquis of Hertford, Seymour was king's man. He accompanied his brother to the West, and rendered service in organising the Royalist forces, and suppressing the parliamentary militia. His own county town, Marlborough, that he had so often represented in Parliament, was—according to Clarendon, who notes the ' obstinacy and malice of the inhabitants '—one of the most notoriously disaffected (towards the king) in all England. There, during the last ten years, Sir Francis had built a very fine house on the site of the old castle.[1] In

---

[1] The royal castle at Marlborough had been undoubtedly made up on the site of the old Roman castrum. It was one of the dower gifts of Henry VIII. to his unfortunate queen, Katherine of Arragon. Later, it was granted to the Protector, and was restored to him in 1550 with the other of his Wiltshire possessions. His estates were forfeited after his

this house, which must have been considered of great strength, he left his wife and daughter when in service in the west. Hence they were there at the first siege of Marlborough, and were taken prisoners. Parliament sent orders for them to be kept in safe custody in Marlborough. When the Royalists were gaining ground Sir Neville Poole, with halberds and pikemen, retreated to the mound near Lord Seymour's house, carrying with him Lady Seymour and her daughter. Then, setting up two lay figures on the top of the mound, dressed in white aprons and black hoods to represent the ladies, he sent word to the enemy that if they approached the mound the prisoners would be shot. This not very creditable ruse answered and the prisoners were safely conveyed to London, where Parliament settled their ransom. In November 1644, the king himself fortified Lord Seymour's house at Marlborough, on his way through the western counties. The Parliamentary war budget, *Mercurius Civicus*, for January 1644-5, reported that ' The cavaliers and townsmen of Marlborough have cut down most of [the] woods of [the] Marquis of Hertford: and some of the Lord Seymour's own tenants have cut down and much defaced his houses and buildings there. So courteous are that party even to their best friends.'

Meanwhile Lord Seymour, with his son Charles, was in Oxford, and was in 1645 made Chancellor of the Duchy of

attainder for felony, but early in Elizabeth's reign were restored to Edward, Earl of Hertford, his heir. After the death of the latter in 1621, Marlborough passed to his younger son, Francis, who also inherited the manor of Trowbridge (known in early days as Straburgh), from which he took his title (see *supra*). Both Marlborough and Trowbridge passed as family estates to Charles, second Baron Trowbridge, and Francis, third baron and fifth Duke of Somerset, thence to Charles, the fourth baron and sixth duke. On the marriage of Francis Seymour, daughter of the latter, to John Manners, Marquess of Granby, afterwards Duke of Rutland, Marlborough and Trowbridge were settled on her and her husband. From the Duke of Rutland, Marlborough reverted to the Bruce family (Earls of Ailesbury). Trowbridge was sold to the Timbrells, and later to William Stancourt of Blount Court, Potterne.

Lancaster, and one of the commissioners for preserving the city and university of Oxford.   Like his brother, he was in Oxford when that city surrendered in June 1645, and was admitted with his son, Charles, in November 1646, to composition on the Oxford articles for the Trowbridge estates, upon a fine of £8725.   Attempts had been made both by the commissioners for Wiltshire, and by several private persons in the county, to lighten the burden of delinquency for Charles Seymour.   The commissioners certified that, although he had been four years past appointed one of His Majesty's commissioners for sequestrating Parliamentary estates he had only once come to the meetings of the commissioners, and had never, to their knowledge, executed anything, '*but did get many of the Parliament's friends freed from trouble* that were quartered by the king's party.'   Concerning the sequestration of his estate he had informed the commissioners in the last year that he was willing to pay £60 for it, and for the present year £80.   They were credibly informed that he had not supplied the king with money or taken up arms against Parliament.   The private petition also showed that for all the undersigned knew or had heard, Mr. Seymour did never take up arms against the Parliament, but whilst he lived at 'Allington, near Chippenham, behaved himself very nobly, friendly and lovingly amongst us and others.'

In May 1650, Lord Seymour placed a request before Cromwell for the exemption of both his son and himself from the decimation tax.   Cromwell, acting with his unfailing wisdom, wrote to stay proceedings against them. The commissioners were 'very unsatisfied' with the request and the case was referred to Desborough, the major-general for the district.   He, with a characteristic hatred of the cavalier species, wrote to Cromwell that he was far from satisfied with Seymour's profession of peace.   'I have . . . perused his (letter) to your Highness,' he writes,

' wherein I find no more than any cavalier in west of England
shall pretend for himself.   I must confess I should be glad
of a real change, but I humbly conceive that without some
public declaration made by him to the world of alteration
of his spirit and principles, and of his real engagement to
the present Government, it will but open the door and give
occasion to the enemy to cry out of our partiality, especially
if favour and respect be shown to him and denied to others
who will do as much if not more than he hath done.'   ' If,'
the major-general continues, ' his spirit be such that he can
cordially close with the people of God as Captain Burgess
seems to hold forthe, he will not be ashamed to disown that
interest wherein he formerly engaged, and for the satisfaction of friends manifest his integrity to the public.'   For
the present, however, according to Cromwell's pleasure, the
commissioners were willing to ' let Lord Seymour alone until
they ascertain whether there be any difference betwixt him
and his former practices.'   Seven or eight of the county
gentlemen had already been taxed, among them Sir James
Thynne, who, at first, ' did plead as much innocency as my
Lord Seymour hath done, but at last, having no refuge, was
constrained to comply.'   The result in Lord Seymour's case
is not given, but in all probability Desborough had his
way.

The Civil War once over, Lord Seymour seems to have
willingly turned to a quiet life at Marlborough, taking no
part in the politics of the years of the Commonwealth.   His
house at Marlborough, which had undoubtedly suffered in
the Civil War, was soon restored, and there, at Christmas
1648, Aubrey, the garrulous Wiltshire historian, visited
him.   ' I never saw the country about Marlborough,'
Aubrey writes, ' until Christmas 1648, being then invited
to Lord Francis Seymour's by the Honourable Charles
Seymour, with whom I had the honour to be intimately
acquainted, and whose friendship I ought to mention with

a profound respect to his memory.' The Penruddock Rising of 1655 somewhat disturbed the complacency of Lord Seymour's life, since he and his brother, Lord Hertford, were suspected of aiding the plot. Penruddock had, indeed, been so confident of gaining their help, that he had at first designed to make Marlborough the centre of his plans. A troop of Cromwell's horse was stationed there; twelve of Penruddock's men were to enter the town concealed in a cart, and were to seize all the horses preparatory to Penruddock and his followers entering and falling on the soldiery. However, since both Hertford and Seymour were too cautious to be drawn into the ill-managed schemes, Penruddock was obliged to change the scene of action to Salisbury. Major-General Desborough, however, was determined, if possible, to connect both Hertford and Seymour with Royalist confederacies. The story of Cornet Joyce's treacherous entrapping of William Houlbrook, the smith of Marlborough, is well known. Joyce, acting as a tool of Desborough, disguised himself as a farmer, and bade the honest smith, who was known to be a Royalist agent, drink to the king with him. 'Dost know,' he added, 'of any who have money or horses to carry on our master's interests ? What think you of Lord Seymour and Lord Hertford ?' The smith hesitated. Both the Marquis and Lord Seymour had been ' so pulled and baited up and down,' he informed Joyce, 'that it was clear they had but small stomach to meddle any more in such matters unless they saw a fair opportunity.' However, Cornet Joyce and his companions seized the smith and, strapping him on a horse, rode off with him to London, where Desborough attempted to browbeat him into a confession of knowledge of the implication of Lord Seymour and Lord Hertford in Royalist designs. But the smith had nothing to tell him and Desborough's attempt was foiled.

There is a little manuscript book in the British Museum

entitled Lord Seymour's Meditations,[1] written down by his daughter, Frances Seymour, between the years 1655 and 1664.[2] It contains both meditations and prayers and a ' Tract one userie,' composed by him. ' Usury and charitie are opposite one to another '—this is the keynote of the tract. ' The usurer hath so much of self love as he hath no mercy for the poor nor kindness for his friend.' The meditations are for the most part paraphrases of well-known biblical stories and ideas. Perhaps the most characteristic of the man are the words on religion, summing up his general conclusions. ' However religione may be thought by some to be a burthen, yet,' he meditates, and his daughter faithfully transcribes, ' is it but a light one, and only seems heavye to those who are not acquainted with it and care not for it, to God's children it is not only light but delightfull not taking away their mirth and libertye, but rather qualifies them, making them to diserne aright betwixt the carnall man's revellying and the rejoycinge of a godly man.' He then goes on to speak of the way men deceive themselves by imagining that the outward profession of religion is all they need, ' denying the power thereof in their lives and conversations.' ' These are,' he shrewdly remarks, ' but almost Christians it brings with such, and God's rule as with a crooked rule and a straight line, although they may meet in some parts, if not in all places, for the crooked hearts of disemblers, they may in some duties agree with the strict rule of God when in most things they will not come neare.' Others ' deall with religion as with fashions, if great men use it they will be their apes, but if they cast it off soe will they.' Some, of course, deride religion altogether, others are content that they are ' of the visible church and soe as holly as the best, but

[1] Egerton MS., 71.
[2] A duplicate volume, written in his own hand, was sold at Sotheby's, 18th June 1844, lot 238.

as the eagle casteth her younge ones out of the nest which cannot indure to looke uppone the sunne, as thinking them none of her owne, soe will it be with counterfeit Christians and formallists who, although they bee bread up in the church, yet soe longe as they cannot looke up untoe the sunne of righteousness, God will not owne them to be his.'

Sir Francis Seymour lived to see the Restoration, and to be reappointed as Chancellor of the Duchy of Lancaster. He also royally entertained Charles II. at Marlborough on his progress through the western counties in 1668. The ' Prince of Denmark ' also came privately to England, and was brought to Marlborough to be entertained in the July of that year.[1] On the 12th of July 1664, Sir Francis died at Marlborough, but was buried in the chancel of Great Bedwyn Church, which was so intimately connected with the Seymour family as the parish church of their sixteenth-century manor of Wolf Hall.

It is evident that for some years, probably throughout the Commonwealth period, Charles Seymour, the only son of Sir Francis, had, with his wife and young family, been living in his father's house at Marlborough. The parish registers, both of St. Peter's and Preshute (Lord Seymour's house was partly in both parishes), contain numerous entries of the birth of children (two of whose deaths are also registered) to Charles Seymour and his wife, Elizabeth, daughter of William Alington, first Baron Alington. A fragmentary series of for the most part undated letters preserved in the British Museum,[2] gives us a more intimate picture of the husband and wife than is generally possible, when the figures are so small in the crowded scene of the history of their day. Incidentally too, some of the letters written by Lady Alington to her daughter quaintly describe some of the happenings of the day, and in their gossiping style already suggest the letter writers of the

[1] Add. MS., 32,324, fol. 146.   [2] *Ibid.*

ELIZABETH (ALLINGTON), LADY SEYMOUR, WIFE OF CHARLES,
SECOND BARON SEYMOUR OF TROWBRIDGE.

From an engraving in the British Museum. (J. J. Van den Berghe sculpt., 1700.)

eighteenth century.   However, we must not here deal with
them at any length, except as they affect Charles Seymour
and his wife.

Early in January 1657, Lady Alington wrote to her
daughter at Lord Seymour's house at Marlborough, ' there
would be no newes more wellcome to me (if you be come
to your full time) then to heare of thy safe delivery of
either Boye or Girle, shall be very wellcome to me (*sic*) but
if it please God a boy shouldbe most wellcome. I shall now
never be quiet till I hear you are safe layd for I assewer
thee, my dear, nothing can be more entirely beloved by me
than thy selfe.' Her anxiety was natural since the year
before two of her daughter's children had died, as we see
in a later letter, and it almost seemed as though the old
grandfather would be disappointed and his only so have
no children to carry on his name and title. However,
on the 17th of January 1657, twin children, Francis [1] and
Elizabeth, were born.

It was on this occasion that Charles Seymour received
a letter from an old servant, that deserves quoting, if only
from its human interest. He writes, ' I doe not give you
the Trouble of this out of an expectation to receave any
from you in return becos I know your great affayres formerly
would not permitt you to Answer scarce a tenth, and nowe
certainly you must bee soe employed in playinge with your
newe little ones (to whom I wish all Health) and kissinge the
pretty mother well againe that I expect not to receave A
lyne from you whilst this man is mayor. But if you will
needs fayle my expectation And because I could not bee at
ye groaning (*sic*) will send me uppe A great Pige that shall be
Pregnant with a Brace of Turkeyes you shall by the next
Returne of the Carrier After Receave such An Account of
the employinge of your ffavour that you shall not but think

---

[1] This Francis was destined to become not only Baron Seymour of
Trowbridge, but fifth Duke of Somerset.

it worthily Bestowed.[1] Sir to wish you joy of your newe gotten wealthe is An old complement, myne therfore shallbee that you may every yeare growe so rich till each corner of your Table bee planted with such olive Branches that when hereafter I come to wayt on you I may bee Turned out for want of Roome to sitt Amongst the Boyes.' He concludes ' with my most humble duty *where due* with my Prayers for my deare mistress And my service to your noble sister— Your oune servant A . . . (the name is obliterated). Lady Alington wrote to Seymour at the same time, congratulating him on her dear child's safe delivery of two hopeful children, and expressing her delight that she should be godmother to the little girl, ' little Betty.'

At the Restoration, Charles Seymour and his wife evidently went to London to ' my Lord Seymour's house in St. Marten's Lane—a corner house neare the churche.' There, in September 1660, Lady Alington wrote to her daughter, ' I am extreame sory for the Duke's death [the Duke of Gloucester], but being in the countrey wee shall not change our morning, if your maide give a right carector of the maide I think you cannot doe beter for I like the maide very well, send me certaine word what wages you will give hir and what time you will appoynte hir to come, we are all going to the Faier therfor I can say no more.' Later in the year Charles Seymour was at Marlborough, pursuing his duties as one of the Lieutenants of Wiltshire, raising militia and suppressing Anabaptists, Quakers and others. This work he continued throughout the next two or three years, while his wife for the most part remained in London, and with her mother. Towards the end of 1660, not daring yet ' to tast of ye London ayre,' he wrote to his wife concerning her ' removall to the new House.' She had written to him that she was ' very buisy,' and thus he wrote back to her, 'to over buisy thy Deare selfe will not only be a prejudice

[1] This looks very like a suggested bribe for an election vote.

to thy selfe but to thy second selfe, and therefore let me
entreate thee not to trouble thyselfe any wayes lest sadde
periele ensue.' ' I will not absolutely promise to meet you
at Reading on Thursday night,' he continues, ' because
of my country buisinesse, but if not then on Friday I
would have mett you at Newberry where a dish of crafish
should have been our repast, but considering my Father
not using to make halts for himselfe I shall perhaps
suspende it.'

In March 1661, Charles Seymour and Henry Hyde were
elected as the members representing Wiltshire in the coming
Parliament. An account of the election expenses of the
two members is in existence and, at the risk of wandering
from the immediate subject, it is so interesting as illustrating
seventeenth-century electioneering methods that it may be
quoted here. ' Spent in wine at the Bell in Wilton, £10, 10 ;
For 82 men's dinner with the undersheriff at 12d, £1, 12 ;
For 5 Hogsheads of beere there and for tobacco, £6, 10 ; For
horsemeat there, 10s ; At the signe of the Badger payd for
4 hogsheads of beere, £6 ; For tobacco, bread and fyre, 16s ;
For wine sent thither by Francis Deverell from The
Swanne, £10, 10s ; For bottles and glasses lost and broken,
14s 6d ; For wine spent at Parhams there, 10s ; Delivered
to Mr. Walter Sharpe, major of Wilton, for the Poore there,
£10, 10s ; Given the undersheriff for his care and paynes and
providinge the Indentures, £10, 10s ; To his clarke, 10s ; To
the sheriff's Bailif, the Cryer, 5s ; To the Hall keepers, 10s ;
To the Ringers at Wilton, £1 ; To servants and attendants
at ye Bell, 10s ; To Hostlers there, 2s, 6d : Paid Henry
Hervet at the King's Armes in Sarum for provision Monday
night and all Tuesday and Wednesday, Breakfast—the first
table being at 4s ordinary, the second at 2s, 6d, and the third
at 12d, together with Tobacco, four Hogsheads and one Barell
of Beere, 5 Barells of ale with sugar and spice for burning
of wine, And for fyre in the chamber, and for Bottles and

glasses lost and broken, £61, 6s ; For Horsemeat there, £5, 14s 9 : Payd Roger Langley at the Mermayd in Sarum for A Hogshead of sack and a Hogshead of clarett And for sugar, £40, 1s ; Paid to John Gilbert at the Bell in Sarum for several expenses there as by this Bill, £9. 8. 2 ; Payd John Smedmore at the White Hart in Sarum for severall expenses there, £2. 2. 8 ; given to servants at the King's Arms, being by number 17, £8 ; given the servants at the White Hart and Bell, £1 ; given the servants who kept and drew the wine, £1 ; To the poore in Sarum, £5 ; given the 2 Beadles, 5s ; To foure Trumpeters, £1 ; To the Ringers for two dayes, £1. 10 ; given Richard Thomas for ridinge severall journeys about the election and his expences, £5. 5 ; Payd at the Swanne in Sarum for generall expences there, £1. 7 ; Payd a second Bill at the White Hart, 9s 6d ; given the vintner's man for his care and paynes in orderinge the wine, 2s 6d ; given A poore woman servant at the Bell wch was forgotten amongst the other servants, 1s ; Payd a second Bill at the Bell in Wilton, £1. 10. The total charges for this entertainment, £195. 8. 2.' Sir Francis Seymour's idea evidently was to secure parliamentary influence in Marlborough, as well as in the county, for his family. The mayor and Corporation thought differently. They wrote, in March 1661, to Sir Francis concerning his lordship's recommendation of Lord John Seymour as one of the members for the borough—' a person of noble birth and virtuous disposition, whom we truly honour for the sake and memory of his truly noble father—' It was ' a great grief ' to them to offend his lordship, but they were ' already pledged to a discreete, modest and pious gentleman.'

Meanwhile, during this year, Charles Seymour and his wife were frequently corresponding with one another, since he remained in Marlborough and she in London. On the 2nd of April she wrote to him, evidently in answer to a letter of his :—

' DEARE HEARTE,—I am sorey you tacke my kind expressions as complements and to be as winde, as you say words, I knowe not howe to cary myselfe when you wilt (*sic*) nether beleave actions nor expressions but I hope the absence of your company will make a stronger beleavef that I am reall in all my expressions to you, for at a distance when we feall the want of on a nothers componeys we then cane expres in riten what our hartes is : and expres in riten what wee canoute expres with so moch confedancs in wordes to eache other therfore nowe beleave what I have not poure to shoue in actions . . .' She concludes this letter as ' your most reall affectionat wyfe if you please to account her so.'

In another letter written a few days later she describes how 'On Maunday Thursday the kinge washed 81 oulde mens feate with a bounch of Leves and wipte them with a towell on his knesse . . . and kiste their feate when he had doun.' At the same time he bestowed gifts upon them, linen and cloth and new shoes and stockings, and 'a pource of 81 peaces,' and 'a pourse with 1 pounde in it,' and a measure full of 'samen and shellfish and herens and loves of brede.' Many letters follow, dealing for the most part with personal and family news, and but rarely with political affairs. There is one other letter of a different type in the series, which, written as it is by Charles Seymour to his sister Frances, gives a sidelight on his tastes and character. 'In this summer's progresse,' he writes, 'I have light upon twoe most excellent songs or Ballads chuse you whether, wich I thought very fitt to recommende unto you but with this provisoe that you either returne them to me when I come to London or else lett me have coppyes of them for they are originals as to my perticular, and unlesse I fancye the musicke I cannot regaine any more coppyes, having lately distasted them by refusing them to weare my Livery. As for the tunes, I forgott to bid them pricke

K

it, and for my oune part I am soe unskillfull in ye mistery that I must crave yor pardon and begge you to picke (*sic*) it out yourselfe, wch favour I hope you will not give a flat deniall to.' This is written from ' neare unto Marlborough ' and is dated 12 October 1663.

As we have seen, Sir Francis Seymour died in July 1664. His son became second Baron Seymour of Trowbridge, but only held the honour just over a year, dying on the 25th of August 1665. His death is entered in the Preshute parish register, and he was buried in the chancel of Trowbridge Church on the 7th of September.

His eldest surviving son Francis, whose birth we noticed above, was only eight years old when his father died, and he became third Baron Seymour of Trowbridge. The following years of his life, until he was about eighteen, seem to have been for the most part spent at Marlborough, where he lived with his mother and sisters and his brother Charles. In 1675, by the death of his Uncle John,[1] he became fifth Duke of Somerset. Like his cousin William, the third duke, he was to hold his honours but a short time and die young. In the spring of 1678 he was travelling in Italy, and on the 20th of April arrived at Lerici near Genoa. At his entrance to the town he had the misfortune to fall into the company of some Frenchmen, who travelled, like the duke, ' out of curiosity.'[2] It was about the middle of the day when they arrived, ' a time when the churches usually are open, and consequently when the Italian ladies were most likely to be seen.' Upon this motive they went into the church of the Augustinians where, it is said, the Frenchmen were guilty of some indecencies towards certain

---

[1] Among the MSS. of the city of Salisbury, there is a council order of September 1694, bidding ' the Chamberlin doe procure the picture of His Grace, late John Duke of Somerset, and that the same shall be paid for out of the chamber Revenue, his grace having been a worthy bene-factor to the poor of this city.'

[2] Lansd. MS. 722, fol. 133.

ladies of the family of Botti. Horatio Botti, the husband of one of the ladies, having ascertained where the gentlemen dined, watched his opportunity, and shot at the first one of them who appeared at the door of the inn. The Duke of Somerset was the victim, and died instantly—'an act of barbarity, the more to be resented because the duke's part in the rudeness offered to the Ladies was least offensive.' The duke's uncle, Mr. Hildebrand Alington, who seems to have been travelling with his nephew, immediately notified the crime to the Republic of Genoa with a demand for justice. That Government 'seemed to be highly incensed against the criminal, and in all appearance used its utmost to apprehend him and bring him to justice, but he timely quitted the Genoese dominion and so escaped.' All the Government could then do was to affix a brass plate over the door where the murder was committed, declaring the crime, and promising a reward to those who should apprehend the murderer.

At a later date King James II. was petitioned by the family of Botti to consent to the pardon of Horatio Botti. James consented out of resentment, it is said, towards Charles, Duke of Somerset (only brother and heir of the murdered man), for refusing to attend the Pope's nuncio on his arrival in England. However, the full tale of this event must come later, for it belongs to the life of the man who was now to become sixth Duke of Somerset—Charles, the Proud Duke.

CHAPTER VII

THE PROUD DUKE: HIS CHILDREN AND HIS CHILDREN'S CHILDREN

' Pride in their port, defiance in their eye,
I see the lords of human kind go by.'
                                  ' GOLDSMITH, *The Traveller.*

' HE was probably the most ridiculous man of his time ; he had the pomp of an Eastern Pasha without the grave dignity which Eastern manners confer. He was like the Pasha of a burlesque or an *opéra bouffe.*' And again, ' All his rank, his dignity and influence could not protect him against the ridicule and contempt with which his feeble character, his extravagant pride and his grotesquely haughty demeanour invariably brought upon him.'

Thus McCarthy pithily sums up the character of Charles Seymour, sixth Duke of Somerset, better known as the ' Proud Duke.' His preposterous pride in his rank and dignity was indeed calculated to make him the sport of satirists, hiding, as it did then and afterwards, from the general conception of his character what common-sense he had. The anecdotes that keep bright the picture of his absurd pride are well known, but some bear repetition. It was he who, whenever he travelled in England, had the roads in front of him scoured by a body of outriders to see that none of the lower orders looked on his sacred person. Apropos of this we find among the list of his household servants, four running footmen. One of these received £6 a year, two others £8, one of them also getting 2s. 6d. a day when he ' ran by himself,' with ' a livery, and waistcoats, drawers, stockings, pumps, cap, sash and petticoat breeches.' The fourth agreed on a salary of £10 a year, ' with 2s. 6d. a day when I run by myself a journey, and 1s. a day when I run by his Grace's coach. No money allowed when I run any way under twenty miles. To find my own stockings and pumps, and to have my running clothes washed in the house.' [1]

Several anecdotes concerning the duke's travelling are preserved among the Memoirs of the Kit Cat Club. One tells how Sir James Delaval having laid a wager of £1000 that he would make the duke's carriage give his precedence, stationed himself in a narrow lane in a coach emblazoned with the arms of Howard, and setting his servants shouting, ' Way, way, for the Duke of Norfolk,' forced the duke's carriage to give way as it entered the lane. On another occasion the duke's servants shouted, ' Get out of the way ! ' to a man leading a pig by the roadside. ' Why ? ' asked the man. ' Because my Lord Duke is coming, and he does not like to be looked at.' ' But I will see him, and my pig shall see him too,' retorted the man, and he held the pig up by the ears until the duke had passed.

All his servants obeyed the duke by signs, and his wife and children were kept almost in the same state of servility. It certainly says much for the man that he was able to crush the spirit of his haughty first wife, Elizabeth Percy, but perhaps he exaggerated when he rebuked his second wife, one of ' the Black Funereal Finches,' who dared to tap him with her fan :—' Madam, my first duchess was a Percy, and *she* never took such a liberty.' His daughter, Charlotte, paid dearly for the forbidden pleasure of sitting down in his presence. She lost £20,000 of her inheritance. It is really cheering to come across one or two stories of his election campaigns in which, as we shall see later, his dignity must have been grievously spoiled. And although

[1] *Gentleman's Magazine*, lxi. p. 199.

one realises that Swift's biting sarcasms were mainly
political, one can imagine how he must have enjoyed
wielding the only weapon that could be directed with any
effect against the duke's invulnerable fortress of pride.
Anthony Henley must have enjoyed the same pleasure
when, according to Walpole, he directed a letter to the
duke, 'over against the trunk shop at Charing Cross,'
meaning, of course, Northumberland House.

At the same time there is another side to Somerset's
character, a side hardly ever emphasised, simply because the
absurdities of his all-absorbing pose have dwarfed every other
interest where he is concerned.   There is no question that
both Whig and Tory parties regarded him as a tower of
strength to the Hanoverian cause, not only because of his
great territorial and political influence, but also because he
was steadfast in his principles, and because his pride ever
saved him from descending to the acts of duplicity which so
many of his contemporaries, caring little for public opinion,
performed smilingly and with an easy conscience.   True, he
did not, as we shall see, shrink from nocturnal meetings with
Harley, but that he regarded as making for the welfare of
the Hanoverian cause and preserving, as he wrote to Harley,
' the future quiet and happy reign of the Queen, whose happiness and welfare you and I both ought in the highest sense
of gratitude to have the preference of all other consideration in our thoughts.'   Moreover, his share in the political
situation at the end of Anne's reign must always be remembered.   It was his prompt action in combination with the
Dukes of Shrewsbury and Argyll that thwarted Bolingbroke's Jacobite schemes, when Anne lay dying, and brought
the Elector of Hanover to the English throne.

Macky describing the duke in 1702, says he was 'of a
middle stature, well-shaped, a very black complexion, a
lover of music and poetry, of good judgment [" not a grain,"
interpolated Swift, " hardly common sense "], but by reason

CHARLES SEYMOUR, SIXTH DUKE OF SOMERSET: THE PROUD DUKE.
From an engraving in the British Museum. (I. Smith fec.)

of a great hesitation in his speech wants expression.' Kneller's portrait of him, in a full-bottomed wig, shows him to have been a handsome man of the true Seymour type, large-eyed and full-lipped, holding himself with the arrogant air that might well have hindered any poor relation from claiming kinship.[1] The death of his brother Francis in 1678 had brought him the title and estate of the dukedom of Somerset, when he was only sixteen years of age, and had recently entered Trinity College, Cambridge.[2] The estate was not suitably adapted to the title, as a contemporary expressed it. Many of the estates which had belonged to the second duke had gone, at the death of his grandson William, to the only sister of the latter, Elizabeth, the wife of Thomas Bruce, second Earl of Ailesbury.[3] Hence the Trowbridge Seymours had more dignity than territory. An ambitious marriage was

[1] Walpole tells an amusing anecdote concerning James Seymour, the animal painter, who, being employed by the duke to decorate a room at Petworth with portraits of his racehorses, dared to claim kinship with him. ' Cousin Seymour, your health ! ' the duke one day drank to the artist at dinner. The artist replied, ' My lord, I really do believe that I have the honour of being of your Grace's family.' The duke, enraged, bade his steward dismiss Seymour for his impudence. Another artist was engaged, but, failing to continue the work successfully, advised the duke to recall Seymour. This he eventually did, and then Seymour replied, ' My lord, I will now prove myself one of your Grace's family, for I won't come.'

[2] In the March of 1678-9, the young duke fell ill of smallpox, and Colonel Cooke wrote to the Marquess of Ormonde. ' Mr. Seymour (Edward Seymour, afterwards fourth baronet, and the Speaker) now bids fair for Duke of Somerset, the young duke yesterday falling sick of that fatal disease to that family, the small pox, and if he miscarries there is no thing but his father (the third baronet) betwixt his worship and his grace ' (Marquess of Ormonde's MSS.).

[3] This Earl of Ailesbury was an ardent supporter of the Stuarts. He refused to take the oath to William and Mary, and being suspected of complicity in Sir John Fenwick's plot, was arrested and put into the Tower. The shock of the news brought about the death of his wife (Elizabeth Seymour), in premature childbirth. See his *Memoirs* (Roxburghe Club).

surely a tradition in the Seymour family, but the marriage on which this wiser Seymour had set his heart was one of solid wealth or territorial aggrandisement, with no drawbacks such as those which had handicapped his ancestors.

Elizabeth Percy was the sole heir of Josceline, eleventh and last Earl of Northumberland. In 1671, when she was only four years old, her father had died, and she succeeded to all the honours and estates of the house of Percy, holding in her own right six of the oldest baronies in England—Bryan, Fitz Payne, Latimer, Lucy, Poynings, and Percy. Brought up under the care of her grandmother, the old Dowager Countess of Northumberland, she was soon the centre of attraction for interested suitors. Her grandmother guarded her well, refused her hand to Charles II. in February 1679, for his natural son, the Duke of Richmond, but bestowed her a few weeks later on Henry Cavendish, Earl of Ogle, and heir of Henry, second Duke of Newcastle ; the ' ugliest and saddest creature ' that Sacharissa, Elizabeth's great-aunt, had ever looked upon. The bridegroom was only fifteen, the bride twelve. It was arranged that he should take the name of Percy, and travel abroad for two years, while the bride finished her education. Before the first year was over, the weakly boy was dead, and the old countess was planning a new marriage for her ward. This time she chose a middle-aged man of the world, a well-battered rake, Thomas Thynne of Longleat in Wiltshire. In the summer of 1681, Elizabeth was married to Thynne, but fled immediately after the marriage to the protection of Lady Temple at the Hague. The second husband was as distasteful to her as the first, but she was again to be delivered by his death. Count Charles Königsmark, who had been one of the rival suitors for her hand, caused Thynne to be murdered by hired assassins in Pall Mall in the February of 1681-2.[1] This paved the way for a new suitor, and this time

[1] There is a memorial to Thynne in Westminster Abbey. Swift

for one whom Elizabeth, now a girl of fifteen, delighted to honour, Charles Seymour, Duke of Somerset. On the 30th of May 1682, she became his wife, and he became lord of her estates, and master of Alnwick Castle, Petworth, Syon House, and Northumberland House in the Strand. The only stipulation was that he should assume the arms and name of Percy, and even from this agreement his bride released him when she came of age.

Wealth and territorial influence secured, Somerset was open to any favours that the court might shower upon him. In 1683 he was appointed a Gentleman of the Bedchamber, and 1684 was installed as Knight of the Garter. Soon afterwards he was sworn one of the Privy Council, and was one of those who signed the order for the proclamation of James II. At the funeral of Charles II. he was one of the supporters of Prince George of Denmark, who was chief mourner.

The duke had been appointed by the late king colonel of a regiment of Dragoons, and in 1685 he put himself at the head of the militia in the county of Somerset for the purpose of opposing the Duke of Monmouth's rebellion. On the 16th of June 1685 he wrote from Wells to the Earl of Sunderland : ' I intend to march myselfe to-morrow towardes Crookeherne [Crewkerne] and will gett there as soon as I can. . . . Pray my lord acquaint the king that there shall not be any thing wanting in me to put a stope to this rebellion which (sic) I hope now in ten dayes you will find a very alteration for the best.' ' I have here stopt ten idle lusty fellowes,' he continues, ' we suspected to be going into Lime that could give noe account of themselves, and one of them confessed that he believed the Duke of Monmouth an honest man, and was sure that he was a friend of his, and upon this we have sent them all to the jaile of this

later accused the Duchess of Somerset of having been privy to the plot to murder Thynne. She revenged herself by keeping him out of the bishopric of Hereford.

town.' He had found all the gentlemen of the town very well inclined to do the king's service and the militia in very good order, for militia, and likely, with the encouragement of their officers, to do their part well. Yet he advised that a foot regiment should be sent to lead on the militia, ' since almost any report would startle them,' and ' the common sort of people if they durst would rise every minute.' Five days later Somerset sent an urgent message to Lord Albemarle to come to his help. Lord Stawell's regiment had fled, and for the most part gone over to the enemy, who were only ten miles away at Bridgewater, and Somerset had ' onely one regiment and one troop of horse which,' he wrote, ' I am afraide will hardly stand, because the others have showed them the way to run.' He was forced to retire to Bath, whence he wrote to King James that he hoped assistance would soon be sent, or the whole county would be lost.[1] However, by the end of June the Royalist troops had come into the county, while Monmouth's army was every day becoming more demoralised for want of adequate training and adequate weapons. The Earl of Feversham, who was the Royalist commander, seems to have spent most of his generalship in writing long reports of events in execrable French to the king, but Churchill was commanding under him, and the genius of Churchill won the Battle of Sedgemoor. Yet in the story of the rebellion the work of the militia of Somerset and of the Duke of Somerset in heading and organising it must not be forgotten.

Although Somerset rejoiced in court favour, and was a keen supporter of the royal cause, ' an accident' prevented him from continuing in the king's good graces. James, misled, as it was said, by the persuasions of his queen and such of his Council as were her creatures and dependants, permitted the Pope openly to send a Nuncio to England, and admitted him to a public audience

---

[1] MSS. of Mrs. Stopford Sackville.

'which was so contrary to his prerogative as King of England, and head of the national Church, also so repugnant to Protestantism that it mightily disgusted the whole nation.' The Duke of Somerset, to whom, as first Lord of the Bedchamber, James assigned the duty of introducing the Nuncio d'Adda to St. James's, absolutely refused the task, 'leaving that part of his office,' as a contemporary puts it, 'to be performed by some abject court sycophant that stood in need of rise and favour.' [1] He grounded his refusal on the fact that the carrying out of such a task would involve him in heavy penalties according to English law. 'I would have you fear me as well as the law,' replied the infuriated king. 'I cannot fear you,' the duke suavely answered, 'as long as I commit no offence I am secure in your Majesty's justice.' Still more infuriated, James dismissed him from office, and took from him the command of his regiment, 'to the duke's immortal honour,' as his biographer remarks. It was after this event that James pardoned Horatio Botti, the murderer of the late duke, and 'by this act the Somerset family were so highly disobliged that their respect for that unhappy prince was much abated.'

It was not wonderful that Somerset was one of those who heartily welcomed the Prince of Orange in 1688, and was at first handsomely treated by the new king, having the honour of carrying the queen's crown at the coronation, while his duchess was one of the queen's train-bearers. And though at a later date he was less popular with the king because he sided with Princess Anne in her quarrels with the queen, yet in 1694, when Queen Mary died of smallpox, the duke was one of the supporters of her pall and the duchess was chief mourner.

The first office to which Somerset was installed during William's reign was that of Chancellor of the University of

---

[1] The task was performed by the Duke of Grafton, son of Charles II., by the Duchess of Cleveland.

Cambridge,[1] to which he had been elected a few months before James II. fled to France. He began a more prominent career in Parliament in 1690, when he succeeded Halifax as Speaker of the House of Lords. In 1699 Edward Harley wrote to his father, Sir Edward Harley, that it was generally supposed the Duke of Somerset would be Chamberlain. The death of the Duke of Gloucester (Princess Anne's son), in the spring of 1700, threw open the question of succession to the throne after Anne's death. The Tory ministry which William was obliged to appoint at the end of 1700 settled the succession on the children of Sophia, Electress of Hanover, granddaughter of James I., but in the meantime wild schemes as to the possibility of establishing a commonwealth whenever Anne should die, the ideal of Lord Somers and Lord Montague, had been concocted. Further, one unknown correspondent wrote to another unknown (probably Sir Edward Harley), ' I will tell you one pleasant thing, they have made Duke Somerset believe he has a fair pretence, but at all adventures he is to have an eminent post, and some other such men they say are to be wrought on by suitable application.'[2]

Certainly Anne's reign opened well for the Duke of Somerset's ambitions. He was in high favour with the queen, since she well remembered that when in April 1692 she had been summarily ejected from her lodgings at the

[1] The most noticeable feature of his chancellorship was his action in regard to the ejection of Dr. Bentley of Trinity College, Cambridge, from the Regius Professorship (*Hist. MSS. Com.*, Duke of Portland's MSS., vii. pp. 2, 3). From 1714 to 1724, Bentley, as Master of Trinity College, had ruled with despotic power, in spite of the intermittent resistance of the Fellows. In 1718, the Vice-Chancellor summoned him to appear at his court, at the suit of Conyers Middleton (the biographer of Cicero), who, when he had received his D.D. degree, had been forced by Bentley to pay him a fee, which he now sought to recover. Bentley failed to appear, and the Chancellor ordered him to be deprived of his degrees by the University.

[2] *Hist. MSS. Com.*, Duke of Portland's MSS.

Cockpit [1] for continuing her friendship with the Duchess of Marlborough at the time when Marlborough was disgraced, it was Somerset who had opened his doors and given her warm welcome at Syon House.[2] Hence at her Coronation her train, which was passed through the back of the chair (since being disabled by gout she had to be carried through most of the ceremony), was borne by the Duchess of Somerest as Mistress of the Robes, assisted by Lady Elizabeth Seymour and other women of the Bedchamber, while the duke carried the orb. Both the duke and duchess sat at the centre table with the queen in the reception after the ceremony.

In 1702, by the queen's influence, Somerset was made Master of the Horse, although there were two other candidates, Ormond and Marlborough, and the general opinion was that Marlborough would be successful. In December 1708 Marlborough and he were sent to Spithead to welcome the Archduke Charles as King of Spain. Charles Goring (M.P. for Steyning) wrote to Robert Harley,

[1] Charles II. had bought the Cockpit lodgings for her use when she was married.

[2] She was carried in a sedan chair to Syon House, ' being then with child, without any guard or decent attendance, where she miscarried, and all people forbid waiting upon her : which was complied with by everybody but the Duke of Somerset, whose house she was in, and Lord Rochester, who was her uncle' (Burnet). The following entry occurs in the *London Gazette*, for April 17, 1692 (No. 2758) : ' Her Royal Highnes was taken ill last night at Syon House, and fell in Labor this morning, near two months before her time, and about 11 of the clock was delivered of a son, who was immediately christened by name of George and dyed about an hour after. The queen (Mary) went in the afternoon to see her Royal Highness, who is as well as can be expected.' The queen's visit, as described by Duchess Sarah herself, could hardly have been welcome to the invalid. As she approached the bedside she remarked, ' I have made the first step by coming to you, and I expect you should make the next by removing my Lady Marlborough.' Anne protested and refused, whereupon the queen swept out of the room in high dudgeon, and came no more to Syon House. See App. ii.

Speaker of the House of Commons, that the Dukes of Somerset and Marlborough had come on board about four o'clock, and after waiting about half an hour the Duke of Somerset was called first, and delivered his letter and compliment. After a little time the Duke of Marlborough, who was impatiently waiting, went in and the other came out. In the elaborate ceremonies which followed in celebration of this visit of the King of Spain both Somerset and his wife took prominent part.

So far Somerset had not openly expressed any strong political views, though he was necessarily pledged to the Hanoverian cause. The Whig Parliament, which had sat for six months after King William's death, had been followed by a strong Tory majority, but a majority which on the whole tended for a time to support Marlborough and the war. The High Tories, headed by Rochester, were one by one weeded out of the ministry, and Marlborough made an attempt to govern through the moderate men of both parties. But the Church question, expressed in the Occasional Conformity Bill, brought the Tories into a fresh opposition to Marlborough, and it was evident in 1704 that his popularity with the Tory party was irretrievably shaken. Thus it was obvious at the beginning of 1705 that he was being fast driven into the hands of the Whigs and into virtual opposition to the queen, who loved the Tories. So far Somerset, steering according to Marlborough's course, had pursued a moderating Whig policy. In February 1703, when Charles Montague, Lord Halifax, was attacked by the Tory commissioners for the examination of public accounts, it was Somerset who presented a report to the House of Lords, acquitting him of the neglect and breach of trust imputed to him by the commissioners. The Lords agreed, and Halifax, whose conviction would have been disastrous to the Whigs, was saved.

Two years later when, as we have seen, Marlborough was being forced into Whig sympathies, Somerset used

every direct and indirect means in his power to influence
the elections at Marlborough and elsewhere, but more
especially at Marlborough where his own family interests
were centred. The election of the knights of the shire
for Lewes (Sussex) took place in the May of 1705. Charles
Goring wrote describing the election to Harley. There were
four candidates, Mr. Lumley, Sir George Parker, Sir Harry
Peachy and Mr. Trevor. But what added, if not to the
interest of the two latter, yet the splendour of their party
(Whig) was that the Dukes of Somerset and Richmond appeared at their head, and ' such a sight having been seldom
seen at Lewes, it was thought by all the inhabitants it must
of necessity carry the election, but *multa cadunt*, etc., for
before they began to poll the High Sheriff (Turner) produced the resolves of the House of Commons against the
Lords of Parliament appearing at elections, and told their
Graces they should go off the Bench before one man should
be polled.' The Duke of Richmond swore he would not go ;
the Duke of Somerset began to argue, telling the Sheriff that
the resolve of the House of Commons was no law. The
Sheriff answered that he would ever abide by whatever was
done by the Commons, as his representatives, even to the
last drop of his blood, and ' if you do not go immediately off
the bench,' he added, ' I 'll adjourn the court.' ' Mr. Sheriff,'
quoth the Duke of Somerset, ' you had acted more like a
gentleman had you told us of this before we came here.'
' My Lords,' the Sheriff answered, ' till I came here I had
nothing to do to tell you, neither could I believe you would
have come where you knew you had nothing to do, and I
would have you to know I am as good a gentleman as yourself, and know as well how to behave myself.' He then
ordered the Under Sheriff to make way, and he himself went
off, 'and our Dukes immediately with their stars disappeared,
which brought all their party under a cloud.' The writer
adds, as a postscript, that the two dukes employed the rest of

their time in seeing a puppet show. As a matter of fact, the resolve of the House of Commons seems to have done little to check the interference of the Lords with the elections. ' They have done more in the electing this Parliament than ever before,' wrote a contemporary. At Salisbury, the bishop's candidate for the town was defeated, and the bishop's friends were very ill-treated by the clergy at the county election. The bishop's gentlemen, the Dukes of Somerset and Bolton received strange insults, and Daniel Defoe[1] wrote to Harley, ' His Grace of Somerset was insulted in the streets of Salisbury by the mob, his coach being stopped in the street.' The indignation of the Proud Duke may be imagined.

At Marlborough the duke represented the Whig interest, while Charles, Lord Bruce,[2] represented that of the Tories. In 1705, Roger Williams, who was mayor at that time, was the duke's agent, while Charles Beecher represented Lord Bruce. Beecher wrote to Lord Bruce in April 1705 that the Marlborough people were very mercenary, and resolved to serve the highest bidder, for they had no sort of honour or conscience, being now as corrupt as any other borough. The duke had lately nominated the son of Mr. Ash that stood last time for the county, ' which Wat Shropshire and all that party say will certainly lose him the election, for all the Church party that are voters are resolved to be against him.' However, the election went in favour of the duke's candidate, partly because the Whig cause was more popular, partly, doubtless, because the duke's bribes were the highest. Beecher wrote to Robert Bruce in May 1705, ' I went to every person that voted for you and thanked them as ordered; they all took it very kindly, and expressed great concern at

---

[1] It was at this time that Defoe having been delivered from Newgate by Harley, had become his pliant tool in the queen's secret service.

[2] Son of the second Earl of Ailesbury, who had married Elizabeth Seymour, grandchild of the second Duke of Somerset. (See *supra*.)

your disappointment, and promised to serve you on another
occasion. As to Bedwin, the portreeve engaged to me that
his man shall give evidence of his being bribed to give his
vote, and that he himself would make it his business to get
other proofs privately, and did not doubt but to succeed
well in it.'

The general outcome of the election of 1705 was that the
nation, having become thoroughly interested in the war and
altogether disgusted with the Tories, returned a large Whig
majority. The ministry was composite ; on the one hand
a number of Whigs led by Sunderland, on the other a section
of the moderate Tories led by Harley and St. John. But
at the very moment when Marlborough seemed to have
succeeded in forming a moderate ministry which would
uphold the war, his authority with the queen was under-
mined by the machinations of Harley, who used as his instrument the quiet, even-tempered Mrs. Abigail Hill, his
own cousin. Harley knew well that the power of the Tories
over the queen lay in their High Churchism. This then
should be his point of attack on Marlborough and his duchess.
Mrs. Hill was to ingratiate herself into the queen's favour,
was to rouse in the queen a dread of the subversion of the
church, and inch by inch, quietly but relentlessly, to undermine the influence of the Duchess of Marlborough over the
queen, and make herself the queen's indispensable friend.
The plot succeeded well. Anne was captivated by the quiet
respectful attitude of her new friend, and though for a time
the Marlboroughs retained their influence, yet Mrs. Hill,
who had now become Mrs. Masham, was soon to utterly
supplant the duchess.

In the meantime the absolute failure of the composite
ministry was proved in the winter of 1707, and in the
beginning of 1708, it was certain that Marlborough must
break with Harley and the moderate Tories, and give his
whole-hearted support to the Whigs. This at least was

L

his only alternative if the war was to continue.   In this
ministerial crisis, the Duke of Somerset played an important
part.   It was he who read the report, which lasted about
three hours, in the House of Lords concerning the treason of
the man Greg, a clerk in Harley's office, whose correspondence with France, easily construed into infidelity on the part
of his master, was a convenient excuse for Marlborough to
insist on Harley's dismissal.   That Somerset recognised the
flimsy character of the charge against Greg is shown by the
fact that before reading the report he told some lords in
the House ' that he thought it was not worth anybody's
hearing, and for his own part, if he was not obliged to
read it he should not stay to hear it.'

In the heat of the struggle in the Council when Marlborough
and Godolphin withdrew, having given the queen the option
of their withdrawal or Harley's dismissal, Somerset made
a very definite stand for Marlborough.   Harley attempted
a discussion on the imperial contingent of troops since business with the Court of Vienna was in his department.
Somerset quickly rose and interrupted him.   How, he asked,
could they deliberate on such a question when the general
was not with them.   He offered to withdraw himself from
the Council if the discussion continued, and his lead being
followed by Lord Pembroke, the President of the Council,
Harley was completely foiled.   The queen was left unsupported in her attempt to retain Harley, whose influence was
strong upon her through his High Church leanings, and his
medium Mrs. Masham.   Hence, by the force of circumstances and by the persuasion of her husband, Prince
George, Anne was forced to consent to Harley's dismissal.
Marlborough had triumphed, but he had triumphed by
means of the Whigs, and the Whigs were prepared to be
his taskmasters, or to subvert his authority.   The Duke
of Somerset for one was already conceiving an idea of
forming a party on Harley's lines, but on the basis of

moderate Whiggism. In the height of his elation at the triumph of the Whigs he wrote ' a very haughty letter ' to the electors of Marlborough, bidding them choose his son (Lord Hertford) and stating that he knew his interest to be so well assured, that his son or whom else he pleased to recommend would always be chosen. ' This,' Beecher wrote to Lord Bruce in April 1708, ' has disgusted many.'

The triumph of the Whigs was to be short-lived. Once in power they had become dictatorial and overbearing, and the Duke of Marlborough was bound to accept their terms and obey their dictation. They were working their own destruction as the more moderate Whigs, Somerset among them, were quick to realise. The Tory party saw their way to win over the discontented moderates. Already in the beginning of the year 1709-1710, the Duke of Shrewsbury wrote to Harley. ' The Duke of S[omerset] is much out of humour, talks very despairingly, as if he sees nothing would be done, and sometimes doubtfully of the above-mentioned Council. I wish he and Lord Rivers and you and I might talk together soon, and if the motion came from you it were the better. I doubt he was nothing more out of humour because you and I were together yesterday, but for that I have slight ground.' He added a postscript, ' since I writ so far I have seen the Duke of S[omerset]. He is in better humour, but not quite as I wish.' Somerset had personal as well as impersonal grounds for opposition to Marlborough and the extremist Whigs at this juncture. It was well known that Marlborough had explained to his wife that he never dreamed of employing so witless a person ' in anything that is of any consequence.' Thus the Mastership of the Horse was the only office Somerset held. Further, the duke had refused a regiment to Lord Hertford, Somerset's son, and ' the high spirited father bore this repulse with deep Resentment.' Now this ' witless person ' was preparing to turn on Marlborough, and hand in hand with Rivers to play a wrecking

game against the Whig Government, with his little following
of discontented moderates, nicknamed ' the Juntilla.'

Meanwhile his duchess was teaching Sarah, Duchess of
Marlborough, that her imperious rule over the queen was
ending.   Poor Duchess Sarah had not learned to suffer
gladly.   She had lost all command of her temper at Mrs.
Masham's success with the queen, and now she realised a
new and dangerous rival was subtly preparing a still more
final defeat.   The trial of Dr. Sacheverell, the test which
finally proved to the Whig ministry that its day was
done, was the moment chosen by the Duchess of Somerset
for a special stratagem by which Duchess Sarah should be
placed at a disadvantage with the queen.   Duchess Sarah
told the story herself in a letter : ' The Duchess of
Somerset came to the trial, and before I sat down I asked
if her Grace would not be pleased to sit, at which she gave
a sort of start back with the appearance of being surprised,
as if she thought I had asked a very strange thing, and refused sitting.   I observed that it was always the custom
to sit before the queen in such cases, and that her Majesty
had ordered us to do so the day before, but that her refusing
it now looked as if she thought that we had done something
not proper.   To which she answered that she did not care
to sit and then went and stood behind the queen as Lady
Hyde had done the day before, which I took no notice of
then, but sat down with Lady Burlington.   But when I came
to reflect on what the ladies had done, I plainly perceived
that in the Duchess of Somerset especially this conduct
could not be thought to be the effect of humility, but that
it must be a stratagem to flatter the queen by paying her
more respect, and to make some public noise of this matter
that might be to my disadvantage or disagreeable to me.'

For the time being there was peace between Mrs. Masham
and the Duchess of Somerset, for they were leagued against a
common enemy.   When in the January of 1710-11 the queen

was finally persuaded to deprive Duchess Sarah of all her offices, the duchess, after gratifying her spite by carrying off the brass locks and the marble chimney-pieces from her apartments in St. James's, departed ignominiously, and her gold key as groom of the stole was handed to the Duchess of Somerset, while Mrs. Masham was made keeper of the Privy Purse.

The part that Mrs. Masham was playing towards the Duchess of Somerset in the arena of the queen's feelings, was the part that Harley was playing towards the Duke of Somerset in the arena of the politics that the queen's personal likes and dislikes so much affected. As Mrs. Masham was well content that the active attacks on Duchess Sarah should proceed from the Duchess of Somerset rather than from herself, so Harley was more than content that the attack on the Whig Government should proceed from the duke as a moderate Whig, rather than from himself as a Tory. A contemporary (Dr. Burnet) said of Somerset that he was 'so humoursome, proud and capricious, that he was rather a ministry spoiler than a ministry maker'—and this was Harley's conception of his usefulness. It had first of all been necessary that Sacheverell should be allowed to go free, with light, even nominal, punishment, and Somerset had to be won over to procure this. The doctor's acquittal would have been too violent a triumph for the Tories and High Churchism. Harley had seen that, and desired rather to win a Tory majority by slow means and sure. Hence it had been good news to him, when the Earl of Orrery wrote in the March of 1709-10, that though the Duke of Argyll could not vote for the acquittal of Sacheverell, since he thought that 'a man who had made so bad a use of the pulpit ought never to come into it again,' he would warmly oppose fine and imprisonment, and would endeavour to persuade the Duke of Somerset to do the same.

The result of the trial and the triumph of Harley's policy is too well known to need repetition here. His next move was to win the confidence of the Duke of Somerset, and encourage him to play the wrecking game which, as we have seen, he was already scheming to play. The Duke of Shrewsbury, as already indicated, was willing to act as go-between. At the end of May 1710, Somerset wrote from Kensington to Harley. ' The Duke of Shrewsbury says you desire to talk with me, if so, let me know before eight o'clock, if you can be at home or at Northumberland House this night at nine o'clock, accordingly I will come from hence. In case you choose to come to me I will have a servant to conduct you, and if I come to you then have your back door open for me ; but if this notice has not the good fortune to fall into your hands by eight o'clock, then any time you shall appoint to-morrow morning I shall obey.' Harley's plans were succeeding well, and for the next two months we constantly have the picture of Somerset slinking in at Harley's back-door, or admitted in a hackney chair with the curtains drawn round it, or of Harley paying nocturnal visits to the duke. All this in comparative detail the Harley papers reveal, while they also show how cleverly Harley used the duke to instil his own opinions into the queen. On the 18th of June 1710 the duke wrote to Harley, ' I have spoken to the queen on the last part of your letter. She was pleased to express her own thoughts on that matter in such a manner that she will not only consider it, but will in a few days speak to Mr. Secretary Boyle about it ; the further particulars I will at present refer till we meet, which I hope may be to-morrow morning at eleven o'clock at your own house. I desire your porter may be instructed to admit a hackney chair with the curtains drawn round it, into your hall without examining the chairmen, or if this time be not convenient let it be at your own house, for it will be the same to me morning, noon or night.'

On July 8, he wrote to Harley, ' Your humble servants do desire you to come here (Kensington) this night to any other lodging than mine, soon after nine o'clock, it being very necessary to have half an hour's conversation with you before your other engagements.' Two days later he wrote, ' If you please to come to Kensington to-morrow night between the hours of nine and ten, I will have a servant at the gate under the clock who shall conduct you to me.' Later in July he wrote offering his services as special ambassador to Hanover, to ' discourse with the Pensioner,' concerning the state of affairs in England. On the 30th of July he wrote off in haste to Harley, at six o'clock in the evening, that some affairs had already happened, but that more would before the Cabinet Council had risen. The queen had therefore commanded him (Somerset) to write to Harley to come that night to the Duke of Shrewsbury's lodging, from whence he was to be conveyed by Somerset to a place unnamed. Four hours later, since Harley had not appeared, he wrote off to him that he was sorry for the cause of his not coming that night. ' Therefore,' he adds, ' I must desire admittance to-morrow morning between the hours of nine and ten into your own house, to discourse on some matters of consequence.' In a postscript he reminds Harley, ' Don't forget to order your porter to open the door to a hackney chair with curtains drawn.'

Every day was bringing the impending crisis nearer and nearer. On the 8th of August the secret machinations of Somerset and his ' Juntilla,' inspired by the craftiness of Harley, had succeeded. The queen was persuaded of her own power, and without consulting Godolphin made the Duke of Shrewsbury Lord Chamberlain. This was the blow that Somerset had been planning. It was followed by the dismissal of Godolphin himself, and then, probably to the genuine surprise of Somerset, Harley was made Chancellor of the Exchequer, and was virtually Prime Minister. The letters between Somerset and Harley ceased for a time, and before the end of August Somerset was reckoned by the friends of Harley 'to be against us.' Thus Thomas Conyers wrote to Harley, 'I hear the Duke of Somerset is now against us. I thought he was for us, and therefore went twice to Newcastle to prevent their setting up another to throw out Lord Hertford (Somerset's only son), so if you would have him out be pleased to let me know, and I dare engage to remove him . . . but this must be known as soon as may be.'

On the 11th of September Erasmus Lewis wrote to Harley that the Duke of Somerset, in a conversation the night before with Sir Peter King, desired him to acquaint all their friends ' that he was, is, and ever would be a Whig, that he would serve them in all elections, and would oppose a dissolution to the utmost.' On the 22nd of September the Honourable Robert Bruce reported to Lord Bruce at Marlborough, that rumour had it that the Duke of Somerset was certainly out of his place, and gone away from court for good and all in very great heat, and that the Duke of Beaufort was sent for to take the place of the Master of the Horse.[1] But the rumour was premature. Neither Somerset nor his duchess were to fade away from the scene so quickly as Harley wished they might do, now that their usefulness was over. The queen was certainly induced to dissolve Parliament in the November of 1710, and Harley formed an entirely Tory ministry, but the power of the duke and duchess was still strong with the queen.

Swift was quick to see the danger of the influence of the duchess with the queen, and to see that although Somerset played up to Harley, writing him polite and submissive letters, he might well be trying his hand once more as a ministry spoiler. Hence, in the February of

[1] *Hist. MSS. Com.*, MSS. of Duke of Ailesbury.

1711 (1710-11) Swift wrote to ' Stella ' concerning Harley's peace policy and the general state of affairs :—' The ministry is on a very narrow bottom, and stands like an isthmus between the Whigs on one side, and the violent Tories on the other. They are able seamen, but the tempest is too great, the ship too rotten, and the crew all against them. Lord Somers (Whig leader) has been twice in the queen's closet—once very lately; and your Duchess of Somerset, who has now the key, is a most insinuating woman, and I believe they will endeavour to play the same game that has been played against them.[1] . . . They have cautioned the queen so much against being governed that she observes it too much. I could talk till to-morrow upon these things, but they make me melancholy.' Two months later Somerset was writing to Harley on his return from abroad, inquiring for his health, congratulating him on his escape from the murderous attack of the French refugee, Guiscard, and promising that the next day he (Somerset) returned to town he would either visit Harley or his ' grave porter.' His advances were evidently rejected, since in May he wrote again from Kensington, ' Since I cannot obtain leave to wait on you, I must try for leave to write on this condition, that I do promise to give you as little trouble as any man, but as you are, and are to be very soon declared *le premier ministre*, I hope you will allow me to make application to you as occasion shall require; but if I am not to do it, tell me so, and I will have done.' Probably Harley granted an interview after this, since chiefly through the influence of his duchess with the queen, the use of Somerset's friendship

---

[1] During the autumn of 1710, Mrs. Masham had made use of her influence with the queen to persuade her to admit Harley to private audience, in which the dissolution of Parliament and the creation of a Tory ministry had been planned. The Duchess of Somerset now had the opportunity of playing the same game against the Tories.

could not be despised. But there was war between Secretary St. John and the duke. On the 18th of August 1711 Swift wrote to ' Stella,' ' The reason why the Cabinet Council was not held last night was because Mr. Secretary St. John would not sit with your Duke of Somerset. So to-day the duke was forced to go to the race while the Cabinet was held.'

Throughout the early autumn Mrs. Masham was ill, and the duchess held the queen's ear more completely for the time being. In September Swift wrote to ' Stella ' that Mrs. Masham was better, and would be at court in three or four days—' she had need,' he added, ' for the Duchess of Somerset is thought to gain ground daily.' Indeed, things were looking well for the Whigs. Harley was now Earl of Oxford and Lord Treasurer, but his peace policy was not popular. ' I hope your Lordship has prepared your mind for any change of fortune,' Dr. Stratford wrote to him in September. ' The Whigs give it out with great joy here (Oxford) that there will be a new scene, or rather the old again, before Christmas. I believe, too, it is concerted to hearten their friends with the same news in other places too.' ' You see,' he continues, referring to the struggle between Bolingbroke and Somerset concerning attendance at the Council meeting the month before, ' what use has been made of that affair.'

The Tories, in despair, tried to terrify the queen with tales of Whig designs. The *Post Boy*, of the 12th of November 1711, charged the Kit Cat Club, of which Somerset, as a Whig, was a prominent member, with ' conspiracy to raise a mob to confront the best of queens against her ministry, pull down the houses of several honest, true, worthy English gentlemen, having had money distributed to them by G., G., G., S., S., S., W., H., M. (Grafton, Godolphin, Dr. Garth, Somerset, Sunderland, Somers, Warton, Halifax, and Montague), an insatiable junto, *cum multis aliis*, who made subscription, and gave out the queen was very ill, if not dead, in order to have acted their treason with greater freedom.' The whole story was a gross exaggeration of the fact that the Whigs had designed some midnight Guy Faux processions that November, on which, according to Swift, they had laid out £1000 to dress up the Pope, devil, cardinals, Sacheverell, etc., and ' carrying them out with torches about to burn them.' Swift, like the *Post Boy*, could not refrain from enlarging on the ' very foolish and mischievous designs ' contemplated by the Whigs, saying ' it was thought they would have put the rabble upon assaulting my Lord Treasurer's house and the Secretary's, and other violences.'

These tales accomplished little for the Tory cause. The ministerial arrangements were unpalatable, not only to the Whig Lords, but to that section of the Tories who had been excluded from office.   Hence, on the opening of Parliament, at the beginning of December 1711, Nottingham, who headed a coalition of these two parties, moved as an amendment to the Address, that no peace could be safe or honourable to Great Britain or Europe if Spain or the West Indies were allotted to any of the Bourbons. This was a distinct challenge to Harley's peace negotiations, and in spite of hot discussion, the Government was beaten. Swift was furious. ' Yesterday,' he wrote to ' Stella ' on December 8th, ' when the queen was going from the House, where she sat to hear the debate, the Duke of Shrewsbury, Lord Chamberlain, asked her whether he or the Great Chamberlain Lindsay ought to lead her out, she answered short, " Neither of you," and gave her hand to the Duke of Somerset, who was louder than any in the House for the clause against peace. She (Mrs. Masham) gave me one or two more instances of this sort, which convinces me that the queen is false, or at least very much wavering. . . . This is a long journal and of a day that may produce great alterations and hazard the ruin of England. The Whigs are all in triumph ; they foretold how all this would be, but we thought it boasting. Nay, they said the Parliament should be dissolved before Christmas, and perhaps it may : this is all your d——d Duchess of Somerset's doings. I warned them of it nine months ago, and a hundred times since. The Secretary always dreaded it.' He tells Stella, further, how the Lord Treasurer (Harley) had come to see him after the Government defeat. ' I rallied him, and desired him to give me his staff, which he did : I told him if he secured it me a week I would set all right. He asked how ? I said I would immediately turn Lord Marlborough, his two daughters, the Duke and Duchess of Somerset, and Lord Cholmondeley out of their employments : and I believe he had not a friend who was not of my opinion.' The next day Swift wrote : ' I was this morning with Mr. Secretary. We are both of opinion that the queen is false . . . my friend Lewis . . . gave me reasons to believe the whole matter is settled between the queen and the Whigs, he hears that Lord Somers is to be Treasurer, and believes that sooner than turn out the Duchess of Somerset, she will dissolve the Parliament and get a Whiggish one, which may be done by managing elections. Things are now in the crisis, and a day or two will determine.' Two days later he wrote : ' The Lord Treasurer talked confidently . . . I could not forbear hinting that he was not sure of the queen, and that those scoundrel starving lords would never have dared to vote against the Court if Somerset had not assured them it would please the queen.' Secretary St. John was also confident that ' things would be well,' to Swift's dismay. ' Will you believe it,' St. John asked him, ' if you *see* these people turned out ? ' Swift answered, ' Yes, if I saw the Duke and Duchess of Somerset out.' St. John swore if they were not he would give up his place.

In fact, the Tories were now using every effort to displace the duke and, if possible, the duchess. Boyer states, in his *Annals*, that there was a consultation about the middle of December concerning the removal of the duke from his place as Master of the Horse, but the queen having a great affection for his duchess, could not be prevailed upon to comply, since it was thought that ' the conjugal love ' of the duchess ' would not suffer her to remain at Court if her consort were in disgrace.' More than affection determined Anne's action. She had learnt how eminently convenient it was to balance her favours between Mrs. Masham and the duchess. The tyranny of Duchess Sarah had made her fear an unrivalled favourite. ' We must certainly fall,' wrote Swift on December 21, ' if the Duchess of Somerset be not turned out, and nobody believes the queen will ever part with her.'

He himself was preparing to play his trump card—the famous *Windsor Prophecy*. Three days later he wrote to Stella : ' My *Prophecy* is printed, and will be published after Christmas Day : I like it mightily. I don't know how it will pass. You will never understand it at your distance without help. I believe every one will guess it to be mine, because it is somewhat in the same manner with that of " Merlin " in the *Miscellanies*.' On the 26th he wrote again : ' I called at noon at Mrs. Masham's, who desired me not to let the *Prophecy* be published for fear of angering the queen about the Duchess of Somerset, so I writ to the printer to stop them. They have been printed and given about, but not sold.' The card had been played, and it was impossible to recall the *Prophecy*. In this cruel lampoon he bids ' dear England '

> ' Beware of *Carrots* [1] from Northumberland.
> *Carrots* sown *Thyn* a deep root may get,
> If so they are in *Sommer* set.

---

[1] Referring of course to the red hair of the duchess.

Their *Conyngs mark* them, for I have been told
They assassine when young and poison when old.[1]
Root out these *carrots*, O thou whose name
Is backwards and forwards always the same,[2]
And keep close to thee always that name
Which backward and forwards is almost the same,[3]
And, England, wouldst thou be happy still,
Bury these *Carrots* under a *Hill*.'[4]

Probably the only result of the *Prophecy* was that Swift managed to concentrate the bitter hatred of the duchess on himself. She had her revenge in later days when Swift was wanting preferment.[5] For one brief day, he imagined that his *Prophecy* had accomplished something. On the 29th of December he wrote to Stella : 'The queen has made no less than twelve lords to have a majority, nine new ones, the other three peers' sons, and has turned out the Duke of Somerset. She is awaked at last, and so is the Lord Treasurer, I want nothing now, but to see the duchess out. But we shall do without her. We are extremely happy.' The next day he wrote disappointedly, ' I writ the Dean and you a lie yesterday : for the Duke of Somerset is not yet turned out.' The next day he determined to be ' very civil to the Whigs' at court, but found few there. Lady Burlington and he ' gave one another joy of the change,' but sighed when they reflected ' on the Somerset family not being out.'

Early in January, Swift was still bewailing the fact.

---

[1] Here Swift accuses the duchess of complicity in Count König-mark's murder of her second husband, Thomas Thynne, in Pall Mall.
[2] Anna.   [3] (Mrs.) Masham.
[4] Mrs. Masham's maiden name was Hill.
[5] Swift made his famous retort in *The Author upon Himself*, 1713 :

　　　' Now angry Somerset her vengeance vows
　　　On Swift's reproaches for her ******* [murder'd] spouse
　　　　[Thomas Thynne]
　　　From her red locks her mouth with venom fills
　　　And thence into the royal ear instits.'

' I sat this evening,' he writes, ' at Lord Masham's with Lord Treasurer ; I don't like his countenance ; nor I don't like the posture of things well :—

> " We cannot be stout till Somerset's out,"

as the old saying is.' A few days later, on the 11th of January, he wrote in high spirits : ' It is told me to-day as a great secret, that the Duke of Somerset will be out soon ; that the thing is fixed : but what shall we do with the duchess ? They say the duke will make her leave the queen out of spite if he be out. It has struck upon that fear a good while already.' Seven days later Swift could still give no definite news. ' We want to have this Duke of Somerset out and he apprehends it will not be, but I hope better.' His hopes were fulfilled the next day. ' The Duke of Somerset is out, and was with his yellow liveries at Parliament to-day. You know he had the same with the queen when he was Master of the Horse : we hope the duchess will follow, or that he will take her away in spite. The Lord Treasurer I hope has now saved his head.' A few days later Swift wrote, that he had seen the Duchess of Somerset at court, ' she looked a little down, but was extremely courteous.' Rumour went that the duke was being persuaded by his friends to let the duchess stay with the queen. ' I am sorry for it,' wrote Swift.

However, nothing could induce the queen to part with the duchess, and the Tories had to be content with the displacement of the duke only. Even so he still influenced the queen, sharing with his wife in her confidences, and it was he whom she charged in event of her death, to burn the sealed packet which she always carried about with her. To Harley he remained severely, if not sarcastically, polite. Thus he wrote to him in April 1712, concerning the payment of some of the salaries appertaining to his late office, ' as everything is so absolutely in your power, and you do just as you will in much greater things, you may do the same in this. It is very indifferent to your lordship's most humble servant.'

During the next years the Duke of Somerset was busy at Marlborough, bribing right and left, with the design of influencing the elections both of mayors and members of Parliament.

In January 1711-12, the day before the duke was removed from office, Beecher wrote to Lord Bruce that he (Somerset) had offered Solomon Clarke ' a pension of £20 per annum for his life and his wife's, and to make him porter of Sion House besides,' if he would vote for the duke's candidate for the mayoralty. Clarke rejected the offer, and ' vowed he would not serve him if he would give him the castle and Barton farm.' In July 1712 Beecher wrote to Lord Bruce : ' I came hither (to Henham Park) on Monday, and went to Marlborough yesterday, where I found that the D[uke] himself had been driving very high bargains with the burgesses, for the next mayor and Parliament men, and advised them to submit all differences to him, or the fittest person to set them right, intimating as if all the affairs of this corporation properly belonged to him to determine, and told them if they did not come to oblige him this time, he would never come among them more, and bid them mind that.'

There follows a list of the bribes offered by the duke, so remarkable that they can only be appreciated when one or two are quoted in their fulness. ' He offered Mr. Meggs to become his servant in the nature of a surveyor, and to settle £40 per annum on him and his wife for their lives, and to make his place worth £40 a year more to him. To John Clarke he promised to put him into a place in the Bluecoat Hospital, worth £50 or £60 per annum, to pay his debts, and employ him in all business at his farms. This not prevailing, he offered

Clarke £200 ready money.' To William Garlick he offered
what ready money he would ask, and to pay all his debts,
and, ' in the hope to make him comply (or to rid him out
of the way, as some say), Mr. Pigott (the duke's agent)
drank the poor old man to such a pitch that he was very
near death.' Thomas Hunt was ' too full of banter,'
so they made no offers to him. All these flatly refused
the duke, and rejected his offers. Thomas Smith,
tobacconist, took £20, but swore afterwards he would not
serve the duke, ' saying he owed him this much and more
for former services.' In the next month report ' went that
the duke had declared publicly he would give £50 a man for
as many as would desert Lord Bruce and come to him. He
had actually given a certain John Smith £100 down, and
engaged to be at the charge of educating a son of Smith's
of seven years old at school and at the university, and to
present him with a good living when he was capable of it.

The mayoral election ended, in spite of the duke's
efforts, in favour of Lord Bruce's candidate. ' I never
saw more rejoicing in all my life,' wrote Beecher, ' than
all the Church party showed at carrying this point when
they were so violently attacked. It is hardly possible
to express the Duke's passion or credit his extravagant
expressions, if report does not bespatter him.' He remained with his duchess at Marlborough, and asserted,
according to Beecher, that the election should be judged
invalid because Kimber, the appointed mayor, was not
one of the three nominated for election—' But,' asks
Beecher, ' why did his Grace then take so much pains now
to purchase votes at any rate.' The same struggle ensued
at the parliamentary elections of 1718. At the beginning
of the election, Beecher wrote to Lord Bruce, in November,
' the two Birds and old Dorritt put Harry Wilmott upon
riding about the country to get Parliament men, and sent
him to the Duke of Somerset, and swore, God d—— them,

M

if they could get him to recommend a man it would be harder for my Lord Bruce and better for them, for then they should get more money from him, for they did not care who was chosen so they could get the money, for when my Lord Bruce was not chosen the better he paid them.' In December, John Fowler wrote to Beecher, ' The Duke of Somerset came to this town last night, and this morning Loe, the Duke's gardener, is very busy going up and down among the burgesses desiring them to give one vote as the Duke shall direct.' If the burgesses obeyed him the duke promised to serve them on all occasions, and invited them to meet him at the castle. If they refused he threatened to set up ' a popular election ' in the town and ruin them.

Such were the typical proceedings at the Marlborough elections. The correspondence concerning them, and the continued fight between the duke and Lord Bruce, lasted until 1720. However, from 1716 onwards, after the passing of the Septennial Act,[1] elections were less frequent, and less bribery was therefore possible. Moreover, the struggle at Marlborough was probably less bitter since Somerset, resigning office as Master of the Horse in 1716,[2] retired from court, and contented himself with wielding despotic rule as lord of his estates and his family.

His first duchess died on the 28rd of November 1722. ' She was,' wrote Burnet, ' the best bred, as well as the best born lady in England. . . . The Duke of Somerset ' (for whom Burnet could feel no respect) ' treated her with little gratitude or affection though he owed all he had, except an empty title, to her. She was by much the greatest favourite when the queen died, and it would have continued, for she

---

[1] It was on the occasion of the passing of this Act that the Tories talked ' like old Whigs,' and against monarchy, the Whigs vilified the mob and exalted the court. ' A new strange jumble,' commented an onlooker. The Duke of Somerset as a Whig, voted against the Bill. (MSS. of the king at Windsor.)

[2] George I. had reinstated him at his accession in 1714.

[the queen] thought herself justified in her favour to her when she was ashamed of it elsewhere.' Further, Burnet looked on her as in all respects ' a credit and an ornament to the court,' and contrasted her forcibly with Mrs. Masham, who was ' extremely mean and vulgar in her manners, of very unequal temper, childishly exceptious and passionate.'

The duchess left one surviving son, Algernon, Lord Hertford, who afterwards succeeded to the dukedom, and three daughters, all of whom were already married.[1] It was through Sir William Wyndham, the husband of the second daughter, Katherine, that the Duke of Somerset had retired from court in 1716. In the Rebellion of 1715 the ministry suspected Sir William, and to prevent him from joining the rebels, or making any movement in their favour in the West, where his interest was very powerful, they determined to take him prisoner. The duke, hearing of the design, went to court and offered himself as security for his son-in-law's appearance whenever he should be called. The king, it was said, ' in order to make the Duke easy,' gave him his royal word that Sir William should not be taken into custody, and the duke went away content. But the ministers seem to have had too sure intelligence of Sir William's proceedings to allow themselves to be bound by the royal word, and two messengers were sent west to take him prisoner. They seized him at his house in Somersetshire as he was asleep in bed, but, on pretence of going into the next room to take leave of his wife, who was with child, he made his escape through a postern. A proclamation offering a reward of £1000 for his discovery was then issued, and Sir William, finding one of his letters had been intercepted, surrendered

---

[1] Elizabeth married Henry O'Brien, Earl of Thomond ; Katherine married Sir William Wyndham, and Anne married Peregrine Osborne, afterwards Duke of Leeds. Three children had died young and unmarried, two sons, Percy (who died in 1721 having served as member for Cockermouth), Charles, who died in 1711, and a daughter, Frances, who died in 1720.

himself to his brother-in-law, Lord Hertford. The duke was enraged, flew to court, and made resignation of all his places and employments, to which, as we have seen, he had been restored by George I. All the uniforms and badges, belonging to himself and his servants in his office of Master of the Horse, he caused to be carried in a common dust cart to St. James's, where he commanded his servants to 'shoot the rubbish' into one of the courtyards. 'He could not refrain,' wrote a contemporary, 'from using many virulent expressions against the king, and felt so great a disgust towards both the king and his ministers that he never appeared any more at court until the next king's (George II.) accession, when he was sworn of the Privy Council, and carried the orb at the Coronation.'

In the meanwhile the duke had married his second wife. Dr. William Stratford of Christ Church, Oxford, Harley's voluminous correspondent, wrote to the latter in January 1725-6: 'The Duke of Somerset's marriage at present is the entertainment of the town. No one of the duke's family had the least suspicion of it till it was over. He had with her £5000, but has made settlements proper for a Duchess of Somerset.' Early in February, Stratford wrote further: 'The account that Lord Nottingham [1] gives of the match is that he had no reason to expect it till six weeks ago he received a letter from the Duke of Somerset to desire him to give him leave to make his addresses to his daughter, and that, when he was received, the duke desired the utmost secrecy. He had with her only the usual portion of the daughters of that family—£5000, and he is said to have presented her with £2000 of it on the wedding-day.' A few years later the duke retired to Pet-

---

[1] The father of the bride, commonly known as 'Dismals,' from his lugubrious appearance. Gloom was a family characteristic, and Sir Charles Hanbury Williams nicknamed them 'The Black Funereal Finches.'

worth, where his wife endured most of those twenty odd
years of what Walpole termed her ' slavery ' with him.

During these years his son, Lord Hertford, who had won
for himself a military reputation in the early campaigns in
Anne's reign, under Marlborough, was awarded several
preferments. In 1739 he was made Lieutenant-General of
the Horse, the next year Colonel of the Royal Horse Guards,
and in 1742 Governor of the Island of Guernsey. He did
not, however, take up residence at Guernsey, probably
through his chronic ill-health, but that year rented a house
called Richings Park (afterwards Percy Lodge), west of
Colnbrook, from Lord Bathurst. For several years after
his marriage with Francis Thynne in 1718, Hertford and his
wife had lived at the Trowbridge Castle at Marlborough.
Lady Hertford loved Marlborough, and wrote of it to a
friend : ' Whether it is because this was the first habitation
I was mistress of in those cheerful years when everything
assumed a smiling aspect from vivacity that attends that
season of life, or because almost every little ornament has
been made either by my lord's or by my own contrivance,
I cannot tell, but I certainly feel a partiality for this place
which an indifferent person would be at a loss to account
for.' She was full of happiness in watching the growth
and character of her only son, George Seymour, Lord
Beauchamp. She wrote to Dr. Watts in 1731 : ' I assure
you my little boy is grown a great proficient in your " Songs
for Children," and sings them with great pleasure.' Six
years later she wrote again to Dr. Watts : ' I own I find a
pleasure in thinking that I perceive dawnings of an honest
heart and tolerable reasonings in Lord Beauchamp and his
governor and I flatter ourselves that we see a clearness of
judgment and distinctness of ideas in the themes he com-
poses, which are infinitely the favourite part of his studies,
and always performed with good humour, though he is
obliged to write them in three languages—English, Latin,

and French.'   Of her only daughter, Lady Elizabeth (Betty) Seymour, she wrote : ' I have the happiness to see her a very good-natured, sensible young woman, with a sincere sense of religion and virtue, and the same observance from affection to my lord and me at almost one-and-twenty years old that she had in her earliest childhood.'   The death of Lord Beauchamp in 1744 was not only a terrible grief to his mother and father, but a severe blow to the pride of his grandfather, the Proud Duke.   ' It is a most terrible loss to his parents, Lord Beauchamp's death,' wrote Horace Walpole.   ' If they were out of the question one could not be sorry for such a mortification to the pride of old Somerset. He has written a most shocking letter imaginable to poor Lord Hertford, telling him it is a judgment on him for all his undutifulness, and that he must always look upon himself as the cause of his son's death.   Lord Hertford is as good a man as lives, and has always been most unreasonably used by that old tyrant.' [1]   Lord Beauchamp had died of smallpox at Bologna on the eve of his nineteenth birthday, and now the title would revert, after the death of Lord Hertford, to the descendants of the Protector by his first wife, Katharine Filliol.   Between Sir Edward Seymour, baronet and Speaker of the House of Commons, and the Duke of Somerset, there had been no love lost.   Now his eldest son, as representative of the Filliol line, would be Duke of Somerset.

The old duke lived four years longer, dying on the 2nd of

[1] There had been a temporary reconciliation between the father and son two years before.   Lord Hertford had been desired to resign his regiment in favour of the Duke of Argyll.   He declared he had received it from the king, and if His Majesty pleased to take it back he might, but he did not know why he should resign it.   Afterwards he sent a letter to the king by Lord Beauchamp resigning his regiment, his Governorship of Guernsey and his wife's pension as Lady of the Bedchamber to the late queen.   ' His old Grace of Somerset ' was pleased, and sent for Lord Hertford to tell him he had behaved like his son. But his dislike for his son was proverbial.

December 1748, at the respectable age of eighty-six.[1]   A few
days later Walpole wrote : ' Old Somerset is at last dead.
. . . He tendered his pride even beyond his hate ; for he
has left the present Duke all the furniture of his palaces,
and forbore to charge the estate according to a power he
had with £85,000.'   To his duchess he left only £1000 and
a small farm, besides her jointure, while the whole of his
unsettled estate went absolutely to his two daughters by
her, though neither of them was of age.   Lindsay, or
Ancaster House,[2] in Lincoln's Inn Fields, which the duke
had bought of the Duke of Ancaster, was left to the
elder daughter, in the hope that she would allow her
mother to live in it.   To Sir Thomas Bootle, whom he
had befriended in his earlier years, the duke left half a
borough, and to his own grandson, Sir Charles Wyndham,
a whole borough, with an estate costing £14,000.   Other
legacies were £1000 to another grandson, Mr. O'Brien
(brother of Sir Charles Wyndham, and afterwards Earl of
Thomond), and £100 a year to Miss Wyndham, ' just such
a legacy as you would give to a housekeeper to prevent her
from going to service again.'   Horace Walpole speaks also
of the ' famous settlement ' of the Percy estates having
been found.   The first duchess had settled her estates, in
case her son died without heirs male, on the children of her
daughter Katharine, who had married Sir William Wyndham,
while the barony of Percy was to go to her son's daughter.

[1] He was buried in Salisbury Cathedral, where a statue by Rysbrack
surmounts a commonplace Latin epitaph.

[2] The house is on the west side of Lincoln's Inn Fields, next door to
' James Forster's house,' the dwelling of ' Mr. Tulkinghorn,' that ' tight,
unopenable oyster of an old school ' (cf. *Bleak House*).   Lindsay
House was built by Inigo Jones, and was formerly considered very
handsome, the open balustrade on the top of the house being ornamented
by four urns.   It is now converted into two houses, 59 and 60 Lincoln's
Inn.   A neglected stone path leads round a crescent-shaped piece of
rough gravel to the house ; on either side are high bare brick walls,
on each of which stands an ornate stone urn.

Hence Sir Charles Wyndham, by this settlement, inherited about £12,000 a year of the Percy estates, while £5000, with the barony of Percy, went to Lady Betty Seymour, then Lady Betty Smithson.[1] The old duke had 'refused to allow his writings to be seen during his life,' so that the whole affair of the granting of the earldom of Northumberland, after the duchess's death, had dropped, everybody believing that she had made no settlement. In July 1749, the king consented to give two earldoms ' to replace the great families of Somerset and Northumberland in their descendants.' After the then Duke of Somerset's death (Algernon, the seventh duke), his daughter, Lady Betty Smithson, was to have the title of the Duchess of Northumberland, with the barony of Percy, and Sir Charles Wyndham some other title he might choose, with the Percy estates. The duke, it seems, wanted the earldom of Northumberland to be given to his son-in-law (Sir Hugh Smithson) instead of his daughter. Eventually, in the October of 1749, the duke obtained a new patent of creation as baron and earl, Baron Warkworth of Warkworth Castle in Northumberland, and Earl of Northumberland, to hold the same to him and the heirs male of his body, and in default of such to Sir Hugh Smithson of Stanwick, in Yorkshire, his son-in-law, and his heirs by the Lady Elizabeth.[2] At the same time he was created Earl of

---

[1] The story of her marriage goes thus :—Sir Hugh Smithson, descended from commercial ancestry, since his grandfather was ' a man that let or drove coaches,' was of comparatively low rank, but very handsome in person. Lady Betty admired him, and when she heard that a certain lady had refused to marry him, expressed her surprise that any one could have the heart to reject so handsome a man. Sir Hugh heard of her remark, went off and proposed to her, and was accepted. Thus he became heir, in his wife's right, to the Percy barony, and was eventually created Duke of Northumberland. See *infra*.

[2] The king would not entail the dukedom on Sir Hugh's children by another wife. Thus, in May 1775, Walpole writes, ' Another of our number is dying, the Duchess of Northumberland. Her turtle will not be so impatient for a mate, as his patent does not enable him to

Egremont and Baron Cockermouth, with remainder to Sir Charles Wyndham.

Overshadowed during his father's lifetime by his tyrannising pride and jealousy, and living scarcely more than a year to enjoy his freedom and his title, Algernon, seventh Duke of Somerset, leaves little mark on the pages in the history of his family. His health had been sorely tried in the campaigns under Marlborough in his early life, and some years after his death his wife wrote that ' a long series of pain and infirmity, which was daily gaining ground upon him, shewed me the sword, which appeared suspended over my head by an almost cobweb-thread, long before it dropt.' This knowledge runs like a sad undercurrent through the pages of the letter that she wrote to Lady Luxborough in June 1749, describing the alterations that the duke intended to make in Northumberland House, ' in order to make it look less like a prison.' ' I find, by living long in strait circumstances, one contracts a narrowness of mind which makes launching out at once into great expence not appear so desirable as it would be thought by young gay people. . . . I am looking to a resting-place in Northumberland House, where, perhaps, I may never come ; the probability is much stronger against me than it was this time five years ago against my ever lamented Beauchamp.'

The alterations to the house included a new wing on the right hand side of the garden, containing a library, bed-chamber, dressing-room, and waiting-room, and besides many important additions and minor internal alterations, the court was paved and the footway altered. The stair-case,[1] the duchess thought, was ' very noble,' but would

beget Percys—a Master or Miss Smithson would sound like natural children.'

[1] It was this staircase that Mr. Leyland bought, and had fitted into his famous house of the Peacock Room, at Prince's Gate, when Northumberland House was pulled down in 1876. Whistler painted the panels for the dado on the stairs, but, as is well known, reserved his energies for the Peacock Room.

require ' as large a lanthorn to light it as that at Houghton, so much celebrated in the newspapers.' ' My lord is in treaty for nine houses on the other side of the way,' wrote the duchess, ' in order to pull them doun and build stables, whose gates are intended to open directly over against those of the Court.'   In the following January, the duchess wrote to Lady Luxborough that the duke had returned to Percy Lodge from Bath, where he had been drinking the waters for gout, ' with his health and appetite much improved.'   She adds, ' Our servants and goods have all been removed to Northumberland House since before Michaelmas, but when we shall get into it ourselves is yet among the secrets of Fate.' The house itself was still hidden in the scaffold towards the street, but the duchess thought it would be very handsome. The alterations to the house itself would not cost above £14,000, but ' the houses purchased to widen the street and build his stable, and the remainder of the Duke of Chandos's grant for Scotland Yard, which he is in treaty for in order to carry down his garden and open a view from his House to the Thames, will cost at least as much more.' When she wrote, the duchess herself was suffering from a fall, of which she had taken too little care at first, but owing to which she was now forbidden all sort of exercise, ' which gives me but a melancholy prospect as to my Health for the future.'

On the 7th of February, less than three weeks after this last letter, the Duke of Somerset died, and the duchess, left alone with her own shattered health, having lost her husband and her son, but having as consolation her religion and her friends, retired to Marlborough, and lived there the quiet life of a chronic invalid, quiet but not unhappy. Her daughter's[1] children were very dear to her, the youngest especially, since she thought

---

[1] Lady Betty Smithson, then, by the death of her father, Duchess of Northumberland.

him so like her son. ' My daughter,' she wrote, ' who is
very good to me, has sent me her youngest son, just turned
of four years old, to amuse me in my solitude, because he is
a great favourite of mine, and shows a great deal of his
uncle's disposition and some faint likeness of his person.'
To Lady Luxborough she wrote : ' The little boy is called
Algernon, after his grandpapa, and is, though less handsome,
the counterpart of his poor uncle, Lord Beauchamp. His
innocence, his temper, and his voice are just the same, and
every motion of his body. Judge if I am not fond of him.'

The duchess had also her literary interests to employ her
time. At Longleat, in her youth, she had first come into
touch with the literary circles which had gathered round
her grandfather, Viscount Weymouth, and these had been
continued at Alnwick, at Marlborough and at Percy Lodge,
and now, in her old age, again at Marlborough. She aspired
more than to the patronage of literature, since she was herself a writer of verses,[1] and it was her practice to invite
some young poet to the country every summer to hear her
verses and assist her studies. According to Dr. Johnson,
the poet Thomson was one year one of these, but he took
more pleasure in carousing with Lady Hertford and her
friends than in helping her ladyship to write poetry, and
in consequence was not asked again. Lord Buchan, in his
memoir of the poet, indignantly denies this statement, and
although Johnson's authority cannot be lightly passed over,
it is certain that Lady Hertford makes no reference in her
own letters to any such facts about Thomson. In June
1789, she was writing to her niece, Lady Pomfret : ' I
hope your route will lead you to the Fontaine de Vaucluse
which Petrarch has made so famous by his sonnets. Mr.
Thomson told me he had seen this fountain, and he promised
to give me a description of it in verse ; but the promises

---

[1] Four pieces of her poetry appeared under the signature, *Eusebia*,
in Dr. Watts's *Miscellanies*, which were also inscribed to her.

of poets are not always to be depended on.' However, he had already, in 1727, dedicated to her his poem *Spring*,[1] probably as a result of his visit to Alnwick.

> 'O Hertford, fitted or to shine in courts
> With unaffected grace, or walk the plain
> With innocence and meditation joined
> In soft assemblage, listen to my song
> Which thy own season paints ; when nature all
> Is blooming and benevolent, like thee.'

The story of her intercession for the life of Richard Savage, the poet, when, in 1727, he was convicted of homicide, is well known. Johnson, in his *Lives of the Poets*, relates how the news of the ' merits and calamities ' of Savage ' happened to reach the ear of the Countess of Hertford, who engaged in his support with all the tenderness which is excited by pity, and all the zeal which is kindled by generosity.' She placed his case before the queen so successfully that he was soon after admitted to bail, and pleaded and received the king's pardon. William Shenstone also owed much to her patronage, and, as late as 1758, dedicated a poem to her. Thus she wrote to him in the November of that year, declining the dedication, and asking him to put dashes instead of names, since he had taken his conception of her character from the warped judgment of a partial friend (Lady Pomfret). ' The world will blame the choice of the person to whom it is inscribed,' she writes, ' and draw mortifying comparisons between the ideal lady and the real one.'

Her interests were not only with poetry, but with literature in general. ' I want to know what you think of the *Peruvian Letters*,'[2] she wrote to Lady Luxborough in 1748,

---

[1] In an unprinted preface, he wrote to her, ' Should you read it with approbation, its musick shall not droop ; and should it have the good fortune to deserve your smiles, its roses shall not wither.'

[2] *Lettres d'une Péruvienne*, par F. Huguet de Grafigny, published in 1747. They are the love-letters of a certain Princess Zilia, to her

' and especially of the Fifth in the suite. I have been very well entertained lately. with the two first volumes of *The Foundling*,[1] written by Mr. Fielding, but not to be published till the twenty-second of January, if the same spirit runs through the whole work, I think it will be much preferable to *Joseph Andrews*.' She was right. At another time she asked her friend, 'Have you seen a little French book called *Conseils à une Amie*, said to be written by Madame de Pompadour : the name of the author will not incline you to expect any very exalted sentiments of religion or morality ; but it contains good rules for making a proper figure in high life.' At the same time she speaks of the Letters and some Memoirs of M. Racine père she had been reading : ' they give me a greater esteem for him as a man than as the author of *Esther* and *Athaliah* ' (*Esthère* and *Athalie*). She further speaks of a reply made by ' the minister of B.'s ' to Dr. Middleton's *Free Enquiry about Miracles*. ' I cannot imagine how he can reply to it without owning himself a Deist or explaining some of his innuendos in a different way to what they appear at first sight.'

In the summer of 1753 the duchess was extremely ill, and for some weeks believed to be in great danger. However, in November, she was well enough to write to her friend, Lady Luxborough, ' by the Blessing of God, upon Dr. Shaw's prescriptions, I am at present, though lean and ill favoured, much better.' She died on the 7th of July 1754, and was buried beside her husband in Westminster Abbey.

One last glimpse at the old duke's children, and his

beloved Aza, whom in the end she does not marry, but gives herself instead to a Frenchman, Deterville, who had cherished in flowery language what seemed a hopeless passion. The letters are tinged with the sentimentality of the time, and are of much the same calibre as the *Paul et Virginie* of Bernardin de St. Pierre.

[1] The name was afterwards changed to *Tom Jones* of famous memory.

children's children, before we leave the story of his line, the Seymours of Trowbridge. His widow, the second duchess, still lived, and Sir Thomas Bootle was making love to her. His two daughters, by this second marriage, were spending the good fortune he had left to them as recklessly as possible. In September 1750 Walpole wrote:— 'Lord Granby's [1] match, which is at last to be finished to-morrow, has been a mighty topic of conversation lately. The bride (Lady Frances) is one of the great heiresses of old proud Somerset. Lord Winchelsea, who is her uncle, and has married the other sister (Lady Charlotte) very loosely to his own relation, Lord Guernsey,[2] has tied up Lord Granby so rigorously that the Duke of Rutland has endeavoured to break the match. She has £4000 a year; he is to have the same in present, but not to touch hers. He is in debt, £10,000. She was to give him ten, which now Lord Winchelsea refuses. Upon the strength of her fortune Lord Granby proposed to treat her with presents of £12,000, but desired her to buy them. She, *who never saw nor knew the value of ten shillings while her father lived*, and has had no time to learn it, bespoke away so roundly that for one article of plate she ordered six sauceboats : besides this, she and her sister have squandered £7000 apiece [3] in all

[1] John Manners, Marquess of Granby (1721-1770), son and heir of the Duke of Rutland. It is in his honour that no less than eighteen public-houses, in London alone, have the sign of 'The Marquis of Granby.' He owed this signboard popularity, partly to his personal bravery as a general, partly to the baldness of his head. One naturally remembers that it was my Hostess of ' The Marquis of Granby,' at Dorking, who married Mr Weller, senior, in *Pickwick*.

[2] Heneage Finch, the eldest son of the second Earl of Aylesford.

[3] Some of the undesirable methods by which the money was squandered are suggested by Horace Walpole's description of an incident, three months before the marriage. 'Here' (at Vauxhall), he says, ' we picked up Lord Granby, arrived very drunk from " Jenny's Whim," a tavern at the end of the wooden bridge, at Chelsea, where . . . he had dined with Lady Fanny (Lady Frances Seymour), and left her and eight other women, and four other men, playing at " Brag." '

kinds of baubles and frippery, so her £4000 a year is to be
set apart for two years to pay her debts.' 'Don't you
like this English management ? ' Walpole asked Sir Horace
Mann, ' two of the greatest fortunes meeting, and setting
out with poverty and want ! Sir Thomas Bootle, the
Prince's Chancellor, who is one of the guardians, wanted
to have her tradesmen's bills taxed ; but in the meantime
he has wanted to marry her duchess-mother : his love-
letter has been copied and dispersed everywhere.' However, the dowager-duchess refused to be won, and died a
widow at Sutton Court, Chiswick, on the 21st of January
1778. Lady Frances had died of fever and sore throat
thirteen years before her mother. Thus, in January
1760, Horace Walpole writes concerning the epidemic in
London, ' All the houses in town are laid up with sore
throats. There has been cruel havoc among the ladies ;
my Lady Granby is dead.' Lady Charlotte survived her
mother, dying in 1805, and leaving a numerous family.

Of the children of the Proud Duke by his first wife,
his only son, Algernon, had, as we have seen, left an only
daughter, Elizabeth, who became Duchess of Northumberland. She died in 1775, predeceasing her husband, and
leaving a family of children, the eldest of whom became
second Duke of Northumberland, of the Smithson creation,
and ancestor of the present line. He was the subject
of the clever parody of the Ballad of Chevy Chase, which
appeared in the *Anti-Jacobin* in 1798. His Smithson
ancestry is supposed to have prevailed over his nobler
blood, and he avoided full payment of Pitt's Income Tax
by claiming the deduction of ten per cent. which was
allowed to persons with above a certain number of
children.

> ' No drop of princely Percy's blood
> Through these cold veins doth run,
> With *Hotspur's* castles, blazon, name
> I still am *poor* Smithson.

I at St. Martin's Vestry Board
To swear shall be content
That I have children eight and claim
Deductions ten per cent.'

Charles and Percy, the sons of the old duke's eldest
daughter, Katherine, became respectively Earls of Egremont
and Thomond, the latter succeeding to the estates of his
uncle, the Earl of Thomond, who had married the old
duke's second daughter, and died childless in 1741. Lady
Anne, the third daughter, predeceased her father, dying
childless in 1722.

At the risk of becoming tedious, one is tempted to
look back once more at that ' absurd vain man,' the old
Duke of Somerset. Absurd, vain, pompous, frail of intellect,
and devoid of commonsense—such is his general reputation.
And we may leave him with the words of Burnet re-echoing
in our ears : ' He always acted more by humour than by
reason . . . and was so humoursome, proud and capricious,
that he was rather a ministry spoiler than a ministry maker.'

CHAPTER VIII

THE SEYMOURS OF BERRY POMEROY AND THE 'GREAT SIR EDWARD'

'Now been ther two maneres of Pryde: that oon of hem is with-
inne the herte of man, and that other is withoute. . . . But natheless
that oon of thise speces of pryde is signe of that other right as the
gaye leefsel [1] atte taverne is signe of the wyn that is in the celer.'—
CHAUCER, *The Persones Tale.*

RETURNING for a brief moment to the middle of the sixteenth
century, one remembers the story of the Protector and his first
wife, Katherine Filliol, whom he repudiated for real or supposed unfaithfulness, preparatory to marrying Anne Stanhope, the lady of 'haughty stomach.'   Katherine Filliol had
two sons, John and Edward, the former of whom was supposed to have been born when the Protector was in France.
His legitimacy was thus, rightly or wrongly, suspected, but,
by the persuasion of Anne Stanhope, both sons were excluded in 1540 from their mother's, as well as their father's,
inheritance and all their claims to their father's dignities
were postponed to his children by his second wife.   Yet in
the irony of things it was his two elder sons who remained
faithful to their father in the years of his misfortunes.   In 1550
and 1551 both John and Edward Seymour were sent to the
Tower with their father, and John Seymour paid the price
with his life, dying in the Tower in the December of 1552.
Until quite recently the name JOHN SEYMOUR was inscribed
on the wall of the Beauchamp or Cobham Tower, where
he spent the last months of his life, being nursed by

[1] The bush at the tavern door which, the proverb says, good wine
does not need.

N

two stranger women through a long and trying illness. He was buried in the Savoy Hospital on the 19th of December, and according to Henry Machyn 'ther was a dolle.' Already, from the Tower, John Seymour had petitioned for restoration to the lands which had belonged to his mother. The estates of Katherine Filliol had already been sold, but Parliament ordered that compensation should be made to her children. Hence the manor of Maiden Bradley, excepting the land of Yarnfield and Baycliff, was awarded to John Seymour, with the proviso that, as the manor was considered more valuable than the properties in lieu of which it was given, the estimated difference should be yearly paid to the children of Anne Stanhope, to whom the manor was secured.

However, it was not John Seymour, but his younger brother, Edward, who was to benefit by the award of Maiden Bradley,[1] and it was for his brother's sake that John Seymour had made the effort. In his will, which was proved on the 26th of April 1558, after leaving legacies to the two women who had nursed him as a reward for their patience, he adds : ' Also I make my brother, Sir Edward Seymour the elder, my full executor, and I give him all my lands and goods that is unbequeathed. He to pay and discharge all my debts.' Edward Seymour

---

[1] Maiden Bradley is a long, straggling, but neat village, between Stourhead and Longleat. According to Camden, it derived its name from a daughter of a certain Manasser Bisset, who, being herself infected with leprosy, founded here a house for leprous women, and endowed it with her estate, in the reign of Henry II. Gough and Tanner both assert that this story is fabulous, and that the founder was Manasser Bisset himself. Anyhow, it seems that Hubert, Bishop of Salisbury, about 1190, transformed the house into an Augustinian priory. At the dissolution, Henry VIII. granted the site, in 1537, to Edward Seymour, then Viscount Beauchamp (see *supra*), and thus it now passed to John Seymour. Maiden Bradley is one of the seats of the present Duke of Somerset. The house is a plain stone structure, with no important architectural features.

had, from the first, been more favourably treated than his
elder brother, and in 1540, when both were disinherited,
arrangement was made that the titles and honour of his
father should come to him in case of the failure of the
younger branch.   In 1547 he shared in his father's expedition to Scotland, and was knighted for his services by the
Protector.   Having been in constant attendance on his
father during the years 1549 and 1550, he shared in his
imprisonment in the latter year, and again in 1551 ; in the
first case he was released after a few weeks, and in the
second after a few months.   The following year, as we have
seen, he succeeded to his brother's estate in the manor of
Maiden Bradley, and was restored in blood and confirmed
in the estate.   Moreover, he had been previously granted
the reversion of an estate in Somersetshire, and early in
1553 the king, who held him in good favour, granted him
the manor of Barnwell, in Somersetshire, following up this
grant by a transaction, lasting for many years, by which
Sir Edward acquired the manor and castle of Berry
Pomeroy in Devonshire, the manor of Bridgetown, and the
manor of Middleton or Milton, all part of the possessions
of the late Priory of Taunton.   Exchanges were later
enacted with regard to these properties, but Berry Pomeroy
Castle remained the chief seat of this branch of the Seymour
family throughout the sixteenth century.

For the rest, this Sir Edward Seymour's life furnishes
scanty interest.   His marriage to Jane Walsh, daughter of
John Walsh, Serjeant-at-Law, unlike that of his half-brother,
was made for businesslike rather than politically ambitious
reasons.   He had early learnt that his part in life was to
work for the aggrandisement of his family by the procuring
of solid wealth, not political honours.   Thus the events
of Elizabeth's reign, like those of Mary's, passed him
by unmoved.   He devoted himself to his own private
interests, and, dying at a good old age in May 1593, left

his son and grandson to profit by the unassuming, but prosperous part he had played in life.

In the very early years of his life the schemes of his father had been drawn around Edward Seymour, the only son and heir of Sir Edward. The Champernowne estate and their residence, Dartington Hall, lay close to Berry Pomeroy. Sir Arthur Champernowne was thus a near neighbour and intimate friend of Sir Edward Seymour. Sir Arthur had a daughter and heiress of three or four years old. Sir Edward had this son born in 1562-3, and about the same age. There was nothing more natural to the minds of the two fathers than that these children should be betrothed. Ten years later they were married. On the death of his father, in 1593, Edward Seymour succeeded to all his father's extensive, but hardly compact estates—the castle and honour of Berry Pomeroy and Bridgetown Pomeroy, with the advowson of the church of Berry, the castle and honour of Totnes, the manors of Cornworthy, Loddiswell, Huish, Zeal Monachorum, the manor of Loxbeare, a moiety of the hundred of Haytor, the site of the monastery of Torr, and many other lands in Devon, besides the manor and lordship of Maiden Bradley, and many other lands in Wilts, and the house called Lord Cheyne's house in London.

Already Edward Seymour had been appointed Deputy-Vice-Admiral for the county of Devon, and Sheriff of Devon in 1583, and in 1595 he was again appointed Sheriff of Devon, and in reward for his services in staving off a Spanish attack on Torbay, received a commission as Colonel from the Lord-Lieutenant. In this capacity he did much useful service during the critical years at the end of Elizabeth's reign. On the accession of James I. he was chosen as member of Parliament for the county of Devon, but was pricked as Sheriff of the same county.

The year 1611 was the year of King James the First's clever expedient for raising money by the creation of baronets, who, when their patents were granted, found themselves bound to pay a large sum for the honour. The *sine qua non* of creation was the maintenance of a certain number of foot soldiers for service in Ireland, or, and here was the loophole, the payment of a sum of money as an equivalent. Edward Seymour was one of those on whom the expensive honour was conferred, and, although in his patent he was supposed to have maintained thirty men at his own expense for service in Ireland, he discovered shortly afterwards that £1095 had to be paid as a supposed equivalent for the necessary service. Whether the new baronet had been aware of his liabilities is not clear ; he certainly made no mention of them in his letters to Salisbury concerning his creation, in the one thanking the latter for deeming him worthy to be recommended for advancement, and in the other thanking him for his creation.

The new baronet, first Baron Seymour of Berry Pomeroy, enjoyed his honours scarcely two years, dying in April 1613. He was buried in great state in Berry Pomeroy Church, as his father before him, and his funeral sermon was preached by Barnaby Potter, afterwards Bishop of Carlisle. The monument to his wife and himself in Berry Pomeroy Church is in wonderful preservation. The five sons, two of whom died young, and the four daughters kneel in the filial way along the base of the monument, on the separate shelves of which recline Sir Edward and his wife, not side by side, but one above the other.

Edward, the eldest son and second baronet, had been knighted by King James in 1608 at the age of thirty-one.[1] In April 1613, he succeeded to his father's possessions, and was appointed Governor of Dartmouth later in the year. By some strange chance this Sir Edward seems to have inherited a certain taste for privateering from his quite

[1] By his own computation, since he stated in 1652 that he was eighty years old. (See *infra*, p. 200.)

distant relative, Thomas Seymour of Sudeley, the Lord
Admiral. His opportunity seems to have been his employment as an officer of the Admiralty on the Devonshire
coast, and various entries concerning his exploits suggest
that his privateering was not only winked at, but acknowledged by the Crown.

In May 1622 a petition was presented to the Privy
Council on behalf of certain merchants of St. Malo, whose
ship had been taken and brought into Plymouth by a
Rochelle pinnace. The officers of the Admiralty, one of
whom was Sir Edward Seymour, had not taken the
pirate pinnace into charge, but had aided the pirates
in selling the captured goods and ill-treating the master
and mariners. No notice was taken of the complaint. In
April 1626, the Mayor of Dartmouth wrote to the Council
that a warlike ship belonging to Sir Edward Seymour had
come into Dartmouth with a prize, an Irish barque bound
from Newhaven to Dundalk. The mayor wrote not to
report on the taking of the vessel, but to inform the Council
that in searching the prize a priest from Douay had been
discovered on board. In the next month Sir John Eliot
wrote complaining to the Council that, whereas he himself,
as Vice-Admiral, should have received half of the value of
the ship *Joshua*, which had lately been captured in his
district, the Duke of Buckingham had unfairly given the
reward of £1000 to Sir Edward Seymour. The fact probably was that one of Sir Edward's own ships (one of which
was named *The Reformation of Dartmouth*) effected the
capture, and its owner claimed the reward. In 1628, Sir
Edward was endeavouring to secure the post of Vice-Admiral
of Devon. Both Sir James Bagg and Sir John Drake were
weary of the work, he wrote to Secretary Nicholas, while
he himself should be a 'thankful debtor.' However, it
was not until 1636 that he gained the coveted appointment.

The dislocation of affairs on the outbreak of the Civil War

drew Sir Edward, by that time an old man, from his privateering expeditions to throw in his lot with the king. He
was taken prisoner at the outset of the war, but was soon
released, and retiring to Berry Pomeroy, lived quietly there,
leaving his son Edward to engage in active service in the
king's cause. In March 1646 the father and son were called
upon to answer for their estates. The son, who was imprisoned in Exeter, compounded for delinquency in serving
against Parliament. He had quitted his command in 1644,
but had been in Dartmouth when that town was taken.
He had been ignorant of the time fixed for the coming
in of delinquents, but, in the previous December, had
sent his wife [1] (Anne, daughter of Sir William Portman, of
Orchard Portman in Somerset) to London to tender his
submission. He begged to be admitted to his liberty on
bail. He was fined at one-third of his estates, namely
£3133,[2] and in June was allowed to go on security to the
counties of Devonshire and Wiltshire. The fine remained
unpaid in January 1647, and his estates were to be se-
questered. In March, he was first granted and then refused,
a reduction of his fine to £1200 on the Exeter Articles. In
April, he remonstrated against the alteration, and prayed
for a hearing. Nothing was settled until June, when
Thomas, Lord Fairfax, urged that Seymour ' having so
clear a claim to those Articles (the Exeter Articles), as, in
my judgment, nothing can be more clear,' should have ' the
same fruit of them as others therein comprehended.' The
fine was thus once more reduced to £1200, and Edward
Seymour, having paid that sum, had his estate fully discharged in the following October, and he himself was released

[1] On that occasion he had written to the Council, advising them ' in
relation to their own quiet,' to grant his request, ' rather than be
punished with her (his wife's) importunity.'

[2] His father had, in 1638, given over the manor of Maiden Bradley
and the other Wiltshire estates to his son, contenting himself with
the Devonshire manors.

from imprisonment.   However, in January 1652, his father, the old baronet, made complaint that on some misinformation his name had been returned to the commissioners for his estate to be sold.   He was eighty years old, and had never committed any delinquency, and though his son had been a delinquent, he had compounded and had his discharge.   The old baronet's plea was successful, but his son still remained under suspicion, and there is evidence that even Cromwell believed the younger Seymour to have involved himself in several of the conspiracies for the king's restoration.   Hence, in November 1655, he was obliged to promise that he would surrender himself, whenever required, into the hands of General Desborough or Sir John Copplestone ; that he would not act against the Protector or the Government, nor go out of the county of Devon, except to Exeter, without leave of the Protector or of one of his officers.   In the autumn of 1659, the old baronet died at the age of eighty-seven, according to his own computation, since he stated in 1652 that he was eighty years old.[1]   He was, according to Collins, ' very much lamented, having, by an obliging temper, attracted the love of his country, and, by a prudent management, gained the character of a person of honor, conduct, and experience.'

His son Edward now became third baronet, and was made Deputy-Lieutenant for Devon at the Restoration, and shortly afterwards Vice-Admiral for the same county. After years of diligent duty in these offices in the West, he was chosen member of Parliament for Exeter in 1688, but,

---

[1] This reckoning, however, sadly disagrees with the term of years usually allotted to him. It means that if he was correct he must have been born in 1572 when his father, according to his usually ascribed birth-date, was only ten years old, and four years before the date usually given of his father's marriage to Elizabeth Champernowne, *i.e.* 1576. Either the old baronet was in error in 1652 or his father's birth-date must be put back, in which case his grandfather's marriage to Jane Walsh, generally given as 1562, must also be put back.

except for an attack on Lord Danby, he took no leading part in the House of Commons. That was reserved for his greater son. He died in the December of 1688, at the age of seventy-eight, and was buried at Berry Pomeroy.

Before passing on to the life of his greater son, ' the great Sir Edward,' as Guthrie termed him, a few words must be given to the castle of Berry Pomeroy, the ruins of which now stand among high woods on the shoulder of the hill which towers above the village of Berry Pomeroy. It has been generally supposed that the castle, on the improving of which the second baronet had spent vast sums of money—£20,000, according to Prince—was plundered and burnt during the Civil War, but from a settlement made in 1664, it seems that it was still remaining uninjured. However, by the year 1701 it was certainly ruined, since Prince wrote in that year, ' it is now demolished, and all this glory lieth in the dust buried in its own ruins, there being nothing standing but a few broken walls which seem to mourn their own approaching funerals.' The probability seems to be that the castle was burnt down during the late seventeenth century, and only the great gate with the walls of the south front, the north wing of the court, and two or three rooms were left intact.

In these rooms, up to the end of the eighteenth century, the steward of the estate was accustomed to live. One was a large ill-proportioned room panelled with carved oak, still lighted by a stained window, in which were emblazoned the arms of the former lords of Berry Pomeroy. In one corner, to the right of the wide fireplace, was a flight of oaken steps forming part of a staircase leading apparently to some chamber above. Such, at least, is the account of one of the rooms given by Dr. Walter Farquhar, who was summoned one day, in the year 1796, to attend on the wife of the steward who was lying dangerously ill. The doctor waited for a moment in this outer apartment alone while the steward went to inform his wife the doctor was at hand.   As he waited there the door opened, a richly-dressed lady came into the room, hurried across to the staircase, and, wringing her hands in agony, mounted the stairs to the room above. Calling the next day, he found the steward's wife better, and then bethought himself to ask who this strange lady was. The steward, greatly agitated, cried out again and again, ' My poor wife ! my poor wife ! ' Then he told the doctor he knew his wife must die. The lady was the ghost of a daughter of one of the early barons of Berry Pomeroy, who had borne a child to her own father, and strangled it in the chamber above. The omen, he knew, was sure. If ever she was seen, some one in the house must die. The doctor assured him his wife was much better, and all danger was over, but the same day, in spite of the doctor's faith, the poor woman died.

Many years afterwards, the doctor was called to attend a lady who had one morning driven over to Berry Pomeroy with her brother and sister to see the ruins. The steward was ill, and there was a difficulty in getting the keys, but the brother and sister went in search of them, while she remained in the outer apartment in which the doctor had waited years before. On their return she was in great distress, telling them she had seen an apparition, a richly-dressed lady, who passed across the room, wringing her hands, and mounted the staircase. They had laughed at her, but she had persisted in her statements, and was now suffering from the shock. The doctor learnt that the old steward had died the very day they had visited Berry Pomeroy. The lady recovered, and the apparition was not seen again, for the old steward was the last person to live in the castle.

Other stories have grown up round the ruined castle. Guides at the present day tell of some old Pomeroy, who, at the end of a long siege, finding that his castle must surrender, mounted his horse, and, blowing his bugle in token of the fall of the castle, leapt down the precipice and was dashed to pieces.[1] Or there is another tale connected with the old pleasaunce which still exists, though sadly overgrown, near the ruined castle gateway. Once a Pomeroy surprised his sister in an arbour in this pleasaunce with an enemy of their house. His revenge was swift, he slew them both ; and, as the tale goes, their shadowy forms still haunt the castle, standing on either side of a high embrasure on the castle walls, struggling always to reach one another, but parted always by the brother's curse.

It is both interesting and remarkable that Charles, the Proud Duke of Somerset, and Sir Edward Seymour the Speaker should have been cousins, contemporaries and rivals. They were men of much the same temperament, overburdened with a fantastic pride, yet whereas in the one it became ridiculous, in the other it added a certain dignity to his bearing, and helped to make him one of the most successful, if not one of the most estimable Speakers of the House of Commons. Thus Manning says of him that he was the most arrogant man who ever presided over the House, and yet that quality was advantageous in preserving order in the proceedings of an unruly House torn and distracted by factions. So much fear did he inspire by his haughty bearing, dignity and courage, that, it is said, one day when the House was sitting in Committee, and so violent a discussion had taken place that not only were blows struck, but members had begun to draw swords, Mr. Seymour resumed the chair as of right, although contrary to all usages of Parliament, and instantly reduced the House to obedience. Burnet describes him as ' the ablest man of his party . . . a graceful man, both bold and quick. But he had a sort of pride so peculiar to himself that I never saw anything like it. He had neither shame nor decency with it.'

[1] See Elizabeth Barrett Browning, *The Rime of the Duchess May*.

Of this pride there are many anecdotes.   On one occasion when driving through Charing Cross his carriage broke down, upon which he ordered the beadles to stop that of the next gentleman who should pass.   They did so, much to the unfortunate gentleman's annoyance.   The Speaker replied it was fitter that another should walk the streets than the Speaker of the House of Commons.   At another time he was congratulated by the House for ordering the Mace to take Serjeant Pemberton into custody for not paying him sufficient respect.   'He saw me, and paid me no respect, though I was near him, or very slightly.'   Still another anecdote relates how a message was once brought to the Speaker that the king was on his throne, and required his presence to hear the prorogation of Parliament, but the Speaker refused to stir until the Bill of Supply had been returned from the House of Lords according to precedent. Warning was brought him that the king was both impatient and angry, but Seymour replied 'he would be torn by wild horses sooner than quit the chair.'   Then there is also the unforgettable incident connected with the landing of the Prince of Orange.   'You,' said the Prince, wishing to be gracious, 'are of the Duke of Somerset's family?' 'Pardon me, Sir,' said Sir Edward, 'the Duke of Somerset is of *my* family.'

It was in 1661, when he was twenty-eight years old, that Edward Seymour had first entered Parliament, and being in favour at court on account of the loyalty and service of his father and grandfather, he was almost immediately made Commissioner of Prizes in the Navy.   Six years later he was winning the eternal hatred of Clarendon, by being the first man in the House who had the courage to accuse the earl openly of the crimes on which his impeachment was to be based, and it was Seymour who was chosen to lay the impeachment before the House of Lords.   In 1668 he was appointed Deputy-Lieutenant for Wiltshire, and

SIR EDWARD SEYMOUR, FOURTH BARON SEYMOUR OF BERRY POMEROY:
THE SPEAKER.

From an engraving in the British Museum. (Roth. delt.)

Treasurer of the Navy with a salary of £3000 a year. Four years later he was again appointed a Commissioner of the Navy, and was made Clerk of the Hanaper in Chancery for life. In the February of 1678 he was unanimously elected Speaker of the House in the place of Sir Job Charleton, and was, the following month, sworn a member of the Privy Council. The latter preferment gave considerable annoyance to some of the members of the House, one of whom, Sir Thomas Littleton, informed the Speaker in debate, ' you are too big for that chair and us, and you that are one of the governors of the world, to be our servant, is incongruous.' In the end, the debate on the subject turned entirely in Seymour's favour. The latter then rose from his chair, which he had refused to vacate during debate, and assured the House ' that he held no employment a greater honour to him than that which he had in their service.' Later in the session, in May 1677, another hot discussion arose in the House concerning the French alliance, and the evil councillors about the king. Several members did their best to persuade Seymour to put the matter to the vote immediately, but he, not desiring to let the motion pass, refused to do so. Some idea then arose of holding him forcibly in the chair until the motion was passed, but Seymour ' very nimbly ' skipped out, leaving the House to rise in great confusion.[1]

A new Parliament met in March 1678-9, but there was ' a difference . . . about the choice of a Speaker, the House being for one [Edward Seymour], and the king recommending another [Sir Thomas Meers]. . . . The Commons began to be angry with the Treasurer [Danby], for that the Speaker they had proposed had been rejected by the king, saying he was the cause of it, because, truly, the gentleman was not his Lordship's Friend.' Finally, the Commons having refused to enter into business presented an address to the

[1] *Memoirs of Sir John Reresby* (1875 ed.), p. 118.

king, begging him not to invade ' their undoubted privilege of chusing their Speaker.' Charles remained obdurate until it was clear that the Commons would not give way. At last, after a delay of eight days, a compromise was arrived at, and Mr. Serjeant Gregory was adopted as Speaker. As Burnet's annotator adds : ' It certainly was a most unpropitious mode of beginning what the king said he wished to be " a healing Parliament " ; such a piece of ill policy would be without any assignable reason if Sir William Temple had not recorded that Seymour's rejection arose from a pique that existed between him and the wife of the Lord Treasurer [Danby].'

Within two years Seymour had lost his popularity with the House, notwithstanding the fact that he was the prime mover in the passing of the Habeas Corpus Act. They bitterly resented his strong opposition to the Bill for excluding the Duke of York (afterwards James II.) from the succession to the Crown. After complaining in Parliament that even his life had been threatened by some of the duke's enemies, Seymour went on to show how little probability there was that the duke would ever dare, even if he were king, ' to offer any such alteration of the religion established by us as is needlessly, nay, unjustly apprehended.' Further, ' to disinherit him for his religion is not only to act according to the Popish principles, but to give cause for war with all Catholic princes in Europe, and that must occasion a standing army, from which there will be more danger of Popery and arbitrary government than from any Popish successor or a Popish king.[1]

In spite of this defence the Exclusion Bill passed the Commons, but was rejected by the Lords. The wrath of the Commons then fell upon Seymour. They first

[1] At the same time Seymour was urging the duke to change his religion, and when he found his persuasions unavailing, he proposed that the Prince of Orange should be appointed Regent when James became king.

addressed a request to the king that Lord Halifax, the opposer of the Bill in the Lords, and Edward Seymour, for his defence of the Duke of York in the Commons, should both be removed from the Privy Council. Charles was not likely to consent, for the rejection of the Exclusion Bill had been a royal triumph. The Commons resorted to another method—the impeachment of Seymour on the grounds of corruption and maladministration in his office as Treasurer of the Navy. Four articles were exhibited against him by Sir Gilbert Gerrard, his accuser. The first stated that out of a sum of £584,978, 2s. 2d. raised by Act of Parliament for the speedy building of thirty men-of-war, and appropriated to that use only, he had, in 1677, lent £90,000 at eight per cent. towards the support and continuation of the army after such time as the army, by order of Parliament, should have been abandoned. The nation had, therefore, owing to the consequent disturbance, hazard, and danger of the peace and safety of the kingdom, been put to the charge of raising £200,000 for disbanding the army. (This certainly reads strangely when one remembers Seymour's allusion to a standing army, in the speech in favour of the Duke of York lately quoted, and to his opposition to standing armies in 1688.) The second article declared that, whereas £40,000 had been paid by certain East-land merchants for the supplying of stores for the war against France, according to the Act of Parliament allowing moneys to be raised by poll for this purpose, Seymour had spent the money otherwise by paying certain victuallers of the navy as advance for provisions not then brought in, against the meaning of the Act and to the prejudice of the merchants. In the third place, having a salary of £8000 a year as Treasurer, he had, while Speaker of the House of Commons, received £8000 yearly out of the moneys appointed for secret service. In the fourth place, when, during the war with the Nether-

lands, he had been one of the commissioners for prize
goods, he did 'fraudulently, unlawfully and in deceipt of
His Majesty unlade a certain prize ship, taken from the
subjects of the States without order or authority for the
same, and did house the lading and goods of the ship and
lock up the same without presence of any storekeeper, and
did sell the same, pretending it to be only Muscovado
sugars, and did account with His Majesty for the same as
such, whereas in truth, cochineal and indigo, rich merchan-
dises of great value, formed the ship's cargo.'

'Whether Sir Gilbert Gerrard had any particular quarrel to
Mr. Seymour or affection to his place is no where specify'd,'
says Ralph in his *History of England*.   It seems, at any rate,
difficult to say why, at this crisis, matters which had so long
lain dormant were brought forward and made the basis for
an impeachment, but whether private hatred or party views
or both were the cause of the attack, it is certain that the
House was unanimous against him upon every article,
and an order was made that he should be taken into the
custody of the serjeant-at-arms, and so continue until he
had given sufficient security for his appearance to answer
to the impeachment.   Thus his brother, Harry Seymour,
wrote to his father, Sir Edward, in December 1680: 'My
brother Seymour is under no other restraint than a bond
to answer the impeachment.   Sir William Portman, Sir
Thomas Thynne, my Uncle Seymour, Mr. Wallop, Mr. Ash
and myself are his bail in a bond for £10,000.   They (the
Commons) pressed hard for his committment, the chief
design of the impeachment being to have a pretence to move
him from the King's ear that they might the better carry on
their designs.   His prosecutors quickly found themselves
disappointed of the hopes they entertained for committing
him, and compounded for taking bail which we readily
accepted.'   The truth was, the House of Commons had
developed a wild frenzy of fear, lest the accession of James

should mean Popery, and Seymour, though he was as true to their cause as they themselves were, was to be punished for his opposition to the Exclusion Bill. They tried further to coerce the king, promising supplies if he would secure them against Popery by passing the Exclusion Bill, and putting the militia and navy into Protestant hands. A dissolution of Parliament was the only possible course, and the dissolution necessarily put an end to the proceedings against Seymour. They had failed to effect their purpose, and were never revived.

For the next two years, 1681 and 1682, Seymour continued his associations with Lord Halifax, endeavouring with him to obtain the restoration of Monmouth to favour. But their ways parted when Halifax, to Seymour's disappointment, was granted a gift he himself coveted—the Privy Seal. Seymour was henceforward under the banner of Rochester,[1] to whose influence he owed many of his preferments in later years. In keeping with his opposition to the Exclusion Bill, Seymour was loyal to James II. when he became king in 1685, but he showed the spirit he would inculcate in the House when he alone opposed the king's request for the settlement of the revenue by stating that, before such business could be discussed, measures should be taken to remedy the constitution of the House, packed as it was with men corruptly and illegally elected. He spoke, says Burnet,[2] 'very high and with much weight. He said the complaints of the irregularities in elections were so great that many doubted whether this was a true representative of the nation or not. He said little equity was expected upon petitions where so many were too guilty to judge justly and impartially. He said it concerned them to look to these, for if the nation saw no justice was to be expected from them other methods would be found, in

[1] Laurence Hyde, son of Lord Clarendon.
[2] *Hist. of His Own Time* (ed. 1823), iii. 38.

which they might come to suffer that justice which they would not do.' Macaulay has drawn a picture of him as he must have stood, ' looking like what he was, the chief of a dissolute and high-spirited gentry, with the artificial ringlets clustering in fashionable profusion round his shoulders and a mingled expression of voluptuousness and disdain in his eye.' He sat down in silence ; many in the House thought with him, but the court nominees were too strong, and moreover, ' he was a haughty man, and would not communicate his design in making that motion to any, so all were surprised with it, but none seconded it.'

During the same session James demanded a standing army. The court nominees brought specious arguments as to need for secure defence, and the futility of half-trained militia. But Seymour now expressed the feeling of the House and of the nation when he utterly opposed the placing of such a weapon in the hands of the king. A standing army was at the best but a drain on the public resources, and in the hands of James it would become something worse, namely, a Popish standing army. The trained bands must be disciplined, and the navy strengthened ; this was the solution of all questions of defence. The debate was long and tedious, and in the end a supply was granted to the king, and a Bill was passed for making the militia more efficient.

The inevitable end came, as we know, to the reign of James II. The king dared to attempt what Seymour, for one, had not believed possible, the subversion of the Established Church. Loyal as he had been to the Stuarts, so loyal that he had faced the unpopularity that attended his defence of the Duke of York in 1681, and had himself been charged with being a Papist, Seymour was one of the first to invite the Prince of Orange to England, to stand between the people of England and their king ; between the Established Church and Popery. He met the prince at Exeter nine days after his landing, and as the head of the ' western alliance ' was instrumental in drawing up the articles of association,

which all who might join the party of the prince were forced
to sign. Yet he could not immediately share the general
desire that the Prince of Orange should be king. His aim
was rather that he should be Regent in order to ensure the
Stuart king's faithfulness to his coronation vow. ' He was,'
says Reresby, ' much for continuing the power in the king's
name, and even in his person, could we but be secured from
the danger of Popery.' Thus he joined Rochester in protesting in the Parliament of January 1689 that the throne
was not vacant, and could not therefore be filled by the
Prince and Princess of Orange.

The Regency idea was impossible; William declared he
would not be Regent. The idea of placing the princess
on the throne was impossible; William declared he
would not be tied to his wife's apron-strings, and Mary,
with wifely modesty, refused to take upon herself any
office except as the prince's wife and subject to him.
The Princess Anne, a tool in the hands of the Whigs,
made it known that she was willing the prince should
reign for life. Slowly relinquishing these hopes one by
one, Seymour and the Tory party, still clinging to a
vague and impossible dream that James might repent
of his Popery, and return to his kingdom, were at last
brought to consent to the only working solution of the
difficulty; William and Mary must be king and queen.
' We thankfully accept what you have offered us,' William
answered for himself and his wife, and the English
Revolution was finished. Henceforward Seymour, now Sir
Edward, and fourth baronet through the death of his
father, gave a grudging support to the House of Orange.

In the following November, he rose in the House and
proposed that an address should be presented to the king
for the apprehension of Colonel Ludlow, the regicide, and
for the settlement of a reward for whoever should apprehend
him. Tindal, speaking of Ludlow, declares that many
were surprised at his coming to England in 1660, and none

more alarmed by it than Sir Edward Seymour, because his seat and estate at Maiden Bradley had belonged to Ludlow.   Therefore, he says, Sir Edward represented the case against Ludlow's return very strongly in the Commons, and obtained the votes of the Commons for an address to the king recommending his apprehension.   Smollett, in his *History of England*, follows Tindal, and repeats this story. The facts, of course, are wrong, as Maiden Bradley had come to Sir Edward from Edward, Duke of Somerset, the Protector.   Ludlow had only held the little manor of Yarnfield in the parish of Maiden Bradley,[1] which was obtained by Sir Edward when forfeited by Ludlow's treason.   A writer in the *Gentleman's Magazine* for 1764, praises the conduct of Sir Edward as ' legal, constitutional, and meritorious,' and declares he should be ' commended for his zeal in driving that infamous regicide from the kingdom.'   Yet, it certainly seems unfortunate that, having profited by Ludlow's forfeiture, he should have been the one to speak against him in the House.

Early in March 1692, Sir Edward was made a Lord of the Treasury.[2]   His Tory followers were annoyed, and his own ambitious pride was not satisfied, for he was indignant to find he would have to sit below Richard Hampden at the Board of Treasury.   This, at first, he flatly refused to do until he had been pacified by being given a seat in the Cabinet, and by a special recommendation to the queen.

---

[1] An old house in Maiden Bradley, formerly the New Inn, and now used as stores, was once the residence of the Ludlow family.   It contains a fine old stone fireplace, beautifully carved.

[2] While in the Treasury, he opposed the proposed reform of base coinage, advising the king to look on and let the matter have its course : the Parliament would in due time take care of it ; but, in the meanwhile, the badness of money quickened the circulation, while every one studied to put out of his hands all the bad money ; and this would make all people the readier to bring their cash into the Exchequer ; and so a loan was more easily made.   Burnet, *op. cit.*, iv. 246.

I bring you,' said King William, ' a gentleman who will, in my absence, be a valuable friend.' Burnet comments thus on the fact :—' The taking off Parliament men who complained of grievances by places and pensions was believed to be now very generally practised. Seimour, who had in a very injurious manner, not only opposed everything, but had reflected on the king's title and conduct, was this winter brought into the Treasury and Cabinet Council.' The wisdom of the king in thus preferring Seymour, who was only 'violent against the court until he had forced himself into good posts,' was evident in the debates of 1692 on the events of the war by sea and land. Members complained of the preference given to aliens over Englishmen. ' Let English soldiers be commanded by Englishmen,' was the general desire. Seymour, who would once have scorned the idea of foreign generals, now that he was in office on the Board of Treasury, had modified his opinions. ' I have no love for foreigners as foreigners,' he stated in the House, ' but we have no choice. Men are not born generals ; nay, a man may be a very valuable captain or major, and not be equal to the conduct of an army. Nothing but experience will form great commanders. Very few of our countrymen have the experience, and therefore we must, for the present, employ strangers.'

The justice of this imputation on the English officers might be disputed, but Seymour had served the king's cause, and the debate ended in nothing more effective than the expression of a hope that the king would not disregard the general wish of the country. In January 1692-3, Seymour opposed the Bill for the annual sitting of Parliament and Triennial elections. ' He said,' wrote Robert Harley[1] to his father, ' it was a Bill against the Crown and against the Commons, and ought not to be countenanced.'

[1] See *Hist. MSS. Com.*, MSS. of Duke of Portland, which contain all the Harley Papers.

In March 1693-4, Sir Edward lost his place through the
creation of a Whig ministry ' in order to soften the distaste '
that might have arisen on account of the king's refusal to
pass the Triennial Bill, though it had come through both
Houses.   Sir John Somers had the Great Seal, Trenchard
was Secretary of State, and the Whig party was ' brought
to a much better opinion of the king.'   However, to counter-
act this, ' a party came to be formed that studied to cross
and defeat everything,' and the heads of that party were
Seymour and Musgrave.   Although the Tory party was too
small to effect much harm on the Whigs, yet on many
critical occasions the king had to pay liberally to win the
silence or consent of Seymour and Musgrave.   On Lord
Pelham's authority (he was a lord of the Treasury), Burnet
relates that Musgrave had £7000 for settling the king's
revenue for life, and that he carried the money himself in
bank-bills to the king's closet for that use.   On one of
these occasions Seymour said to him, ' Kit, Kit,[1] I know
where you have been and what you have got, but it was
first offered to me.'   ' Yes,' said another person, ' it was so,
and the offer was £5000, but Seymour stood for £10,000.'

During the year 1694 the country was plunged into excitement by a rumour that the two great corporations, the
City of London and the East India Company, had bribed
and corrupted many of the prominent Tory members of
Parliament, chief among them, Seymour, Trevor, and
Leeds.   The Whigs saw a golden opportunity for attacking
their opponents.   They concentrated all their efforts to
bring about an official inquiry into the matter, but before
their plans were perfected an unexpected incident brought
the subject before the House.   One day in March 1695,
while a Bill of little interest was being discussed in the
House, the postman arrived with letters for the members,
who hurried helter-skelter to the Bar, amid a buzz of con-

[1] He was Sir Christopher Musgrave.

versation, to receive them. Seymour, 'whose imperious temper,' says Macaulay, 'always prompted him to dictate and to chide, lectured the talkers on the scandalous irregularity of their conduct, and called on the Speaker to reprimand them.' A wild scene ensued,—one of the angry members turning on Seymour with the retort: 'It is undoubtedly improper to talk while a Bill is under discussion; but it is much worse to take money for getting a Bill passed. If we are extreme to mark a slight breach of form, how severely ought we to deal with that corruption which is eating away the very substance of our institutions!'

The moment for the Whig attack had declared itself, and Wharton, one of the chief Whigs, who had impatiently awaited its coming, seized it unerringly. An immediate and strict inquiry was instituted, and a committee was appointed to examine the books of the City of London and East India Company. Sir John Trevor, the Speaker, was found to have been bribed right and left, and was dismissed the House, and an informal verdict of guilty was pronounced against the Duke of Leeds by his impeachment, abortive though it was in formal effect. The accounts of the East India Company showed that the company had entered into agreement with a certain Colston, an agent for Seymour, for the furnishing of two hundred tons of saltpetre. The arrangement was such that, whatever contingency arose, Seymour would be the gainer and the company the loser by ten or twelve thousand pounds. Yet so cleverly was this obvious bribe disguised that no amount of twisting could make it a punishable case. Seymour was perforce allowed to keep his seat in the House, and escaped a vote of censure. Only the satirist could attack him, as in the *Prophecy* of 1708, in which one finds the line quoted by Macaulay:—

'When Seymour scorns saltpetre pence,'

or in another line in another satire referring to his later ,
attack on corruption,

'Bribed Seymour bribes accuses.'

In the elections of 1695 the Whig party was triumphant ;
the nation was zealous for the king and the war. Seymour's
seat at Exeter was assailed by two Whig candidates, and
what seemed to be the impossible happened. In spite of
his ability, eloquence and fortune, Seymour bore no un-
impeachable moral character ; the saltpetre scandal was
not forgotten, and the contrast between his fierceness in
opposition and his meekness in office had justly weakened
his hold on the minds of his constituents. The whole
kingdom watched while the Whigs concentrated all their
forces on Exeter. Seymour fought to the death in the
fiercest political contest that even that age of bribery had
ever seen. For five weeks the poll was open, and for five
weeks the freemen of Exeter made their proverbial hay as
the sun of heavy bribes and luxurious fare shone on them
day by day. It was not till the last day that enough
votes came in to decide the contest. Seymour was unseated,
and ignominiously retired to win the seat of the small
borough of Totnes.

During the next two years Seymour's policy was, to a
certain extent, conciliatory towards the king. Thus, in
December 1696, George Bridges wrote to his son-in-law,
the Earl of Shrewsbury, that Sir Edward had lent the
king £10,000, and was security to the butchers and glaziers
of Wiltshire for £20,000 worth of fat cattle, to be delivered
to the victualling office for the Fleet, ' which makes some
people judge the preparations at Brest grow as cold as the
weather.' [1] However, to balance this, he urged the House,
in 1697, to postpone the question of supply until the king's
speech had been thoroughly discussed, and later in the

[1] *Hist. MSS. Com.*, MSS. of Duke of Buccleuch at Montagu House,
ii. (pt. 2) 430.

same year made a remarkable speech on behalf of Sir John Fenwick, the most dangerous of the conspirators, whose efforts were directed against William's throne.

A new Parliament was called in 1698. The mind of the nation was changed. In the crisis of 1695, the Whigs had been eagerly welcomed ; in the period of prosperity and security that followed on their statesmanlike government, the nation desired a change, and the Tories had three magnificent battle-cries :—No standing army ; no grants of Crown property ; and no Dutchmen. Seymour was returned for Exeter by a large majority, although he was absent from the city at the time. In October 1698, Edward Harley had written to his father, ' I perceive Sir Edward Seymour has a great inclination to the chair.' In December, Dr. William Aglionby wrote to Matthew Prior, ' We are like to have a great intrigue about a Speaker, but I believe it will be Sir Thomas Littleton, for Sir Edward Seymour has been chid by his party for dining with Mr. Montague [1] and him [Lord Jersey], and his answer was, he would dine with them again next day.' Aglionby was right, and Seymour's inclination to the chair was unsatisfied : when, at a later date, he might have become Speaker, he declined the office in favour of Robert Harley.

A personal sorrow gave him, in the autumn of 1699, what Macaulay has termed ' a fertile theme for invective.' His son, Popham Conway Seymour, was wounded in the neck, early in the June of that year, by a certain Captain Kirke, who began a quarrel with him, without provocation, in St. James's Park. On the 17th of June, the wounded man was dangerously ill, and on the 20th, he was dead. Evelyn notes in his *Diary,* ' This week died Conyers Seymour, son of Sir Edward Seymour, killed in a duel,

[1] Afterwards Lord Halifax. The old Marquess of Halifax had been his patron, and he took his title in memory of his benefactor. He was a favourite of William III., and was Chancellor of the Exchequer (1694-8).

caused by a slight affront in St. James's Park, given him by one who was envious of his gallantries : for he was a vain, foppish young man, who made a great *éclat* about town by his splendid equipage and boundless expense. He was about twenty-three years old ; his brother (Francis Seymour Conway), now at Oxford, inherited an estate of £7000 a year, which had fallen to him not two years before.' Macaulay tells the story in his own picturesque way. London had nicknamed Conway Seymour ' Beau Seymour,' and as he was 'displaying his curls and his embroidery in St. James's Park, on a midsummer evening, after indulging too freely in wine . . . a young officer of the Blues, named Kirke, who was as tipsy as himself, passed near him. " There goes Beau Seymour," said Kirke. Seymour flew into a rage. Angry words were exchanged between the foolish boys. They immediately went beyond the precincts of the Court, drew, and exchanged some passes. Seymour was wounded in the neck. The wound was not very serious : but, when his cure was only half completed, he revelled in fruit ice and burgundy until he threw himself into a violent fever.' ' Yet,' the historian confesses, ' though he was a coxcomb and a voluptuary, he seems to have had some fine qualities. On the last day of his life, he saw Kirke. Kirke implored forgiveness, and the dying man declared he forgave as he hoped to be forgiven.'

However, his father was not so forgiving, and, in his violent determination to avenge his son's death, he magnified a common brawl, of which his son had partly by chance, partly by his own foolishness, been the victim, into an attack on the liberties of the nation by an attempted military tyranny, of which tyranny Captain Kirke and his behaviour were the result. A motion was before the Court of the King's Bench, that Kirke should be admitted to bail or given immediate trial. Seymour, in the madness of his fury, and fearing his revenge would slip away from him if this were allowed, contrary to all custom and all decency, pushed his way into Westminster Hall and delivered an informal harangue against standing armies. ' Here is a man who lives on money taken out of our pockets. The plea set up for taxing us in order to support him, is that his sword protects us, and enables us to live in peace and security. And is he to be suffered to use that sword to destroy us ? ' This speech effected nothing. Kirke was only convicted of manslaughter, and the attempted appeal made by Seymour against this sentence failed utterly.

When Parliament met once more in the November of 1699, after a six months' interval, all his pent-up rage broke forth. The king's speech, couched in gentle conciliatory terms though it was, provoked debate from the fractious Parliament. Seymour took part, and, with a strange indelicacy, harangued the Commons as he had harangued the King's Bench concerning the death of his son, and the insolence of soldiers such as Captain Kirke. His words fell on deaf ears. The Tories were too keenly determined on an attack on the Whig Chancellor, Lord John Somers, to notice this private trouble, and Seymour, as the Tory leader, was soon hand in hand with Harley in an attempt to carry a vote of censure against Somers, without giving the House time to read the papers concerning Kidd's expedition.[1] But the Tories had overreached themselves in their accusations against the Chancellor, and the House

---

[1] William Kidd had been commissioned, by the Earl of Bellamont, to clear the Arabian Gulf and the Bay of Bengal of pirates, and secure the highways for trade. A privateer ship, *The Adventure Galley*, was fitted out for the purpose, and to this Somers had subscribed £1000, and had given Kidd a commission under the Great Seal. Kidd turned pirate himself, and *The Adventure Galley* became the terror of the merchants of Surat. The Tories turned on Somers and accused him of a knowledge of Kidd's character and designs, and of employing the Great Seal to sanction a piratical expedition.

acquitted him by 188 Ayes against 18 Noes. A few months later, in April 1700, the Tories warmed to the attack again when the House of Lords objected to the report on the alienation of the Crown lands and the debated Resumption Bill. Somers was ill at the time, and, though he had privately objected to the conduct of the House of Lords, had been unable to express his opposition. Seymour, however, had no hesitation in attacking him in the House. ' No doubt the Chancellor is a man of parts. Any one might be glad to have for counsel so acute and eloquent an advocate. But a very good advocate may be a very bad minister; and of all the ministers who have brought the kingdom into difficulties this plausible fair-spoken person is the most dangerous.' Further, ' the old reprobate,' as Macaulay terms him, was not ashamed to add that Somers was ' no better than a Hobbist in religion.' The next day Seymour, as chief manager for the Commons, returned the Resumption Bill and the amendments to the Lords, and reported to the Lower House, ' If I may venture to judge by the looks and manner of their lordships, all will go right.' He was mistaken. The Lords returned the Bill with the amendments the next day. The Commons sent it back, bidding Seymour tell the Lords that their decision was unalterable. The Bill passed without amendments, and, pained and humiliated, William, on the 11th of April, abruptly closed the session without any speech from the throne. Seymour went to Kensington, to take leave of the king, after the prorogation. William, adopting a conciliatory attitude, told him he did not mean to think of the past, but hoped they would be better friends next session. Seymour, with characteristic lack of delicacy, knowing the king's sense of defeat, and anticipating a Tory reaction, replied abruptly, ' I doubt it not.' [1]

In the following December, 1700, being influenced by a

---

[1] Bonnet, *Despatches.*

desire to gain popular support by any possible channel, the king determined to ally with the Tory party. A dissolution was pronounced, and while His Majesty's health failed from ' his great thoughtfulness in relation to the public,' Seymour and the Tories prepared themselves for the New Year with its undoubted train of successes in the impending elections. Lord Godolphin wrote to Robert Harley that he had had ' an opportunity to discourse with Sir E. S[eymour] about filling the chair of the House of Commons,' and finding him totally decline it for himself, had named Harley to him, and ' he came as entirely into that as I could wish.' ' I had no mind,' Godolphin continues, ' to lose any time in acquainting you with this, because he seemed to think of speaking to you of it this day.' [1]

On the 10th of February Harley was elected Speaker, and this first triumph of the Tories was the omen of their entire success in the elections. Despite their strength in the House, they were dissatisfied until they had cleared it of many that were engaged in another interest. Report was rife that the new East India Company had scandalously purchased many of the elections for the Whigs. Seymour, who, according to Burnet, ' had dealt in this corruption his whole lifetime,' and whom the old East India Company had, as we have seen before, bought at a very high price, brought the discovery of some of the practices of the new company before the House. He made his attack ' with all the skill and dexterity which he had acquired in such a length of practice, and which shew'd him to be a master in Parliamentary management, for . . . it was resolved without a division that he had made good his general charges, and then, *Nemine contradicente*, That the thanks of the House should be given to him for the great service he had done the public in

---

[1] *Hist. MSS. Com.*, MSS. of Duke of Portland, iv. 14.

detecting the bribery and corruption which had been practised in elections.' [1]

Several Whig elections were declared void, while those of the Tories were carefully excused. The Whig members proved to have been so elected were kept in prison for a time, and were afterwards expelled the House. Seymour was also to the fore in pushing with more vigour the attack on Lord Somers, and the resolutions of impeachment against the Earl of Portland, the Earl of Oxford and Lord Halifax. William was in the hands of his Tory Parliament and could do little. However, the death of James II. in September 1701, followed by the recognition of the Pretender by the French king,[2] roused a fierce flame of indignation in England, and William, at last a popular king, dared to break with this Tory Parliament.

In the elections which followed the Whigs were triumphant, while even Seymour and the Tories modified their zeal, and were willing to help the king in beginning a fresh campaign in the Netherlands. At this moment, the high-water mark of his life, King William died.[3] The accession of Anne with her Tory partialities brought Seymour into high favour at court, and in April 1702, he was appointed Comptroller of the Household, a member of the Privy Council, and in May, a Ranger of Windsor Forest. It was now that his more marked rivalry with his cousin, the Duke of Somerset, began, since the duke, although a Whig, was in favour with the queen on account of his loyalty to her in former years. Anne offered Seymour a peerage. He declined for himself, on the grounds that there was every probability the dukedom

---

[1] Ralph, *Hist. of England*, ii. 926.

[2] France was anxious to seize the Spanish fortresses, which protected the Netherlands from her ambition. Holland would suffer, and an invasion of England, in the cause of the Pretender, would be within the bounds of possibility.

[3] On the 8th of March 1702.

of Somerset would revert to his descendants by his first
marriage, but accepted it in the person of his eldest surviving
son by his second marriage.

The first Parliament of the reign, which met on the
20th of October 1702,[1] had a large Tory majority, for the
partiality of the queen was well known, and indirectly
influenced the elections. The House met in full fury
against the late king, settled the question of supplies, and
proceeded to bring in a Bill against Occasional Conformity.
Seymour was a supporter of the Bill since ' all hot men were
for it,' but, as is well known, it failed to pass the Lords.
He also, in December 1702, made a menacing proposal
against the alien peers, moving for leave to introduce a
Bill to resume all the grants of crown lands made by
William III., and to apply them to the use of the public.
Sir Robert Walpole rescued the Whigs from this dilemma
by proposing as an amendment, that all the grants made by
James II. should also be resumed. The amendment was
rejected, but it effected this, that although the Tories carried
Seymour's motion by 180 to 78 the Bill was dropped.

Throughout the session the struggle between the Whigs
and Tories was intense. The Lords who sided with the
Whigs finally threatened the appointment of a committee
to examine the accounts of the Tory officials. Among the
most unpopular of these was Seymour, who, it was
rumoured, had never rendered an account of the office of
Treasurer of the Navy, held by him from 1673 to 1681.
This was more than the Tories could tolerate. They persuaded the queen to close the session the 28th of February
1703, seeing that if this campaign against the officials were
continued they would be obliged to influence the queen to

---

[1] William's last Parliament had been dissolved on the 2nd of
July 1702. In the following September, the month before the new
Parliament met, a false report was rife, according to Evelyn, that
Seymour was dead.

dissolve Parliament, in which case the Whigs might triumph. Moreover, within the Tory ranks there was dissension. Nottingham, the new Secretary of State, was determined to render the war in the Low Countries as far as possible defensive, and to press hard on the Dissenters at home. Marlborough and Godolphin desired the war, and thought the time unseasonable for attacking Occasional Conformity. Seymour was Nottingham's right hand. He and Sir Charles Hedges undertook in the Commons the support of Nottingham, which the Duke of Buckingham and the Earl of Jersey undertook in the Lords. Moreover, he was Nottingham's lieutenant in the dismissal of the Whig justices of the peace in the March of 1708.[1] Already, in November 1702, Godolphin had expressed his impatience at Seymour's conduct. ' I can submit in most things to better judgments,' he wrote to Harley, ' but am at present so out of patience with Sir Edward Seymour, that I am sure I can meet him nowhere but to scold.' By the summer of 1708, he was still more impatiently writing to Marlborough, ' We are bound not to wish for any body's death, but if Sir Edward Seymour should die, I am convinced it would be no great loss to the Queen nor the nation.'

[1] Thus Mr. Richard Duke (of Otterton, near Exeter) wrote to Secretary Harley, in September 1704. ' Sir Edward Seymour, when he had the white staff, prevailed with the Lord Keeper to throw out several of our most valuable justices, five round me worth about £100,000, and put in one of £100 per annum. I desire you may have the honour to rout Sir Edward by inducing the queen to restore the justices of this great kingdom county, as has been done in lesser counties' (*Hist. MSS. Com.*, MSS. of Duke of Portland, iv. 122). Later in the month Duke wrote to Robert Harley, ' And for our outed justices, I have some confidence my Lord Poulett and my constant friend hath not occasioned the laying aside any of them, nor so much as knows one half of them, nor ever advised with Sir Edward Seymour thereabouts, who is a man of so many passions and perturbations, and swears and swaggers amongst the seamen in his late progress here within five miles of me, that I would rather whisper in your ears than write what I hear ' (*Ibid.* 134).

In November 1703 the Parliament met again, and the High Tories under Nottingham were determined to press the Occasional Conformity Bill. Godolphin wrote to Harley that it was certain Seymour would do his best to thwart all the plans of the moderate Tories. This Marlborough and he had foreseen, and they were being fast driven to throw in their lot with the Whigs. The queen, influenced by Marlborough and Somerset, was outwardly no longer willing that the Dissenters should be attacked at this moment, when foreign affairs were so critical. But the High Tories persevered. The Occasional Conformity Bill failed, though Marlborough and Godolphin voted for it, against their principles, in order to preserve the queen's favour. Seymour in his wrath not only made unjust and intemperate attacks on Godolphin, but threatened to renew the attempt to 'tack' the Occasional Conformity Bill to the Bill of Supplies in the next session.

Marlborough and Godolphin decided that the ministry must be cleared of the High Tories. They could not make a direct attack upon Nottingham, but they could attack his lieutenants in the Lords and Commons, and thus force him to resign. Their opportunity came when Nottingham, blind to his own insecurity, and trusting in the queen's favour, demanded the dismissal of the Dukes of Somerset and Devonshire from the Privy Council. The queen, a tool in the hands of Marlborough and his duchess, instead of striking off the dukes from the Privy Council list, dismissed Lord Jersey and Sir Edward Seymour. The latter could only retaliate by sending word to the queen that he would return his staff by the common carrier. Godolphin was satisfied. Seymour certainly was not dead, but he was, it seemed, rendered powerless. Yet in the anxious weeks of the summer of 1704, while Marlborough was marching to Blenheim, Godolphin had need to fear the attacks which Seymour and Rochester hurled against the waste of blood and

treasure involved in the war, and their threatened impeachment of Marlborough. The victory of Blenheim (the 13th
of August 1704) saved Godolphin's ministry, and defeated
the schemes of Seymour and Rochester. On the 12th of
August, the day before the Battle of Blenheim, Thomas
Foley was writing to his brother-in-law, Robert Harley.
' 'Tis reported Sir E[dward] S[eymour] did not shave his
beard from the time he lost his place till last Warminster
Sessions, where he appeared very gay, new shaved, with a
fine long periwig, and was a very great beau, and *having
had the misfortune to lose his staff* ordered it to be cried in
open court in Warminster.'

However, in spite of the new periwig and the gay manner,
Sir Edward's spirit had been broken by his dismissal. He
retired to his seat at Maiden Bradley, and died there on the
17th of February 1708, at the age of seventy-five. The
manner of his death is told by Tindal in his continuation
of Rapin's *History of England*, as follows : ' After he had
been the terror of his enemies ; and lived among his friends
with a haughty superiority, a mean wretch hurried him out
of the world, its most imperious disturber. When infirmities
had confined him to his chair, his house was deserted by
the servants on account of some new diversions ; and in
the meantime an old female beggar of the maddish tribe,
happened to wander into the apartments. Finding the
great man thus alone, she reproached him for all his cruelty
and oppressions, threatened, terrified, and handled him
in a manner, the effects of which soon put an end to a
life through the whole course of which he seemed equally
insensible of crimes and punishments.' An elaborate
monument bearing a still more elaborate inscription,
was raised to his memory by his grandson, Francis
Seymour, in 1730, in Maiden Bradley church, where he
was buried.

Of the person of the Speaker, one word picture, written by

a contemporary, remains. 'He hath,' said John Macky, writing in 1708-4, 'a very erect countenance, and is a stately man for his age; of a fair sanguine complexion' (contrasting with his cousin, the Duke of Somerset).

Dryden introduced Sir Edward Seymour as 'Amiel' into his *Absalom and Achitophel* :—

> 'Indulge one labour more, my weary muse,
> For Amiel, who can Amiel's praise refuse?
> Of ancient race by birth, but nobler yet
> In his own worth and without title great:
> The Sanhedrin long time as chief he ruled
> Their reason guided and their passion cool'd.'

Another satirist, Elkanah Settle, was pleased to dip his pen in gall, and describe Seymour as 'Jonas,' in his *Absalom Senior* :—

> 'Next Jonas stands bull-faced but chicken-soul'd
> Who once the silver Sanedrin controul'd,
> Their gold-tipped tongue. Gold his great councels Bawd,
> Till by succeeding Sanedrins outlaw'd
> He was prefer'd to guard the sacred store.[1]
> There Lordly rowling in whole mines of oar
> To Diceing Lords, a cully favourite,[2]
> He prostitutes whole cargoes in a night.
> Here to the top of his ambition come
> Fills all his sayls for youthful Absolom.[3]
> For his religion 's as the season calls
> Gods in possession, in Reversion Baals.[4]

---

[1] Referring, of course, to Seymour's appointment as Lord of the Treasury in 1692.

[2] Seymour's enemies declared he was the channel through which gratuities were distributed to court favourites.

[3] His contemporary, John Macky, wrote of him in his *Characters* of great men, 'He hath established his family very well, his second son being a major-general in the army, and a lieutenant in the Band of Pensioners; his third son is created a peer, by the title of Lord Conway, and the fourth is a gentleman of the Bedchamber to the Prince of Denmark.' See *Memoirs of the Secret Services of John Macky* (1733).

[4] The reference is political, for his general reputation was, as Evelyn worded it, that he was not at all sincere, but would be head of a party,

He bears himself a Dove to mortal Race,
And though not man, he can look Heav'n i'th' Face ;
Never was Compound of more different stuff—
A heart in Lambskin and a conscience Buff.'

While every Whig historian has delighted to exaggerate the
insincerity and immorality of Seymour, it is not too much
to say that after taking into account the natural bitterness
provoked by party feeling, one is left with the conclusion,
that beneath their exaggerations there is a deep layer of
truth. His attack on Lord Clarendon was made on personal motives, and to please a corrupt court ; and the same
is true of his attack on Lord Somers. Moreover, as we have
seen, his tirade against standing armies was the immediate
result of his son's death following a duel with a soldier ; a
duel which need not have ended fatally, if it had not been
for his son's uncontrollable debauchery. While he declaimed
against real or imaginary corruption in others, he himself
was not slow to accept service money, or to stay his violence
against the court when he had once forced himself into
good posts. Of his private character we cannot well judge.
Tindal states that he was often reproached by members
in the House, for ' the licentiousness of his morals, which
they declared to be a disgrace to the station which he bore
in the House.' Burnet calls him ' the most immoral and
impious man of his age,' and declares that ' in all his private
dealings, he was the unjustest and blackest man that has
lived in our times.' His power in the House of Commons
arose solely from his illustrious descent, his eloquence, and
his knowledge of the House. ' He was,' says Macaulay,
' so useful an ally, and so mischievous an enemy, that he
was frequently courted even by those who most detested

at any time prevailing in Parliament. Except for his defence of the
Duke of York, in 1685, his worst enemies could not accuse him of any
defection from his high church principles, although those principles
had little influence for good on his character.

ISABELLA ANNE (INGRAM SHEPHERD), SECOND WIFE OF THE
SECOND MARQUESS OF HERTFORD.

From an engraving in the British Museum. (Reynolds pinxt.)

him.' Even Burnet was forced to confess that 'he knew
the House and every man in it so well that, by looking
about, he could tell the fate of any question.' This he used
as a means of serving the court while he was Speaker,
contriving usually to protect the debate when their party
was not assembled in strength.

Be all this as it may, his contemporary, John Macky,
speaks of him as 'the prudentist man in England; of great
experience in the affairs of his country, but extremely carried
away by his passions; does not value scandal, and was
openly visited by the French ambassador when the people
seemed to suspect him in that interest.' Noble, in his continuation of Granger, speaks of him as a man of morose disposition but of great good sense, invincible obstinacy, and
incorruptible integrity. Manning venerates him as the
promoter of the Habeas Corpus Act, and declares, that he
was 'worthy, if not amiable,' in private life, 'true to his
two wives, and to his children careful, if not kind; to his
tenants and attendants a good, though not a bountiful
master.' This is grudging praise, but it is the best and
most that can be given to the 'Great Sir Edward,' even
more, perhaps, than should be given. The one good that he
accomplished was the outcome of his infinite pride; he
was able to control the proceedings of a fractious Parliament, where one less arrogant and less despotic in his
methods would himself have been controlled.

CHAPTER IX

TWO BROTHERS: THE FIRST MARQUESS OF HERTFORD
AND FIELD-MARSHAL CONWAY

'The defects of each being taken away, their virtues might have
made one excellent man.'—HEYLYN.

OF the two sons of the Speaker by his first wife, Margaret,
daughter of Sir William Wale, knight, of London, Edward,
the elder, became fifth baronet, on his father's death, but
being devoid of any ambition, preferred a quiet life at
Maiden Bradley to the excitements of court or Parliament.
Certainly, on his father's death, he once represented Totnes
in Parliament, and twice (1710 and 1718) served for Great
Bedwyn. But he was a silent member at the best, and
after 1718, retired to Maiden Bradley, where he died, in
1740, at the age of eighty or thereabouts. His son, Edward,
became sixth baronet and eighth Duke of Somerset. His
brother, General William Seymour, had a more eventful life,
commanding at the sieges of Namur and Landen in 1693,
serving under the Duke of Ormond in the expedition to
Cadiz in 1702, and being made Lieutenant-General of the
Forces in 1706. He died, unmarried, in February 1728.

The second wife of the Speaker was Letitia, daughter
of Francis Popham of Littlecote, Wilts, by whom he had
six sons and one daughter. Of these, the eldest son was,
as we have seen, killed in 1699. Francis, the second son,
with whose descendants this chapter is principally concerned,
was created Baron Conway in March 1702, and was the
ancestor of the subsequent Marquesses of Hertford. Three
other sons, Charles, Henry, and Alexander, died young; the

sixth, John, became a colonel in the army, and was appointed Governor of Maryland. Anne, the daughter, married William Berkeley of Pill, in Somerset.

The death of Popham Conway Seymour in 1699 gave his brother Francis the estates of the late Earl of Conway, who, dying without heirs in 1688, had willed them to Popham Seymour as the eldest son of his first cousin, Letitia Popham, or in case of his death to his brother Francis. Tradition has it that Popham Seymour was engaged to be married to the only daughter and heir of the Earl of Conway, but that she died on the wedding-day. Her father then summoned Mr. Seymour to his bedchamber, and after deploring the incident, bade him still to consider himself as his son-in-law and heir to his estates, providing he assumed the additional name of Conway. Francis Seymour therefore became Francis Seymour Conway, and when in 1702 his father declined a peerage for himself (see *supra*), he was created Baron Conway of Ragley (in Warwickshire). On the 16th of October 1712 he was further created Baron Conway and Killultagh (co. Antrim).[1]

Ragley Hall, which now passed with the Conway inheritance to Francis Seymour, was to become the chief residence of his descendants, the Marquesses of Hertford. According to Horace Walpole, who was 'much struck with Ragley,' the house was far beyond anything he had seen 'of that bad age,' referring to the late seventeenth century, for, as he found by an old letter in the library at Ragley, the house as it then stood (1751) had been begun in 1680. His friend Francis, second Baron Conway (of the Seymour creation), and afterwards first Marquess of Hertford, made great improvements and alterations in the house, and is generally credited with having built it. In 1758 Walpole

[1] He possessed a large estate in Antrim, as part of the inheritance of Edward, Earl of Conway.

wrote he had just returned from Ragley, 'which has had a good deal done to it since I was there last . . . there are no striking faults, but it wants a few Chute [referring to the Chute mansion, 'The Vine,' near Basingstoke, where he had just been visiting] or Bentley touches. . . . I have recommended some dignifying of the salon with Seymours and Fitzroys, Henry the eighth's, etc. . . . They will correspond well to the proudest situation imaginable. I have already dragged some ancestors out of the dust there, and written their names on their portraits.'   Indeed the situation of the house on high ground in the midst of fine scenery was to Walpole, and is still, its chief charm.   'Ragly is superb,' he wrote, 'that is, the situation and the dimensions of the house, but it has nothing else to occupy or detain one a moment.'

Later the house was altered by Wyatt.[1] It has four fronts, with a chief entrance from the east. The large hall, 80 feet long, 40 feet broad, and 45 feet high, is one of its best features, and has a richly carved ceiling. There are also two fine staircases of polished oak. The surrounding park is 500 acres in extent, and contains a broad lake covering about ten acres. Herds of deer wander at will in the park, and there is a heronry of ancient date. In the church of the Holy Trinity, Arrow,[2] in which parish Ragley is situated, are many monuments to the Conway-Seymours, and several of the Marquesses of Hertford.

Little is known of the life of Francis, first Baron Conway, except that in 1728 he was made a Privy Councillor for Ireland, and in 1728 was appointed Governor of Carrick-fergus. He was three times married, first, to Lady Mary Hyde, third daughter of the Earl of Rochester, by whom he had four daughters who all died young; secondly, to Jane, daughter of Mr. Bowden of Drogheda, by whom he

[1] James Wyatt, architect (1746-1813).
[2] The manors of Arrow, Alcester, Beauchamp Court, etc., belong to the Marquess of Hertford, in this county.

had a son and daughter who both died young; thirdly, to Charlotte, daughter of Sir John Shorter, Lord Mayor of London, and sister to Catherine, wife of Sir Robert Walpole.[1] By this third wife he had four sons and three daughters. Of the four sons the two youngest died young, the eldest, Francis, afterwards became Marquess of Hertford, and the second, Henry, was to become Field-Marshal Conway. Of the three daughters, two, Charlotte and Arabella, died young; the third, Anne, became the wife of John Harris of Haine, in Devonshire, Master of His Majesty's household, after whose death she was appointed housekeeper of Somerset House, remaining in office until her death in 1774. Francis Seymour Conway died in February 1782, at Lisburn in Ireland. His body was brought to England to be buried at Ragley. His third wife, Charlotte, survived him for two years, dying in February 1784.

Francis Seymour Conway, his eldest son, thus became second Baron Conway, and afterwards Earl of Hertford. The first few years after his father's death were spent abroad, chiefly in Italy and in Paris. On his return to London he took his seat among the Peers in November 1739. On the 29th of May 1741 he married Lady Isabella Fitzroy,

[1] Hence by this marriage sprang the relationship between Horace Walpole, and the first Marquess of Hertford. In 1741, Walpole was writing to Henry Conway, ' My dear Harry, will you take care and make my compliments to that charming Lady Conway [wife of Francis Seymour Conway, second Baron Conway], who I hear is so charming. . . . As for Miss Anne and her love *as far as it is decent* : tell her decency is out of the question between us, that I love her without any restriction. I settled it yesterday with Miss Conway, that you three [Anne, Francis and Henry] are brothers and sister to me, and that if you had been so, I could not love you better. I have so many cousins and uncles and aunts, and bloods that grow in Norfolk, that if I had portioned out my affections to them as they say I should, what a modicum would have fallen to each! So, to avoid fractions, I love my family in you three, their representatives ' (Walpole, *Letters*, i. 133). The references to Walpole's *Letters* throughout are to the Clarendon Press edition (1903-4).

second daughter of the Duke of Grafton, the ‘charming Lady Conway’ of whom, as Lady Hertford, we hear so much in Horace Walpole’s *Letters*. Indeed, if it were not for Horace Walpole, garrulous though he be, we should know little of Francis, Earl of Hertford and second Baron Conway and his wife, or of his brother, Henry Seymour Conway. As it is, through the intimate nature of his friendship for the two brothers, we have a picture of their lives and characters which, though undoubtedly biassed, is certainly unique.[1]

By means of characteristic temporising Walpole tried always to keep amiable with both brothers even in the moments of their most strained relations. Yet his preference for Henry Conway was inevitable, in the first place, because Conway appeared to him to be a most remarkable and magnificent man, for whom he had a sincere if unbalanced affection; and in the second place, this ‘remarkable man’ in reality lacked decision and firmness, and being easily influenced by his friends, allowed himself to be the unconscious instrument of Walpole’s inconsistent political views and personal caprices. His brother, on the other hand, less pleasing in person and manner, less imbued with an almost too delicate sense of honour, and far more selfish, cared little for Walpole’s advice and pleasures, but much for his own aggrandisement, and had, what Henry Conway lacked, very decided views of his own which he could keep to himself. There is often a marked irritation in Walpole’s letters to Conway at this secrecy, which being so utterly alien from his own gossiping nature he could not understand or forgive. Thus, for example, in the spring of 1765, after having addressed

---

[1] A collection of Conway’s private letters was made by C. Knight, with the intention of publishing a memoir, but the idea was never realised. The letters, not yet discovered, are apparently hidden away in some private collection.

several tentative questions to Lord Hertford himself, as to his possible appointment to Ireland, he wrote again: ' I was assured last night, that Ireland had been twice offered to you, and that it hung on their insisting upon giving you a secretary, either Wood or Bunbury. I replied very truly that you had never mentioned it to me, and I believed, not even to your brother. The answer was: "Oh! his particular friends are always the last that know anything about him." Princess Amalie loves that topic, and is for ever teasing us about your mystery. I defend myself by pleading that I have desired you never to tell me anything till it was in the *Gazette*.' Hertford still preserved his ' mystery,' and Walpole's subterfuge accomplished nothing.[1] This then would be enough to account for Walpole's preference for the younger brother. However, it is only fair to Walpole to say that he was not alone in his judgment. The *Diaboliad*, that bitter satire of 1777, ascribed to William Coombe, and dedicated ' to the worst man in His Majesty's dominions,' emphasises the greed and selfishness of Hertford, and cannot find any term for him but avaricious. But of this anon. It will be more possible to judge something of the characters of the two men when we have considered their actions and the events of their lives.

It was in the August of 1750 that Francis, second Baron Conway, was created Viscount Beauchamp, and Earl of

---

[1] One other amusing instance of Walpole's irritation at Hertford's ' mystery' is given in a letter written to Henry Conway, in October 1764. ' We have a report here but the authority bitter bad, that Lord March is going to be married to Lady [Anne] Conway [Lord Hertford's eldest daughter]. I don't believe it the less for our knowing nothing of it ; for unless their daughter were breeding, and it were to save her character, neither your brother nor Lady Hertford would disclose a little of it. Yet in charity, they should advertise it, that parents and relations, if it is so, may lock up all knives, ropes, laudanum, and rivers, lest it should occasion a violent mortality among his fair admirers ' (*Letters*, vi. 133). Lady Anne did not marry Lord March, but the next year married Charles Moore, afterwards sixth Earl of Drogheda.

Hertford. The barony of Beauchamp, and the earldom of
Hertford, had become extinct on the death, in that year, of
Algernon, seventh Duke of Somerset, since those dignities,
not being restored in 1660, were subject to the forfeiture of
1552, and lapsed with the death of the descendants of the
second wife of the Protector. Hence, Edward Seymour held
only the titles of eighth Duke of Somerset, and Baron Seymour. Walpole wrote to Sir Horace Mann, 'My cousin, Lord
Conway, is made Earl of Hertford, as a branch of the Somer-
sets. Sir Edward Seymour gave his approbation handsomely.' Five years later, in the February of 1755, Walpole
was writing to Mr. Richard Bentley, that an ambassador was
to be sent to Paris, and ' to my great satisfaction, my cousin
and friend, Lord Hertford, is to be the man. This is still
an entire secret here, but will be known before you receive
this.' In his *Memoirs of George II.*, Walpole further
describes this incident. ' The Earl of Hertford, a man of
unblemished morals, but rather too gentle and cautious, to
combat so presumptuous a court, was named ambassador
to Paris.' However, the journey was suspended, since the
demands of the French were ' too haughty ' to be admitted.

From 1751 to 1766, Hertford was Lord of the Bedchamber to George II. and George III.; in 1756 was made
a Knight of the Garter, and in 1757, Lord-Lieutenant
and Guardian of the Rolls of the county of Warwick,
and city of Coventry. A Magdalen House was founded
in Prescot Street, Goodman's Fields, in 1758, and Lord
Hertford was appointed governor.[1] Thus in 1760, Walpole describes a visit to the said house. ' Lord Hertford
at the head of the governors, with their white staves,
met us at the door, and led the prince [Prince Edward],
directly into the chapel, where, before the altar, was an arm-
chair for him, with a blue damask cushion, a *prie Dieu*,
and a footstool of black cloth, with gold nails. We sat on

[1] He was also vice-president of St. George's Hospital.

forms near him. . . . The chapel is small and low, but neat,
hung with Gothic paper, and tablets of benefactions. At
the west end were enclosed the sisterhood, above an hundred
and thirty, all in greyish-brown stuffs, broad handkerchiefs,
and flat straw hats, with a blue riband, pulled quite over
their faces. . . . The chapel was dressed with orange and
myrtle, and there wanted nothing but a little incense, to
drive away the devil—or to invite him. The sermon was
preached by a young clergyman, a certain Dodd,[1] . . .
entirely in the French style, and very eloquently and touch-
ingly. He apostrophised the lost sheep, who sobbed and
cried from their souls—so did my Lady Hertford and Fanny
Pelham, till I believe the city dames took them both for
Jane Shores.' Amusing, rather than important though it
is, this incident, together with an account of his presentation of Walpole at court, is practically all that is known of
Lord Hertford's life, during the first two years of the reign
of George III.

However, George III. had come to the throne, with
the fixed determination to end the Whig monopoly of
government, which had coloured the events and appointments of the later years of his predecessor's reign. The
peace of November 1762 marked the virtual accomplish-
ment of that purpose. Horace Walpole wrote, ' The die is
cast. I am returning to Strawberry (Hill) for some days,
rejoiced that my friends are secure : and for events, let them
come as they may. I have nothing to do to be glad or sorry,
whatever happens ministerially.' Yet one of the results of
the ' triumphancy of the court,' was the appointment of
Lord Hertford as a Privy Councillor, and his ambassadorship
in Paris, from October 1763 to June 1765. Already, as early
as February 1763, some report was rife that Hertford would
go to Paris, and Walpole wrote to Henry Conway ,' Your brother

---

[1] William Dodd (1729-1777), the forger, who was hanged at Tyburn,
on the 27th of June 1777 (see Percy Fitzgerald, *A Famous Forgery*).

has pressed me much to go with him, if he goes to Paris . . .
but my resolution against ever appearing in any public light
is unalterable.' A series of long and voluble letters, addressed
to Lord Hertford by Walpole, belong to this period of
ambassadorship. On October 18th, when Lord Hertford
had just reached Paris, Walpole wrote, ' I am impatient for
a letter . . . to hear of your outset, and what my Lady
Hertford thinks of the new world she is got into, and whether
it is better or worse than she expected. Pray tell me all :
I mean of that sort, for I have no curiosity about the family
compact, nor the harbour of Dunkirk. It is your private
history—your audiences, receptions, comforts or distresses,
your way of life, your company—that interests me ; in
short, I care about my cousins and friends, not like Jack
Harris, about my Lord Ambassador.' Lord Holland (the
elder Fox), had 'procured his wife's brother-in-law, Mr. Bunbury, to be imposed on Lord Hertford, as secretary of the
Embassy.' [1] Hertford was advised not to 'digest' this affront,
but instead, he acquiesced, and then treated Bunbury with
such cold indifference that he was glad to ' quit the employment.' Walpole refers to this incident in his first letter,
wanting to know particulars ' of my Lord Holland's joy at
seeing you in France, especially without your secretary.'
Lord Hertford himself chose as his secretary David Hume,
the freethinker, historian and philosopher. ' The decorum
and piety of Lord Hertford, occasioned men to wonder at
his choice,' says Walpole, but it was ' the effect of recom-
mendations from other Scots, who had much weight with
both Lord and Lady Hertford.' [2]

[1] Fox was always, according to Walpole, an enemy of both Lord
Hertford and Mr. Conway, ' both most inoffensive men ' ; and the
former ' even a good courtier, and never in union with Fox's enemies.'

[2] In March 1764, the printers of the *London Evening Post and Gazetteer*
were called before the House of Lords, on a complaint put forward by
Lord Marchmont, for printing a letter (written by Wilkes), attacking
Lord Hertford for choosing Hume as his secretary, and representing the

For the moment, we must digress from the incidents of Lord Hertford's term of office in Paris, to consider briefly some of the events of his brother Henry Conway's life, in order to understand the import of many of the letters which Walpole directed to Lord Hertford, and to be able to judge of the causes underlying the strained relations between the two brothers, in the years 1763 and 1764. Henry Conway had entered the army at an early age, and employed his time in the study of mathematics, fortification, and drawing. In 1741, on the marriage of his brother Francis with Isabella, daughter of the second Duke of Grafton, the suggestion was made that Henry Conway should be returned as member for the duke's borough of Thetford. The idea failed, but Conway was, the same year, returned first as member of the Irish Parliament for Antrim, and then as member of the English Parliament for Higham Ferrers, Northamptonshire. From that time he sat in successive Parliaments until 1784. His career as a soldier was sadly marred by the inactivity frequently forced on him by the Government. In his first appointment, as lieutenant-colonel of the 1st Foot Guards, he went with the army to Flanders, but was condemned to spend an idle summer at Ghent, 'employing his time in reading, both morning and evening.' In the winter he returned once more to take his seat in Parliament, and voted against the disbanding of the army in Flanders. After serving in the campaigns of 1743 and 1744, he returned to England, disheartened and

Embassy in Paris as entirely Scotch in its sympathies. Walpole wrote to Hertford concerning it :—' I leave to your brother [Henry Conway], to tell you the particulars of an impertinent paragraph in the papers, on you and your embassy ; but I must tell you how instantly, warmly and zealously he [Henry Conway] resented it. He went directly to the Duke of Somerset [Edward, ninth duke] to get him to complain of it to the Lords. His grace's bashfulness made him choose rather to second the complaint, but he desired Lord Marchmont to make it, who liked the office, and the printers are to attend your House to-morrow ' (*Letters*, vi. 32-3).

discontented with the methods of the war. It was at this time that he wrote to Horace Walpole, asking his advice on a personal affair, his own relationship with Lady Caroline Fitzroy, sister of Lady Hertford. Walpole declined to give definite advice, but showed his friend so clearly that he did not approve of the match, that Conway decided to comply with his wishes.

In 1745, ' by the interest of a near relative,' Conway was ' placed in the Duke's [of Cumberland] family, where he grew a chief favourite, not only by a steady defence of military measures on all occasions, but by most distinguished bravery in the battles of Fontenoy and Laffelt [Lauffeld, where he was taken prisoner], by a very superior understanding, and by being one of the most agreeable and solid speakers in Parliament, to which the beauty of his person, and the harmony of his voice, did remarkably contribute.' [1] Early in 1754, seven years after his marriage to Caroline, widow of Charles, Earl of Aylesbury, Conway was appointed secretary to Lord Hartington, the new Lord-Lieutenant of Ireland. ' He rose,' says Walpole, ' merely on the basis of his merit, to a distinguished situation, entirely unsought, uncanvassed.' Lord Hartington had insisted that Conway should be his secretary, and his choice was wise, for his conciliatory temper did much to pacify the country. His term of office ended in 1755, but his association with Lord Hartington, now Duke of Devonshire, did not cease. Under Walpole's influence, he was led, in the autumn of 1756, to persuade the duke to accept the Treasury, without conditions, and so to allow Pitt freedom of action in the formation of the ministry, and defeat a cabal of Fox, and the Bedford faction. ' Fox

---

[1] *Memoirs of George II.*, i. 41. In these battles he was fighting under the Duke of Cumberland, for whom he had great admiration. He is said to have learnt to be a martinet to his soldiers, through following the duke's methods.

realised who shot the arrow,' writes Walpole, 'especially as Devonshire assured him it was *not* Mr. Conway.'[1]

The summer of 1757 saw the conception of Pitt's expedition to surprise Rochfort as the late autumn saw its disastrous failure. Pitt's idea was that Conway, now major-general, should be put in command, but the king thought him too young. However, he was summoned from Dorsetshire, where his regiment was stationed, and given command under Sir John Mordaunt. Mordaunt was rendered practically incapable through ill-health, and Conway, though brave enough as a soldier, lacked the decision, initiative, and power of leadership which the occasion demanded. One poor attack was made on Rochfort, failed, and was not renewed; Hawke, the commander of the fleet, disgusted with the inactivity and delay, brought back his ships to England, and nothing was accomplished. Naturally Pitt and his ministry were quick to blame the commanders of the expedition, while military men in general blamed the plan. 'You will have seen or heard the fleet is returned,' wrote Walpole to Lord Strafford. 'They have brought home nothing but one little island [the Isle of Aix]. . . . My joy for Mr. Conway's return is not at all lessened by the clamour on this disappointment. Had he been chief commander, I should be very sure that nothing he had done was all he could do. As he was under orders, I wait with patience to hear his general's vindication.' On the 18th of October, he wrote to Conway himself that he had long before 'judged that the ministry intended to cast the blame of a wild project upon the officers. That they may be a little willing to do that, I still think—but I have the joy to find it cannot be thrown on you.' Conway's innocence had already 'broken out and made its way.' 'My Lady Suffolk told me last night,' Walpole reported, 'that she heard all the *seamen* said they wished the general had been as ready as

[1] *Memoirs of George II.*, ii. 265-8.

Q

Mr. Conway . . . your name is never mentioned but with honour . . . all the violence, and that extreme, is against Sir John Mordaunt and Mr. Cornwallis.'

According to Walpole, Mr. Conway was very patient under 'unmerited reproach,' and Walpole desired him to continue so, and advised him not to defend himself but to vindicate Sir John Mordaunt, 'for,' says the crafty schemer, 'as it is known you differed with him, it will do you the greatest honour to vindicate him, instead of disculpating yourself. My most earnest desire always is, to have your character continue as amiable and respectable as possible . . . and your justification not coming from yourself, will set it in a ten times better light. I shall go to town to-day to meet your brother [Lord Hertford], and as I know his affection for you will make him warm in clearing you, I shall endeavour (on these grounds) to restrain that ardour.' In the middle of November, when the inquiry on the case was still pending, Walpole wrote to Sir Horace Mann, ' You may easily imagine that with all my satisfaction in Mr. Conway's behaviour, I am very unhappy about him: he is still more so; having guarded and gained the most perfect character in the world by the severest attention to it, you may guess what he feels under anything that looks like a trial.'

After a perusal of several of the letters that follow, one is left with a sincere compassion for Henry Conway. To be esteemed as Walpole esteemed him and wrote of him to his friends, to be deluged with letters begging him to maintain that ' perfect character ' and ' amiable disposition ' by any sophistical means that Walpole did not scruple to suggest, must, one would imagine, have caused him considerable discomfort and a certain sense of humiliation. And then one hears Walpole smack his lips over tales of Conway's courage and goodness that appear, to some minds at least, to be, on the one hand, foolhardy bravery, and on the other hand, foolhardy softness. Thus he tells how, when on the Isle of Aix, Mr.

Conway was one day discovered trying a burning-glass on a bomb, but was luckily saved by a fellow-officer, who snatched the glass from his hand ' before he had at all thought what he was about.' As an example of his goodness Walpole tells how a groom had refused to follow Mr. Conway on the expedition unless he would provide for his widow, in case of accidents. Mr. Conway told him he had already settled £200 on her. The man said this was not enough, and refused even to go to Portsmouth and see the horses embarked. Walpole proceeds to ' adore human nature ' in the person of Conway.

Trying as these letters are, we must return to them for a moment to finish the history of the inquiry concerning the Rochfort fiasco. First, perhaps, we may quote from the verses written by Walpole to his friend at the time of the inquiry, ' a most hasty performance, literally conceived and executed between Hammersmith and Hyde Park Corner. The Lord knows if it is not sad stuff.'

> ' When Fontenoy's empurpl'd plain
>   Shall vanish from th' historic page,
> Thy youthful valour[1] shall in vain
>   Have taught the Gaul to shun thy rage.
>
> When hostile squadrons round thee stood,
>   On Laffelt's unsuccessful field,
> Thy captive sabre, drench'd in blood
>   The vaunting victor's triumph seal'd.
>
> Forgot be these ! Let Scotland, too,
>   Culloden from her annals tear,
> Lest Envy and her factious crew
>   Should sigh to meet thy laurels there.

---

[1] Fontenoy was Mr. Conway's first engagement. Walpole wrote to him after the battle, on the 27th of May 1745, ' As gloriously as you have set out, yet I despair of seeing you a perfect hero ! You have none of the charming violences that are so essential to that character. You write as coolly, after behaving well in a battle, as you fought in it. . . . Can one ever hope you will make a figure, when you only fight because it was right you should, and not because you hated the French or loved destroying mankind ? This is so un-English, or so un-heroic, that I despair of you !—*Letters*, ii. 101-2.

When each fair deed is thus defac'd,
    A thousand virtues, too, disguis'd,
Thy *grateful* country's voice shall haste
    To censure worth so little priz'd.

Then, patient let the thunder roll,
    Pity the blind you cannot hate,
Nor, blest with Aristides' soul,
    Repine at Aristides' fate.'

This 'sad stuff' was printed anonymously in the *Public Advertiser* on November the 28th, 1757, and dedicated to Major-General H. C.   In January 1758 Sir John Mordaunt was acquitted, and, 'if the commander-in-chief is so fully cleared, what must the subordinate generals be ? ' wrote Walpole to Sir Horace Mann.

Yet, though Conway's name was cleared, he was not allowed a command in America, and when Lord Legonier, the commander-in-chief, told the king how anxious Conway was to be employed, and added, 'he had tried to do something,' George replied, 'Yes, *après dîner la moutarde.*' Walpole was ready with his insidious advice; Conway must not resent not being employed, but might write a letter to Legonier or to Pitt, or even to 'the *person* who is *appointed* to *appoint* generals' [the king], to thank them for not exposing him a second year.' Chiefly through the enmity of Lord George Sackville it was not until March 1761 that Conway was allowed to go on active service, but he was given the command of the first Regiment of Dragoons in March 1759, and had been sent to Sluys in the December of 1758 to settle a cartel with the French. Of this latter appointment Walpole wrote that it 're-established' him, and adds, ' I should say his merit re-establishes him—all the world now acknowledges it, and the insufficience of his brother generals makes it vain to oppress him any longer.'

While he was in France Walpole wrote him some amusing

advice, ' You are so thoughtless about your dress I cannot help giving you a little warning against your return. Remember everybody that comes from abroad is *censé* to come from France, and whatever they wear at their first appearance immediately grows, the fashion. Now if, as is very likely, you should, through inadventure, change hats with a Master of a Dutch smack, Offley will be upon the watch, will conclude you took your pattern from M. de Bareil, and in a week's time we shall all be equipped like Dutch skippers. You see I speak very disinterestedly, for, as I never wear a hat myself, it is indifferent to me what sort of hat I don't wear.'

In October 1759 Walpole visited his friend at his house at Park Place, ' where,' he wrote to the Earl of Strafford, ' one of the bravest men in the world, who is not permitted to contribute to our conquests, was indulged in being the happiest by being with one of the most deserving women, for Campbell goodness no more wears out than Campbell beauty—all their good qualities are *huckaback*.' This picture of domestic happiness was disturbed in March 1761 by what was, to Conway, the more than welcome news of his appointment to command in Germany under Granby. Within a few months he succeeded Granby in command, was in action at Wilhelmsthal, took the castle of Waldeck, and was generally praised by Prince Ferdinand. But Walpole was impatient for a peace to ' nip his laurels.' The resignation of Pitt, who stood practically alone in his support of the war, and the consequent supremacy of the pacific Bute, brought the Seven Years' War to an end with the peace of November 1762. General Conway, under pretence of bringing home the troops, was kept abroad until the peace was voted, ' the ministers apprehending that they should not be able to influence him to approve an event so ruinous and shameful to his country.'

It is now, after this long digression, that we come back

to the year 1763, in the autumn of which Lord Hertford went to Paris as ambassador.   Lord Hertford was ' a perfect courtier,' and not likely to countenance opposition to the court and the Grenville [1] ministry on the part of his brother.   Walpole, however, desired Conway, who had as yet, since his return from Germany, entered into no cabals, and attached himself to no party, to enter into opposition. He knew that Lord Hertford, if suspicious of his intentions, would ' labour to prevent his brother from involving himself against the court.'   He might even, Walpole saw, procure that Conway should be sent on some honourable commission, or ' contrive to have his gratitude dipped in favours from the king before he should be aware with what view they were bestowed.'

Walpole well knew that Conway could be driven into opposition by being persuaded of the illegality of general warrants such as had been issued for the apprehension of John Wilkes for libel on the Government.   However, knowing Lord Hertford's desires, Walpole waited ' in silence and patience ' till Hertford was set out on his embassy to Paris before he ' ever named the term *General Warrants* in the presence of Mr. Conway.'   Then he asked him, ' as by accident,' how he intended to vote on that business, as he himself wished to act as he did.   Mr. Conway declared himself (probably on Walpole's suggestion) disgusted at the warrants, and thence, says Walpole, ' I easily entered into agreement to oppose them.'   The first step was taken in the November of 1763, when Walpole and Conway acted with the Whigs in resisting the arbitrary measures proposed by the ministry against Wilkes.   Walpole wrote off to ' explain ' matters to Lord Hertford.   ' This will be an interesting matter to you when you hear that your brother and I were in the minority.   You know *him*, and therefore

[1] Grenville succeeded Lord Bute on the retirement of the latter, through alleged ill-health, in April 1763.   *Memoirs of George III.,* i. 270.

know he did what he thought right ; and for *me*, my dear Lord, you must know that I would die in the House for its privileges, and the liberty of the press. But come, don't be alarmed : this will have no consequences. I don't think your brother is going into opposition ; and for me, if I may name myself to your affection after *him*, nothing but a question of such magnitude can carry me to the House at all. I am sick of parties and factions, and leave them to buy and sell one another.' A few days later he wrote again, ' You will not have been fond of your brother's voting against the court. Since that, he has been told by different channels that they think of taking away regiments from opposers. He heard it as he would hear the wind whistle : while in the shape of a threat he treats it with contempt : if put into execution, his scorn would subside into indifference. You know he has but one object —doing what is right ; the rest may betide as it will.' [1]

Walpole little knew at that moment that the king himself had already proposed to Grenville that Conway should be dismissed from all his offices, and that it was Grenville (whom Walpole disliked) who had proposed that the dismissal should, at any rate, be postponed. Grenville further arranged a meeting with Conway in the early days of December, and, in the presence of the Duke of Richmond, tried to pledge Conway to support the Government. Conway refused to bind himself, and wrote an account of the meeting to his brother. Meanwhile, Lord Hertford wrote to blame his brother's conduct for the stopping of some bills which he had been anxious should pass. Walpole answered, ' Your brother was not pleased with your laying the stopping your bills to his charge. To tell the truth, he thinks you as too much inclined to courts and ministers as you think him too little so. So far from upbraiding him on that head, give me leave to say you have no reason to be concerned at it. You must be sensible, my dear Lord,

[1] *Letters*, v. 358, 397.

that you are far from standing well with the opposition, and should any change happen, your brother's being well with them would prevent any appearance that might be disagreeable to you. In truth, I cannot think you have abundant reason to be fond of the administration. Lord Bute never gave you the least *real* mark of friendship. The Bedfords certainly do not wish you well : Lord Holland [the elder Fox] has amply proved himself your enemy : for a man of your morals it would be a disgrace to you to be connected with Lord Sandwich,[1] and for George Grenville, he has shown himself the falsest and most contemptible of mankind. . . . In this situation of things, can you wonder that particular marks of favour are withheld from you, or that the expenses of your journey are not granted to you, as they were to the Duke of Bedford ? '

Early in February, Walpole's triumph came. The debate in the Commons arising on the question of Wilkes's privilege was ' hobbling on very lamely,' when Mr. Conway rose and made the first attack against general warrants. In high excitement Walpole wrote to Lord Hertford, ' Imagine fire, rapidity, argument, knowledge, wit, ridicule, grace, spirit : all pouring like a torrent but without clashing. Imagine the House in a tumult of continued applause : imagine the ministers thunderstruck, lawyers abashed and almost blushing, for it was on their quibbles and evasions he fell most heavily, at the same time answering a whole session of arguments on the side of the court. No, it was *unique* ; you can neither conceive it, nor the exclamations it occasioned.'[2] Lord Hertford did not share Walpole's enthusiasm, still less did he appreciate

[1] Popularly known as ' Jemmy Twitcher,' from a line in the *Beggar's Opera*, then being performed at Covent Garden :—
' *That Jemmy Twitcher should peach me, I own surprised me.*'
One of the most dissolute and profane men of his time, he attacked Wilkes in the House of Lords for obscenity and profanity. Walpole once described him as ' the father of lies.'   [2] *Letters*, v. 437, 451.

the news that his brother had not only spoken, but had voted against the legality of general warrants on two different occasions.

Walpole had triumphed; *mais, après dîner la moutarde!* On the 19th of April he wrote hurriedly to Henry Conway that he had heard that night the report that Conway was dismissed, he imagined, from the Bedchamber. The next day, to forestall any other version from reaching Paris, he wrote to Lord Hertford that rumour went about town that Conway was dismissed, not only from the Bedchamber, but from his regiment. He for his part did not believe it, and could not credit the ministry with such folly, it was only 'one of the lies of which the time is so fruitful.' But, on the night of the 21st of April, he was writing to Conway 'with a very bad headache: I have passed a night for which George Grenville and the Duke of Bedford shall pass many an uneasy one! Notwithstanding I heard from everybody I met that your regiment as well as Bedchamber were taken away, I would not believe it, till last night the Duchess of Grafton told me that the night before the Duchess of Bedford said to her, "Are you not very sorry for poor Mr. Conway? He has lost everything." When the Witch of Endor pities, one knows "she has raised the devil."' The loss of income was a serious inconvenience to Conway, and Walpole at once offered him £6000, while the Duke of Devonshire persuaded him to accept £1000 a year until he was restored to command.[1]

---

[1] The case for the Government was stated in an 'Address to the Public on the Dismission of a general officer,' in the *Gazetteer* of 9th May 1764. Walpole answered in a feeble 'Counter Address,' on 12th August, which called forth a still more feeble 'Reply to the Counter Address.' The Whigs, represented by Lord Rockingham (*Rockingham Memoirs*, i. 180), tried to draw Pitt into opposition on this case. He condemned the dismissal, but considered the question 'touched too near upon prerogative.'

Lord Hertford, however, could not reasonably be expected to be willing to share in the consequences of his brother's conduct since it was so entirely opposed to his own sympathies, and doubly unwelcome at a moment when he was employed on the king's service at home and abroad and associated with the ministry. Walpole wrote to him : ' Honour and general interest and personal resentment should have called on him to espouse his brother's cause,' but Lord Hertford's temperament was not disposed to personal sacrifice. Walpole did his best to maintain harmony between the two brothers, assuring Hertford he had never thought of his quitting the embassy, ' that would be the idlest and most unwise step you could take ; and believe me, my affection for your brother will never make me sacrifice your honour to his interest.' Again he writes, excusing Lord Hertford for his conduct, ' you was not circumstanced as I was. You had not voted with your brother as I did ; the world knew your inclinations were different . . . my motives for thinking you had better have espoused his cause were for your own sake.' In the end Lord Hertford was entirely persuaded, and we hear in September that he had offered to help Walpole if by any chance the ministry make him suffer for his defence of Conway by depriving him of his salary as one of the Lords of the Treasury. ' I can never thank you enough for this,' Walpole wrote to him, ' nor the tender manner in which you clothe it.' [1]

On the 10th of January 1765, Parliament met again. Grenville ' took up the defence of the Spaniards,' though he said he only stated their arguments. General Conway rose and declared Grenville had adopted the reasoning of Spain, and exhorted every one to support the king's government, ' which I,' said he, ' ill-used as I have been, wish and mean to support—not that of ministers, when I see the laws and independence of Parliament struck at in the

[1] *Letters*, vi. 59, 96, 112.

most *profligate* manner.' Grenville took this to himself, and asserted that his own life and character were as pure, uniform, and little profligate as General Conway's. A duel of words ensued between the two men, and finally the debate was closed by Lord Granby, who declared against the dismissal of officers for civil reasons, and spoke of Mr. Conway 'with many encomiums.' In May 1765, Walpole was able to write to Lord Hertford that Mr. Conway was perfectly restored to the king's favour, and, if he should continue in opposition, it would be no longer against the king, but against 'a most abominable faction,' headed by Grenville, 'who, having raged against the constitution and their country to pay court to Lord Bute, have even thrown off that paltry mask, and avowedly hoisted the standard of their own power.' [1]

By the summer of 1765, the king had suffered such humiliation that he was forced to turn to the great Whig families. Grenville was dismissed, and an administration was formed under the Marquess of Rockingham. Conway accepted office as one of the Secretaries of State, and became leader of the House of Commons. He now proceeded to attempt the rectification of a wrong done to the American colonies by the last Parliament, at a time when he himself was engaged in personal conflict with Grenville concerning his own dismissal. In February 1766, he moved the repeal of the Stamp Act,[2] and was successful in gaining a majority in spite of violent opposition on the part of the late ministry. Edmund Burke [3] has given us a picture of

---

[1] Grenville, Bedford, and Temple now desired to form, with Pitt, a ministry of their own, neither leaning on Lord Bute and the Tories nor upon the Whig lords.

[2] Lord George Sackville wrote to General Irwin that Mr. Pitt's attitude towards America had given ' a new turn to the minds of many. ... Mr. Conway at once adopted his sentiments ' (MSS. of Mrs. Stopford Sackville).

[3] His cousin, William Burke, had been Mr. Conway's private secretary.

him on this occasion, equalled perhaps, but never excelled, by any elaborate praise that Walpole could bestow on his idol. In his speech on American taxation, in April 1775, Burke called up before the House the memory of how ' in that crisis [of February 1766] the whole trading interest of this empire, crammed into your lobbies, with a trembling and anxious expectation, waited almost to a winter's return of light their fate from your resolutions. When, at length, you had determined in their favour, and, your doors thrown open, showed them the figure of their deliverer [General Conway] in the well-earned triumph of his important victory, from the whole of that grave multitude there arose an involuntary burst of gratitude and transport. They jumped upon him like children on a long absent father. They clung about him as captives about their redeemer. All England, all America, joined to his applause. Nor did he seem insensible to the best of all earthly rewards, the love and admiration of his fellow-citizens. Hope elevated, and joy brightened his crest. I stood near him, and his face, to use the expression of the Scriptures of the first martyr, his face was as it were the face of an angel.' [1]

In the following July, the king, who had always disliked the Rockingham ministry, finding that they ' would not bow the knee to the idol [Lord Bute] that keeps behind the veil of the Sanctuary,' advised each minister separately that he had sent for Pitt. Pitt accepted office as Lord Chatham,[2]

[1] *Annual Register*, xviii. *Characters*, pp. 17, 18.

[2] The French minister wrote to his colleague in London concerning the formation of this ministry, ' quel a été le dessein de My Lord Chatham en quittant la Chambre des Communes. Il nous paroissoit que toute sa force consistoit dans sa continuation dans cette chambre, et il pourroit bien se trouver comme Sampson après qu'on lui eût coupé les cheveux. . . . Je suis persuadé que la querelle de My lord Chatham avec son beau-frère My lord Temple ne durera pas. Ils se raccommoderont et il y aura encore un nouveau changement dans le ministère. C'est pour cela que l'on a laissé la place à M. Conway. Je suis persuadé que le Duc de Grafton la reprendra et cédera la sienne à My lord Temple . . .' Later in the letter, he speaks of ' l'ineptie de M. Conway.'

and offered Conway his old post as secretary, and the leadership of the Commons. The Duke of Richmond did his best to dissuade Conway from accepting; the Rockingham ministry was based on a strict aristocratic alliance which the king and Pitt had determined to destroy; Conway, by accepting, would further this design. However, Walpole, fearing that, if Conway refused, the leadership of the House would go to Grenville, persuaded him to accept. Conway, who had already told Pitt that he would prefer ' returning to the military, but would consult his friends,' agreed to follow Walpole's advice, and taking office, ' laboured to make some accommodation between Mr. Pitt and the fallen ministers.' Rockingham, though feeling some natural dislike that Conway should have deserted his friends, soon came to look upon him as ' the connecting link between the two parties,' and it was not until the disruptive tendencies of Pitt's administration had been too fully declared that Rockingham urged Conway to resign. Walpole wrote to his friend, Sir Horace Mann, that not only had Mr. Conway's friends flown out at him and left him, but Lord Rockingham and the Cavendishes had never ceased endeavouring to persuade him to resign—' Lord Hertford and I, seeing the factions and treacherous behaviour of his friends, and thinking it full as proper that he should govern them as they him, have done everything in our power to stop him : and I now, at last, flatter myself that he will not quit.' Conway, though ' very uneasy, perplexed himself with refinements,' as Lord Rockingham put it, and stayed in.

Meanwhile, Lord Hertford had been appointed Viceroy of Ireland by the Rockingham ministry, in the autumn of 1765. In the first few days that the ministry held office, the appointment had been mooted, and, on the 12th of July, Walpole wrote to Sir Horace Mann, ' The crown of Ireland is offered to Lord Hertford.' A few days later, he wrote again that Lord Hertford had come to London for a few days to make his option between Ireland and

Paris. By the 12th of August, he had decided to go as Viceroy to Ireland, and the Duke of Richmond succeeded him at Paris. On the whole, his embassy in Paris had been very successful, and he and his wife had become very popular by the way they responded to the gay life of Paris, and by their magnificence, of which Horace Walpole reported to the earl, both French and English newspapers spoke well. His appointment to Ireland was generally welcomed.[1] Thus Lord Chesterfield wrote, 'I really think he will be liked [as viceroy], for he is, in my opinion, the honestest and most religious man in the kingdom, and, moreover, very much of a gentleman in his behaviour to everybody.' His administration of Ireland proved they were right. Lord George Sackville wrote to General Irwin, in January 1766, 'affairs in Ireland go on hitherto prosperously for Lord Hertford, but that firebrand, Lucas,[2] is making the mob uneasy, and possibly may create ill-humour in the country.' In the following June, he wrote further, 'The latter part of the session was very satisfactory for him [Lord Hertford], but he underwent for some months every abuse that could be offered to a chief governor. The Speaker [of the Irish Parliament] is not in good humour, he played the old game upon the Lord-Lieutenant of dropping in questions, where popularity might be lost. As soon as he had done it he apologis'd for his conduct, and then the

[1] Realising that David Hume, his secretary, as a Scotsman, was not likely to be popular in Ireland, Hertford left him in Paris. Hume had been lionised in Paris, and his *History*, which Walpole describes as 'so falsified in many points, so partial in so many, so very unequal in its parts,' was looked upon as 'the standard of writing.' When William Burke resigned his office as secretary to Mr. Conway, on the downfall of the Rockingham ministry, David Hume was persuaded to take his place. 'I was pleased with the designation of Hume,' writes Walpole, 'as it would give jealousy to the Rockinghams, who had not acted wisely in letting Burke detach himself from Mr. Conway.'

[2] Charles Lucas, one of the prominent members of the Irish nationalist party. See *Hist. MSS. Com.*, MSS. of Mrs. Stopford Sackville.

FRANCIS SEYMOUR CONWAY, FIRST MARQUESS OF HERTFORD.
From an engraving in the British Museum. (Reynolds pinxt.)

opposition, who thought themselves sure of him, were more angry with him than even Lord Hertford was, so that, finding all sides had abused him, he thinks the best way is to be out of humour with Government, but, in the meantime, he does not object to the being one of the Lords Justices, and of holding the employment of Commissioner of the Revenue. How surprised such people would be if they were treated with that degree of severity which their conduct naturally calls for, but, indeed, the levity of government sets everything afloat in that kingdom.' On the whole, although Lecky [1] passes by Hertford's administration in Ireland unnoticed, it seems to have been generally recognised as 'respectable,' if not brilliant, and to have secured a period of tranquillity under very difficult circumstances. In September 1766, he was recalled to England, and in the same month was made Master of the Horse. Two months later, he was made Lord Chamberlain of the Household. 'Lord Hertford is already remarkably in favour with the king,' wrote Walpole, in the following January.

In the same month the king and Hertford concocted some indefinite plan to put Conway, whom, as we have seen, Walpole had persuaded, at the end of 1766, to retain his office, at the head of a reformed administration. Such a state of affairs, as even Walpole realised, must have been impossible. Conway had neither the ability to formulate a policy nor the decision to carry it out. Lord Hertford thought his brother not averse to the idea, but, says Walpole, ' he never had a settled ambition of being first nor . . . could he determine to yield to the temptation.' [2]

Throughout the year 1767, Conway was holding a practically impossible position. He attempted to uphold the principles of the Rockingham ministry in the March of that year, and proposed lenient measures towards

[1] *Hist. of Ireland in the Eighteenth Century.*
[2] *Memoirs of George III.*, ii. 295.

America, but, being unsupported, he was defenceless against the wit and oratory of Charles Townshend, who had profited to the full from Chatham's forced retirement from office earlier in the month.[1] Conway was forced to follow where Townshend led. At last, on the 30th of May, he summoned up courage to inform the king he wished to retire from office for he was tired of moderating. Walpole had done his utmost to prevent this, for he knew it meant the success of Grenville, but wrote, on the 28rd of May, to the Duke of Grafton, who had become chief minister after Chatham's retirement, ' things are come to such a crisis that my endeavours to prevent Mr. Conway's resignation are almost exhausted.' When he found that he could not for once prevail with Conway, who had been the instrument of his spite against Grenville for so long, he wrote to Sir Horace Mann, ' Mr. Conway, I think, will retire, not from disgust or into opposition, but from delicacy towards his old friends. . . .'[2] To me it will have nothing unpalatable.' A month later he wrote, ' Mr. Conway does quit. It is unlucky ; bad for the public, disadvantageous for himself, distressing to the king ; but he had promised his late friends. I call them *late* for they have by no means shown themselves so this winter nor are half grateful enough for such a sacrifice.[3] He might be minister ; he retires with nothing.'

But it was not to be. The king persuaded him to delay his resignation, and, meanwhile, invited Lord Rockingham to draw up a plan for administration. Rockingham attempted to form a union with the Bedford party, but the latter insisted that agreement as to the American policy was essential, and as this could not be made possible, and as Rockingham insisted that Conway should be leader of the

[1] Chatham was seriously attacked by gout and disabled.

[2] The Rockingham party, against whom, since they had ' espoused Mr. Grenville,' Walpole had done his best to embitter Mr. Conway.

[3] At the eleventh hour !

Commons the project was abandoned. Chatham was still in retirement, through a prolonged illness, but the king persuaded the Duke of Grafton to retain office, and he and Conway jointly undertook the administration. Grafton was as careless as Conway was vacillating, and the king ruled the ministry. However, in December, the Duke of Bedford, weary of opposition, 'sent to lay himself and *his friends* at the Duke of Grafton's feet, begging as alms that they might have some of the first and best places under the Government.' The Government accepted his terms, and this put an end to Conway's long-lasting indecision. At the end of January he resigned the Seals, but remained Cabinet Counsellor and acting minister in the House of Commons. He himself was desirous of quitting in December, but 'it was thought right that as the Duke of Bedford had objected to him in the summer, they should be forced to swallow this submission of coming in under him.' [1]

Conway at once turned to military life, for he was a better soldier than he was statesman. Already, in September 1767, he had been appointed Lieutenant-General of Ordnance, and in February 1768 he received the command of the fourth regiment of dragoons. 'Conway has the regiment *en attendant mieux*,' wrote George Selwyn to Lord Carlisle. During the riots consequent on the imprisonment of Wilkes on his return to England early in 1769, Conway took active steps to secure the safety of the king's palace. Thus 'Junius' comments, 'The security of the royal residence from insult was sufficiently provided for in Mr. Conway's firmness.' Yet while 'Junius' could praise his 'firmness' in matters military, even Walpole had no patience with his indecisive attitude in the first Cabinet meeting to decide the treatment of Wilkes. 'The Chancellor,' he writes, 'was all moderation; Conway as usual fluctuated between both opinions.' The next year,

[1] *Letters*, vii. 154.

R

when Lord Granby for political reasons retired from office, the king offered Conway the post of Master General of the Ordnance. He refused, saying he had lived in friendship with Lord Granby and would not profit of his spoils ; but, as he thought he could do some essential service in the Ordnance office, where there were many abuses, if His Majesty would be pleased to let him continue as he was, he would do the business of the office without accepting salary. The king replied, according to Walpole, ' You are a phenomenon ! I can satisfy nobody else, and you will not take even what is offered to you.'

During the next two years Conway was able to do much useful work at the Ordnance, but in the spring of 1772, hearing that George Townshend, who had retired from the Lord-Lieutenancy of Ireland, was to be Master of the Ordnance, he refused to serve under him. It happened thus : In the March of 1772, when the Royal Marriage Bill [1] was in debate, General Conway had approved the motion, yet owned he thought the Crown claimed more than it was entitled to. He lamented his doubts, feared he must express them in the Committee, wished to combine his affection for the king with his free opinion, was a friend to the principle of the Bill and to the minutest wish of the Crown.[2] All this conveys little, but in short, Conway was an enemy of the Bill, and ' with serious dignity and becoming firmness,' spoke against it in the House. The next day he came to Walpole and showed him a letter he had received from his brother, Lord Hertford, stating that the king had written to him that morning, ' complaining grievously ' of Conway's opposition to the Bill, thinking it was a personal affront. Walpole advised him not to recant for his own

[1] The Duke of Gloucester had married Lady Waldegrave, niece of Horace Walpole and second cousin of Lord Hertford and General Conway. The Bill aimed at the marriages of the Dukes of Gloucester and Cumberland, both married to commoners.

[2] Walpole, *Journ. of Reign of George III.*, i. 44.

sake : ' it ill became his brother to interfere in what concerned his honour ; and . . . if he allowed his brother to
dissuade him from acting as he ought to do, he himself
would have no thanks ; Lord Hertford would have all the
merit, and instead of Conway's receiving favours, Lord
Hertford would be rewarded for governing him.' Conway
agreed with Walpole and censured his brother for his
' unbounded servility.' Lord Hertford ' wrote him more
letters,' but they had no effect, for two days later Conway
again attacked the Bill. ' It ought to be corrected, it was
a law not fit to go down as it was drawn : he would venture
to say the House could not pass it. Were he capable of
paying a compliment, on this occasion, he should think
his tongue would wither in his mouth.' The king was
bitterly incensed, and urged on by the Bedford family, who
declared that Conway would neither accept the post of
Master of the Ordnance himself nor let anybody else enjoy
it, appointed Lord Townshend, a younger man than Conway,
and one who had never seen service.

Conway saw no course open to him but to resign, but
Walpole, knowing that he could ill afford to lose the pay
he received, and knowing that his work at the Ordnance
was ' even his plaything and passion,' determined to use
every effort to remedy or to stop the evil. Lord Hertford,
as Lord Chamberlain, could, if he were not ' too good a
courtier,' influence the king. Walpole went to him, and
told him it would prove he had little credit with the king
when he could not save his brother from affront. Hertford
broke into a temper, declaring he had done his utmost to
reclaim his brother before too late, talked of being head of
the family, and that his brother ought not to traverse his
views, that if Mr. Conway expected favours from court,
he must conform to the king's pleasure or take the consequences of his behaviour. Walpole urged that Conway
owed nothing to Hertford, but rather Hertford owed it to

him that he had been created Lord-Lieutenant of Ireland, and was now Lord Chamberlain. The first Hertford could not deny, the second he said he owed to Lord Chatham. Then Walpole 'touched gently' on Mr. Conway's conscientiousness and scruples, and hinted broadly that Lord Hertford carried his acquiescence to the king's will further, perhaps, than was justifiable. 'It is but justice to the elder brother to say,' adds Walpole in his *Journal*, 'that though he did not love to ask favours for others who might interfere with those he wished for himself or his children ; though he shuddered at dropping a harsh or unpleasant word to the king instead of using a firmness that alone made impression on him ; though he had violent repugnance to soliciting Lord North,' governing himself by that ruling humour of His Majesty that whoever attached himself to any first minister was not ' the king's friend,' still Lord Hertford had, in a sugared way, ' tried to ward off the blow from his brother, and when, in spite of that, it had fallen, he had done his best to sooth the king's wrath, and once or twice negotiated with Lord North for intercession.' He had already asked the king whether it were impossible for his brother to be restored to favour, and the king had replied, ' No, not if you advise it.' Finally the king was mollified by being informed that Conway, though he had voted against the Marriage Bill, would have nothing to do with his cousin, the Duchess of Gloucester.[1] The result was that through Lord North's intervention Conway was offered the Governorship of the island of Jersey. Again,

[1] Conway had been much inclined to visit her, when the king's prohibition had been issued, declaring that those who should visit the duke and duchess must abstain from court, but had been dissuaded by Walpole (*Journal*, i. 156). The duchess was hurt that Conway did not wait upon her, and suspected Lord Hertford of having had a hand in the prohibition. Walpole wrote to tell her that Hertford was innocent of such conduct, and that General Conway's absence was entirely due to his (Walpole's) persuasion (*Ibid*. 157).

on Walpole's advice, he accepted the Governorship, 'which the king gave him with every accompaniment of grace that he could mix with the boon.'

During the summer of 1774, Conway, who had been promoted to general in May 1772, left England 'on a tour of armies, because he has not seen enough of them,' that is to say he was on a tour of 'military curiosity' through Flanders, Germany, Prussia, and part of Hungary. In August, Walpole wrote to him, referring to his kindly reception by his old commander, Ferdinand, King of Prussia. 'Of your honours and glories, fame has told me; and for aught I know, you may be a veldt-marshal by this time, and despise such a poor cottager as me. Take notice, I disclaim you in my turn, if you are sent on a command against Dantzic or to usurp a new district in Poland. . . . For my part, I wish you was returned to your plough. Your Sabine farm [Park Place] is in high beauty.' Late in October Mr. Conway ended his tour in Paris, where his wife, Lady Ailesbury, and his daughter, Mrs. Damer, met him, and where they spent the winter together.

Meanwhile, on the 1st of October 1774, on the very day of the dissolution of Parliament, the king had sent to inform Lady Ailesbury that he had made her husband commander of the royal regiment of horse guards in place of Sir Robert Rich. Lady Ailesbury was 'charmed,' but Mrs. Damer, 'who had more penetration,' said, 'Pho! this is only a sugar plum.' She proved right, for the king's idea was to exclude Conway from the next Parliament. Walpole had already, in the last week of September, suspected that Lord Hertford was privy to some plan with the king to get the Duke of Grafton to leave Conway out of Parliament. Hertford was away from town, but Walpole went to see Lady Hertford, and they discussed together what could be done for Conway if he were excluded from his seat at Thetford.

Lady Hertford said her lord had no seat but Oxford and Coventry for his own three sons, and could not prefer his brother to them. ' To this,' says Walpole, ' I said not a word . . . and yet I thought Mr. Conway of much more consequence than the two younger sons, who never spoke in Parliament.' Lady Hertford then said her lord could speak to Lord North to bring in General Conway, though she thought all the boroughs were full. Again Walpole made no answer, and would not, for he was convinced Lord Hertford meant to ' drop his brother.'

The day after General Conway's commandership had been announced, Colonel Keene, a protégé of Lord Hertford, came to Walpole and said that, seeing Lord Hertford's difficulties, he himself had asked Lord North to bring Mr. Conway into Parliament. Walpole then proceeded to tell Colonel Keene all that Lord Hertford owed to his brother; Keene was astonished and began to speak, but Walpole stopped him, and, in Walpole's own words, ' for fear he should not say all I wished, and what I could not say myself to Lord Hertford, I determined to put my words into his mouth, I said, Sir, I know what you are going to say, but I will not let you. When you are kind to me, I will not be so unjust as to let you say what is not proper for you to say. You are Lord Hertford's friend, not Mr. Conway's. I know you was going to say Lord Hertford ought to bring his brother into Parliament out of gratitude rather than one of his own sons : I don't wonder you think so, but you must not say so to me.' This was, as Walpole guessed, duly reported to Lord and Lady Hertford.

That same evening Lord Hertford returned to London. Walpole at once went to his house and found Lady Ailesbury playing at cribbage with Lady Hertford, but was told his Lordship was busy. Twelve o'clock came, and still his Lordship was busy. Walpole now determined to leave without seeing him, but 'trembled so with passion' that he could hardly walk downstairs. At the last moment Lord Hertford's second son, Henry Conway, went to his father, and came back to say his father would see Walpole, but he would not go to him then, saying, 'I will not trouble him; I have nothing to say.' When he and Lady Ailesbury, who, although she was generally occupied with dress and feminine amusements,[1] was at last alarmed as to her husband's position by Walpole's passion, left the house in their chairs, a porter was sent after them to say that Lord Hertford desired to see Walpole, but Walpole repeated his formula, 'I have nothing to say.' Lady Ailesbury, who was by this time in tears and as angry as Walpole, now began to feel slighted herself that Lord Hertford 'had not seen *her*, since she went to Paris in two days.' Walpole assured her that Hertford wanted to see them both out of town till it was too late to find a borough for her husband, and then he would plead lapse of time as an excuse, and 'I added,' Walpole confesses, 'a great deal of very intemperate invective on him.'

The next morning he wrote off a very passionate letter to Lord Hertford threatening to break off all intercourse with him. However, before he sent his letter, he received one from Lady Hertford, saying her lord was distressed at not having seen Walpole, that his business had lasted until half-past two, and that as soon as he came from *church* that day he would go to *Kew*, and call on Walpole on his way back. Walpole thought it strange

---

[1] Walpole describes her as having been extremely handsome and preserving her beauty well; mild, gentle, and of a temper unsusceptible of strong, at least of lasting impressions. She had read much, was fond of music, and had a wonderful genius for needlework. She seldom thought on politics, and understood them less; nor, though she lived in the happiest union with her husband, did she make any right judgment on the frequent difficulties of his situation (Walpole, *Journal*, i. 407-8).

that Lord Hertford had time for church in moments of
such business, and saw that the visit to Kew meant that
Hertford did not dare to see him until he had seen the king.
He at once wrote off a civil letter to Lady Hertford, but
declared, after the indignity with which her husband had
treated both Conway and himself, he (Walpole) could never
enter his house again, or remain friendly.

Later in the day, Lady Hertford followed him to Lady
Ailesbury's house, entirely acquitted her lord, taxed
Walpole with pride, ingratitude, and injustice, swore
how much her lord loved both Conway and Walpole,
and declared that if Walpole should quarrel with her
husband, she herself would never speak to him again.
'I was charmed with her behaviour,' writes Walpole,
'and treated her with the utmost respect.' After a little
while, he found that Lady Hertford 'would fain have
reconciled me, but I did not think it ripe yet.' Finally,
Lady Hertford said that her husband would give up his
third son, Robert, to bring in his brother, but added
that Robert was the proudest of their children,[1] and ' probably would quarrel with his father about it.' As soon as
the offer was made, Walpole could not bring himself to
consent to it, and refused the idea, both now and later,
when Lord Hertford himself made the proposal.

In the evening Lord Hertford called on Walpole, bringing
his son Henry with him. 'He entered smiling,' says Walpole,
' shook me by the hand, and tried to treat my anger as too

[1] Lord and Lady Hertford had thirteen children, seven sons and six
daughters. Francis, Lord Beauchamp, who became second Marquess of
Hertford; Henry, who had ' very uncommon parts '; Robert, Edward,
Hugh, William, George, Anne, Sarah, Gertrude, Frances, Elizabeth,
Isabella. All eleven children, both sons and daughters, were of fine
figure or handsome; Lady Frances and Lady Elizabeth (see their portraits by Reynolds at the Wallace Collection), very handsome. The
family took the name of Seymour, instead of Seymour Conway, on
their father's death in 1794.

exceptious and to laugh it off, pretending he had not suspected my having been earnest to see him.' But Walpole 'was very cold, and would not answer a syllable,' except very circumspectly, until Henry Conway, the son, had gone out of the room. Then Lord Hertford and he talked the affair over 'with cordiality and better temper.' Hertford protested his innocence ; excused the king ; offered to give up his third son, and finally, promised to lay down any sum to bring his brother into Parliament. The next day, Lord Hertford sent for Walpole. The Duke of Grafton [1] had declared he would not bring Conway into Parliament. The little comedy which had been played for Conway's sake in the last few days was of no avail ; Hertford was powerless.

Then Walpole comforted his soul by the possibilities arising from news that men and ships were required for active service in America. 'I made full use of this,' he writes, 'to imprint on Lord Hertford's mind his brother's importance. . . . I painted to him the necessity there would be of the king calling Mr. Conway to council, and gave him a hint . . . that his brother might be again in a situation to save *him*.' Lord Hertford confessed this might be so, as the king must call in 'some temperate man.' 'I wanted no more than this hint,' says Walpole, 'to assure me Lord Hertford would soon find some way, if possible, to bring his brother into Parliament.' The next thing Walpole had to do was to prevent the king from offering Conway the command of the troops in America, since he was certain to refuse to fight against America, and would be ruined, as an officer, in consequence. He put his fears before Lord Hertford, who

[1] The Duke of Grafton was Lady Hertford's nephew, since he was the son of her brother, Lord Augustus Fitzroy. This action was a deliberate slight to her husband's family. Lord Hertford was not, it seems, privy to Grafton's plan, as Walpole had suspected. Had he been still recorder of Thetford, he might have used his influence for his brother in that borough, but Grafton had persuaded him previously to resign that office.

asked what was to be done.   Walpole suggested he should
tell the king that if his brother refused to serve against
the Americans, the example would spread and be followed.
' No,' said Lord Hertford, ' the king will never bear that !
I should tell him my brother has scruples ; and irresolu-
tion will hurt the service.' [1]

Meanwhile, the hero or victim of all these intrigues was
in Paris, whence he wrote thanking Walpole for all the
trouble he had taken on his behalf.   It was not until the
following May that he came once more into Parliament,
when a seat was found for him at Bury St. Edmunds, vacant
by the succession of Captain Augustus Hervey (the husband
of the famous Miss Chudleigh) to the earldom of Bristol.
Conway accepted grudgingly, since he was chosen by the
influence of the Duke of Grafton, whom Lady Hertford had
persuaded to secure the election for him.   Lord Hertford,
however, was very eager that he should accept, because,
notes Walpole, ' it would save him the expense of bringing
his brother into Parliament.'   Yet neither the king nor the
Opposition were pleased in the end, since Conway opposed
the policy of the Government towards America in April 1775.
Lord Hertford was much hurt at it ; ' the one brother voted
as his conscience directed him, the other considered only how
his brother's vote would affect the interest of the family.'
Again, in November, Conway voted against the address,
since it approved of the war and spoke against the Bill for
restraining trade in the southern colonies.

In the July of the next year (1776) General Conway had
an attack of facial paralysis.   Walpole was glad to find
neither his head nor speech were affected, but he wrote to
his friend, the Rev. William Cole, ' it has operated such a
revolution in my mind as no time, *at my age*, can efface.
It has at once damped every pursuit which my spirits
had even now prevented me from being wearied from.'

---

[1] Walpole, *Journal*, etc., i. 401-418.

However, in less than a month's time General Conway was 'visibly much mended,' and no traces of his disorder remained.[1] 'His countenance is quite come to itself,' wrote Walpole, 'and his disposition was so little disturbed, that in one of the rainy days I passed there he employed all the morning in cleaning his own boat. He is as indifferent about the accident, and talks of it with as much unconcern as if he had only been out on a skirmishing party.' The next day, however, came the news of the death of Mr. Damer, his son-in-law, under the most revolting circumstances. Walpole feared the effect of the shock, but had a very calm letter from Conway showing that his nerves were not affected.

The marriage of his only daughter Anne, in 1767, had greatly pleased Mr. Conway. 'He is in great felicity,' Walpole had written to Sir Horace Mann, for Lord Milton, Mr. Damer's father, was very rich, and £5000 a year was settled on his son. Miss Conway was to have a jointure of £2500 and £500 pin-money. Her own settlement, which was £10,000, the whole of her father's fortune, went in jewels, equipage and furniture. In spite of this provision, Mr. Damer had incurred debts amounting to about £70,000. His father refused to pay the debts. On the 16th of August 1776, Mr. Damer supped, at the Bedford Arms in Covent Garden, with four common women and a blind fiddler. When his companions had left he shot himself, and the master of the house came up and found a scrap of paper on the table beside him :—' The people of the house are not to blame for what has happened, which was my own act.' Lunacy, not distress, was generally supposed to be the reason of his act. Lord Milton forced Mrs. Damer to sell her jewels for the discharge of just debts, but that was all the harm he could do her ; he was obliged to allow her her

[1] Yet, in the following October, Walpole wrote that he certainly had marks of his disorder still (*Letters*, ix. 429).

jointure of £2500 a year. From this time she developed
her real talent for sculpture,[1] and gradually paid off all her
husband's debts without the least obligation upon her to
do so. Her work is often, and not undeservedly praised
by Walpole, and is best remembered in the fine heads of
Thame and Isis, carved on the keystones of the bridge at
Henley that was built near Park Place, the seat of General
Conway, in 1785.[2] The original models for the two heads
in terra cotta were exhibited that year at the Royal
Academy. It was through Horace Walpole's persuasion
that Mrs. Damer herself undertook to carve the stones from
her own models.

From the spring of 1778 to 1781 General Conway was
frequently engaged in performing his duties as Governor
of Jersey, and made constant and lengthy stays in the
island. Walpole wrote to Lady Ailesbury, in June 1778,
surprised at the length of her husband's stay in Jersey : ' Is
he revolting and setting up for himself like our nabobs in
India ? or is he forming Jersey, Guernsey, Alderney and
Sark into the United Provinces in the compass of a silver
penny ? '

In May 1779, when the French attack on Jersey had
become more than a vague possibility, General Conway
went at once to the island. The invasion was attempted,
repulsed, and given up within eight days—' the visionary
monarch [a Prince of Nassau who headed the French
expedition, and was to be declared king of the island]
sailed back to France . . . and King George and Viceroy
Conway remain sovereigns of Jersey—whom God long preserve.' In July another invasion was expected, and the

---

[1] In 1821 she was still alive, ' 70 years of age, and as fresh as if she
was 50' (*Creevy Papers*, ed. Sir Herbert Maxwell). A statue of her
stands in the entrance hall of the British Museum.

[2] Walpole notes that General Conway himself regulated a bend of
the arch of the bridge on three centres.

French had better chances with less risk—' Mr. Conway is
in the midst of the storm in a nutshell [Mont Orgueil ?]
. . . and,' wrote Walpole, ' I believe the court would sacrifice the island to sacrifice him.' At this same moment,
while General Conway was in danger of being attacked
on the island, his daughter, Mrs. Damer, had been taken
prisoner by a French privateer when crossing from Dover
to Ostend. The captain, however, was ' a Paladin in disguise,' and treated all his lady prisoners ' not only with the
continence of Scipio, but with disinterest, a virtue still more
rare in a freebooter,' refused to ' touch a pin,' and told them
they were their own mistresses.

The next month Walpole wrote to Sir Horace Mann,
' General Conway is still in his little island which, I trust,
is too diminutive to be descried by an Armada. I do
not desire to have him achieve an Iliad in a nut-shell.'
A few days later he wrote, ' I am trembling for Mr. Conway, who is chained to a rock.' The French were now
threatening more than Jersey, even England herself, and
grave rumours were everywhere. Yet the next month
Walpole anxiously wrote to Conway to hope he would be
at the meeting of Parliament in October, ' Surely you
have higher and more sacred duties than the government
of a mole-hill ! ' On the 31st of October he wrote to
Sir Horace Mann : ' I trust we shall see General Conway
within a week. . . . He has acted in his diminutive islet with
as much virtue and popularity as Cicero in his large Sicily,
and with much more ability as a soldier, a commander—
I am heartily glad he was disappointed of showing how
infinitely more he is a hero.' Yet early in November he
was writing, ' Mr. Conway is not come : I trust from the
obstinacy of a contrary wind. . . . I have expected him
for this fortnight.' Finally, on the evening of the 21st of
November, as Walpole was sitting with Lady Ailesbury
and Mrs. Damer, ' the door opened and entered General

Conway . . . he had landed at Portsmouth the night before, after being blown to Plymouth.'[1]

The year 1780, the year of the Gordon Riots, Conway remained in England, often speaking severely against Lord George Gordon in the House of Commons. An alarm of another invasion of Jersey reached him in June, but before he could set out it was proved to be false, and it was not until the January of 1781 that the invasion really took place. Eight hundred French troops, led by Baron de Rullecourt, landed at Jersey on the 6th of January, seized Lieutenant-Governor Corbett in his bed, and, it was reported in England, seized the island. Orders were sent to Portsmouth to send what force could be spared, and an express to General Conway to set out for Jersey. He, though at the time suffering from a broken arm, the result of a fall in the previous September, ' came to town on the wings of the wind, and never pulled them off, and in two hours was on the way to Portsmouth.' As soon as he had embarked, more reassuring news came to England. Major Pierson, as second in command, had rallied the British troops, gained a complete victory, and killed or taken prisoner all the invaders. ' Mr. Conway,' wrote Walpole, ' will proceed and thank his little army who, without detracting from their merit, certainly owe some of it to his discipline. . . . These are the troops Mr. Conway himself formed last year. *To me* this battle is worth the day at Blenheim.'

Conway never arrived in Jersey. He had embarked in so great a storm that a transport with sixty men was lost as he sailed, and a cutter that preceded him was not heard of again, while his frigate, after tossing for two days and a night, with difficulty reached Plymouth. There he was relieved to hear the good news of the victory in Jersey. He had done all he could, and was now forced to

[1] *Letters*, xi., 7, 13, 23, 44, 63.

take to his bed from rheumatism and cold, while his broken arm caused him much suffering, since a well-meaning sailor, seeing him awkward at getting up the ladder into the frigate at Portsmouth, gave his arm a tug to help him, and nearly broke it again. By March, however, he had recovered, and went to Jersey with an additional force 'which he obtained only by dint of perseverance,' and was still there in June when Walpole was writing to him: 'I am not afraid for your island when you are at home in it . . . the French would be foolish indeed if they ran their heads a third time against your rocks, when watched by the most vigilant of all Governors.' Conway had, however, so Lord Hertford had informed Walpole, written to Lord Hillsborough, Secretary of State, for leave to return, and at the end of the following August surprised Walpole, one Sunday morning at breakfast, at Strawberry Hill, looking 'well in health and spirits' as Walpole reported.

Meanwhile, affairs in America had become more and more disastrous for England. In the November of 1781, Colonel Robert Conway, third son of Lord Hertford, and aide-de-camp to Sir Henry Clinton,[1] arrived in England with a message from the latter, representing the desperate state of affairs. Lord Cornwallis was in imminent danger of being surrounded and starved by the Americans and French; Clinton was going on a relief expedition, but he and Lord Cornwallis were ' so ill together ' that Sir Henry had owned to Colonel Conway he was determined to challenge Cornwallis after the campaign. Admiral Digby, who was in command of the fleet, was determined to attack the French. Colonel Conway told his father, Lord Hertford, that every captain in the navy disapproved, yet from bravery would not oppose it. He told his father further, ' we had not a friend left in America.' On the 25th of November, news

---

[1] Sir Henry Clinton was at the head of the English forces in America.

came that Cornwallis had been forced to capitulate and
abandon the loyal Americans who had followed him to
their fate. General Conway, who had consistently opposed
the war, then began once more to take a prominent part in
attacking Lord North's administration, since it had thus
reduced England to the necessity of allowing America her
independence. He bitterly condemned the Tenth Article
of Lord Cornwallis's capitulation which abandoned the
loyal Americans, looking upon it as ' so deep a disgrace
that Lord Cornwallis must have been forced by his own
troops to sign it.'

Wraxall, describing him at the time of this speech,
says, ' he had already passed his sixtieth year, yet his figure
and deportment were exceedingly distinguished ; but his
enunciation, embarrassed and often involved,[1] generally
did injustice to his conceptions.'   On the 22nd of February
1782, Conway further moved, ' to implore his Majesty to
listen to the advice of his Commons, that the war in America
might no longer be pursued for the impracticable purpose
of reducing the inhabitants of that country to obedience
by force, and to express their hope that his Majesty's desire
to restore the public tranquillity might be forwarded
and made effectual by a happy reconciliation with the
revolted colonies.' [2]   ' The effect of his speech,' says Wraxall,
' was incredible,' a long debate ensued, the ministers continued to hold the same vague and undetermined language
as before, and finally, the motion was lost by one vote.
This was looked upon as a virtual defeat of the ministry,
and five days later, General Conway put forward the motion
again in ' a most eloquent and animated speech,' answering
the objections which had been urged by his opponents.
He denied that it was unconstitutional for Parliament to
interfere in the executive work of Government ; Parlia-

[1] Probably the result of the facial paralysis of 1776.
[2] *Ann. Reg.* 1782, p. 168.

ment, and more especially the House of Commons, had generally made its voice heard with authority and effect. He denied that his motion had been vaguely and obscurely worded, it was intended to put an end to ' offensive war,' and of this the Government had given no assurance, so their hands must be tied. He attempted to oblige Dundas and Rigby to vote with him, reminding them of their late declarations respecting the war. If he might borrow an allusion from the sacred text he should say that they, as well as many other members of the House, had received the gift of tongues. Cloven tongues had alighted upon them. Not, indeed, tongues of sincerity and truth, but double tongues, one for Parliament, the other for private society.

Lord North made a long and able reply and, referring to Conway's reproach of the ' cloven tongues,' declared, ' I do not wish for the support of any such double-tongued senators. I desire to stand this night on the merits of my cause.' He expressed his willingness to resign should the House have withdrawn its confidence from him, thanking God that ' mere disgrace, in the ministerial sense of the term,' constituted no crime. Soon after one o'clock in the morning, after an all-night debate, 284 voted for Conway, 215 adhered to Lord North, and Conway, ' now completely master of the deliberations of the House on the subject of America,' proposed and carried two addresses to the king, one to stop the prosecution of the war, another to declare all who advised or prosecuted the continuance of the war, enemies of the throne. The king was enraged with Conway, whom earlier in the year he had intended making Commander-in-chief. Selwyn wrote to Lord Carlisle,[1] on the 18th of March :—' Conway was at the Levee yesterday, and scarce noticed ; the king talked

---

[1] Selwyn's correspondence is among the MSS. of the Earl of Carlisle (*Hist. MSS. Com. Rep.* xv., App. vi.).

and laughed a great deal with both Rigby and the Advocate, who were on each side of Conway.'

On the 20th of March, Lord North, much to the king's chagrin, unexpectedly resigned; 'The old ministry is at an end,' wrote Selwyn, 'and of what materials the new one will be composed, the Lord knows.' But Walpole was happy; 'I can only say, with a change in a Scripture phrase, This is *not* the Lord's doing, but the Commons', and it is marvellous in our eyes!' Seven days later, the new ministry formed by a combination of the parties of Rockingham and Shelborne came into office, Conway having been made Commander-in-chief, with a seat in the Cabinet. All went smoothly until Rockingham died on the 1st of July. George was delivered from the Whigs, and Shelborne was made Prime Minister. Fox, Burke, and Lord John Cavendish resigned, refusing to serve under him, and went into Opposition. Both Conway and the Duke of Richmond laboured to prevent disunion, imploring harmony till the peace with America should be established, but in vain. Ten days later Fox was attacking Conway in the House, calling him ' *an innocent* who knew nothing, thought nothing of men, but looked to measures, and had wrought great good and great evil.' Conway avowed it was time he looked to measures not men, and summed up his own political creeds under four headings ; the reduction of the power of the Crown ; public economy ; the independence of America, and the independence of Ireland. By these tests he desired to be tried, and if he abandoned them, to be condemned.

He managed to keep his uneasy seat in the Cabinet until February 1788, when the ministry resigned. In the December following, Pitt accepted office as first Lord of the Treasury and Chancellor of the Exchequer. Fox was in opposition, and Conway supported Fox, taunting Pitt in January 1784, and stating that the Government was corrupt.

Finally, in the following March, Parliament was dissolved as a result of Fox's motion for an address to the Crown for Pitt's dismissal. Conway's political life was finished, he resigned his military command and retired to Park Place, keeping only his governorship of Jersey.

Meanwhile, Lord Hertford, ' one of the " ancient, most domestic ornaments" of the court, who had held the white wand of Chamberlain during more than fifteen years, and whose presence in the circle seemed, from long habit, almost essential to its very existence,' [1] had of course disappeared from court under the changed administration of March 1782. ' Lord Hertford is delivered up at discretion,' wrote Selwyn to Lord Carlisle, ' either he or his son, Isaac [Lord Beauchamp], must be sacrificed. But his lordship has not been thought the father of the faithful, or so himself. Their trimming has released his M[ajesty] from any obligations to protect them.' Already Hertford and his wife had attempted to make friends with the Opposition. Thus Selwyn wrote in the beginning of March, ' Poor Lady H[ertfor]d['s] civilities in inviting so many of the Opposition to her Ball afford a great deal of mirth. Charles [Fox] did not go . . . although invited in so *distinguishing a manner.*'

Within eight months Lady Hertford was dead. She had been nursing her grandson, Lord Beauchamp's son,[2] at Ditton, and caught a violent cold. On Wednesday, the 6th of November, she came to London ' on his account, and not her own,' was not considered dangerously ill as late as Friday night, but on Saturday she was in extreme danger, and on Sunday, the 10th of November, she died between 5 and 6 o'clock in the evening. ' Her life,' wrote George Selwyn, ' has been sacrificed to her affection for that child.' ' There was no one,' he continues, ' more ready to do a kind

---

[1] Wraxall, *Memoirs*, ii. 275.
[2] Afterwards third Marquess of Hertford. (See *infra.*)

office, and no one ever showed me more civility than she did. I have had no particulars of the manner in which Lord Hertford supports this misfortune, but I should imagine with great difficulty, for to him it must be irreparable. Lord Dartmouth has indeed been assisted so much by his religion [as I hear] that, under the loss of a favourite son, he has been resigned. I do not doubt of the cause nor of the effect. I am only afraid that, in a similar case, I should want that and much more to make it tolerable to me.' 'His [Lord Hertford's] loss is beyond measure,' wrote Horace Walpole. 'She was not only the most affectionate wife, but the most useful one, and almost the only person I ever saw that never neglected or put off or forgot anything that was to be done. She was always proper, either in the highest life or in the most domestic. Her good humour made both sit easy; to herself only she gave disquiet by a temper so excessively affectionate.' Already, before the blow had actually fallen, Hertford had written to Walpole, 'With a dagger in my heart, which nothing in the world now can extract, I am determined to exert all my feeble power to tell you, who loved my dearest and beloved Lady Hertford, that I am upon the point of losing her, the best woman, the best friend, and best wife that ever existed. Do not make me any answer, or pity me. I am not able to bear even the condolence of a friend.'

In the new Parliament of the spring of 1784, whereas General Conway retired from office, his brother, Lord Hertford, was 'tricked out of his seat,' and in this 'a *royal* finger . . . too evidently tampered, as well as singularly and revengefully.' Lord Hertford had five sons in that Parliament, yet he himself could not in his old age put off his courtier ways, and in June 1784 he seems to have been hankering after his old office of Lord Chamberlain. Walpole wrote to General Conway, 'with a vast fortune Lord

Hertford might certainly do what he would, and if, at his age, he can wish for more than that fortune will obtain, I may pity his taste or temper; but I shall think that you and I are much happier who can find enjoyments in an humbler sphere, nor envy those who have no time for trifling.' Nine years later Hertford was still looking for titles, ribands, offices of no business which anybody can fill.' Thus, in June 1793, Walpole again wrote to Conway, ' How can love of money, or the still vainer of all vanities, ambition of wearing a high, but most insignificant office [that of Lord Chamberlain] . . . tempt a very old man who loves his ease and his own way, to stoop to wait like a footman behind a chair, for hours, and in a court whence he had " been cast ignominiously " ' ? In July the patience of the old courtier was rewarded by his creation as Earl of Yarmouth and Marquess of Hertford. He enjoyed his title for nearly a year, dying, at the age of seventy-six, on the 14th of June 1794, at the house of his daughter, the Countess of Lincoln, at Putney, as the result of a mortification following on a slight hurt he received while riding.[1] A year later his brother, who had been created Field-Marshal Conway in October 1793,[2] died suddenly at Park Place between four and five o'clock on the morning of the 9th of June 1795. He was seventy-five years of age. The cause of his death was cramp in the stomach caused by his imprudence in exposing himself to cold and damp. Walpole, who outlived both brothers, passes by their deaths unnoticed in his letters.

Thus the tale of their lives is ended, and there is left only the task of considering the truth of the statements made hypothetically before the tale was told. In Lord Hertford there is, it seems, little that we can admire, even though

---

[1] *Gentleman's Magazine*, 1794.

[2] Walpole, *Letters*, xv. 259-60. ' Conway must needs go and kiss hands for his idle truncheon.'

we must perforce respect him with Lord Chesterfield for
his honesty and his religion.   In his home and his relations
with his immediate family circle, his wife and his children,
he appears to have been a devoted husband and father,
bent on raising himself and, like his ancestor, the Speaker,
'doing well' for his children.   In the political world he was
'a perfect courtier'—the 'ancient and most domestic ornament of the court'—and to his courtier spirit was added
an absorbing love of wealth.   William Coombe, in his satire
The Diaboliad, tells how Satan sent his ministers to find
an heir to the throne of Hell before he resigned it himself
through old age.   Some of the ministers searched for his
successor in the English court.

> 'The rest of Hell's industrious Band resort
> To the corrupted purlieus of the court
> To lure the statesman from his deep-laid scheme,
> To wake the Courtier from his golden dream,
> And make the C-b-l-n [Lord Hertford, the Lord Chamberlain]
>   desire to hold
> Hell's mighty Sceptre, for 'tis made of gold.
> Sure he'd resign for such a tempting fee !
> Hell's sceptre far outweighs the Golden Key !
> But cautious * * * * * [Hertford] shrinks when risks are run,
> And leaves such Honors to his eldest son.'

We have seen in his life how he was cautious, reserved,
selfish and mean, a place-seeker, trimming his political
opinions to meet the views of the party in power.   Coombe
tells that his family was held 'in universal disgust,' and
that when Charles Fox proposed to introduce his second
son, Henry Seymour Conway,[1] into one of the fashionable
clubs, he was almost universally blackballed.   Fox thereupon proposed him again, declaring, on his honour, that
young Mr. Henry Conway had not one quality in common
with any of his family, and in the second ballot not a single

[1] After the death of their father the family dropped the name of
Conway, so that he is generally known as Henry Seymour.

black ball appeared against him. At the same time, it is due to Lord Hertford to remember, in the first place, that his work in Paris and Ireland was intelligent and useful, and served more than his own ends, and, in the second place, that the facts of his life, as we know them, are mostly from the pen of Walpole, whose statements were necessarily biassed in favour of his idol, General Conway.

Passing on to consider General Conway himself, we have seen how he was the half-conscious instrument of Walpole's caprices; we have seen how, because of the workings of his mind, he was brave and fearless, yet no strong man; a brilliant speaker, yet no statesman; a capable soldier, yet no general. Fearless, except of wounding the feelings of others, he dared, at the bidding of his friends, to carry their opinions into practical issue and to logical conclusions before which even the thoughts of their originators paled, yet he was powerless to formulate, enforce, or adhere to opinions of his own. With the skill of a scholar and an artist in words, he spoke often and well in Parliament, yet, being without the knowledge and strength of a statesman, it was chance rather than foresight and power that made him more than once a successful leader of the Opposition. Stern yet diffident, brave yet hesitating, he was a lover of discipline, yet a too generous master; a fighter of battles, but an impossible general. Kindly, charming, and lovable in person, he yet had no commanding personality, and was only a hero to one man—Horace Walpole. Finally, he was unfortunate in that this dearest friend and worshipper was certainly his evil genius, who tricked out personal grievances in the garb of political wrongs, and, showing him shadowy cities built by his own intriguing, taught him that the possession of these was, or should be the *raison d'être* of his every thought and action.

CHAPTER X

THE THIRD MARQUESS OF HERTFORD, 'WHISKERS,' 'RED HERRINGS,' OR 'BLOATERS': HIS PARENTAGE AND LIFE

> ' This was a man who might have turned
>   Hell into Heaven—and so in gladness
> A Heaven unto himself have earned :
>   But he in shadows undiscerned
>   Trusted, and damned himself to madness.'
>   —SHELLEY.

SEVERE as he had been in his estimate of Lord Hertford in the *Diaboliad*, William Coombe [1] was still more severe to Lord Hertford's son, Viscount Beauchamp, who became second Marquess of Hertford on the death of his father in 1794. He appears before Satan to plead his fitness for office as Lord of Hell :—

> ' Without one virtue that can grace a name,
> Without one vice that e'er exalts to fame,
> The despicable * * * [Beauchamp] next appears,
> His bosom panting with its usual fears.
> He strives in vain—and fruitless proves the art—
> To hide with vacant smile the treacherous heart.
> The faithful Harry [Hon. Henry Seymour [2]] stands not by his side
> His learned counsel and his constant guide,

---

[1] Coombe had married a discarded mistress of Viscount Beauchamp, and possibly gained some of his information from her.

[2] His younger brother, second son of Lord and Lady Hertford. Walpole, writing of him in 1762 to his uncle, General Conway, says, ' Lord Beauchamp showed me two of his letters, which have more natural humour and cleverness than is conceivable. They have the ease and drollery of a man of parts who has lived long in the world,

Who for an hard-earn'd narrow competence
Supplies his tongue with words, his head with sense.[1]
At length, recovered from his huge affright
He, stammering, reads the speech he did not write—
"Curst with hereditary love of pelf
I hate all human beings but myself,
Cross and perplex my wife   because she prov'd,
Poor girl !—not rich enough to be belov'd.
But all return my hate :—where'er I go
My coward eye beholds a ready foe,
And though to earth's extremes my feet I bend
These arms would ne'er embrace a real friend.
When my breast throbs with unrelenting grief
No friendly spirits bring the kind relief ;
If I sink down beneath oppressing pain
Surrounding foes rejoice as I complain.
I'm scoff'd by those who from my hand have prov'd
That kindness which would make *another* lov'd,
Men, who to other Patrons bend their knee,
Are proud of their Ingratitude to me ;
But without friends on earth I humbly sue
To find, my gracious Liege, a Friend in you.
Hated by all—I 'm fit to be allied
To your Imperial State !"   The king replied :
"If vacant smiles and hypocritic air
Could form pretensions to this sov'reign chair ;
If my pale crown by *meanness* could be won,
Who has so fair a claim as * * * [Hertford]'s son?

---

and he is only seventeen' (Walpole, *Letters*, v. 252).   This Henry
Seymour died, unmarried, in 1830.

[1] According to Coombe, Lord Hertford, like an 'avaricious father,'
had saddled the younger brother for a maintenance on the elder, who,
possessing ' an hereditary baseness,' insisted that his younger brother
should give him ' the use of his understanding ' in return for maintenance. ' It too often happens,' he adds, ' that the elder brothers want
spirit and understanding, and that the younger ones, who have both
in an eminent degree, stand in need of a provision. It is hard that
worth and genius should be so situated.'

[2] His second wife, Isabella Anne Ingram Shepherd, daughter and
co-heir of Charles, ninth and last Viscount Irvine. She became very
rich, by the death of her mother, in 1807.

But meanness is a vice which Devils disdain !
Shouldst thou attempt, base mortal, here to reign,
To wield this sceptre and to wear my crown,
The imperial Host will rise to cast thee down
With furious zeal, where outcast spirits lie
In the dark dens of gnashing Infamy.
Such minds as thine—observe the truth I tell—
Find neither Friends on Earth nor Friends in Hell."
Appall'd the hapless Lordling sneak'd away,
And harpies kiss'd him to the realms of Day.'

'Several of my friends,' the author comments on his
own lines, 'seemed to think that I had frustrated my
intention of marking the insignificance of this character
by giving so many lines to the delineation of it. But as
the bold strokes are more easily imitated than the finer
pencillings of nature, these colourless bad qualities, which
have not sufficient strength or spirit to rise into daring
manly vice, require a great length of description to impress
them properly on the attention of the Reader.' This man's
life, he goes on to declare, is a striking example of a mean
spirit, ' a low, sneaking, base, fixed propensity to what is
bad which it loves, driven by its fears to assume the
semblance of good which it hates.' Much of this satire
is undoubtedly the result of the personal hatred of the
author directed against Lord Beauchamp, yet his character
certainly appears to have been colourless, and not only colourless but mean, for he inherited his father's capacity for
serving his own ends, trimming his political opinions, and
bowing himself down before any of the gods set up by the
king and court. Yet, though it is difficult to say whether
or no he owed his words and his sense to his brother Henry,
he does not seem to have been lacking in understanding,
as William Coombe would have us believe. Wraxall, who
described his person as ' elegantly formed,' and his manners
as ' noble yet ingratiating,' notes that whenever he addressed
the House of Commons he spoke ' if not with eloquence,

at least with knowledge of the subject,' and Wraxall was hardly likely to be taken in by knowledge acquired in parrot fashion from a younger brother. Moreover, his pamphlets and speeches in favour of the freedom of Ireland, with whatever motive they were written, certainly show him a friend to Ireland, and perhaps a friend to liberty. The truth was he had plenty of ability, but, like his son, the third marquess, liked pleasure better than statesmanship and preferred court favours to political fame.

Born in 1748, the eldest son of Lord Conway, Francis Seymour Conway,[1] became Viscount Beauchamp in August 1750, when his father was created Earl of Hertford. He was educated at Eton, matriculated from Christ Church, Oxford, in February 1760, and took his M.A. degree two years later. From 1761 to 1768 he represented Lisburne in the Irish Parliament, was made a privy councillor for Ireland in 1765, the year that his father was appointed Lord-Lieutenant, and was chief secretary to his father during his one year's term of office. He was then appointed Constable of Dublin Castle, but being elected in the same year (1766) to the English Parliament as member for Lostwithiel, transferred his field of action to England, although he still kept a keen interest in Ireland and Irish affairs. For two years he represented Lostwithiel, but from 1768 to 1794 sat for Oxford, since Oxford borough belonged to Lord Hertford. Carefully following in his father's footsteps, he attached himself to the court, and was promoted to be a Lord of the Treasury, under Lord North's administration, in March 1774, at the moment when his uncle, General Conway, was being ejected from Parliament by the king's wish and the Duke of Grafton's schemes. In February 1780 he was appointed Cofferer

---

[1] On his father's death he dropped the name of Conway, and on the death of his wife's mother, in 1807, took the name of Ingram before that of Seymour.

of the Household, and a privy councillor. From 1774 to 1788 he was a frequent speaker in Parliament, favouring the taxation of America, and generally opposing the idea of her freedom from England. Thus, in April 1774, he opposed the motion for the repeal of the American tea duty on the ground that the mother country must preserve the right of taxing her colonies, and in December 1777, spoke against Wilkes's motion to repeal the American Declaratory Act. On the other hand, his sympathies were on the side of freedom as regards Ireland, that is to say, he warmly advocated religious toleration for the country and parliamentary independence, but he looked on the interests of the two countries as inseparable, and their political connection as indissoluble. In May 1778, he strongly declared himself in favour of the repeal of the Penal Acts, directed against the Roman Catholics in Ireland, and in April 1782, declared that the repeal of the Irish De- claratory Act, as suggested by Charles James Fox, would only satisfy Ireland if a counter declaratory clause were inserted assuring the independence of the Irish Parliament. He emphasised these views in a pamphlet entitled ' A Letter to the First Company of Belfast Volunteers,' published in Dublin in that year. Horace Walpole wrote to Lord Hertford concerning this pamphlet, that it was very well written for Lord Beauchamp's purpose and situation in Ireland, yet he himself thought that the less it was seen by any except those to whom it was addressed the better. ' There does not seem to me,' says Walpole, ' to be an argu- ment in it in favour of the freedom and independence of Ireland that is not equally applicable to America,' and this was awkward, since Beauchamp, as a member of the ministry, was an upholder of the repressive policy in America. ' I am certainly glad Lord Beauchamp declares so strongly in favour of liberty and prerogative,' Walpole continues, ' he never can grow an advocate for the latter, or his pamphlet will be a terrible witness against him . . . of all politicians, a politician author is most bound to adhere to the principles he has professed in print, for even posterity in that case will call him to account, and his contemporaries are not likely to wink at his contradictions ' (*Letters*, xii. 352). However, as far as Ireland was concerned, Beauchamp remained consistent always, and in May 1785, unsuccessfully opposed Pitt's proposition concerning the commercial union of England and Ireland, to bind Ireland to accept such regulations as Great Britain should enact. 'The only lasting connexion between the two countries,' he declared, ' can be of freedom and common interest, not of power.' On two other occasions, Lord Beauchamp made speeches of some general interest in the House. In February 1780, he introduced a Bill for the relief of debtors from imprisonment. Edmund Burke, who supported this motion, spoke of Lord Beauchamp in highly complimentary terms. The House of Lords, in February 1784, resolved ' that an attempt in any one branch of the legislature to suspend the execution of law by assuming to itself the direction of discretionary power, is unconstitutional.' Lord Beauchamp, within a few days, proposed six counter resolutions (1) That the [House of Commons] had not assumed to itself a right to suspend the execution of the law; (2) That for them to declare their opinion, respecting the exercise of any discretionary power, was constitutional and agreeable to established usage; (8) That it was a duty incumbent on them [the Commons] to watch over and endeavour to prevent the rash and precipitate usage of any power; (4) That the resolution of the 24th of December [1] last constituted

---

[1] *Ann. Reg.*, 1784. Lord Beauchamp had moved the resolution, in December 1783, that the Lords of the Treasury should not allow the directors of the East India Company to accept any bills without the consent of Parliament. The Lords objected to this, because discretionary power was lodged with the Treasury Lords.

a judicious and regular discharge of an indispensable duty;
(5) That had they acted otherwise the members of the
House would have been responsible to their constituents
for the most alarming consequences; (6) That the House
would persist in asserting its privileges thus firmly. The
resolutions were carried against the ministers by a majority
of thirty-one.

The year 1788 practically terminated Lord Beauchamp's
parliamentary career, but he supported Pitt's Alien Bill
in 1793, and spoke in favour of the augmentation of the
forces. In that year his father was created Marquess, and
he himself took the title of Earl of Yarmouth. Rising in
favour at court, he was employed in work which was much
to his liking, as Ambassador Extraordinary and Pleni-
potentiary to Berlin and Vienna, and was abroad at the
time of his father's death in 1794.

Succeeding to his father's title, he became second Marquess
of Hertford, and took his seat in the House of Lords, but
took no part in the debates on political matters. The whole
of his ambition was centred on accruing to himself court
offices and appointments, and that ambition was certainly
well satisfied. In July 1804 he was appointed Master of
the Horse, and held that office for two years. In July
1807 he was invested Knight of the Garter, and appointed
Lord Chamberlain of the Household in March 1812. He
held the latter office for nine years, and in 1822, the year
of his death, was created Vice-Admiral of Suffolk. The
years of these appointments were the years of Hertford's
close attachment to the Prince Regent (afterwards George IV.),
whose devotion to Lady Hertford [1] was the amusement and

---

[1] This was Lord Hertford's second wife. In February 1768, he had
married Alicia Elizabeth, second daughter and co-heir of Herbert,
Viscount Windsor, rich, but not handsome. Her sister had married
Lord Mountstuart. 'It is odd,' wrote Walpole, 'that those two ugly
girls, though such great fortunes, should get the two best figures in
England, him (Beauchamp) and Lord Mountstuart' (*Letters*, vii. 280).

scandal of London. The year 1806 was an unhappy year for Mrs. Fitzherbert, since ' the young man,' says Creevy, meaning the Prince Regent, whom he more often designates as *Prinny*, ' fell in love with Lady Hertford, and used to cry, as I have often seen him do, in Mrs. Fitzherbert's presence ' [1] (*Creevy Papers*). The tears would run down his cheeks at dinner, so lovesick was he for Lady Hertford, and he would sit dumb for hours sighing of his love. A gracious prince, indeed! Lady Hertford retired to Ireland. ' We have no news here,' wrote Robert Ward to Viscount Lowther, ' except that the Prince has taken it into his head that he is in love with Lady Hertford, and that she has taken it into her head that it would be right to run away to Ireland as the best protection for her modesty ' (MSS. of Lord Lonsdale). It was while Lady Hertford was in high favour with ' Prinny' that Madame de Stael visited England. ' The great wonder of the time,' wrote Lady Holland to Mrs. Creevy, at Brighton, ' is Madame de Stael. . . . Her first appearance was at Lady Jersey's, where Lady Hertford also was, and looked most scornfully at her, pretending her determina-

---

Lady Beauchamp died on the 20th of February 1772. ' A terrible blow which I have long forseen has fallen on Lord Hertford's family,' wrote Walpole. ' His daughter-in-law, Lady Beauchamp, a most amiable and good young woman, is dead, and her husband half-distracted for her loss' (*Ibid.*, viii. 149). On the 20th of May 1776, he married, secondly, Isabella Anne Ingram Shepherd, daughter and co-heir of Charles, ninth and last Viscount Irvine, by his wife, Frances Gibson (born Shepheard). Viscount Irvine died in 1778, his wife in 1807. She left ' a very large fortune ' to the Hertfords.

[1] It was indirectly, through Mrs. Fitzherbert, that the prince had come into contact with Lady Hertford. Mrs. Fitzherbert was ' dotingly fond ' of Mimi (afterwards Mrs. Dawson Damer), the sister of Mr. Horace Seymour and niece of Lord Hertford, and when the Seymour family attempted to remove her from Mrs. Fitzherbert's care, she induced the prince to ' solicit the interest of Lord Hertford, as the head of the family. This brought about the acquaintance with Lady Hertford, and Mrs. Fitzherbert kept the child and lost the prince ' (*Croker Papers*, i. 123).

tion not to receive her as she was an *atheist* ! and immoral
woman !   This harsh resolve was mitigated by an observation very agreeable to the observer, that her personal *charms*
have greatly improved within the last twenty-five years.'
Lady Hertford herself had, it seems, great personal charms,
' such a degree of beauty as is rarely bestowed upon women,'
but her empire over the Regent rested, however, according
to Wraxall, ' from the first moment of its origin, more on
intellectual than on corporeal qualities,' and reposed principally ' on admiration or esteem.'   However, though
Wraxall would persuade us of this fact, the letter-writers,
and the satirists of the day had no such mercy.   A certain
lady,[1] refusing the Regent's advances, one day reminded
him that if all other ladies should fail him :—

> ' You must confess
> You 'll have your fav'rite M[archion]ess
> By whom, if rumour be believed,
> You privately are oft received.'

In one of Tom Moore's *Odes from Horace*, he makes the
Regent say :—

> ' Who will repair
> To M[anchester] Square
> And see if the gentle Marchesa be there?
> Go bid her haste hither
> And let her bring with her
> The newest No-Popery sermon that's going.
> Oh ! let her come with her dark tresses flowing,
> All gentle and juvenile, curly and gay,
> In the manner of—Ackermann's dresses for May !'

Again in a letter in *The Twopenny Postbag* purporting to be
from the Regent to Lord Yarmouth (Hertford's son), Tom
Moore makes the Regent say :—

---

[1] See *infra*.

'We missed you last night at the "hoary old sinner's" [Lord Hertford]
Who gave us as usual the cream of good dinners.[1]

.   .   .   .

Our next round of toasts was a fancy quite new
For we drank, and you'll own 'twas benevolent too,
To those well-meaning husbands, cits, parsons, or peers,
Whom we've any time honoured by kissing their dears,
This museum of wittols was comical rather,
Old H[er]t[for]d gave Massey[2] and *I* gave your father.'

One little fact may be amusing—Lady Hertford seems
to have affected red as the colour to wear while she was
the Regent's favourite.   Thus Lady Jerningham, while
describing a fête of December 1819, writes : ' The Prince
was hissed by the immense mob round the door, and Lady
Hertford, dressed in her scarlet crape, in a chair nearly
overturned.   But Bow Street attendants were in the Hall,
and she was ushered in safely.'   At the Spanish Ball which
was held a few days later, Lady Hertford was to be ' in
Scarlet Satin, Trimmed with crape of the same colour.   This
will make a very conspicuous appearance.'   The effect was
soon lost upon the prince.   He became king on the death
of George III. on 29th January 1820, and in the following
September Mr. Creevy was writing to Miss Ord, ' Do you
know the king is intent on turning out Lord Hertford to
make room for [Lord] Conyngham as Lord Chamberlain.'
Lady Conyngham was to be the new favourite.   ' Lady

---

[1] Lord Hertford's dinners were quite celebrated.

[2] Mrs. Massey had been seduced by Lord Hertford, the *second*
marquess, and it is possible this may have suggested the Becky Sharp
and Lord Steyne episode of *Vanity Fair.* (See *infra.*) In a scurrilous
cartoon, by George Cruikshank, in *The Scourge* of 2nd November 1812,
the Marquess of Hertford is made to say, ' As for business, I never had a
Head for 't, but I have laid the country under a *Massy* load of obligations in other respects . . . so give me the M[arquisateship] of H[ert-
for]d.'   In the same cartoon he is also represented as Lord Chamberlain gazing complacently at Lady Hertford, who is seated with the
Regent under a canopy.

T

Hertford's day is closed,' wrote Lady Jerningham, 'and
Lady Cunningham is now the meteor.' And it was only a
little while since Tom Moore had been laughing in his
Diary of a Politician :—

> 'Last night a concert—vastly gay
> Given by Lady Castlereagh.
> My Lord loves music, and we know
> Has two strings always to his bow.
> In choosing songs the Regent named
> *" Had I a heart for falsehood framed,"*
> While gentle Hertford begged and prayed
> For *" Young I am and sore afraid."* '

In 1821 the king had his way. Lord Hertford was
removed from office, his lady was out of favour, and 'the
old yellow chariot,' the incognito vehicle of the prince,
was seen no more in Manchester Square.[1] Lady Conyngham
was soon installed ' under the king's roof.' Her brother,
Mr. Denison, and her son, Lord Mountcharles, called upon
her ' to leave her fat and fair friend and to go abroad,' but
she treated their interference ' only with bursts of passion
and defiance, always relying on Lady Hertford's case as
her precedent and justification.' [2]

The second Marquess of Hertford died, on the 17th of
June 1822, at Hertford House, at the respectable age of
seventy-nine, and was buried at Ragley. ' Poor old Lord
Hertford is gone at last,' wrote Mr. Croker [3] to Sir

---

[1] Hertford House, Manchester Square (built in 1776, and finished in
1788), the present home of the Wallace Collection, was the residence
of the Marquess of Hertford

> ' Through M-nch-st-r Squ-r- took a canter just now
> Met the old yellow chariot, and made a low bow.'

laughs Tom Moore again in his *Diary*. It was certainly an offence to
recognise ' the old yellow chariot ' in this locality.

[2] *Creevy Papers* (ed. Sir Herbert Maxwell).

[3] Mr. Croker was a friend and sincere admirer of the third Marquess
of Hertford, who in his turn admired Mr. Croker's ability, both as a
member of Parliament, and a man of shrewd commonsense.

B. Blonfield; 'the will has not yet been opened, but it is known by the representation of the Attorney that he has tied up his estates as tight as he could.' All 'the personals' were left to Lady Hertford. 'He judged wisely and kindly,' wrote Croker, 'in making her the object of future attention from his family, and it is but just that he should *share* with her accumulations to which her great property no doubt contributed.' The injustice was, that since she had between thirty and forty thousand a year, that she should have *all* the personals, and his son Yarmouth (the third Marquess of Hertford) not £20,000 for his 'mise en campagne.' The landed estates which came to Yarmouth were supposed to amount to about £85,000 a year (namely £57,000 in Ireland, £8000 in Scotland, £15,000 in Warwick, £10,000 in Sudbourne), and since Lord Hertford had died a few days before Midsummer, the half year's rent then falling due, his successor would have £40,000 to start with, and as he probably would not begin at once to increase his expenses, he might enter the next year with a clear income of at least £90,000.[1]

The old marquess had, like his father before him, hoarded his riches, and ruled his family on a 'narrow and jealous system.' Mr. Croker hoped and believed that his successor, having felt the inconvenience of that system, would be just and liberal himself, and he believed he would, for he 'never knew a man so fixed on doing what he considered his duty.'

Lady Hertford survived her husband until April 1886. She was taken to Ragley to be buried, and was attended out of town 'by the carriages of the king and queen, the royal dukes, and more than thirty of the first nobility.'[2]

'Quite a crowd assembled yesterday (April 22),' wrote Greville, 'to see old Lady Hertford's funeral go by. The king sent all the royal carriages, and every other carriage

[1] *Croker Papers* (ed. L. J. Jennings).
[2] *Gent. Mag.* lxxxiv. 564.

in London was there, I believe—a pompous piece of folly, and the king's [William IV.] compliment rather a queer one, as the only ground on which she could claim such an honour was that of having been George the Fourth's mistress.'

Francis Charles Seymour - Conway, third Marquess of Hertford, the central figure of this chapter, was the only son of the second Marquess by his second wife. He was born in March 1777, succeeded to his father's title of Earl of Yarmouth on the death of his grandfather in 1794, graduated B.A. from St. Mary's Hall, Oxford, in 1796, and represented the family boroughs of Oxford, Lisburne, and Camelford in Parliament until he succeeded his father as Marquess of Hertford in 1822. Yet his reputation has been built up on no fame of Parliamentary career. The favourite and confidant of the Regent at the time when his mother was that prince's mistress ; the man about town commonly known as ' Red Herrings,' ' Bloaters ' or ' Whiskers,' from his fiery red hair and whiskers ; the husband of the many fathered ' Mie Mie ' ; Disraeli's ' Lord Monmouth ' ; Thackeray's ' Marquis of Steyne'—such are Hertford's unmistakable titles to remain in the memory, if not the esteem of posterity. Strange titles, yet sure ; for folly and vice no less, perhaps even more, than wisdom and virtue seem calculated to secure to men and women of all ages the interest of posterity, and a lasting, if not a desirable fame.

First as friend and confidant of the Regent, Hertford, then of course Lord Yarmouth, shared in all the counsels, good, bad, or indifferent of that prince,[1] and took his part

---

[1] In *The Scourge* of August 1st, 1814, a view is given of *the Lilliputian Navy*—' The *Yarmouth*, a stout British ship, lately employed in Russian service, distinguished by its figure head having a large pair of whiskers . . . a repeating frigate to the *Prince George*, in company of which ship it will most generally be seen.'

in the strife of politics concerning the Regency Bill. In February 1812, when the king's madness proved to be permanent, the restrictions on the Regent expired, and a permanent Regency Bill was passed. The prince, directly his chains were thrown off, though, being pacified by the loyal attitude of Perceval, he had determined to still retain the Tory ministry, was yet anxious to secure the friendship of the Whig lords. The result was, that by Yarmouth's advice, he wrote a letter to the Duke of York declaring he had 'no predilections to indulge or resentments to gratify,' but only a concern for the public good, towards which he desired the co-operation of some of his old Whig friends. This letter was parodied by Tom Moore :—

'At length, dearest Freddy, the moment is nigh
When with Perceval's leave I may throw my chains by,
And as time now is precious the first thing I do
Is to sit down and write a wise letter to you.

.   .   .   .   .   .

I meant before now to have sent you this letter
But *Yarmouth* and I thought perhaps 'twould be better
To wait till the Irish affairs were decided,
That is, till both Houses had prosed and divided
With all due appearance of thought and digestion,
For though *Hertford House* had long settled the question
I thought it but decent between me and you
That the two *other* Houses should settle it too.
I need not remind you how curiously bad
Our affairs were all looking when Father went mad,
A strait waistcoat on him and restrictions on me,
A more *limited* Monarchy could not well be.'

The Regent then goes on to say how he had been bidden to choose his own ministers under his restricted office, how he had done ' as old Royalty's self would have done,' [1] and

---

[1] In the political crisis of 1810, when the king's madness made the regency inevitable, the Opposition had hoped that a change of ministry would result. The prince, however, retained the ministry on the

had to his pleasure found that his action met with approbation at Hertford House :—

> 'The Marchioness called me a duteous old boy,
> And my Yarmouth's red whiskers grew redder for joy.'

Now though he had a free hand it pleased him to retain his *new friends* for,

> 'I cannot describe
> The delight I am in with the Perceval tribe.'[1]

Finally, after enumerating the 'successes' of the ministry, he comes to the point of his letter :—

> ''Twould please me if those I have humbugged so long
> With the notion (good men !) that I knew right from wrong
> Would a few of them join me—mind only a few—
> To let *too* much light in on me would not do.
> But even Grey's brightness shan't make me afraid
> While I've Camden and Eldon to fly to for shade.
>
> .   .   .   .
>
> As for Moira's high spirit, if aught can subdue it
> Sure joining with *Hertford* and *Yarmouth* will do it.'

The 'old friends' refused, as is well known. In the following May, Perceval was assassinated in the Lobby of the House; the Regent again unsuccessfully treated with the Whigs, and a Tory administration set in and remained unbroken for no less than fifteen years. In the March 1815, when Napoleon broke from Elba and landed in France, and the 'wonderful Hundred Days' had begun, Yarmouth was on uneasy terms with the Regent. 'Here we are certainly

ground that he wished to do nothing that would retard his father's recovery,

> 'And think,—only think—if our Father should find
> Upon graciously coming again to his mind
> That improvement had spoiled any favourite adviser.'

[1] Lady Jerningham wrote to Lady Bedingfield, on 18th February 1812, 'This is a great political day. The prince's restrictions are at an end, and He cannot find an administration. He wishes to make his Friends coalesce with Mr. Perceval. . . . It is thought that Lady Hertford has been gained by the Percevals.'

for war,' wrote the Hon. H. G. Bennett to Mr. Creevy:
' . . . Lord Spencer, the Carringtons, etc., are for peace,
and what is more amusing still, *Yarmouth*, who preaches
peace at the corners of the streets, and is in open war with
Papa and Mamma (Lord and Lady Hertford) upon that
subject. Prinny of course is for war.' Without doubt,
Yarmouth's opposition to war was in intention opposition
to the Regent, for there was now a coolness between them,
arising from the fact that the Regent had made overtures
to Yarmouth's mistress, Fanny Wilson, which, it is said,
she rejected, and Yarmouth revenged.[1] This was the
occasion of ' Peter Pindar's '[2] satire, '*A kick from Yarmouth
to Wales; Or, The Royal Sprain*' (1812). After describing
a certain banquet the satirist recounts how :—

> '. . . upon this night
> Our R[egent] with his stars bedight
> Had ogled long a lovely dame
> (I dare not now disclose her name)
> 'Twas Cupid's doing, wily lout,
> He plainly saw the *wit was out.*'

The Regent proceeded to seek a private interview with
the lady, she refused his advances in surprise, questioning
him :—

[1] It is quite impossible to say whether the story is true, but some
such circumstances seem to have arisen and to have caused great
scandal at the time. It has been sometimes thought that the Lady
referred to was Lady Yarmouth (Mie Mie), but considering that Lady
Yarmouth was in Paris, and under the care of Marshal Androche, at
least from 1806 onwards, and the incident recited by the poem belongs
to 1812, it obviously does not concern Lady Yarmouth. On the other
hand, Fanny Wilson was Yarmouth's favourite at the time, and in *The
Scourge* of November 2nd, 1812, he is represented as determined to give
up his relationship with ' Fanny Anny,' rather than lose his vice-
chamberlainship. That was evidently after the ' Royal Sprain.' However, the relations between the Regent and he were never so cordial
again.

[2] 'Peter Pindar' was the pseudonym of John Wolcot, the satirist,
(1738-1819).

'Has Dame F[i]tz[her]b[er]t, once your minion,
Entirely lost your heart's dominion?
. . . . .
Are J[e]r[se]y's charms now quite forgotten?'

The Regent continued to protest his love, and the **lady**
threatened him :—

'Should Lord Y[armou]th this way come
Dire evils may arise therefrom.
Excuse my harsh uncourtly tones,
I fear he'd break your Royal bones,
For he's a manly, noble swain.'

The prince kneeling before her, continued his addresses,
but at last ' some pitying seraph heard her cry,' and Lord
Yarmouth soon appeared.

'L—d Y—th's blood began to freeze
To see the R—t on his knees.
He guesses soon his R—l motions,
And swears he'll break up his devotions.'

Forthwith he proceeded to throw ' His H—ss sprawling
on his nose,' where he

'roll'd his fat unwieldy form
About like a porpoise in a storm.'

Then Lord Yarmouth raised him, and proceeded to vengeance.

'Your H—ss do excuse me pray
If I for your amusement lay
(Since we are free from rude beholders)
My cane about your royal shoulders.
There's fever in thy blood, I doubt,
Some exercise will drive it out.

The P—ce he roared like any bull,
L—d Y—th all with rage brim full,
Regardless of his R—l pain,
Brandished aloft the dreadful cane.

> The trembling Regent nimbly tripp'd
> And like a merry Andrew skipp'd,
> The lady, much to laughter mov'd,
> Said how in dancing he'd improv'd.'

Finally the lady begged Lord Yarmouth to desist :—

> 'The Peer complied.—His H—ss swore
> He ne'er had danc'd so much before.'

The result was, the Regent had to thank Yarmouth, not only for a sore back, but a sprained ankle.

> 'So let us sing long live the King,
> The Regent long live he,
> And when again he gets a sprain
> May we be there to see.'

This episode practically marked the end of Yarmouth's popularity with the Regent, and his investiture with the blue ribbon in the autumn of 1822, was due solely ' to his having purchased four seats in Parliament, since his father's death, and to his avowed intention of dealing still more largely in the same commodity.'   However, he still retained until his death in 1842 his office as Lord Warden of the Stannaries, which had been granted to him at the close of his term of office as Vice-Chamberlain of the Household.[1] Tom Moore refers to his tenure of the Stannaries, in one of his parodies of the Odes of Horace, in verses supposed to be addressed by the Regent to Yarmouth, during the wonderful Hundred Days—

> 'Come, Yarmouth, my boy, never trouble your brains
>   About what your old crony,
>   The Emperor boney,
> Is doing or brewing on Muscovy's plains.
>
> Nor tremble, my lad, at the state of our granneries
>   Should there come famine,
>   Still plenty to cram in
> You always shall have, my dear Lord of the Stanneries.

---

[1] March to July, 1812.

Brisk let us revel while revel we may
For the gay bloom of fifty soon passes,
       And then people get fat
       And infirm and—all that,
And a wig (I confess) so clumsily sits
That it frightens the little Loves out of their wits.

Thy *whiskers*, too, Yarmouth ! alas, even they
       Though so rosy they burn
       Too quickly must turn
(With a heart-breaking change for thy whiskers) to grey.' [1]

Concerning the investiture of the new Marquess with the Garter, in 1822, Sir Robert (then Mr.) Peel wrote to Croker, ' I am pleased at Lord Hertford getting the garter, pleased very disinterestedly and for his own sake merely, for I like him. He is a gentleman, and not an everyday one.' While under no delusion as to the fact that, even when he was Lord Yarmouth, and in spite of Peel's praise,[2] Hertford was known as ' a sharp, cunning, luxurious, avaricious man of the world, with some talent . . . and success at play,[3] by which he supplied himself with the large sums of money he required for his pleasures,' [4] one cannot fail to be struck

[1] This latter verse, says the author, is freely translated from the original ! which was—neque uno Luna *rubens* nitet Vultu.

[2] Peel kept his respect for Hertford to the last, even as Hertford kept his admiration of the wisdom and character of Peel. Thus, on Hertford's death, in spite of all the scandal and the shadow of sin that hung around the last years of his old friend, Peel's carriage followed his remains out of London. The Duke of Bedford, who himself dwelt in a glass house, was one of the first to throw a stone. ' What is the use of character and conduct in this world,' he wrote to Grenville,' if after such a life, death and will as Lord Hertford's, such a mark of respect is paid to his memory by the First Minister of this great country, and this not by the loose and profligate Lord Melbourne, but the good and honest and particular Sir Robert Peel ? ' Peel, like many another, probably realised that much of Lord Hertford's later life was the result of a diseased brain.

[3] Algernon Stanhope, brother of the Duchess of Leinster, was dismissed from the army for non-payment of his gambling debts to Yarmouth (see *Creevy Papers*).   [4] *Grenville Memoirs.*

by the contrast between the judgment passed on him by
Peel, in 1822, and the judgment passed on him by another
contemporary, less than twenty years later. John Mills, in
The Follies of the Day, could describe him no better than
as a 'pale, emaciated, dwindled shadow of humanity . . .
a man without one redeeming quality in the multitude
of his glaring vices.' 'He became puffed up with vulgar
pride, very unlike the real scion of a noble house,' says
Grenville, ' he loved nothing but dull pomp and ceremony,
and could only endure people who paid him court and
homage. After much coarse and vulgar gallantry, he formed
a connection with Lady Strachan (an infamous and shame-
less woman), which thenceforward determined all the habits
of his life.'

One cannot but ask the reason that this man so changed
for the worse after he became Lord Hertford, that he
became engulphed in a swirl of nauseating pleasures, that
he was satisfied, in spite of his gifts and his ability, to
live the life of a voluptuary, and to all intents and purposes
to be satisfied with it. There is something to be said for
the fact, that his wife ' Mie Mie ' (Maria Fagniani) was
certainly more fitted to help than to hinder him in his course
of profligacy. With the avaricious instinct of his grandfather he had married her, the child of three putative fathers,
the Marquess of Queensberry ('Old Q '), George Selwyn, and
the Marquis Fagniani (the husband of her mother), solely
for her great fortune, and her prospect of greater fortune
yet to come. In the year of their marriage (1798), she had
reached the mature (for a woman) age of twenty-seven,
while he was barely twenty-one. George Selwyn had
adopted her as his daughter, at the early age of four years,
and, whatever may have been the truth of the general
rumours, that he believed himself to be her father, it is
certain that he had a very real affection for the child, affection that was sorely tried by the whims of her mother, and

her mother's husband, who constantly kept Selwyn in dread of losing the child, by their recalling her to them. '*Combien de tems faut-il que je sois le jouet des caprices des autres ?*' he wrote to Lord Carlisle, in 1779, '. . . *ma patience et ma persévérance sont inépuisables sur ce qui regarde Mie Mie. . . . J'aurais des entretiens avec la mère qui ne sont pas toujours composés avec du miel, Hélas ! Rende, mi figlia mia.*' Finally he managed to keep possession of her,[1] and she grew up under his care and protection, and on his death, in 1791, inherited £30,000. The Duke of Queensberry was made residuary legatee : a quaint concession, considering their rival claims to paternity. In 1798, as we have seen, she became Lady Yarmouth, and in 1810, the Duke of Queensberry (' Old Q ') left her £150,000, and two houses,[2] making her husband residuary legatee. With such indeterminate parentage, and such an undesirable reputation, she was little likely to observe the meaning of the tie which bound her to a husband, to whom that tie probably meant little else but an increased income, and the possibility of a lawful heir. She bore him three children,[3] but even before the third, Lord Henry Seymour, was born, in 1805, she seems to have been carrying on an intrigue with Marshal

[1] In 1781, he wrote to Lord Carlisle, that he hoped he should never hear one syllable more from any one of the family—' It grows every day less likely, and yet when I am out of spirits that Dragon, among others, comes across me, and distresses me ; and the thought of what must happen to that child, if I am not alive to protect her.' On Selwyn's death, the Marquise Fagniani wrote to Lord Carlisle, desiring that the child should be delivered to her care, avowing she should come to no harm by her. ' *Est-il possible, Mylord, qu'une Mère veuille revoir sa Fille pour la rendre malheureuse ?* ' The young heiress was, however, not sacrificed to the schemes of her adventuress mother.

[2] These were 13 Piccadilly Terrace (now 139 Piccadilly) and 105 Piccadilly, afterwards Old Pulteney Hotel. This latter house became the private house of Lord Yarmouth, and many of the valuable possessions now in Hertford House were for a time housed there.

[3] Maria was born 2nd February 1799 ; Richard, Viscount Beauchamp, 23rd February 1800 ; Henry in 1805.

Androche. Yet she was with her husband, in Paris, in 1808, when Chevalier Jerningham wrote ' *Ld et Lady Yarmouth sont encore ici, quoique old quiz*[old Q], *soit mourant à Londres.*' Lord Yarmouth, it seems, had landed in France, *pour venir chercher sa Cara Sposa*, and was unduly detained there, by the rupture of the treaty of Amiens, until 1806. However, when he then returned to England his wife remained in Paris, finally putting herself under the charge of Marshal Androche. It does not appear that Yarmouth and his wife lived together after this date, but some mutual agreement was made as to financial matters. His occasional references to her in his letters are, not unnaturally, anything but cordial.[1]

Such was the state of affairs in 1822, when the second marquess died. For the rest of his life, the third marquess lived for the most part abroad, in Paris, Naples, or Milan, since his amusements were such as could not have been chosen for him in England. In 1827, he was envoy extraordinary to Nicholas I. of Russia, from whom, in 1821, he had received the order of St. Anne, for service before rendered at the Russian Court. Although seldom in England, Hertford took a lively interest in public affairs at home, especially as they affected his personal interest in his estates and fortune. Mr. Croker was his adviser as to the management of his estates[2] during his frequent absences and his constant correspondent, keeping him in touch with political and social happenings. And

[1] George Cruikshank, in *The Scourge*, November 2nd, 1812, makes Yarmouth say, ' My wife 's in a foreign country ; God be praised. I should like to be vice-(chamberlain), that is all.' His wife died in Rue Tailbout, Paris, 2nd March 1856, aged eighty-five, and was buried at Père-Lachaise.

[2] Mr. Croker, in fact, superintended his property, and as he refused to receive a salary, Lord Hertford always declared he would at his death compel Mr. Croker to receive some of the wealth he had preserved. However, he was not responsible for his actions in his last days, and the sum bequeathed to Mr. Croker, though as substantial as £23,000, was much less than he had intended.

here we come to the picture of Hertford as given by Lord Beaconsfield in the character of the 'Lord Monmouth' of *Coningsby*.

Allowing for the novelist's licence to manipulate his facts, Disraeli was writing a *roman-à-clef*, and the minutest comparison of whatever facts one can gather about the life and character of Hertford, with the portrait and character of Lord Monmouth, shows Disraeli with a master-hand pencilling the lines of the figure he had set out to portray with the genius of one who has studied the lines of human nature, in all its curves and contortions. The writer may be sententious, the characters may be sententious—it does not matter !—Lord Monmouth lives, not certainly as the figment of a creative brain, but as a photographic picture of the man he represents, and that man, though nowise idealised, yet at his best. Then there is ' Rigby,' the ubiquitous ' Rigby,' just the animal that Lord Monmouth wanted . . . with his clear head, his indefatigable industry, his audacious tongue, his ready and unscrupulous pen ; with all his dates, all his lampoons, all his private memoirs, and all his political intrigues.' It does not take us long to recognise Mr. Croker in Rigby, member for ' one of Lord Monmouth's boroughs . . . manager of Lord Monmouth's parliamentary influence, and his vast estates . . . his companion when in England, his correspondent when abroad ; hardly his counsellor, for Lord Monmouth never required advice.' And in the end, when we have spelt out the character of Croker from his correspondence, and the known facts of his life, we are left with the conclusion, that, though the sketch of Rigby may be vitriolic, it is nine parts true.[1] And the tenth part, which is, perhaps, after all, only the reservation made by

[1] At the same time, neither Disraeli nor Macaulay were justified in their attack on Mr. Croker, immediately after the death of the latter ; even if his character was irritating, it certainly was not vicious. as they would insinuate.

a private opinion, is the fact, that Croker's respect for the marquess arose from a more real regard for his ability and good-nature, than 'Rigby' would have been capable of feeling, and this was not weakened after the death of Hertford, even when it was discovered that the massive fortune that was supposed to be settled on Croker was not forthcoming.

'Lord Monmouth, who detested popular tumults as much as he despised public opinion,' writes Disraeli, 'had remained during the agitated year of 1831 in his luxurious retirement in Italy, contenting himself with opposing the Reform Bill by proxy. But when his correspondent, Mr. Rigby, had informed him, in the early part of the spring of 1832, of the probability of a change in the tactics of the Tory party . . . his Lordship, who was never wanting in energy when his own interests were concerned, immediately crossed the Alps and travelled to England . . . the Peers were in a fright. 'Twas a pity; there is scarcely a less dignified entity than a patrician in a panic.' Turning to the correspondence between Lord Hertford and Mr. Croker in 1831 and 1832, we find Lord Hertford writing to Mr. Croker from Naples in the spring of 1831 : 'With regard to reform I agree with you . . . that if it could be resisted *entirely* it would be the preferable course ; but is it . . . not well to give up a part to save some part ? . . . My idea in reform is to save as much as maybe, and even if I were in London, and saw an evident desire on the part of Lord G[rey] to throw over his Radicals, I should try to be to him as quinine, to strengthen him to throw off his impurities.' He strongly advised a formation of Government under the Duke of Wellington, and *not* under Sir Robert Peel, 'the worst Tory Government possible would be one under Sir Robert Peel.' [1] 'All I wish,' he concludes, 'is to pre-

---

[1] Yet in 1828, Hertford (then Lord Yarmouth) had seen that Peel must be minister. 'Croker,' he said, . . . 'we must have Peel minister. Everybody wishes for him, everybody would support him . . . I like him personally. I have no other motives than personal liking, and

serve to the king his crown, to myself my coronet and estate,' even though it might be ' burthened with a large property tax, which I should swallow as easily as any of Hawkins's black doses.' A little later, he was writing of the proposed Income Tax : ' I have always liked in the general sense of public advantage, and disliked in the sense of personal disadvantage, the Income Tax. . . . A property tax, valuing what you possess, like the Legacy Tax, is a detestable mode of raising money and purely revolutionary, for the collector could walk into Sir R. Peel's house, and ask him to pay a percentage on the pictures with which he has adorned the country, and into Lord Londonderry's, and ask for one of the diamonds with which he has enriched it.' By the early part of May 1831 it was clear the revolutionary torrent, carrying along with it the Reform Bill, could not be stemmed. ' I regretted the D's [Duke of Wellington's] denial of all change,' wrote Hertford to Croker, ' not as bad in itself, but as unwise and unnecessary. . . . I am glad Alborough and Oxford[1] die quietly in their beds, and with their old bedfellows, and am grateful for the trouble you have taken about them.'

In 1882, Hertford himself came to London on the news of the probably successful passage of the Reform Bill, but though he and the Duke of Wellington brought pressure to bear on ' the Waverers,'[2] whom the duke himself declared to be ' an object of detestation and

public respect, and I should be glad on every account to see him at the head of affairs.' The experiment had proved a failure.

[1] These were pocket boroughs, belonging to Lord Hertford, and were to be disfranchised. Mr. Creevy described Alborough as ' the rottenest of the rotten.'

[2] Lord Harrowby was one of the leaders of the party in the House known as the ' Waverers.' They voted against the second reading of the bill, as originally introduced, and for its second reading in its amended state, while they objected entirely to the principle of the measure, and by their indecision did much to help on the passage of the bill.

jealousy to our friends and supporters,' they could prevail nothing. 'England was lost for ever,' 'Rigby' constantly informed 'Coningsby' (Lord Monmouth's grandson), but the assembled guests still contrived to do justice to his grandfather's excellent dinners; nor did the impending ruin that awaited them prevent the Princess Colonna (Lady Strachan) from going to the opera, whither she very good-naturedly took 'Coningsby.' Having done what he could to prevent this 'ruin,' Lord Hertford once more retired to Italy, being unable to remain in 'this Radical-ridden country.' Before the close of 1884, the popular Reform ministry of 1882 was overturned, the Reform Parliament dissolved, and Peel became first minister.

The year 1886 found Hertford, 'who,' as Disraeli says of Lord Monmouth, 'was never greater than in adversity, and whose favourite excitement was to aim at the impossible,' once more in England, and ready to 'feast the country, patronise the borough, and diffuse that confidence in the Tory party which his presence never failed to do.' Moreover, notwithstanding the Reform Bill, with its Schedule A disfranchising so many boroughs, 'the prestige of his power had not sensibly diminished, for his essential resources were vast, and his intellect always made the most of his influence.' 'The Conservatives are feasting and spouting in all parts of the country, and rallying their forces,' wrote Greville. Meanwhile, there was a split in the Opposition, but it was probable they would reconcile their differences before Parliament met, and be ready to baffle the common enemy. However, the accession of the young Queen Victoria, in whose name both Whig and Tory blazoned their election posters, and shouted their election cries, brought a balance slightly in favour of the Tories, and Tory language was put into the queen's mouth when she delivered her speech, for it was obvious that this alone was palatable to the nation. The Tory majority secured, Lord Hertford retired once more to Paris. This was practically the last time he took any active interest in politics.

Meanwhile, the Strachan family, a mother and three daughters, had succeeded in drawing Lord Hertford into their clutches, playing upon the well-known fire of his desires to secure codicils to his will in their favour. First the mother, Lady Strachan, figured as his favourite. To her he at one time decided to bequeath his whole fortune, but altered his mind, partly because he objected to a cynical reference to her as his ' successor,' partly because he grew tired of her society and preferred that of her daughter Charlotte, afterwards Countess Zichy.   Sir Richard Strachan had left his three daughters to the care of Lord Hertford, and they lived in Lord Hertford's house until they were married.   Charlotte Strachan had been his favourite as early as October 1884.   Thus one of the numerous codicils to his will was written when he was abroad with her at that date.   It is dated at ' Munich, the Inn of the Golden Hirsch,' 18th October 1884.   It directs that in case of his death ' while abroad with Charlotte L. Strachan . . . all the transferable securities for money, cash, diamonds, and banker's travelling notes be given to the said Charlotte. . . . I advise Charlotte to entrust these securities if I die abroad, with the nearest respectable banker. . . . I warn her to beware of her mother's new connection, and as soon as she can to marry some respectable English gentleman.   Charlotte to open my secrets in carriages and boxes.   She knows how and where, and take her legacies. . . . Charlotte to take great care of Belle and Bezuies (two dogs) for love of me.'   In two or three years Charlotte became Countess Zichy, and she and her husband lived with Lord Hertford for some years.   The other sisters also married, after they had secured codicils from Hertford, one becoming Countess Berchtholdt, the other Princess Ruffo.

As the years went on, even the Countess Zichy and

her husband were too respectable company for the man who, with his increasing feebleness of mind and consuming passion for orgies and excitement, was being made the dupe of a still more unscrupulous adventurer than any of the members of the Strachan family—his valet, Nicholas Suisse, 'my head valet, an excellent man.' Willing to be employed in any work that his master might desire, Suisse, 'a showily dressed man, with features bearing a striking resemblance to those of a fox,' made himself indispensable to Lord Hertford, and introduced to him 'the company he liked to have sometimes to dine with him.' With these, 'the parasites that lived and throve upon a diseased mind,' his last days were spent. They ruled his movements, and kept him from his friends. He wrote a piteous note to Croker, 'I believe we are going to change, because *they* say so, but I do not know.' 'They' were determined to get rid of the Count and Countess Zichy, who had come over from Paris with Lord Hertford in 1841, and resided with him at Dorchester House, Park Lane, and imbued Hertford with that idea. At first when he was at all well he dined out at Richmond or Greenwich to be quit of the society of the Zichys, and enjoy that of his parasites, but finally determined that the Zichys should go. Hence he resolved to lie in bed as long as they remained, and 'this and some other broad hints induced them to go.' Then he got up, and 'by a strange *inconsequence* did that which he might have just as well have done if they had stayed '—went to dine with his usual company at Richmond. The drive to Richmond on a damp February night, the cold, unaired rooms of the hotel, and the late return at night, brought on a severe chill from which he never recovered. In less than a week Mr. Croker found him dangerously ill, but obstinate in his refusal to see a physician, 'being satisfied with Mr. Copeland, his old surgeon, and Mr. Fuller, his old apothecary.' When the physician was at last called in he could do nothing; the catarrh, which was little or nothing in itself, was too strong for organs enfeebled by palsy. On Tuesday, the 1st of March 1842, the week to the day after his last orgie at Richmond, he died peacefully among his own relations and friends, 'as he lay in a *chaise longue* in his library while they were making his bed in his bedroom.' His will was necessarily 'curious' with its codicils and its legacies. His own family was 'mentioned rather unkindly and little benefited,' his son, the fourth marquess, was residuary legatee, but the bulk of the estate went in legacies, which were disputed, to the Strachan family, while in seven different codicils separate sums were left to Nicholas Suisse, who altogether was to receive upwards of £20,000. Mr. Croker, as one of the executors of the will, incurred many calumnies for his prosecution of Suisse as the thief of a missing package containing a hundred thousand francs. Suisse was acquitted, but being put on trial on a second charge was found guilty, and ordered to pay the costs.

'In height, about the middle size, but somewhat portly and corpulent. His countenance was strongly marked; sagacity on the brow, sensuality in the mouth and jaw. His head was bald, but there were the remains of the rich brown locks, on which he had once prided himself. His large, deep-blue eye, morbid and yet piercing, showed that the secretions of his brain were apportioned, half to voluptuousness, half to commonsense. But his general mien was truly grand; full of a natural nobility, of which no one was more sensible than himself.' Such is Disraeli's description of the person of the Marquess of Hertford in his description of that of Lord Monmouth. In contrast, comes Thackeray's less dignified portrait of the 'Marquis of Steyne.' 'The great Lord of Steyne was standing by the fire, sipping coffee. . . . The candles lighted up his shining bald head, which was fringed with red hair. He

FRANCIS CHARLES SEYMOUR CONWAY, THIRD MARQUESS OF HERTFORD.
From an engraving in the British Museum. (Lawrence pinxt.)

had thick bushy eyebrows, with little twinkling bloodshot eyes, surrounded by a thousand wrinkles. His jaw was under hung, and when he laughed, two white buck teeth protruded themselves, and glistened savagely, in the midst of the grin. He had been dining with royal personages, and wore his garter and ribbons. A short man was his lordship, broad-chested, and bow-legged, but proud of the firmness of his foot and ankle, and always caressing his garter-knee.' For the rest, the Lord Steyne of *Vanity Fair* is too familiar a character to need any further description. He is to us, as he was to little Rawdon, ' that bald-headed man, with the large teeth,' and more ; and worse. But as for identifying Lord Steyne, whole heartedly, with the third Marquess of Hertford, that is an impossibility.

The facts of that veracious history of *Vanity Fair* puzzle us at every turn, if we slavishly pursue the idea, that Thackeray was intending a portraiture of the third marquess. If he was intending a portraiture at all, it was a composite photograph, for some of the facts and events of the career of Lord Steyne might belong to the second marquess, some to the third. But the most important thing to remember is that Thackeray was writing a novel, and he could play with his facts and his characters as he pleased. At the most, he singled out the Marquesses of Hertford, one or both, and clothed in stories of their lives the puppet of his own making, ' the richly dressed figure of the wicked nobleman . . . which Old Nick will fetch away at the end of the singular performance.'

Gaunt House is of course Hertford House, as Gaunt Square is Manchester Square. The mansions round are still in the comatose state of dowagerism. The famous ' *petits apartements* of Lord Steyne—one, Sir, fitted up all in ivory and white satin, another in ebony and black velvet,' [1] are unrecognisable in the elaborate

---

[1] The notorious Harriet Wilson describes these in her *Memoirs.*

alterations that necessarily took place before even Hertford House could become extensive enough to hold the vast treasury of art collected by the Marquesses of Hertford.

Maria Fagniani is hardly recognisable as the Marchioness of Steyne. At the same time, if Thackeray had been picturing Lady Hertford, the Regent's favourite, he would have chosen different facts to tell about her. Moreover we may, without stretching probability, assume that the Count de la Marche, otherwise the Abbé de la Marche, with whom Lord Steyne, when Lord Gaunt (the third marquess when Lord Yarmouth), fought a duel in '86, is none other than the Marshal Androche, on whose protection Maria Fagniani relied. The two sons of Lord Steyne, Lord Gaunt and Lord George Gaunt, are undoubtedly Lord Yarmouth (fourth marquess) and Lord Henry Seymour. Here again, in his account of their lives, Thackeray juggles with facts, and yet gives a distinct impression of the prototypes of his creations. Wenham, again, who puts 'his hand on his waistcoat, with a parliamentary air'; the smooth-tongued Wenham, of 'the fluent oratory which, in his place in Parliament, he had so often practised,' is unmistakably Mr. Croker; while Mr. Fiche, 'his lordship's confidential man,' who, after his lordship's death, returned to his native country, where he lived, much respected, and became Baron Ficci, can be none other than our fox-faced friend, Nicholas Suisse. And Becky? We may suggest many prototypes for Becky; we may suppose her career was suggested by the seduction of Mrs. Massey by the second marquess;[1] we may suppose she found her origin in Fanny Wilson, or Amy Wilson, sisters of the more notorious Harriet, and once the reigning favourites of the third marquess; we may suppose she was one of the many unknown admirations, of the 'worn-out, wicked old man.' But we had far better not suppose at all. She is Thackeray's own creation, 'the

[1] A *most* improbable suggestion.

Becky puppet . . . uncommonly flexible in the joints, and lively on the wire '—and she is incomparable.

' Lord George Gaunt,' so Thackeray tells us, was invested with ' the Order of the Straight Waistcoat,' and the dark presentiment, lest the awful ancestral curse should come down on him, continually haunted Lord Steyne, for once or twice the evil had before broken out in his own family. ' He tried to lay the horrid bedside ghost in Red Seas of wine and jollity, and lost sight of it sometimes in the crowd and rout of his pleasures. But it always came back to him when alone, and seemed to grow more threatening with years.' One of the medical men who attended the third marquess of Hertford on his deathbed, wrote to Mr. Croker that ' the brain of the late Marquess of Hertford was a diseased brain, and had long been so—the partial paralysis, speechlessness, and other long-standing direct cerebral symptoms, demonstrate it.' Mr. Croker himself firmly believed this was true. Thus, he wrote to the Marquess of Wellesley, ' the lamentable doings of his latter years were neither more nor less than *insanity*. You know, and he was himself well aware, that there is hereditary madness in his family.[1] He often talked, and even wrote about it to me.'

This, then, was the secret of the wasted, misguided life of the third Marquess of Hertford. It has been easy for a smug, self-humbugged, early Victorianism to condemn him, to look askance at the mention of his name, to remember suggestive facts, without attempting to search for causes. But while this attitude is easy, it is not profitable, not healthy, and not just. There is also the dispassionate, ' un-moral ' attitude of a philosopher, who discusses ethics from a logical standpoint. Professor Goldwin Smith writes of the

---

[1] Edward Seymour, ninth Duke of Somerset, and second cousin of the third marquess, was a harmless maniac. He died in 1792. There are probably other examples among the less well-known characters of the family.

'Marquis of Steyne,' he ' is an organism, and like all other organisms, so long as he succeeds in maintaining himself against competing organisms, is able to make good his title to existence under the law of natural selection.   He has his pleasures ; they are not those of a St. Paul, or a Shakespeare, or a Wilberforce, but they are his.   They make him happy, according to the only measure of happiness which he can conceive. . . . In the name of what do you peremptorily summon him to return to the path of virtue ? In the name of altruistic pleasure ?   He happens to be one of those organisms which are not capable of it.   In the name of a state of society which is to come into existence long after he has mouldered to dust in the family mausoleum of the Gaunts ?   His reply will be, that as a sensible man, he lives for the present, not for a future in which he will have no share. . . .' [1]

Tiresome though a middle course may be, we have here, as so often, to steer towards it, for neither of these attitudes can satisfy or convince.   The facts which the early Victorian blushes to think on, which the dispassionate philosopher looks straight in the face, and defies another man to condemn, cannot be contradicted, but they may be put aside and forgotten, as the ravings of a fever patient are forgotten, when the cause is known.   In an honest attempt to realise something of the character of the third Marquess of Hertford, one is bound to conclude that his last years were overshadowed by madness, and that the direction his madness took was not unnatural for one whose mother had been a king's mistress, and who had himself spent his early days as a favourite under the Regency.

Meanwhile, there are other sides to his character which are generally forgotten, the hundred and one little acts of kindness and generosity which are constantly appearing through-

---

[1] Goldwin Smith, *Guesses at the Riddle of Existence*, pp. 191-244.

out the earlier years of his life, made Mr. Croker call him 'the most generous and most friendly of men . . . a bitter foe, but an unbounded friend.'   On the other hand, he 'always stickled about *right*, and while he was giving away hundreds as *bounty* and *favour*, he would resist a *claim* of twopence.' Apropos of this, Mr. Croker quotes an amusing incident. One day, when out of Parliament, he came all the way from Seymour Place to the Admiralty to *frank* a letter to his servant in the country, containing an order for a reception which would cost him at least £500.   He saved six-pence by his walk, and yet if he had been tired, he would have got into a hackney coach and paid half-a-crown fare to save sixpence !   On the other hand, there is one instance of his kindness and thoughtfulness which, approved or not, may not be forgotten.   When Fanny Wilson, his once mistress, lay dying, she asked that he should come and see her.   He answered her call directly, and though he 'seemed afraid of feeling too much,' spared no care or expense to see that everything possible should be done for her, and himself wished her a ' God bless you ' before she died.

Further, when we feast our eyes at the Wallace Collec-tion, we must not forget that we owe much of our pleasure to the third Marquess of Hertford.[1] ' He showed us,' says Harriet Wilson, ' miniatures by the most celebrated artists of at least half a hundred lovely women . . . all beauti-fully executed, and no one with any knowledge of painting could hear him expatiate on their various merits without feeling that he was qualified to preside at the Royal Academy itself.   The light, the shade, the harmony of colours, the vice of English painters, the striking characters of Dutch artists.   *Ma foi !* No such thing as foisting sham Van-dykes or copies from Rubens, on Lord Hertford.'   And

[1] As early as 1810, pictures, etc., were being acquired by him in open market, and the year 1823 witnessed many purchases at Christie's. Disraeli mentions the wonderful pictures of Boucher belonging to Lord Monmouth.

besides miniatures, he had ' a vast collection of gold and
silver coins, portraits, drawings, curious snuff-boxes and
watches.' How well we know the look of them, as they
recline silently in their long glass cases. And how often
they rouse the admiration of a strict and conventional
visitor, who would hardly dare to mutter the name of the
' Marquis of Steyne.'

We must turn to Harriet Wilson again, if we would
put one more characteristic touch to the picture of
Lord Hertford. ' Lord Hertford possesses,' she wrote,
' more general knowledge than any one I know . . . he
appears to be *au fait* on every subject one can possibly
imagine. Talk to him of drawing, or horse-riding, painting, or cock-fighting ; rhyming, cooking, or fencing ; profligacy or morals ; religion of whatever creed ; languages,
living or dead ; claret or burgundy ; champagne or black-
cap ; furnishing houses or riding hobbies ; the flavour of
venison or the breeding of poll parrots, and you might
swear that he had served his apprenticeship to every one
of them.' ' I always liked him,' she remarks elsewhere.
' I like a man who can talk, and contribute to the amusement of whatever society he may be placed in.'

The picture of the third marquess is finished. It may
be crude, it may be whimsical, but it is sincere, and, if for
this reason only, may ask for consideration. The shadow
may not be taken for the light, nor ugliness for beauty, but
too often we fail to see anything beyond the shadow, and
too often forget that the ugly and the beautiful are very
near allied.

Richard Seymour Conway, eldest son of the third marquess,
known from 1822 until his father's death as Earl of Yarmouth, became fourth marquess in 1842. Like his brother,
Lord Henry Seymour,[1] he had already spent much of his

---

[1] Lord Henry (1805-1859) was the founder of the Jockey Club at
Paris, in 1830. He is said to have been rarely, if ever, in England, but

life in Paris, and after he became marquess he abandoned
his career as a diplomatist and politician, to which he had
been inclined,[1] and devoted himself, his life, and his wealth
to continuing and enriching his father's collection of art
treasures. For a long time he lived in rooms in a house at
the corner of Rue Laffitte, and during his later years at
Bagatelle, a mansion on the outskirts of Paris. He never
married, and spent only a minimum of his income on the
ordinary needs of life. He was in truth a born collector,
and was gifted with all the patience, knowledge, wealth,
enthusiasm and opportunity, which are the *sine qua non* of
a collector, whose attention is directed to securing some of
the masterpieces of every school of painting, and some of
the most exquisite pieces of craftsmanship that the world
has ever seen. And chief among his agents and assistants
was his half-brother, ' Monsieur Richard,' the natural son of
his mother, Maria (Fagniani), Marchioness of Hertford.[2]
This ' Monsieur Richard,' afterwards Sir Richard Wallace,
had been born in London on 26th July 1818, and had been
known in his early life as Richard Jackson. Being
educated entirely under the supervision of his mother, his
tastes, as hers, were more French than English, and yet

to have lived an eccentric life in Paris, interesting himself mostly in
horses, and horse breeding. He was a well-known character in Paris,
and figured in the carnivals of 1834 and 1835, when he attempted to
introduce the Italian custom of throwing comfits and coins among
the crowd. He inherited his mother's fortune, in 1856, and on his
death three years later, left the residue of his property to the Paris
hospitals, and ' legacies' for the support of four favourite horses,
which were never to be saddled again.

[1] He had been Attaché at the embassies of Paris and Constanti-
nople, and had sat in Parliament as member for Antrim. He was
made Commander of the Legion of Honour of France, 14th November
1855.

[2] Possibly by Marshal Androche. The theory that ' Monsieur
Richard' was the natural son of the fourth marquess, when only a boy
of eighteen, is most improbable.

he was always proud of his English extraction, and in later years, from 1878 to 1885, represented Lisburn (Ireland) in Parliament. All his early life he was, however, well known in French society, especially among art circles, and as long as his half-brother lived he was his devoted friend, adviser, and agent. When, in 1870, the fourth marquess died,[1] the whole of his collection, his houses in London and Paris and estates in Ireland, which secured an income of £50,000 a year, were bequeathed to ' Monsieur Richard.' The titles and other estates belonging to the marquess went, in failure of heirs in the direct line, to his cousin and heir-male, Francis Hugh George Seymour, son and heir of Admiral Sir George Francis Seymour,[2] son of Lord Hugh Seymour, and grandson of the first Marquess of Hertford.[3] His son, Hugh de Grey Seymour, is the present marquess (see later).

' Monsieur Richard,' afterwards Sir Richard Wallace, may still remain within our horizon as the child of ' Mie Mie ' (Lady Hertford), and as the possessor of the Hertford collection, to which he himself made very large additions. During the siege of Paris (1870-1),[4] which took place immediately after the death of the fourth marquess, Wallace equipped an ambulance under the name of the Hertford Ambulance, attached to the 13th corps d'armée, and two others, one under English and another under French doctors, for service in Paris itself. . He also founded and endowed the Hertford British Hospital for the use of British subjects, and subscribed 100,000 francs to the fund in aid of those whom the bombardment had ruined. His

[1] He was buried at Père-Lachaise, as his mother had been before him, and as his half brother and friend, Sir Richard Wallace (Monsieur Richard), was to be twenty years after him.

[2] His only brother, Lord Henry Seymour, had died in 1859.

[3] Lord Hugh Seymour was fifth son of the first marquess. His three elder brothers had died without heirs.

[4] See *La Guerre de* 1870-1, Paris, 1908.

sympathy for Paris was not one of words but of deeds and gifts, and his name was and is both honoured and loved in France.[1]   At the close of the Franco-Prussian war he came to England, and bringing with him his wonderful collection, added it to the treasures already gathered in Hertford House. He was in 1871 made a baronet for his services in France, and in 1878 a Knight Commander of the Bath for his services as Commissioner to the Paris Exhibition.   France had already given him the Legion d'honneur.

The death of his only son,[2] about 1875, left him without an heir, and instead of turning to France and offering his valued possessions to the Louvre, he offered them before his death to the British Government, on condition that the collection should not be dispersed but retained in Hertford House in the surroundings he himself had devised.   Government officials demurred, and received the offer so coldly that one less impersonal and less patriotic than Sir Richard would have turned to France.   On his death in 1890 he left the whole of his possessions to his wife, Lady Wallace, who on her death finally conceded all the treasures of Hertford House to the British nation, on condition that the Government should house them in a central part of London, in a special museum built to contain ' The Wallace Collection ' only, ' unmixed with other objects of art.'   Finally, the original wish of Sir Richard was fulfilled.   Hertford House itself was altered, arranged, and adapted to hold the collection for public view, and the Hertford treasures rest, as far as possible, in the atmosphere of their original surroundings.

[1] Even to the naming of drinking fountains in Paris, ' *Fontaines Wallace.*'

[2] Wallace had, in 1871, married Julie Amelié Charlotte, daughter of Bernard Castelnau, a French officer.

CHAPTER XI

SOME 'OCEAN SWELLS' AND OTHERS: A CHAPTER OF PEOPLE AND FACTS

'The full sea rolls and thunders
  In glory and in glee.
O bury me not in the senseless earth,
  But in the living sea !

Ay, bury me where it surges
  A thousand miles from shore,
And in its brotherly unrest
  I 'll range for evermore.'

W. E. HENLEY, 1876.

THE sea has made its call to many members of the Seymour family, from the time of Thomas Seymour of Sudeley, the Lord High Admiral, and his nephew Henry, the admiral of Spanish Armada fame, to the present day.

Hugh Seymour Conway, the fifth son of the first Marquess of Hertford, being born on 29th April 1759, entered the Navy in 1770 'in hopes of becoming a lasting ornament and support to his country.' He was stationed on board *The Pearl* on the Newfoundland station, under the command of Captain John Leveson Gower. Six years later, after service in the Mediterranean and the West Indies, he was promoted to be lieutenant. In 1778 he was made commander, and in the next year captain. As Commander of *The Ambuscade* in the Channel in 1780, and of the *Latona* in 1782, when the latter vessel was attached to the fleet under Lord Howe for the relief of Gibraltar,[1] he did good service at this critical period of England's imperial

---

[1] His brother, George, was also present, and according to Walpole, was ' delighted to have tapped his warfare with the siege of Gibraltar, and was burning to stride to America' (*Letters*, xii. 5).

life. The relief of Gibraltar, following close upon West
Indian victories, made France anxious for the peace which
came in January 1788. Conway [1] retired to England, took
a house in Conduit Street with his younger brother George,
and his friend 'Jack' Payne (John Willet Payne), whose
restless energy made him an excellent soldier, but a bad
friend. The three men led an irregular and convivial life,
and were soon on intimate terms with the Prince of Wales
and his undesirable company. However, Captain Conway
was more or less rescued from these surroundings by his
marriage with Lady Horatia Waldegrave on 3rd April 1786.
Horace Walpole, to whom both the bride and bridegroom
were related,[2] and who therefore could find no fault in either
of them, wrote the news of the engagement to Sir Horace
Mann, adding of bridegroom, 'he is one of the first marine
characters, and has every quality that would adorn any
profession, but the striking resemblance between the lovers
are good-nature and beauty.' To another friend he wrote :
'It makes me very happy indeed, as she (Lady Horatia)
has found one of the most amiable men in England, and of
a character the most universally esteemed.' A few months
later, Walpole was proudly writing that he had been
presented to the Prince of Wales, 'and by my niece, Lady
Horatia's marriage with Captain Conway, who is a principal
favourite of his Royal Highness, I have dined with the
Prince at Lord Hertford's, and since at his own palace, where
he was pleased to give a dinner to the two families who
in fact were one before.' [3]

During the Spanish armament of 1790, Captain Conway
commanded the *Canada*, and while at sea was accidentally

[1] He should not, by rights, be called Seymour, until after 1794, as
until the death of the first marquess, the whole family retained the surname of Conway.

[2] Lord Hugh's grandmother was sister to Lady Horatia's grandmother, who was Horace Walpole's mother.

[3] *Letters*, xiii. 383.

struck on the head by the lead as soundings were being taken. He had to live in retirement in the country for some time after this, and in May 1791, Walpole wrote, 'Poor Hugh Conway, though his life has long been safe, still suffers at times from his dreadful blow, and has not yet been able to come to town, nor will Lord Chatham's humanity put his ship in commission.' However, in February 1798, he was appointed to the *Leviathan*, in which he accompanied Lord Hood to the Mediterranean.[1] His active service then covered a long period, as, after being sent home with dispatches, he resumed his command of the *Leviathan* which, being attached to the fleet under Lord Howe, took distinguished part in the actions of May and June 1794. Early in 1795 he was moved to the *Sanspareil*, which he had captured in June 1794, and being promoted to flag rank, hoisted his flag on that ship, and in it took part in the action off Lorient on 23rd June of that year. In March 1798 he was appointed one of the Lords of the Admiralty, and in February 1799 became Vice-Admiral.

In the following summer he was appointed as Commander-in-chief of the Leeward Islands, and effected the capture of the Dutch settlement of Surinam. At the beginning of 1800 he was removed to the Jamaica station, where he was seized with fever, and died on the 12th of September 1801. He was at sea at the time of his death on board the *Tisiphone*, having been ordered by his physicians to leave the island on account of his health.[2] His wife, Lady Horatia, had already been obliged to return to England on account of her ill-health, and had died a few months before her husband. Their family consisted of seven children, four sons and

---

[1] In this year, by the creation of his father as marquess, he became Lord Hugh Seymour Conway.

[2] His body was brought to England, and buried in great state at Ragley.

four daughters. Of the two eldest sons, Walpole wrote in 1795 that 'Lady Horatio with her two glorious eldest boys' had arrived on a visit to him, 'the second especially is a bold miniature of his mother, and consequently beautiful.' These 'two glorious boys' were George Francis Seymour, afterwards Admiral of the Fleet, and Hugh Henry John Seymour, afterwards Lieutenant-Colonel.[1] The third son, Horace Beauchamp Seymour, interests us here, more especially for the sake of his son, Frederick Beauchamp Paget Seymour, Lord Alcester, who also became Admiral.

George Francis Seymour was born in 1787, and ten years later entered the Navy, on board the *Princess Augusta*, and from March 1798 to September 1801 was with his father, on the *Sanspareil*, in the Channel and West Indies. From 1802-3 he was on the *Endymion*, mostly on home station, but towards the end of 1803 was sent out to the *Victory*, the flagship of Lord Nelson. In 1804, he was confirmed lieutenant, and was on the *Donegal*, when she took part in the chase of the allied fleet to the West Indies, and back, and in the capture of the Spanish ship *El Rajo*, immediately after Trafalgar. He was appointed commander in January 1806, and joining the *Northumberland*, the flagship of Sir Alexander Cochrane, took part in the battle of St. Domingo, in the following February. Here he was severely wounded in the jaw by grape shot.[2] Two days later, he was appointed to the

---

[1] Hugh Henry John (1790-1821), was equerry to George IV., and M.P. for County Antrim. He married Lady Charlotte, only daughter of George, first Marquess of Cholmondeley, and had an only son, Hugh Horatio. The latter had two children, Hugh Francis and Charlotte Susan. Frederick Charles William (1797-1856), fourth son of Lord Hugh, married, firstly, Lady Mary Gordon, (died 1825) daughter of George, ninth Marquess of Huntly, by whom he had one son (Conway Frederick Charles), and one daughter (Hon. Mary Frederica) ; secondly, Lady Augusta Hervey, eldest daughter of Frederick, first Marquess of Bristol, by whom he had three sons (Frederick, Arthur, Horace) and three daughters (Eliza Horatia, Augusta, and Charlotte).

[2] He received a pension of £250 for this wound in 1816.

Kingfisher sloop. On the 14th of May, the *Pallas*, commanded by Lord Cochrane (tenth Earl of Dundonald), when detached from the squadron, and reconnoitring the French fleet, was roughly handled by a French frigate, *Minerva*, having lost her fore-topmast, and her main topsail yard, would probably have perished if it had not been for the *Kingfisher*, which ran in, and took her in tow.

In the following July, Seymour was appointed to the *Aurora*, in the Mediterranean, from which, in February 1808, he was transferred to the *Pallas*, the vessel he had saved, now on the home station. A year later, in April 1809, the *Pallas* was attached to the fleet, with Lord Gambier, off the Basque Roads. While stationed there, he made a gallant attempt to support Lord Cochrane in his hazardous attack on the French fleet. As is well known, the attack failed, simply through the tacit refusal of Lord Gambier to support Lord Cochrane. The great opportunity was wholly lost. Cochrane returned to England, opposed the vote of thanks to Lord Gambier, in the House of Commons, was court-martialled and disgraced. Seymour, however, supported him loyally, declaring at the court-martial, that Cochrane was right, the whole of the French fleet might have been destroyed had Gambier allowed him even half the fleet.[1]

After several other appointments, Seymour was made a C.B. in 1815, was Sergeant-at-arms to the House of Lords from 1818 to 1841, naval aide-de-camp to William IV. from August to November 1830, and from that date to the king's death, Master of the Robes. Raised to the rank of rear-admiral in November 1841, he became a Lord of the Admiralty from that year, until 1844, when he was appointed Commander-in-chief in the Pacific. Difficulties with regard to George Pritchard, missionary and consul at Tahiti, arose during his term of office in the Pacific, and by his 'tact,

[1] Dundonald, *Autobiography of a Seaman*.

ADMIRAL GEORGE FRANCIS SEYMOUR.
From an engraving in the British Museum. (Francis Holl sculpt.)

ability, and decision,' he was instrumental in quieting
the antagonism between France and England at that
date.[1]   In March 1850 he was made vice-admiral, two years
later K.C.B., was Commander-in-chief on the North America
and West Indies station from January 1851 to November
1853, and from 1853 to 1859 at Portsmouth.   In May,
1857, he was promoted to the rank of admiral, was nominated
a G.C.B. three years later, was made rear-admiral in April
1863, vice-admiral in September 1865, and admiral of the fleet
in November 1866.   He died in January 1870 leaving a widow
(Georgiana, daughter of Sir George Cranfield Berkeley, whom
he had married in 1811), and seven children, three sons
and four daughters.   In the following August, his eldest son,[2]
Francis George Hugh, became fifth Marquess of Hertford.

[1] George Pritchard took the part of Pomare, the queen of the Society
Islands, who having received the religion he brought her, refused to
allow two French priests to land in her dominions. A long quarrel
ensued, resulting in the annexation of the islands by France, in 1843.
Pritchard came to England to lay the case of the dispossessed queen
before the Government, and to describe the outrages inflicted on
several British subjects. Finding his efforts unavailing, he returned
to the Pacific, was imprisoned by the French for encouraging disaffec-
tion among the natives, but was released on condition that he left
the islands for ever. The English Government demanded an apology
and pecuniary reparation of Pritchard's losses. The difficulty was
adjusted in 1845.

[2] The other sons were (1) Henry George (1818-1869), vice-admiral
R.N., C.B., and M.P. for County Antrim, and from 1865 to 1869, a
Lord of the Admiralty. He married Sophia Margaret, eldest daughter
of Derick Hoste, of Barwick Hall, Norfolk, and had two sons, George
Hoste and Charles Derick, and two daughters, Alexandra and Emily ;
(2) Lord William Frederick Ernest, K.C.V.O. (b. 1838), created general
1902, who served with the Baltic fleet during the Russian War 1854,
and in the Crimea 1856, and has seen much other active service, and
held many important appointments. He married, on the 31st of August
1871, the Hon. Eva Anna Caroline Douglas-Pennant, daughter of
Edward Gordon, Baron Penrhyn, and has a son and four daughters.
The four daughters (of Sir George Francis Seymour) were Georgiana
Isabella (married Charles Corkran of Long Ditton), Emily Charlotte
(married William, second Baron Harlech), Matilda Horatia (married

Francis George, fifth Marquess of Hertford, was born on 11th February 1812, and was educated at Harrow, entered the Army, as lieutenant in the Scots Fusilier Guards, in July 1827, and after a series of promotions, finally reached the rank of general in 1876, and was placed on the retired list in 1881. For several years he was attached to the household of the Prince Consort, as Equerry and Groom of the Robes, and was appointed Lord Chamberlain; four years after he became marquess, being at the same time made Privy Councillor. In 1879 he resigned his office as Chamberlain, and was made a G.C.B. He died at Ragley on the 25th of January 1884, from injuries caused by a fall from his horse while hunting with the Warwickshire hounds. In May 1839 he had married Lady Emily Murray, sixth daughter of William, third Earl of Mansfield, by whom he left surviving issue, four sons and five daughters. His eldest son,[1] Hugh de Grey Seymour, is the present and sixth Marquess of Hertford.[2] George Francis Alexander, Earl of Yarmouth (born 1871), the eldest son of the present marquess,[3] like his ancestor, the third marquess, rejoices in the nickname, ' The Bloater.' Having been for two years lieutenant in the 3rd Battalion Black Watch, he is now lieutenant in the Warwickshire Yeomanry. With the experience of over five years on the American stage behind him, he is now known

Lieut.-Col. Cecil Rice), Laura Williamina (married H.S.H. Prince Victor of Hohenlohe Langenburg, Count Gleichen).

[1] The other three sons were Lord Albert Charles (died 1891); Lord Ernest James; Rev. Lord Victor Alexander. The five daughters Lady Horatia Elizabeth, Lady Florence Catherine, Lady Georgina Emily, Lady Constance Adelaide, and Lady Mary Margaret.

[2] He married the Hon. Mary Hood, daughter of first Viscount Bridport, in 1868.

[3] The other children of the present marquess are Lord Henry Charles Seymour (served in S. Africa, 1900-2, and as A.D.C. to Lord Milner); Lord Edward Beauchamp Seymour, also served in S. Africa; Lord George Frederick Seymour, Lieut. R.N.; Lady Emily Walker; Lady Victoria de Trafford, and Lady Jane Carleton.

as a writer of musical comedy, his play, *The Pigeon House*,
having been produced first at Cardiff, and afterwards at
the Court Theatre, London, this year (1910). He himself
played the principal part of Victor de Meneval, under his
stage name of Eric Hope.

Horace Beauchamp Seymour, third son of Lord Hugh
Seymour, was a soldier, and served as Lord Anglesey's aide-
de-camp at Waterloo. Mr. Croker recounts how he sometimes told tales of the battle. On the eventful day, he
himself had been sent about 2 o'clock to the extreme left
by the Duke of Wellington, with some orders. He there
heard a report that the Prussians were near, and thinking
it best to ascertain the fact himself galloped on until he met
and spoke with the Prussian advance, and then hastened
back to tell Lord Wellington. The duke ordered Seymour
to ride back to Bülow, with a request to send him 4000
infantry to fill up his lines. In crossing the Jenappes
Chaussée to fulfil this mission, Seymour was taken by the
French cavalry, but the duke seeing his capture sent some
dragoons to rescue him. In the midst of the fight, in which
he had five horses shot under him, he was next Lord
Anglesey when he was shot, and heard him cry out, ' I
have got it at last,' and heard the duke's answer, ' No ;
Have you, by God ? ' One moment, when the smoke
cleared away, he was riding near the duke, and saw the
cuirassiers so close to them that it was only by a very
sudden run they avoided being taken. This was when the
French cavalry had possesssion of the Plateau, and the
English squares and French squadrons seemed almost for
a short time hardly taking notice of each other. It was
almost impossible to distinguish Buonaparte and his staff
to be sure of them, but ' early in the day, we saw a body
moving along the French line, which we guessed was him
and his staff.' While the cuirassiers had possession, Seymour
saw one Frenchman place his sabre on one of the English

cannons, ' as much as to mark it, and say this is mine.'[1]
Sir Horace married twice, first, in 1818, Elizabeth Malet,
daughter of Sir Lawrence Park, baronet, who died in 1827 ;
secondly, in 1835, Frances Isabella, daughter of William
Stephen Poyntz, and widow of Robert Cotton St. John,
eighteenth Baron Clinton. By his first wife, he had two
sons and a daughter.[2]   He died in November 1851, and his
elder son, Charles Francis, was killed at Inkerman, three
years later.

Frederick Beauchamp Paget, his second son, entered the
Navy in January 1834. From 1844 to 1847 he served as
flag-lieutenant to his uncle, Sir George Francis Seymour,
then Commander-in-chief in the Pacific, and was promoted
to be commander in 1847.   After distinguished service as
a volunteer on the staff of General Godwin in Burma, in
1852 he was commissioned for the West India Station,
whence he was recalled in 1854 to serve against Russia,
in the White Sea, in the squadron under Commander
Erasmus Ommanney.   In May 1855 he took the *Meteor*
floating battery out to the Crimea, and in the summer of
1856 brought it back to Portsmouth, ' two feats of sea-
manship scarcely less dangerous than any war services.'
From 1857 to 1865 he was commanding the *Pelorus*, on
the Australian Station, and in 1860-1 commanded the
Naval Brigade in the atrocious Maori War in New
Zealand.   In the end, ' the victory and the earthworks '
remained to the English, but the glory lay with those
whose message that they would fight for ever and for ever
and for ever (aké, aké, aké !) may not be forgotten in
England or New Zealand.

Commander Seymour was made a C.B. for his services.
After various promotions and commands, he was finally

---

[1] *Croker Papers.*

[2] This daughter was Adelaide Horatia Elizabeth, who married
Frederick, fourth Earl Spencer. She died in October 1887.

made a vice-admiral in 1876, a K.C.B. in 1877, and from 1880 to 1888 was Commander-in-chief in the Mediterranean. Thus in 1880 he was commanding the European squadron at Gravosa, when Mr. Gladstone's proposal that the fleet should sequester the Customs due at Smyrna, until Turkey consented to surrender Dulcigno, was met by the submission of the Sultan (Abdul Hamid), who yielded 'not to a threat of coercion from Europe, but to the knowledge that Great Britain had asked Europe to coerce.[1] On the dispersal of the fleet, Seymour received the thanks of the Government, and was made G.C.B. in 1881. In 1882 he commanded as admiral, in the bombardment of Alexandria, consequent on the revolt of Arabi Bey, and the riots among the Arab population. Seymour had been instructed to demand that the works on the fortress should be stopped, and the fortress surrendered, and no notice having been taken of his summons within the given twenty-four hours, the admiral fired on the forts, and speedily silenced them. A catastrophe 'which might have deluged Egypt with blood'[2] was averted by England. All that England got, however, by her intervention was an increased and indefinite responsibility. Sir Beauchamp Seymour was made Lord Alcester, and received a parliamentary grant of £20,000, the freedom of the city of London, and a sword of honour. He had been a Lord of the Admiralty from 1872-4, and was again holding that office from 1888 to 1885. In April 1886 he was placed on the retired list. He was now a man of sixty-five, but he retained the manners of a beau, and not only won for himself popularity in society, but was given the nickname of ' The Ocean Swell.' His was a familar figure in St. James's, for he lived in chambers in Ryder Street. Towards the end of his life, his eyesight failed, and his health was badly broken. His death took place at his chambers, on

[1] From a speech delivered by Mr. Gladstone at the time.
[2] Herbert Paul, *Modern England.*

the 80th of March 1895, and he was buried at Brookwood, on the third day of the following month. As he died un-married, his title became extinct.

It remains to say something of those branches of the Seymour family who settled in Ireland, since to the Irish Seymours belong two at least of the most distinguished sailors of the family, Rear Admiral Sir Michael Seymour (1768-1884), and Admiral Sir Michael Culme-Seymour. The descent of these branches is still very doubtful, but according to Playfair (and this statement is generally accepted by the family), John Seymour, the second son of Sir Edward Seymour (first baronet) of Berry Pomeroy settled in Ireland, and was the head of the family which claims the two distinguished admirals.[1] This John Seymour, who is noticed in the State Papers of his time as Captain John Seymour, settled, it appears, in Ireland, and there married the sister of Sir Richard Stanning. Of his sons we know nothing, but he seems to have had five grand-sons, four of whom survived him. From John, the eldest grandson, descended the Rev. John Crossley Seymour (*ob.* 1881), the head of the Crossley Seymours, while William, the second grandson, left one heir John, Rector of Palace in Limerick. From this point Playfair is in agreement with the other peerages, who state that this John and William were sons of one John Seymour of Limerick, who was Alderman of Limerick, and afterwards Mayor (1720). If Playfair is right, then obviously this John, Mayor of Limerick, was son of John, son of Sir Edward Seymour of Maiden Bradley. However the statement must remain hypothetical, and it must be remembered that the Crossley

[1] The other Irish families are the Seymours of Ballymore Castle, who claim descent from a certain Thomas Seymour, who went to Ireland, as an officer of the English army in the reign of William III. ; and the Seymours of Killagally, who claim descent from the Seymours of Knoyle House, Wilts. (viz. from Francis Seymour of Sherbourne, younger brother of Edward, eighth Duke of Somerset).

Seymours claim descent from Sir Henry Seymour, brother of Queen Jane, and it is certain, although the peerages generally state that he died without issue, that he had a son and heir John, who succeeded him in his estates.[1]

Leaving the family of Crossley Seymour with only a brief mention of the hymn-writer, Aaron Crossley Seymour (1789-1870), and his younger brother, the well-known Michael Hobart Seymour (1800-1874), the controversialist and theologian, we pass to the children of John Seymour, Rector of Palace, co. Limerick, the head of the Culme Seymour family.[2] The eldest son, William Hobart Seymour, died in the West Indies in 1797, after a brief but adventurous life. The second son, Michael Seymour, was born in 1768, and entered the Navy in November 1780, serving first in the *Merlin* sloop with Captain James Luttrell. Two years later, when on board the *Mediator*, he took part in a very severe action. His ship of only 44 guns attacked five French frigates, mounting between them 186 guns. The *Mediator* captured two, the *Alexandre* and the *Meleager*, and put the rest to flight. Promotion to lieutenancy on board the *Magnificent* came to Seymour in October 1790. Three years later he was commissioned to the *Marlborough* as junior lieutenant, and was badly wounded in June 1794 when the *Marlborough* took part in Lord Howe's memorable action.[3] He lost his left arm as a result, but for his services was appointed commander in 1795. From 1796 to 1800 he was employed on board the *Spitfire* in guarding the Channel, and watching the north coast of France, where he took a great number of prizes, privateers and armed vessels attempting to carry

[1] Chan. Inq. p. m., 20 Eliz., ser. 2, No. 24.

[2] He married Grizelda, youngest daughter and co-heir of William Hobart, of High Mount, and died in 1795.

[3] His younger brother Richard, who was killed in a naval action in March 1806, was also present in the action of June 1794, on board the *Impregnable*.

on the coasting trade. In August 1800 he was appointed
to post rank. However, it was not until June 1806 that
he was appointed as commander of the 36-gun frigate,
Amethyst, which was to be employed in independent cruising
on the French coast. On the 10th of November 1808 the
Amethyst effected the capture of the French frigate *Thetis*,
after one of the most desperate sea-fights of the whole war.

It was in the evening off the Isle Groix that the *Amethyst*
sighted the *Thetis*, bound for Martinique with a detachment
of troops. The *Amethyst* gave chase, a duel of shots
followed, and an hour later, the two frigates were in close
action. Pinsum, the captain of the *Thetis*, though the
decks of his vessel were crowded with men, attempted to
close with the enemy and carry her by boarding on the
port side, but at the same moment the *Amethyst* luffed, and
passing at the rear of the *Thetis* took up a new position
on the starboard. Then the fight began again in this
changed position. By half-past ten both vessels had lost
their mizen-masts; the cannons roared on; the French
captain again attempted to board. At that moment he
fell mortally wounded. Then the two vessels grappled
together, swaying to and fro, but never was there a moment
when they were near enough for one to board the other.
The French guns were failing for want of rammers; the
broadside fire of the *Amethyst* never ceased. A few minutes
past midnight, with over two hundred men lying dead or
wounded on her decks, with the terror of a spreading fire
in her midst, with her starboard portholes shattered, her
guns dismantled, and her main and foremasts falling, a
battered, hideous wreck, the *Thetis* yielded to her enemy.[1]
The *Amethyst* had won, but she had paid dearly for her
victory, for seventy men had fallen of her crew of about
two hundred. However, as soon as the ships were made
safe for the return journey, the *Amethyst* brought her prize

[1] Troude, *Batailles Navales de la France*, iii. 548-9.

to Plymouth. Seymour was presented with a gold medal, the freedom of the cities of Limerick and Cork, and £100 by the Patriotic fund for the purchase of a sword of honour.

In February 1809 he started out again on the *Amethyst*, and on the early morning of the 6th of April fell in with the French frigate *Niemen* off Ushant. After a short cannonade, the two ships engaged at close quarters, about half-past eleven in the morning. One change of position followed another, each captain attempting to take his enemy by surprise. By two o'clock the tactics of the English captain had secured him the advantage, the mizen-mast of the *Niemen* had fallen, and a fire had broken out in her riggings. The fire was mastered, and the French vessel began the fight with fresh vigour. By three o'clock the main-mast and the mizen-mast of the *Amethyst* had fallen, according to the report of the French captain, and it seemed as though the English must yield. At that moment the English frigate the *Arethusa* came up, and though the *Niemen* bravely continued the fight with the new adversary, she was forced soon after four o'clock to surrender, for fire had declared itself, and her main-mast had fallen.[1] The English version of this fight differs in some details. It is said that the English captain had no intention of yielding to the French, that the main-mast of the *Niemen* had fallen before the arrival of the *Arethusa*, and that the victory was practically assured to the *Amethyst*.[2] However that may be, both French and English fought long and bravely and well, and the captain of the *Arethusa* certainly disclaimed any part in the action beyond firing a few shots, which probably made the *Niemen* surrender sooner than she would otherwise have done.[3]

[1] Troude, iv. 66.   [2] W. James, *Naval Hist.*, v. 17.
[3] See *Memoir of Sir Michael Seymour*, printed for private circulation by his fifth son, the Rev. Richard Seymour, Canon of Worcester.

On his return to England, Seymour was created a baronet
as a reward for his distinguished conduct, and received a
special compliment from the king.   In the following October
he was appointed to the *Niemen*, and in 1812 to the *Hannibal*, which he commanded for two years.   On the 26th of
March 1814 the *Hannibal* fell in with the French frigate
Sultane about thirty-six miles from *l'île de Bas*, and
succeeded in capturing her without much resistance.   Thus
Sir Michael added a third frigate to the British navy.   The
following year he was made K.C.B., and the pension for the
loss of his arm was increased to £800 a year.   After various
other appointments he was, in January 1829, made Commissioner of Portsmouth, and held the office until it was
abolished in 1882.   Then he chose to return to active service,
and to go to South America as Commander-in-chief.   With
his flag in the *Spartiate*, he sailed in February 1888 for Rio,
which was to be his headquarters.   In April 1884 he was
attacked by a low fever, died on shore in the following July,
and was buried in the English cemetery at Rio.   In 1794
he had married Jane, daughter of Captain James Hawker,
by whom he had many children.   The eldest son, John
Hobart, became second baronet.   He was Canon of
Gloucester, Rector of Berkhampstead St. Mary, Chaplain
in Ordinary to Queen Victoria and Prebendary of Lincoln.
He died in September 1880, leaving two sons and one
daughter by his first wife, Elizabeth, elder of the two
daughters of the Rev. Thomas Culme [1] of Tothill, Devon,
and one son and four daughters by his second wife, Maria
Louisa, youngest daughter of Charles Smith of Suttons,
Essex.   Admiral Sir Michael Culme-Seymour, third and
present baronet, is his eldest son. [2]

[1] Sir John Seymour assumed, by royal licence, 6th May 1842, the
surname of Culme, before his patronymic name of Seymour.

[2] John Hobart Seymour, lieutenant-colonel in the Army, who
died in 1887, was the second son by the first wife, and Elizabeth

Admiral Sir Michael Seymour (1802-1887), second son
of Rear-Admiral Sir Michael Seymour, and uncle of the
present baronet, must here first claim our attention. He
entered the Navy in December 1813, at the early age of
eleven years, on board the *Hannibal* with his father, but
in March 1816 was entered as a scholar at the Royal Naval
College at Portsmouth. In 1818 he was appointed to the
Rochfort, and afterwards to the *Ganymede*, in which he continued until his promotion as lieutenant in September 1822.
The *Sybille*, to which he was appointed in July 1823, was one
of the ships commissioned to blockade the Algerian coast
in April 1824, and was in the squadron afterwards assembled
to once more bombard Algiers as in 1816. At the last
moment the Dey of Algiers came to terms, so that no active
warfare took place. However, in the following December,
Seymour was promoted to be commander, and in January
1827 he was appointed to the *Menai* for service on the
South American station, and did not return to England
until the spring of 1829. His father, Sir Michael, was,
as we have seen, appointed to the command of the South
American station, and wished to have his son, who had
already had experience on that station, as his flag captain.
This the Admiralty inconsiderately refused, but in June
1833 appointed him to the *Challenger*, in which he joined his
father at Rio.

After a brief stay at Rio he was transferred to the
Peruvian coast, but returned to Rio on the news of his
father's death. Later, in May 1835, on his way back to
the Pacific, the *Challenger*, by some abnormal and unfore-
seen reversal of the current, was wrecked on the coast of
Chili near Leubu. The *Diary of the Wreck of the Challenger*,
written by one of the officers, is a fascinating story of the

Culme Seymour, the daughter, who married the Rev. J. Rawlin-
son, M.A., William Hobart Seymour, and Laura Maria, Jane, Caroline,
and Charlotte Augusta Mary, were the children by the second wife.

actual happenings; of the wreck itself; of the encamp-
ment of the crew on the desolate shores of the west coast
of South America for seven long weeks until help could be
brought to them from Conception, the nearest island;
of the constant alarm lest the hostile Indians, ' Enemigos '
Indians, should attack the little camp; and of the cunning
of the friendly Indians, who, learning the value of their provisions to the hungry sailors, whereas they at first had been
satisfied with a button in payment for a bird, began finally
to demand the whole coat.   And in that ' wild and distant '
spot June the 18th did not pass forgotten, but ' the glories '
of Waterloo, and the health of the Duke of Wellington were
drunk with cheers in the officers' tent.   At last, after many
disappointments, about 7.30 A.M. on the 5th of July ' a
sail was reported in sight from the look-out on the hill . . .
and when, after a most anxious examination through the
few glasses we possessed, she was pronounced to be a man-of-
war, it was received by a cheer throughout the camp, and
every heart expanded with joy.'   The sail was finally discovered to be the *Blonde*, and after fires were lighted on
the hill, and the temporary flags vigorously waved, she was
seen to hoist her colours and fire two guns as signal that
she had seen, and in eighty-four days, including a stay
of a week at Rio, the wrecked crew reached Spithead.
Only one of the crew, a supernumerary clerk, succumbed
to the hardships of those seven unforgettable weeks.   And
now the captain, who had been the centre of discipline,
and sound commonsense, and whose personality had been
the means of bringing his men safely through a most trying
adventure, had himself to face a court-martial for the loss
of the ship.   Obviously only one verdict was possible.
Seymour and his officers were cleared of all blame, the
cause of the loss being the unusual and unexpected current.
The court was, moreover, gracious enough to express its
' high sense . . . of the conduct of Captain Michael Seymour,

his officers and his crew . . . when placed in circumstances of the greatest danger, as well as afterwards, during a period of seven weeks that they remained on a wild and inhospitable coast.'

From 1845 to 1848 Seymour was on the North American and West Indian Station, commanding the *Vindictive*, as flag-captain, to Sir Francis William Austen. For the next few years he was employed in an inspection tour in France, and as superintendent of Sheerness dockyard, whence, in September 1851, he was transferred to Devonport, and promoted to the rank of commodore of the first class. In March 1854, when war with Russia became imminent, and the Governments of Great Britain and France resolved to take action in the Baltic, Great Britain hastily dispatched a composite fleet of fifteen ships, steam and sailing vessels, eight of which were battleships. They sailed from Spithead, under the command of Sir Charles Napier. Seymour was appointed as captain of the fleet, under Napier, being commissioned to the *Duke of Wellington*. The fleet was ill-prepared, and Napier had been advised not to engage in any desperate venture, but to assume a defensive, rather than aggressive policy. The declaration of the war reached the fleet on the 4th of April, and Napier himself, as his much criticised signal showed, was ready to meet the enemy, and dispose of them. However, in the end, the fleet retreated without attacking Helsingfors, and Seymour, as captain of the fleet, could do nothing against the will of his commander, who was ' too shaky, nervous, and borne down by responsibility, to have such a charge on him.' In the following December Napier, angered by the tantalising messages of the Admiralty, brought back his fleet to Spithead, and the campaign of 1854 was ended.

In the campaign of 1855, Seymour, now rear-admiral, was again ordered to the Baltic, under the command of the Hon. Richard Saunders Dundas. The fleet was this time much more powerful, being composed wholly of steam vessels, and supported by various small crafts, mortar vessels and gun-boats. Seymour was appointed second in command, with his flag in the *Exmouth*, a ship of ninety guns. The fleet made a rendezvous off Nargen Island, on the 10th of May 1855, and on following days, the two admirals, Dundas and Seymour, in the *Merlin*, reconnoitred Reval and Swea-borg, and later Cronstadt. Cronstadt was known to be well guarded with infernal machines, and stationary tor-pedoes, and after several minor accidents had occurred, the ships stationed before Cronstadt began to sweep and creep for machines. Within seventy-two hours thirty-three of the torpedoes were fished up. Rear-Admiral Seymour and Captain William Hall, having found one ' hauled it into their gig, and began to play with it.' They then took it to the Commander-in-chief, and again played with it : finally, they carried it on board the *Exmouth*, and once again played with it on the quarter-deck. In a few minutes it exploded, knocking down all who were near, and wounding many. Seymour himself was wounded in the face, and conse-quently lost the sight of one eye.[1]

In June, Seymour temporarily transferred his flag from the *Exmouth* to the *Snap*, having left the fleet to reconnoitre the mouth of the Narva, and entered into some brisk engagements with some coast batteries, but to no purpose. The attack on Sweaborg made in the following August was the one event of that campaign, successful, but costly beyond its worth. Towards the end of September the fleet began to return to England, Dundas was made K.C.B., and Seymour, among others, C.B.

The next field of action in which we find Seymour engaged is in the second China War of 1856. In the spring of that

[1] His chief, Admiral Dundas, followed his example another day, and nearly lost his sight through trifling with an apparently empty infernal machine.

year he went out overland, to take charge of that station, and after visiting Japan, had returned to Hong Kong, when, on the 11th of October, he received news of the seizure of a British lorcha, the *Arrow*, by the Chinese authorities at Canton, four days before. Twelve of the crew had been bound, and carried off, and the British flag hauled down. The first China War, of 1839-42, had accomplished little if such seizures were possible. The Consul brought the matter before the Chinese Imperial High Commissioner. The men were eventually sent back, but not in the public manner required, and no apology or assurance was offered by the Chinese. Sir John Bowring, the Governor of Hong Kong, thereupon put the matter into Seymour's hands, suggesting that an Imperial junk should be seized by way of reprisal. A junk was captured, but as it proved to be private property, was immediately released. On the 18th of October, Seymour sent the *Encounter* and the *Samson* to join the *Sibylle*, in the river before Canton, hoping to overawe the High Commissioner by display of forces in the river. This proved unavailing, and he thereupon determined to seize the defences of Canton. Several forts were occupied, but the Commissioner remained unmoved. All the defences were in British hands by the 25th of October, but the Commissioner hardened his heart, and still vouchsafed no reply. Forces were landed, and Canton was attacked, the gate of the city was blown to pieces, and a desultory warfare ensued. Seymour visited the Commissioner, and at sunset re-embarked with all his force, nominally because he had only wished to demonstrate his power to enter the city, more probably because he had found it impossible to make a lodgment.

The moral effect of the retirement was bad.[1] Several days of firing from the ships followed, but Seymour could

[1] Clowes, *Brit. Navy*, vii. The whole account is given here in full detail.

obtain no answer from the Commissioner, the nearest approach to an answer being an attempt to destroy the squadron by fire-vessels. Four large junks were sailed down the river and anchored near to those of the British ships. In a few moments they were ablaze, and the ships only escaped by quickly slipping anchor. To prevent another occurrence of this kind, Seymour caused a line of junks to be drawn across the river, above and below the shipping. By the 15th of November, he had secured the river by the capture of the Bogue forts. He then wrote to England for further orders, but meanwhile, being tormented by the harrying tactics of the Chinese, who made hourly attacks by day and night on the squadron, he realised that without help from England he could not hold the river.

It was not until the following April that he heard with relief England would send 5000 troops, since Seymour and Bowring, by their 'rash action,' had put her credit at stake. The help was grudgingly given, for it was difficult for those at home to realise the situation, and the principles on which Bowring and Seymour had based their vigorous policy. However, in the meantime, the momentous action in the Fatshan Creek, on the 1st of June 1857, resulting in the destruction of the Chinese Junk fleet, had a great moral effect upon the Chinese.[1] If it had been possible to follow up that victory by prompt and vigorous measures, they would in all likelihood have been speedily brought to concede to Seymour's demands, which simply involved satisfaction for the *Arrow* outrage, and permission for foreign representatives to enter Canton, as they entered the other four ports. And, even now, the reinforcements were on their way from England, and Lord Elgin had reached the scene of action with full powers to negotiate.

The troops were never destined to arrive. Lord Elgin

[1] Seymour wrote in his dispatch, ' This engagement opens a new era in Chinese naval warfare.

heard at Singapore of the outbreak of the Indian Mutiny, and realising that a greater danger was at hand, he diverted the troops from China to India, and himself followed them to Calcutta.   Seymour was left to blockade the Canton River as best he could.   On the 29th of December 1857, since 1500 men, chiefly Royal Marines, had been placed at his disposal, and the French squadron had now come to his aid, Seymour pushed up the river, and, after a clever feint, attacked and captured Canton with a very small loss. The Commissioner, Yeh, hoping that the Tartar troops who were assembling would overpower the allied French and English, remained stubborn to the end.   But on the 5th of January 1858 he was taken prisoner and sent to Calcutta. Even so, China remained obdurate.   Lord Elgin, who had returned to China after waiting in vain for the plenipotentiaries from Peking, determined to move the scene of action to the north, hoping that by bringing it into the vicinity of the capital he would hasten the course of events.   In May 1858 Seymour took the forts of the Pei-ho, and forced the passage up the river as far as Tientsin.   Tientsin was garrisoned ; China dared to dally no longer, and on the 27th of June peace was signed. Yet China was not subdued ; an undercurrent of hatred and rebellion, which could not be stemmed, was running through the empire, even when Peking was negotiating with the allies.

Throughout the rest of the year 1858, Seymour, after accompanying Lord Elgin to Japan, was stationed at Hong Kong.   In the spring of 1859 he returned to England, having completed his term of service.   On the 20th of May he was rewarded for his work in China with a G.C.B., and was shortly afterwards presented by the China merchants with a handsome service of plate, since the benefits he had rendered to their trade were inestimable.   On the 1st of November he was promoted to the rank of vice-admiral, and in March, 1864, to be admiral. From March 1863 to March 1866 he was Commander-in-chief at Portsmouth. In 1870 he was put on the retired list, and in 1875 was nominated to the then honorary office of Vice-Admiral of the United Kingdom. His death occurred on the 23rd of February 1887, at the age of eighty-five. He had married, in 1829, his first cousin, Dorothea, daughter of Sir William Knighton, by whom he had one son and three daughters.[1]

We must now pass on quickly. Two other distinguished sailors yet remain to be mentioned. One we have spoken of before, Admiral Sir Michael Culme-Seymour, the third and present baronet. The details of his career are too fresh in our minds to need repetition. Suffice it to say that he is a G.C.B., and an admiral in the Navy; was Commander-in-chief in the Pacific from 1885 to 1887; commander of the Channel squadron from 1890-2; Commander-in-chief in the Mediterranean from 1893 to 1896; Commander-in-chief at Portsmouth from 1897 to 1900, and first and principal A.D.C. to Queen Victoria. In 1866 he married Mary Georgiana, elder daughter of the Hon. Richard Watson, of Rockingham Castle, and has had issue, three sons and two daughters.

His cousin, Sir Edward Hobart Seymour, is the second son of the Rev. Richard Seymour (1806-1880), Canon of Worcester, and grandson of Sir Michael Seymour, first baronet. The details of his career, like those of Sir Michael Culme-Seymour, are fresh in our memory. He served in the Black Sea, throughout the Russian War (1854-5), and in the China War (1857-60), was wounded in a skirmish, on the coast of Africa, in 1870, served in the Egyptian War of 1882, and again in the war with China in 1900. It was in this latter service in the June of 1900, that by his advice

---

[1] Michael Francis Knighton Seymour, born 1841; Dorothea, died 1901; Georgiana, died 1881; Blanche, died 1875.

and under his leadership, an allied naval expedition was undertaken to Tientsin to defend the foreign settlers from the threatened attacks of the Boxers. The expedition was criticised, since it temporarily crippled four British ships, so great was the number of seamen killed and wounded before the Armoury at Tientsin was destroyed, but the necessity was urgent in the extreme, and it was ' one of the rare occasions when something very like rashness becomes a duty.' [1] He holds the Grand Cross of the Order of the Red Eagle, and of the Spanish Order of Naval Merit, and first class of the Order of the Rising Sun of Japan, and a Royal Humane Society's medal. In the May of this year (1910) he has hauled down his flag and closed his career in the Navy, for the sole reason that he has reached the age limit of seventy years.

[1] Clowes, Royal Navy, vii. 523.

CHAPTER XII

THE LINE OF THE LATER DUKES

WE must return now to the main line of the Dukes of
Somerset. Edward, the eldest son of Sir Edward Seymour,
fifth baronet of Berry Pomeroy, son of the Speaker, by
his first wife, Margaret Wale, took but small part in public
affairs, serving only once in Parliament as member for
Salisbury in 1741. In the next year his wife, Mary,
daughter of Daniel Webb of Monkton Farley, died, and
he retired. Some suggestion seems to have been made
that he should marry the Duke of Somerset's (Algernon,
seventh duke) eldest daughter, since by Lord Beauchamp's
death the title must revert to him, but the idea came to
nothing.

The death of the seventh duke came sooner than was
expected. In February 1749-50, when Sir Edward, who
was on his road to London, was playing chess in a country
inn, the host brought him news of the duke's death, and
congratulated him on his accession to the title. Sir
Edward said nothing, but continued his game of chess.
Riding to London the next day, he happened to meet
Lord Holland, who greeted him through the carriage
window, and persuaded him to hasten to town and make
his claim at once. This he did, but not without difficulties.
In April 1750, Walpole wrote to Sir Horace Mann that
the title was disputed, ' my Lord Chancellor has refused
him (Sir Edward) the writ, but referred his case to the
Attorney-General (Sir Dudley Ryder), the present great
opinion of England, who, they say, is clear for Sir Edward's

succession.'   Even by the following August the settlement
had not been made, for Walpole wrote that Sir Edward
had not yet got his dukedom, ' as there is started up a
Dr. Seymour who claims it, but will be able to make nothing
out of it.'   This was only one of many intrigues, but, as
was inevitable, Sir Edward's title was finally assured.   His
right to the succession was proved by Sir Dudley Ryder,
and on the 25th of November he was summoned to the
House of Peers.   Of the few public offices he served, one
was as chief mourner at the funeral of Frederick, Prince of
Wales, in April 1751.   In February 1752 he obtained a
grant of the offices of Warden, and Chief Justice in Eyre
of all His Majesty's forests, parks, chases and warrens
beyond Trent, and was constituted Lord-Lieutenant of the
county of Wilts.   He died at Maiden Bradley on the 12th
of December 1757.   Of his four sons, Edward, Webb,
William, and Francis, the two eldest were both destined to
become Dukes of Somerset.

However, before we pass to the somewhat uneventful lives
of these two men, we may centre our interest on Francis
Seymour of Sherbourne, Dorset, grandson of the Speaker, and
younger brother of the eighth duke.   He is interesting, not
so much for himself as for his only son, Henry, who is best
known to history as a lover of Madame du Barry.   Francis,
like his father and grandfather before him, had married into
the Popham family, his wife being Elizabeth, Dowager
Lady Hinchinbroke, mother to John, Earl of Sandwich,
and daughter of Alexander Popham of Littlecote.   They
had two sons, Henry (1729-1805) and Francis, but the latter
died when an infant.   In July 1758 Henry Seymour
married Lady Caroline Cowper, only daughter of the second
Earl Cowper.   He had, it seems, been jilted the year before
by Lady Diana Egerton.   According to Horace Walpole,
the only answer that Seymour could get on the subject was,
' that Di has her caprices.'   However, the reasons she

herself gave were 'the badness of his temper, and the imperiousness of his letters, that he scolded her for the overfondness of her epistles, and was even so unsentimental as to talk of *desiring to make her happy instead of being made so by her.*' Seymour went abroad in despair, finding an additional cause of discomfort in the fact that his father refused to resettle the Sherborne estates on him, since the entail had been cut off by mutual consent to make way for the settlements on the marriage. However, Lady Caroline Cowper was to step into the breach before a year was over. In June 1778 Seymour became a widower, since Lady Caroline died of 'a putrid fever.' She left two daughters; Caroline, who married William Danby, the bibliophile and mineralogist, and Georgiana, who married Count Louis de Durfort. It was of one of these that Walpole wrote to Henry Conway in 1782. 'I saw another proud prince yesterday, your cousin Seymour from Paris and his daughter. She was so dishevelled, that she looked like a pattern doll that had been tumbled at the Custom House.'

Two years after the death of his first wife, Seymour married Louise Thérèse, widow of Counte Guillaume de Panthou, by whom he had one son, Henry [1] (1776-1849). In 1778 he and his family settled in Paris, and having obtained letters of domicile to protect his property from forfeiture to the Crown in the event of his death, he bought an estate at Prunay, between Versailles and St. Germain. The house at Prunay was 'un élégant petit château avec un parc; de là l'on jouit de la vue magnifique qui s'étend de Saint Germain-en-Laye à Paris.' On Sundays the park was opened to the public, 'et le soir il faisait danser les paysans dans des salles de verdure qui n'ont pas été détruites.' 'Il existait en 1870,' writes Charles Vatel, 'à Port-Marly de vieilles femmes qui se rappelaient avoir dansé dans leur jeunesse au château de M. le Comte

[1] He was high sheriff of Dorset in 1835.

Seymour.'[1] He himself was remembered as 'un gentil-
homme accompli très beau de sa personne, de manières
distinguées et en même temps toutefois populaires.' However, the importance of his life at Prunay lies for us in the
fact that he' became a near neighbour of Madame du Barry,
from whose terraces at Luciennes the chateau de Prunay
could be clearly seen. And as Abbé Georgel remarks,
'elle parut se consoler de sa grandeur passée en vivant
avec le comte de Seymour.' At this date Madame du
Barry was thirty-seven years old while Seymour was fifty.
But age mattered nothing—'Madame du Barry redevint
Jeanne Bécu ; elle fut subjuguée, elle aima.' 'L'assurance
de votre tendresse mon tendre ami, font le bonheur de ma
vie. Croyes que mon cœur trouve ces deux jours bien long
et que s'il était en son pouvoir de les abréger il naures plus
de peine. Je vous attends samedi avec toute l'impatience
d'une âme entièrement à vous et jespere que vous ne
desirerais rien.' Thus runs one of her early letters to
Seymour. And it is no court favourite writing ; it is a
woman. It was not long, however, before Seymour was
complaining that Madame du Barry's heart was not wholly
his. She answered him, 'croyez *quoique vous en disiez*
vous serais le seul amis de mon cœur.' In a following
letter she again mentions his reproach, adding that she was
also obliged to bear the reproaches of M. le duc de Brissac,
who was in his turn as jealous of Seymour as Seymour of
him. 'Sa visite (of the Duc de Brissac) m'a fort embarassé,
car je crois que vous en étiez l'objet. Adieu, je vous
attends avec l'impatience d'un cœur tout à vous et qui
malgré vos injustices sent bien qu'il ne peut être à un autre.
Je pense à vous, vous le dit, et vous le répètte et n'ai d'autre

---

[1] Charles Vatel, *Madame du Barry* (1883), iii. 30. The title is, of
course, inaccurate, but serves to signify his high social rank. M. Huot
de Goncourt improved on the title by stating that he was a Lord, and
was ambassador from England to France. (*La du Barry* [1878], 208.)

regret que de ne pouvoir vous le dire à chaque instant.'
But Seymour refused to be convinced and persisted in his
jealousy ; Madame du Barry wrote her farewell. ' Il est
inutile de vous parler de ma tendresse et de ma sensibilité,
vous la connoisé. Mais ce que vous ne connoissés pas
ce son mes peines, vous navez pas daigné me rassurer sur
ce qui affecte mon âme. Ainsi je croit que ma tranquillité
et mon bonheur vous touche peu, c'est avec regret que
je vous en parle mais c'est pour la dernière foit (*sic*). Ma
tête est bien ; mon cœur souffre. Mais avec beaucoup
d'attention et de courage je parviendrai à le dompter ;
l'ouvrage est pénible et douloureux, mais il est nécessaire,
c'est le dernier sacrifice qu'il me reste à lui faire ;—mon
cœur lui a fait tous les autres, c'est à ma raison à lui faire
celui cy. Adieu, croiie que vous seul occuperai mon cœur.'[1]
The episode was finished. Seymour kept her letters and
a lock of her hair until, in his hasty departure from France
in the August of 1792, they were forgotten, and passed
into the hands of Barrière, an autograph collector.
Finally, after many vicissitudes, they were sold in Paris
in 1892.

During the Revolution all Seymour's papers were con-
fiscated and are now, including even bundles of his tradesmen's bills, in the Archives Nationales of Paris. He himself remained in England until his death in 1805, and, after
the Battle of Waterloo, his heirs obtained compensation for
his losses out of the fund for indemnifying British subjects.

Apart from Seymour's attachment to Madame du Barry,
he is remembered also as the anonymous translator into
French prose of the *English Garden*, by William Mason.
And there is one other interest. He had an illegitimate
daughter who was born in France, and her daughter,
Harriette Félicité, married Sir James Tichborne, and was

---

[1] The letters are quoted as they stand (as regards spelling, etc.) from
Vatel, *op. cit.*, iii. pp. 33-36.

the mother of the young Sir Roger, personated by ' the claimant,' Arthur Orton, in the famous case of 1871. She it was who identified the latter as her son, but died before the trial began.

Edward, the ninth Duke of Somerset, eldest son of Edward, grandson of the Speaker and eighth duke, was born in 1717, and succeeded his father as duke in December 1757. At this date he was engaged to be married to Lady Dungarvon, widow of Charles Boyle, Lord Dungarvon, but he already began to show some signs of the eccentricities which were to develop into a harmless madness, and the lady broke off the match in the summer of 1760. She soon became engaged to Charles, Lord Bruce, who wrote in December 1760 to his friend the Earl of Charlemont : ' I am going to be married to Lady Dungarvon. Don't accuse me of not treating you sooner with confidence on this occasion. Her match with the Duke of Somerset *from his absurdity* broke off in the summer, and mine did not begin till since we broke up camp, and has been concluded on within the last few days only.'[1]   In spite of the fact that his own absurd conduct had caused the failure of the match, the duke seems to have been genuinely disappointed, and this disappointment was a last blow to his reason. He took no part in politics in the future, but settled down at Maiden Bradley, where he lived an eccentric existence in complete seclusion. For several years before his death this seclusion was more and more severe, since he developed so intense a dread of smallpox that he would never touch a letter, but made one of his servants hold it against a pane of glass through which he read it. He was sufficiently reasonable to be conscious of his weakness, but not sufficiently reasonable to control it. Thus he wrote to the Earl of Hertford in 1767 that he would be pleased to come to town and vote in the House of Lords for the Government,

---

[1] *Hist. MSS. Com.*, MS. of James, first Earl of Charlemont.

'but your lordship knows there is an invincible obstacle in my way, which, however weak it may seem, my constitution will not suffer me to get over, sensible I am that it deprives me of most of the comforts of life, as well as of the advantages of my rank and situation; for whilst houses for innoculation are open to the great avenues to the town, and people with the smallpox on them are suffered to walk about the street, it is scarce possible, in my apprehension, to escape infection; nay, in the House of Lords itself, filled as it generally is with strangers on days of great debate. . . . Was it possible to persuade me out of my fears, your lordship would have the power to do it, and my own inclinations on occasions like these would strongly second your arguments; but there is no getting the better of nature, and this particular sort of dread is so rooted in me that I despair of its ever being eradicated.'[1] On the 2nd of January 1792 this pathetic life ended. The years of solitude and seclusion had accomplished one thing. By his parsimony the estates of the Dukes of Somerset were increased in value, and became more suited to their title and position. For it was an empty title that had come to his father, the estates of the dukedom having been divided among the heirs of the other line.

Dying unmarried, the ninth duke was succeeded in his title and estates by his younger brother, Webb Seymour. The latter, only one year younger than his brother, was seventy-four years old when he thus became Duke of Somerset. He held the title only for a year, dying in 1793. He had, in 1765, married Mary, daughter and heiress of John Bonnel of Stanton Court, by whom he had four sons, two of whom died young. The third, Edward Adolphus, became eleventh Duke of Somerset, and the fourth, Webb John Seymour, was well known in the early nineteenth

[1] H. St. Maur, *Annals of the Seymour Family*, p. 448.

century as a philosopher and scientist.[1]   Edward Adolphus, eleventh Duke of Somerset, was not only a man of letters, but a scientist and an antiquarian.   Born at Monkton Farley (Wilts.) in 1775, he was educated at Eton and Oxford, and matriculated in 1792, the year that his father became Duke of Somerset.   The next year he himself succeeded to the title, but continued at Oxford, where he took his M.A. degree in July 1794.   A long tour in the next year through England, Wales, and Scotland, was occupied chiefly in the study of geology.   In 1797 he was elected a Fellow of the Royal Society, and in 1816 a Fellow of the Society of Antiquaries.   From 1801 to 1838 he was president of the Royal Literary Fund, and vice-president of University College, London.   From 1826-1831 he was vice-president of the Zoological Society, and from 1834-7 president of the Linnean Society, and member of the Royal Asiatic Society.   Fulfilling all these offices apart from all business [2] and social duties, it is little wonder he wrote to his brother, Lord Webb Seymour, in March 1816 : ' My occupations are not very uniform, but I am much less

[1] Much has been written about him.   He was a friend of the geologist Leonard Horner, brother of Francis Horner, and of many other well-known Edinburgh men of that period.   See A. Hallam, *Biog. Notes of Lord Webb Seymour*.   See also Lady Gwendolen Ramsden, *Correspondence of Two Brothers*.

[2] In June 1810 he improved the ducal estates by the purchase of Bulstrode Park (Bucks.) from the Duke of Portland.   His son, the twelfth duke, devised it to his daughters.   See *infra*.   Bulstrode is of chief interest from the fact that, having belonged from the time of Edward IV. to the Bulstrode family, it passed, in the seventeenth century, to the infamous Judge Jeffreys.   On his attainder, at the English Revolution, it passed to the Crown, and William III. granted it to William Bentinck, first Earl of Portland.   The house stands on high ground in a park of 800 acres ; it is built of brick, and forms three sides of a quadrangle, with two wings.   The chapel attached is wainscoted with cedar, and ornamented with painted glass.   There are paintings in it by Marco and Sebastian Ricci, and an altarpiece, a Madonna and Child, by Vandyke.

distracted by business than I was.   I feel, however, a great
relief when my attention is absorbed by the history of the
Middle Ages ; or when I can follow the course of a curve
as it meanders upon its axis. . . .'   'I occasionally,' he
adds, 'take up an occupation which is connected on one
side with the drudgery of details and on the other with
general literature.'[1]   In these terms he describes his work
of collecting facts and details about the Seymour family
in a mass of notes and papers which were practically edited
and published by Mr. Harold St. Maur in 1902, in *The
Annals of the Seymours*.   The latter also has in his possession numerous manuscript notes of mathematical and
scientific researches made by the duke.   It was doubtless
some of these that were described by Sir Alexander Johnston in 1820 as 'a model of correct mathematical reasoning
. . . affording one of the best and most useful exercises for
the intellect which I ever read.'[2]

There was one other study among the many subjects
that interested the eleventh Duke of Somerset that has a
special bearing at the present day in view of the advances
that have been made in that yet embryonic science, the
science of 'Psychical Research.'   He collected accounts of
'dreams, visions, and presensions,' and prefaced his manuscript collection with the following definition :—'Any
seeming affection of the senses by absent objects during sleep
is a dream.   Any such affection during vigilance is a vision.
A presension is an ungrounded but true apprehension of
what is happening or going to happen.'   Of vision, he
further remarks, that 'our perceptions came from within,
they are suggestions of the mind, which may indeed be
under the influence of some other mind, but does not receive
its visions directly from external objects.   There is no
real phantom before us, much less is there any object of

[1] Lady Gwendolen Ramsden, *Correspondence of Two Brothers*, p. 177.
[2] *Ibid.*, p. 275.

sense; what we perceive is a thought, vivid, indeed, and often ultimately derived from something real, but not in the ordinary way. It may come from some other mind which may be sensibly informed of its reality.' Another manuscript collection is entitled 'An enquiry into the nature of remote perception.' In his preface the duke observes that of the two classes of phenomena exhibited by nature, the very common and the very rare, the one class is looked upon as a matter of course, the other as a matter of impossibility. 'The subject (of the second class) has hitherto been little more than a matter of wonder. It has excited the fears of the credulous and the contempt of the sceptical. It has never been fully subjected to the observation of the philosophical enquirer.' In spite of all his researches and notes, the Duke of Somerset published nothing but two small mathematical treatises. One, *The Elementary Properties of the Ellipse deduced from the Properties of the Circle*, was published in 1842; while the other, *Alternate Circles and their connection with the Ellipse*, followed in 1850.

In June 1800 the duke had married his first wife, Charlotte, second daughter of the ninth Duke of Hamilton and Brandon, by whom he had four sons and four daughters. Three of the sons,[1] Edward, Archibald, and Algernon, survived, and became successively twelfth, thirteenth, and fourteenth Dukes of Somerset. Their mother, Charlotte, whom Mr. Creevy was pleased to term 'the false devil who robbed her brother Archie of his birthright,'[2] died before her husband, in June 1827, and he married as his second wife, Margaret, eldest daughter of Sir Michael Shaw-Stewart of Blackhall, Renfrewshire. She survived her husband for twenty-five years, dying in July 1880.

---

[1] The daughters were, Charlotte Jane (Lady Charlotte Blount), *ob.* 1889, aged eighty-six; Jane Anne, *ob.* 1895, aged ninety; Anna Maria (Tollemache), *ob.* 1873; Henrietta Jane, *ob.* 1890, aged eighty-one.   [2] *Creevy Papers*, p. 406.

Edward Adolphus, the eldest son of the eleventh duke, succeeded his father in the title and estates on the death of the latter in the August of 1855. He was born in the December of 1804, and much of his early childhood was spent at Mitcham with his grandfather, the Duke of Hamilton, whose idol he became. When he was scarcely eleven years old there was some idea of sending him to Eton, for his mother feared he was being spoiled by his grandfather. ' He is very quick,' she wrote to her brother-in-law, Lord Webb Seymour, ' extremely idle, but his mind is activity itself. You would be surprised at the questions he asks, and the subjects upon which he reasons, the more so as his manner is particularly childish—which I attribute to his being so long the pet at Mitcham. His character is very downright and open ; and *I* think too much destitute of pride and ambition. I should like a little of the former, and a great deal of the latter.' [1] His uncle, Lord Webb Seymour, wrote of him as a ' thoughtless, loving, kind-hearted creature,' but feared lest he should carry his amiability through life, and not acquire ' forethought, the power of application and steadiness of pursuit.' ' I fear his turning out one of those men who are nobody's enemies but their own,' he wrote. ' An incapacity for the cares of business joined to an easy complying temper, may lead him to neglect and mismanagement of every sort, and he may perhaps become the dupe of some designing knaves who will undertake to manage for him.' However, Eton seems to have ' made him manly ' as his father hoped, and from Eton he went on to Christ Church, Oxford, where he matriculated in October 1828, but left the university without a degree.

After a period of travel, which included a visit to Russia, he returned to England, and in June 1830 married Jane

---

[1] *Letters and Memoirs of Edward, Twelfth Duke of Somerset* (ed. 1893, by W. H. Mallock and Lady Gwendolen Ramsden), p. 8.

Georgiana, youngest daughter of Thomas, only son of Richard Brinsley Sheridan. 'Your Georgy is going to be turned into a chaperone,' she wrote to her brother in India; 'Lord Seymour, the Duke of Somerset's son, asked me yesterday to marry him and I, being very civil and polite, said yes. . . . The Duke his father has no objections and is very kind indeed. So are his sisters; but my acquaintances are rabid and frantic at my daring to do such a thing, and they turn round, after first congratulating mamma, and say, "Good heavens, is Lord Seymour mad? What a fool!" with other pleasing intimations of their good wishes towards me.'[1] A few weeks after his marriage, Lord Seymour was elected as Liberal member of Parliament for the town of Okehampton, and began to take an active part in politics. 'His whole soul is in politics,' his wife wrote to her brother, 'and though very shy he does not mind, but rather likes speaking; and so as he is very clever, I am in hopes he will make a figure in the House of Commons.' In 1881, and again in 1884, Parliament was dissolved, and he was elected for Totnes in both the new Parliaments. He had been but three months in Parliament after his second election for Totnes when, on another change of Government, he was appointed Lord of the Treasury under Lord Melbourne. He immediately proceeded to Totnes to present himself for re-election, and in April 1835 wrote to his wife, 'You see, I am again the honoured representative of Totnes. My election took place this morning; no opposition was attempted.'

It was during this same year, 1835, that he fought a duel with Sir Colquhoun Grant, who challenged him with having been an accomplice in the elopement of his only daughter and heiress with Lady Seymour's brother, R. B. Sheridan. Lord Seymour, who knew nothing of the matter, but suspected that his wife might have helped her

[1] Lady Gwendolen Ramsden, *Letters and Memoirs*, etc.

z

brother, refused to either acknowledge or deny the charge. Shots were exchanged without injury to either duellist, and then Seymour proceeded to explain his ignorance. The fact was, his wife had helped her brother without mentioning the fact to her husband. In 1839 Seymour, on Lord Melbourne's advice, resigned his post as Lord of the Treasury, and was appointed Secretary to the Board of Control, holding that position for a year. In the spring of 1839 came the famous Eglinton tournament over which Lady Seymour presided as Queen of Beauty. She herself refers to the tournament, without mentioning her own share in it, in a letter to one of her daughters, ' We saw a fine sight at Eglinton Castle ; a great many gentlemen dressed themselves in armour like old knights, and fought with spears and shields, riding on horses which were covered with silk robes.' We, in these days of pageants, are familiar with such sights.

The next few years of Lord Seymour's life, before he became twelfth duke of Somerset, were passed for the most part abroad, in Italy with Lady Seymour, and in a yachting cruise in the Mediterranean with Mr. Bentinck. Yet his political life was not neglected, and he continued to represent Totnes until it was disfranchised in 1855. On succeeding his father in that year he took his seat in the House of Lords, and became first Lord of the Admiralty. Although not very popular, he concentrated all his force in fulfilling the duties of this office, and was an eminently efficient administrator. He was created K.G. in May 1862, and Earl St. Maur of Berry Pomeroy in June 1863. On his retirement from office in 1866 he took an active part in supporting most of the Liberal measures which came before the Lords, including the Bill for the Abolition of Purchase in the Army. He declined to join Mr. Gladstone's [1] ministry

---

[1] He is said to have described Mr. Gladstone as an enthusiastic politician, trying to set everything to rights, and ' a very good Chan-

of 1868-74, but gave it a half-hearted and intermittent support. However, his lukewarm Liberalism of later years was the result of a private sorrow, the death of his two sons, of his younger son, Edward Percy, in December 1865,[1] and of his elder son, Edward Adolphus, Lord St. Maur, in September 1869.[2] In point of time the death of the younger son almost coincided with the duke's retirement from the Admiralty, and the death of his elder son was a final blow to his interest in public affairs.

For the remaining years of his life, for the most part passed at Bulstrode, the duke devoted himself to a study of the historical aspects of Christianity, which resulted in a small volume on *Christian Theology and Modern Scepticism,* 'thorny subjects' as he himself termed them in his preface, published in 1872, and another on *Monarchy and Democracy,* published eight years later.   In December 1884 the Duchess of Somerset died after much suffering and a partial loss of her sight. Her husband survived her for less than a year, dying in the autumn of 1885.   Three daughters survived,[3] but no son, and the title thus passed to

cellor of the Exchequer, but a very bad Prime Minister ' (*Ann. Reg.* 1885).

[1] In 1865, he started for a tour in India, and while shooting at Jellapoor, was badly bitten by a bear. His leg was amputated, and he had not the strength to recover from the operation.

[2] This son had, on the breaking out of Garibaldi's war of independence, thrown in his lot with those who were fighting for freedom, and enrolled himself as a private, under an assumed name. He had already served as a volunteer in the Indian Mutiny, and there, as in Italy, won himself honour for his bravery. However, his health was delicate, and in September 1869, he was suddenly taken ill, and died in his father's house in Dover Street.

[3] They were Jane Hermione, who, in 1852, married Sir Frederick Ulric Graham, Bart. of Netherby, Cumberland ; Ulrica Frederica, who, in 1858, married Lord Henry Frederick Thynne, second son of the third Marquess of Bath ; Helen Gwendolen, who, in 1865, married Sir John William Ramsden of Byram, Yorks. Bulstrode Park, near Gerrard's Cross, Bucks., where the family had resided since 1810, was devised by the twelfth duke to these daughters and co-heirs.

the younger brother of the duke, Lord Archibald St. Maur or Seymour, who became thirteenth Duke of Somerset. He it was who took the name of St. Maur instead of the corrupted form Seymour, and his example has been followed by his successors. He died unmarried in January 1891, at the age of eighty-one, and was succeeded by his younger brother, the third and youngest son of the eleventh duke, Lord Algernon St. Maur, who became fourteenth Duke of Somerset. He married his distant cousin, Horatia, third daughter of John Morier by Horatia, daughter of Lord Hugh Seymour (*q.v.*), fifth son of Francis, first Marquess of Hertford. In his eighty-first year he died suddenly of heart disease, and was succeeded by his eldest son and heir Algernon (St. Maur), who is the fifteenth and present Duke of Somerset.

APPENDIX I

SOMERSET HOUSE

AMONG the acts of Edward, Duke of Somerset, the Protector, must not be forgotten the foundation of Somerset House,[1] which many have tried unsuccessfully to vindicate, and many more have unhesitatingly condemned. At the beginning of his Protectorate the duke occupied Chester Place, outside Temple Bar, as granted to him when Earl of Hertford, by the late king in 1539 for services at Calais and Guisnes. A more important residence was soon necessary for his almost royal household, and he chose a site for the contemplated palace in the vicinity of Chester Place. This necessitated the seizure and demolition of all the surrounding buildings. Stow, in his *Survey of London and Westminster*, enumerates these :—'A fair cemetery or churchyard . . . and a parish church called of the Nativity of our Lady and the Innocents at the Strand, and of some (by means of a Brotherhood kept there) called of St. Ursula at the Strand . . . Chester Inn situate by St. Mary-le-Strand . . . an house belonging to the Bishop of Llandaff . . . the Bishop of Chester, his inn or London lodging . . . the Bishop of Worcester's Inn . . . Strand Bridge . . . and all the tenements adjoining.' The site, coinciding almost entirely with that of the present day Somerset House, was thus cleared, but even when it was cleared fresh difficulties arose. The stones of the church and of the houses were not likely to be sufficient for the ambitious scale on which Somerset meant to build. Materials must be found, but materials in those days were not easy to procure. Hence Somerset decreed that other surrounding buildings must

[1] *Somerset House, Past and Present*, by R. Needham and A. Webster, is both excellent and complete.

357

be sacrificed.   The steeple and most part of the church of St. John of Jerusalem (Clerkenwell) were ruined and overthrown with gunpowder, and the stones carried to contribute towards the building, and the cloisters on the north side of St. Paul's Cathedral and the charnel-house on the south side, together with the chapel, the tombs, and the monuments therein, were beaten down, and the bones carried away into Finsbury Fields. Such is the charge in the attainder of the Protector, and there is added a further note that he was designing to pull down St. Margaret's Church at Westminster, but was prevented by his fall.   Hayward tells more picturesquely that the workmen of the Protector were preparing to pull down St. Margaret's when 'the stout men of Westminster, fearless of the vengeance of the powerful noble, resenting the wrong and abhorring the sacrilege, rose with one spirit and commenced such a vigorous defence with staff and stones, and at last with clubs and bended bows, that the unhappy carpenters and masons were bewildered and fled, so greatly terrified that no persuasion could induce them to resume the perilous undertaking.' [1]

Except that it is probable that the designer of Longleat, who-ever he was,[2] was also the designer of Somerset House, the architect of the Protector's palace is unknown.   One thing is certain, namely, that at the time of the Protector's death, when Somerset House passed to the Crown, the building was not finished.   As late as 1580 Norden, in his *Speculum Britanniæ*, described it as 'not fully finished, yet a most stately house and of great receyte, having chief prospect towards the south, and the sweet river Thamise offereth manie pleasing delights.   The fields also and the aire are sweet and pleasant.'   At that date the Lord Chamberlain had 'under Her Majestie the use thereof.' As late as 1603 Stow notes that the palace was 'unfinished,' and it seems possible it was left untouched from the reign of Mary until it was transfigured by the genius of Inigo

---

[1] *Life and Reign of Edward VI.*

[2] Longleat is generally attributed to John Thorpe (fl. 1570-1610), but on very insufficient evidence.   All the evidence of Thorpe's professional work is now in the Soane Museum in Lincoln's Inn Fields.

Jones.   Meanwhile the palace had remained in the hands
of the Crown, was several times visited by Elizabeth both as
princess and queen, was partly granted to the Protector's son,
the Earl of Hertford, to be occupied as a place of residence,
but was chiefly used for the accommodation of distinguished
foreign visitors. With the reign of James I. it became the favourite
residence of Anne of Denmark, his queen, and became the centre
of court life.   Then it was that Anne frequently employed
Inigo Jones in architectural changes in the palace,[1] while she
converted the adjoining herbalist garden of John Gerrard into
a formal garden in the Italian style.   King Christian of Denmark, the queen's brother, visited her at Somerset House in
1605, and for the time being her Majesty 'affected to call' her
residence Denmark House in honour of her brother, for the
'affection between the queen and her brother was very great.'
On the death of Anne the palace was conveyed to the Prince
of Wales, but ceased to be used except for occasional festivities
and the lodgment of ambassadors.   On the death of James the
First, his body lay in state at Somerset House. 'The mourners,'
says D'Ewes in his Diary, 'set out from Somerset House about
10 o'clock in the morning, and the last came not to Westminster
till about four in the afternoon ; and no marvaile, seeing the
number of the mourners was near upon eight thousand. . . . I
was a spectator of the whole funeral pomp, and in a most convenient place in the Strand near Somerset House on the other
side of the way.'   In 1626 Somerset House (termed Denmark

[1] Strype says, 'the palace was greatly improved and beautified by this
queen, who added much to it in the way of new buildings, Inigo Jones being
called in to furnish the designs.'—*Survey*, Ed. 1720, Bk. iv.

Daniel, in his dedication of his pastoral, 'Hymen's Triumph,' of 1614 to
the queen, writes :—

> ' Here where your sacred influence begat
>   Most loved and most respected majesty,
> With humble heart and hand I consecrate
>   Unto the glory of your memory,
> As being a piece of that solemnity
>   Which your magnificence did celebrate
> In hallowing of those roofs you reared of late
>   With fires and chearefull hospitality.'

House) with twenty-four tenements adjoining was granted to Queen Henrietta Maria for life, with a stipulation that the king will grant her all the ornaments and household stuff there. The palace was then said to belong particularly to the queen, and to be 'the finest palace in all England.' Here it was that the queen was most easily able to promote the cause of Roman Catholicism, here open masses were held, and here, in 1635, she finally persuaded her indulgent husband to allow her to build a chapel on a site hitherto occupied by 'the Tennys Courte, and tenementes adjoining to Denmarke House.'[1] When Charles had been brought to the scaffold Somerset House with adjoining tenements was ordered to be sold, but at the Restoration no question of ownership was raised,[2] and it was recognised as belonging of right to the Crown. During the interregnum certain members of Parliament seemed to have enjoyed the comfort of the State apartments, while the priceless pictures and furniture were put up for auction that some part of the palace might be cleared to accommodate the army. In Henrietta's chapel 'audacious viragos,' 'feminine tub-preachers' propounded Puritanical doctrines, 'clapping their Bibles and thumping the pulpit cushions with as much confidence as honest Hugh Peters himself'—the seventeenth century 'Hyde Park orator and well-known divine.'

At the Restoration, Henrietta Maria returned to Somerset House as her dower palace, but many preparations, repairs, and alterations were necessary before she could take up residence, and at last the designs which Inigo Jones had long ago prepared[3] were to be carried out. Pepys described the new building as 'mighty magnificent and costly,' Cowley wrote some very poor verse on the subject, and an anonymous poet burst into

---

[1] See description of this chapel in *John Inglesant.*

[2] The Quakers were at one time anxious to take advantage of the offer of sale, but George Fox forbade them: 'when some froward spirits that came among us would have bought Somerset House that we might have meetings in it, I forbade them to do so; for I then foresaw the king's coming in again.'—*Journ.*

[3] The designs are now preserved in the Library of Worcester College, Oxford.

a doggerel effusion on the 'great queen' who had raised such
a pile from such ruins, and declared :—

> 'This by the Queen herself designed
> Gives us a pattern of her mind ;
> The state and order does proclaim
> The genius of that royal dame.'[1]

In spite of all her elaborate preparations to live at Somerset
House, Henrietta Maria, finding her influence at court declining, left England for France, in the midsummer of 1665,
ostensibly 'to drink the Bourbon waters, she being in a
consumption.'   Once more Somerset House became a convenient palace for gentlemen and ladies of the court whom
the king desired to provide with apartments.   Thus the Earl
of St. Albans and Dr. Godden, the king's chaplain, held suites
of rooms there, as did the famous beauty and friend of the king,
the Duchess of Richmond.   The funeral pageants of two bitter
enemies, Marck, Duke of Albemarle, and the Duke of Sandwich, Pepys's hero, passed through the gates of Somerset House,
and it was the scene of various wedding and christening ceremonies.   While the Duchess of Portsmouth reigned at Whitehall, Queen Katharine of Braganza began to occupy the state
apartments of Somerset House about 1675, and while there she
had mass regularly celebrated in the chapel which Henrietta
Maria had provided.[2]   It was this Romanist revival at Somerset
House which helped to give colour to the 'Popish Plot' story
which Titus Oates fabricated.   The mysterious murder of Sir
Edmund Godfrey, the London magistrate before whom Oates
made his deposition on oath, was followed by a search of Somerset House, where it was believed the murder was committed,
according to the evidence of one Miles Prance, a silversmith, who
had been arrested as a Catholic conspirator.   Prance declared

---

[1] B. M. 806, K. 16 (57).   *Upon her Majesty's new buildings at Somerset
House*.   These lines have been attributed to Edmund Waller, but they would
scarcely add credit to his name.

[2] It was at this period that Matthew Locke, as 'composer ordinary to
His Majesty,' was organist to the queen at the Somerset House chapel, and
composed there some of his most notable works.

that certain Catholic priests had decided on Godfrey's murder and enticed him into the courtyard of Somerset House, where the queen was in residence, on the pretext that two of her servants were engaged in a fight.   He was then seized by three murderers, Green, Hill, and Berry, servants at Somerset House, and strangled in the presence of the priests, while Prance himself guarded one of the gates.   Green, Hill, and Berry were at once taken prisoners, while Dr. Godden, the queen's chaplain, who was also supposed to be involved in the murder, fled to Paris.   The three supposed murderers were hanged on the sole evidence of Prance's story,[1] and Somerset House was nicknamed Godfrey Hall.   Queen Katharine, who had been accused of complicity in the plot, returned to Whitehall, and never visited Somerset House again until Charles was dead and she had become queen-dowager.   Then she returned to her old apartments and lived there in quiet retirement, cherishing her own religion, until William of Orange was forced, in view of 'the great meetings and caballings against his government at her residence at Somerset House,' to desire her to leave the town and take up her residence either at Windsor or Audley End.   She stood her ground for a time, but finally, in 1692, left Somerset House for Portugal, giving over her palace to the keeping of Lewis de Duras, Earl of Feversham, jocularly known as king-dowager.   Two years later Government took over the palace, and the buildings were put in repair for the use of the poor nobility.   Thus Churchill describes it in *The Ghost* of 1762 as :—

> 'that building which of old
> Queen-mothers was designed to hold,
> At present a mere lodging pen,
> A palace turned into a den.'

However, the character of Somerset House was soon to change from 'a mere lodging pen.'   In 1775 Sir William Chambers, the Surveyor-General of the King's Works, was

---

[1] He retracted his story in 1686, asserting he had concocted the whole evidence.

appointed to rebuild the then ruined palace for the public service. Thanks to the persuasions of Edmund Burke and others the first designs for the new building, somewhat on the lines of a substantial barracks, presented by a Mr. Robinson, Secretary of the Board of Works, were rejected, and Chambers was allowed to prepare an entirely new series.[1] The first stone of the present building was laid in 1776. By February 1779 the scaffolding had been removed from the Strand front, and by May 1780 Sir William Chambers was able to submit a report on the state of the works to the House of Commons. In March 1790 estimates for the completion of Somerset House were laid before the House, showing that £334,703 had been already spent, and that £33,500 were yet required. This sum represents the outlay on the river façade, the west and east wings and the north block only. The Inland Revenue Office and King's College were later additions.

Architecturally, Somerset House is certainly the best eighteenth century example of secular classic architecture that London possesses. It is sometimes questioned whether sculptural decorations are legitimate additions to the architectural success of a building, but one thing is certain, the success of Somerset House is to a great extent owing to the beauty of its sculptural decorations and the happy way in which sculptor and architect have combined forces.

[1] These are preserved in the Soane Museum in Lincoln's Inn Fields, that unpretentious and little appreciated museum that holds many treasures.

APPENDIX II

SYON HOUSE

SION or SYON HOUSE, another of England's fine buildings owing its existence to Edward, Duke of Somerset, the Protector, was built by him on the site of the dissolved Sion Abbey, which was granted to him by Edward VI. in 1547. On his attainder it was granted to his enemy, the Duke of Northumberland. On the attainder of the latter in 1553 it again reverted to the Crown, but being granted by Elizabeth, in 1604, to the Earl of Northumberland (of the second Percy creation) came back to the Seymour family, in the irony of things by the marriage of Charles, 'the Proud Duke' of Somerset, with Elizabeth Percy, heiress of Joscelin, fifth Earl of Northumberland (of the second Percy creation). And although, on the death of the Proud Duke, Sion House reverted to the Dukes of Northumberland of the new (Smithson) creation, it calls for some brief notice here as the work of the Protector. The shell of the house as he built it still stands, with its embattled terrace and in its quadrangular form, enclosing a flower-garden about eighty feet square. Much trouble was spent over the grounds of Sion House, and the botanical garden was built under the supervision of Dr. Turner, 'the Father of British botany.' At the present day the house is much as it was left by Algernon Percy, tenth Earl of Northumberland, who thoroughly repaired and altered it under the superintendence of Inigo Jones. It is three storeys high, and is an impressive building because of the dignity of its proportions and its massive solidity.

APPENDIX III

I. THE DUKES OF SOMERSET

Arms: The arms proper of the ducal house as borne by Queen Jane Seymour and by the descendants of Edward, first Duke of Somerset, by his second wife, Anne Stanhope, were :—

Quarterly: 1st, Or, on a pile gules between six fleurs-de-lis in pale azure, three lions passant guardant of the field, or (the coat of augmentation granted by Henry VIII. on his marriage with Jane Seymour): 2nd, Gules, pair of wings conjoined in lure or, for St. Maur: 3rd, Vairy argent azure, for Beauchamp of Hache[1]: 4th, Argent, three demi-lions gules for Sturmy[2]: 5th, Per bend argent and gules, three roses bendways counter, changed, for MacWilliam[3]: 6th, Argent, on a bend gules three leopards' faces or, for Coker.[4] The arms as borne by the later dukes since 1750, descendants of the Seymours of Berry Pomeroy, and of Edward, first Duke of Somerset, by his first wife, Catharine Filiol, are :—

Quarterly: 1st and 4th, Or on a pile gules between six fleurs-de-lis in pale azure, three lions passant guardant of the field, or the coat of augmentation (see *supra*): 2nd and 3rd, gules, two wings conjoined in lure or, for St. Maur.

Crest: Out of a ducal coronet or, a phœnix in flames issuant proper.

[1] Introduced by the marriage of Roger, younger son of John Seymour of Undy, with Cecilia de Beauchamp.

[2] By the marriage of Roger Seymour (1366-1420) with Maud Sturmy.

[3] By the marriage of that Roger's son John with Isabel MacWilliam or Williams.

[4] By that of John's son John with Elizabeth Coker.

II. THE MARQUESSES OF HERTFORD.

Arms: The arms of the Marquesses of Hertford of the late creation are :—

Quarterly: 1st and 4th, Sable, on a bend cotised argent, a rose between two annulets gules, for Conway; 2nd and 3rd, quarterly, 1st and 4th, or, on a pile gules, between six fleurs-de-lis in pale azure, three lions passant guardant of the field or, the coat of augmentation (see *supra*), 2nd and 3rd, Gules, two wings conjoined in lure or, for St. Maur.

Crest: On a wreath, the bust of a Moor, sidefaced, couped proper, wreathed about the temples argent and azure.

INDEX

Hoste, Derick, *n.* 323.
—— Sophia Margaret. See Seymour.
Houghton, 186.
Houlbrook, William, 138.
Howards, the, 36.
Howard, Francis. See Hertford.
—— Lord, of Effingham, 88.
—— Thomas. See Norfolk, Duke of.
—— Thomas, Viscount, of Bindon, 89.
—— Lord William, 21.
Howe, Lord, 318, 329.
Hubert, Henry. See Pembroke, Earl of.
Huish, manor of, 196.
Hume, David, 238; *n.* 254.
Hunt, Thomas, 177.
Husee, John, letters from, 15, 18, 19.
Hutton, John, 18.
Hyde, Henry, 143.
—— Lady, 164.
—— —— Mary. See Seymour.

INGATESTONE, 84.
Inkerman, 326.
Irvine, Charles, ninth Viscount, *ns.* 281, 287.
—— —— —— —— Frances, wife of, *n.* 287.
Irwin, General, letters to, 254; *n.* 251.
Isabella, Archduchess of Holland, *n.* 118.
Isham, Mrs., *n.* 83.

JACKSON, CANON, 5, 106.
—— Richard. See Wallace.
Jane Seymour, Queen, 2, 5, 7-28, 31, 34, 97, 365; *n.* 4; childhood of, 8, 9; description and character of, 12, 13, 15, 16, 26-7; married to Henry VIII., 15; death of, 21; funeral of, 22-23.
Jamaica, 320.
James I., 89, 90, 91, 95, 100-2, 107-8, 112-13, 115, 117-18, 120-1, 127, 132, 196-7, 359.
—— II., 147, 153-6, 206-10, 222.
—— IV. of Scotland, 95.
Jeffries, Judge, *n.* 349.
Jellapoor, *n.* 355.
Jerningham, Chevalier, letter from, 301.
—— Lady, letters from, 289, 290; *n.* 294.
Jersey, 30, 260, 268-71, 275.

Jersey, Earl of, 217, 224.
—— Lady, 287, 295.
Johnson, Dr. (quoted), 187.
Johnston, Sir Alexander, 350.
Jones, Inigo, 359-60, 364; *n.* 183.
Joyce, Cornet, 138.

KATHERINE OF ARAGON, 8, 10, 26; *n.* 134.
—— of Braganza, Queen, 122, 361, 362.
—— Parr, Queen, 25, 57-61, 64; letters from, 53-55; marriage with Sir Thomas Seymour, 53-6; death, 58.
Keene, Colonel, 262.
Kenloth, manor of, 31.
Kensington, 167, 220.
—— letters dated at, 166, 169.
Ket's Rebellion, 67.
Kew, 263, 264.
Kidd, William, 219.
Killagally, *n.* 328.
Killultagh (Antrim), 231.
Kimber, mayor of Marlborough, 177.
King, Sir Peter, 168.
Kingston Deverell, manor of (Wilts.), 31.
Kirke, Captain, 217-19.
Kirton, Edward, 106.
Kit-Cat Club, 170.
Kneller, 151.
Knightley, Elizabeth, wife of Sir Richard, 75.
—— Sir Richard, 75.
Knighton, Dorothea. See Seymour.
—— Sir William, 340.
Knoyle House (Wilts.), *n.* 328.
Knyvet, Lord, 102.
Königsmark, Count Charles, 152; *n.* 174.
Kyston, a lawyer, 96.

LAFFELT, 240, 243.
Lambeth, 105, 106, 108.
Landen, siege of, 230.
Langden, manor of, 30.
Langley, Roger, 144.
Lansdown, 124.
Lasco, Doctor de, 10.
Latimer, 63-5.
—— letter from, 20.
—— barony of, 152.
Lee, 110-12.
Leeds, Duke of, 214-15.
—— Peregrine Osborne, Duke of, *n.* 179.
—— —— Anne, wife, 192; *n.* 179.

Printed by T. and A. CONSTABLE, Printers to His Majesty
at the Edinburgh University Press

Lightning Source UK Ltd.
Milton Keynes UK
UKHW022300080223
416651UK00001B/435